Untamed Urbanisms

One of the major challenges of urban development has been reconciling the way cities develop with the mounting evidence of resource depletion and the negative environmental impacts of predominantly urban-based modes of production and consumption. The book aims to re-politicize the relationship between urban development, sustainability and justice, and to explore the tensions emerging under real circumstances, as well as their potential for transformative change.

For some, cities are the root of all that is unsustainable, while for others cities provide unique opportunities for sustainability-oriented innovations that address equity and ecological challenges. This book is rooted in the latter category, but recognizes that if cities continue to evolve along current trajectories they will be where the large bulk of the most unsustainable and inequitable human activities are concentrated. Drawing on a range of case studies from both the global South and global North, this book is unique in its aim to develop an integrated social-ecological perspective on the challenge of sustainable urban development.

Through the interdisciplinary and original research of a new generation of urban researchers across the global South and global North, this book addresses old debates in new ways and raises new questions about sustainable urban development that will be of interest to researchers, city managers and a wide range of policy actors in government, civil society and the private sector.

Adriana Allen is Professor of Development Planning and Urban Sustainability at the Bartlett Development Planning Unit (DPU), University College London, UK.

Andrea Lampis is Associate Professor at the Department of Sociology, National University of Colombia, Colombia.

Mark Swilling is Programme Coordinator: Sustainable Development in the School of Public Leadership, University of Stellenbosch, South Africa.

Routledge Advances in Regional Economics, Science and Policy

Untamed Urbanisms

Edited by Adriana Allen, Andrea Lampis and Mark Swilling

LONDON AND NEW YORK

First published 2016
by Routledge

2 Park Square, Milton Park, Abingdon, Oxfordshire OX14 4RN
52 Vanderbilt Avenue, New York, NY 10017

Routledge is an imprint of the Taylor & Francis Group, an informa business

First issued in paperback 2019

British Library Cataloguing in Publication Data
A catalogue record for this book is available from the British Library

Library of Congress Cataloging in Publication Data
Untamed urbanisms / [edited by] Adriana Allen, Mark Swilling,
Andrea Lampis.
pages cm
Includes bibliographical references and index.
1. Sustainable urban development. 2. Urban policy–Environmental aspects.
3. City planning–Environmental aspects. 4. Urban ecology (Sociology) I.
Allen, Adriana. II. Swilling, Mark. III. Lampis, Andrea.
HT241.U585 2015
307.1'416–dc23
2014038781

ISBN: 978-1-138-81542-1 (hbk)
ISBN: 978-0-367-86987-8 (pbk)

Typeset in Times New Roman
by Swales & Willis Ltd, Exeter, Devon, UK

Contents

Liberating alternatives   217

15 Negotiating and creating urban spaces in everyday practices:
    Experiences of women in Harare, Zimbabwe   219
    Manase Kudzai Chiweshe

16 A conversation in a dentist's chair: Employment, marginality
    and freedom on the borders of a Brazilian favela   232
    Moises Lino e Silva

17 Contested taming spatialities: The micro-resistance of
    everyday life in Buenos Aires   244
    Jorge Sequera and Elvira Mateos

18 Public spaces and transformative urban practices in
    Cape Town   257
    Diana Sanchez Betancourt

19 Everyday practices in Greece in the shadow of property:
    Urban domination subverted?   270
    Irene Sotiropoulou

20 Free-ing foods? Social food economies towards
    secure and sustainable food systems   284
    Ferne Edwards

    Untamed Urbanisms: Enacting productive disruptions   296
    Adriana Allen, Andrea Lampis and Mark Swilling

    Index   307

Figures

Tables

Contributors

Editors

Adriana Allen is Professor of Development Planning and Urban Sustainability at the Bartlett Development Planning Unit, University College London (UCL), UK, where she leads the Research Cluster on Environmental Justice, Urbanisation and Resilience, and is the UCL Environment Institute co-director on Sustainable Cities. Both as an academic and as a practitioner, her work focuses on the interface between development and environmental concerns in the urban context of the Global South, and more specifically on establishing transformative links between spatial planning, environmental justice and sustainability in urban and peri-urban contexts.

Andrea Lampis is Associate Professor in the Department of Sociology of the Universidad Nacional de Colombia (UNAL), Bogotá, Colombia. He holds a PhD in social policy from the London School of Economics. His research combines the study of urban vulnerability and poverty with environmental risk and the socio-institutional implication of climate change adaptation. He co-coordinates the research group 'Global Environmental Change, Climate Change, Social Movements and Public Policy' for the Latin-American Social Research Council (CLACSO). His research group at UNAL is called 'Global Risks and Local Vulnerabilities'.

Mark Swilling is Distinguished Professor of Sustainable Development in the School of Public Leadership, University of Stellenbosch, South Africa, and academic director of the Sustainability Institute. He is responsible for the design and implementation of its master's and doctoral programmes in sustainable development. He also heads up the TSAMA Hub, a new centre for the transdisciplinary study of sustainability and complexity at Stellenbosch University. The TSAMA Hub hosts a new transdisciplinary doctoral programme which involves collaboration between seven of Stellenbosch University's faculties. Professor Swilling obtained his PhD from the University of Warwick in 1994.

Contributors

Mauricio Dominguez Aguilar is a professor in the Dr Hideyo Noguchi Regional Research Center at the Autonomous University of Yucatan, Mexico. He holds a PhD in geography and is a member of the World Social Science Fellows Programme, the Mexican National Research System, and the Poverty and Urban Development Network of the Mexican Council of Science and Technology.

Manase Kudzai Chiweshe, PhD, is a senior lecturer in the Institute of Lifelong Learning at Chinhoyi University of Technology, Zimbabwe. His research interests include African gender and youth studies. His other interests include agrarian studies, sport studies, and urban and rural sociology.

Ferne Edwards, PhD, is a cultural anthropologist specializing in sustainable cities, urban food systems and social movements. She has published widely on topics of food waste and freeganism, food mapping, alternative food networks, climate change and urban beekeeping. She has recently conducted research on the Venezuela food sovereignty movement.

Maarten A. Hajer is director-general of the PBL Netherlands Environmental Assessment Agency and professor of public policy at the University of Amsterdam, the Netherlands. He is the author of over ten books. His *The Politics of Environmental Discourse* (Oxford University Press, 1995) is regarded as a classic study of environmental politics.

John Harris is an assistant professor of regional and city planning at the University of Oklahoma, USA. His research interests involve the connection between urban informality, everyday practices of urbanization and sustainable development as well as urban livelihood productivity in Africa.

Gareth Haysom has an MPhil in Sustainable Development from the University of Stellenbosch and a PhD from the University of Cape Town. His research focus is on urban food governance with particular attention to African cities. He has lectured in sustainable agroculture and food security.

Taibat Lawanson, PhD, is a senior lecturer in the department of Urban and Regional Planning, University of Lagos, Nigeria. Her research focuses on the interface of health, governance and livelihoods in urban communities. She is interested in how formal and informal systems can synthesize for sustainable development in the emerging African city.

Philip Lawton is currently a lecturer in the Department of Technology and Society Studies at Maastricht University, the Netherlands. He obtained his PhD from Trinity College Dublin in 2010. His research is focused on a critical analysis of urban public space, the creative city, and wider urban policy formation.

Moises Lino e Silva, PhD, is an urban anthropologist who specializes in the question of freedom and its relationship to different pressing topics such as violence, religion, sexuality, poverty and social justice. He is currently a lecturer at Brandeis University, USA, teaching anthropology, and international and global studies.

Elvira Mateos is a PhD student from the Universidad Autónoma de Madrid, Spain. She finished her academic training in social anthropology at the

Universidad Complutense de Madrid. Her interest areas are linked to the construction of subjectivities arising from urban segregation, gender studies and social movements, always from ethnography and qualitative methodologies. Since 2012 she has been working on the research project 'Contested Cities: Contested Spatialities of Urban Neoliberalism'.

Chipo Plaxedes Mubaya holds a PhD in development studies from the University of the Free State, South Africa. She is currently deputy director and senior research fellow in the Directorate of Research and Resource Mobilisation at the Chinhoyi University of Technology, Zimbabwe. Her research interests lie in rural development, natural resource management and rural/urban climate change adaptation.

Jenia Mukherjee, PhD, is an assistant professor of history of ecology and environment at the Institute of Development Studies, Kolkata, India. She did her PhD on the social biography of canals and wetlands in Kolkata, funded by the Indian Council of Historical Research. Her research interests include urban planning, urban sustainability and ecosystem resource management.

Patience Mutopo holds a PhD magna cum laude from the University of Cologne, Germany. She is currently a senior lecturer at the Chinhoyi University of Technology, Zimbabwe. Her research interests are in land and agrarian reforms, gender relations, market analysis and bio-fuel sciences.

Mzime Regina Ndebele-Murisa is an ecologist with a PhD in biodiversity and conservation biology from the University of the Western Cape, South Africa. She has extensive experience in biodiversity and conservation, natural resources management, environmental change analysis, aquatic and wildlife ecology, and climate adaptation. She is the author of numerous peer-reviewed publications.

Franklin Obeng-Odoom's research interests are centred on the political economy of development, cities and natural resources. His PhD in political economy was supervised by Frank Stilwell, a well-known public intellectual and Australia's first full professor of political economy. Franklin is the editor of the *African Review of Economics and Finance*.

Jorge Pacheco Castro holds a PhD in social anthropology and is a senior professor in the Dr Hideyo Noguchi Regional Research Center at the Autonomous University of Yucatan, Mexico. Over the past 20 years, he has worked and published widely in the field of social and cultural studies. He now specializes in the social impacts of extreme environmental phenomena and sociocultural change in the context of globalization.

José Palma is a graduate student in the Department of City and Regional Planning at California Polytechnic State University San Luis Obispo, USA. He holds a bachelor's degree in anthropology and psychology from the University of California, Merced. He has been working as a research assistant at the Transit

Coalition, and his research interests include urban planning and sustainable transportation.

Dominik Reusser, PhD, works at the Potsdam Institute for Climate Impact Research, Germany, in a research group on cities as focal points for climate adaptation and mitigation and on transition to more sustainability. His interest is the interactions between nature and society, which are at their extremes in city surroundings.

Natalie Rosales, PhD, is an urban sustainability scientist interested in building an alternative urbanism. Her work focuses on developing innovative urban planning instruments (contextual and procedural) that can be used to institutionalize sustainability. At the time of writing she was coordinator of the urban sustainable platform at *Observatorio Mexicano de la Crisis (OMEC)*.

Diego Rybski, PhD, works at the Potsdam Institute for Climate Impact Research, Germany, in a research group on cities as focal points for climate adaptation and mitigation and on transition to more sustainability. He is interested in the analysis and modelling of structural features of cities as well as the assessment of climate change impacts and adaptation of cities.

Diana Sanchez Betancourt is a senior researcher at the Human Sciences Research Council of South Africa, a junior lecturer on Community Based Research with Stanford University centre in Cape Town and co-founder of the Non-Profit Organisation Open Streets Cape Town. Her research and urban interests include processes of socio-economic transformation and social cohesion, citizen engagement, public spaces, and applied community research and collaboration.

Jorge Sequera, who has a PhD in sociology, is currently a postdoctoral researcher in the Department of Political Science and International Relations at the Universidad Autónoma de Madrid, Spain. His doctoral thesis focused on the processes and consequences of socio-spatial reconfiguration from gentrification in the city centre of Madrid. As part of the Contested Cities research network he is developing studies about micro-resistance in gentrifying neighbourhoods in Buenos Aires, as well as comparative studies in gentrification and resistance among several Latin American cities.

Irene Sotiropoulou, PhD, is a heterodox economist and researcher. She specializes in solidarity economy, parallel currencies, non-monetary transactions, traditional economies and non-capitalist economic institutions, as well as feminist economics.

Anna-Lena Winz is a PhD student in mathematics at the Free University of Berlin, Germany. Her interests are in the applications of mathematics and computer science to predict and explain phenomena in climate impact research. She has spent two months working at the Potsdam Institute for Climate Impact Research.

Mintesnot Woldeamanuel, PhD, is an associate professor in the department of Urban Studies and Planning at California State University Northridge, USA. He has conducted extensive research on the relationship between travel behaviour and urban form. His research interests include community development and sustainability, urban transportation planning, land use and travel behaviour analysis.

Foreword

In March 2013, 22 social scientists from all over the world and from a wide range of academic disciplines found themselves in Quito, Ecuador, at the invitation of the International Social Science Council (ISSC). They were brought together by a shared desire to push forward the limits of knowledge on cities and their future. And push forward they did, as I hope you will find as you read this book that reflects some of the thinking started at the seminar.

This gathering of researchers was the first seminar in the ISSC's World Social Science Fellows Programme. With this programme, generously supported by the Swedish International Development Agency (Sida), we hope to help build a network of future social science leaders who will work together to help address some of the most pressing global challenges of our time, with particular relevance for developing countries. Sustainable urbanization is one such challenge, calling on the joint insights and contributions of scholars from different disciplines and different parts of the world.

Working with us on the first seminar in the programme, and critical to its results, were the former International Human Dimensions Programme on Global Environmental Change (IHDP, now part of Future Earth) and the Comparative Research Programme on Poverty (CROP), as well as our generous host, the Universidad Andina Simón Bolívar, Quito, Ecuador, Area de Estudios Sociales y Globales.

The greatest factor in making the seminar a success, however, was the 19 competitively selected early career scientists and three senior scientists who came committed to developing new, multidimensional perspectives on transitions to a more sustainable future in urban areas. With a lot of hard work, a necessary sense of humour and the use of a surprising number of sticky notes, they developed a compelling sense of urbanities as spaces shaped by practices, experiences and imaginaries that are much richer and more complex than mainstream models of urban development have it. It is this 'untamed urbanism' that the Fellows and senior scientists explore in this book. As they say, 'what matters is how we comprehend and work with both taming and untaming urban dynamics'.

And that it matters is clear. The world is faced with a number of converging crises (of climate, inequality, food, water, finance and social discontent) at a time when the majority of its population lives in cities. The challenge is on to find effective, socially just and sustainable solutions. In seeking 'productive disruptions' in our understanding of the issues at hand, the authors of this book boldly confront that challenge.

Alberto Martinelli
ISSC President

Acknowledgements

This book has been produced as a truly collective endeavour and a great debt is owed to the team who made this possible. Sincere thanks are due to the International Social Science Council (ISSC), which supported and financed both the initial seminar from which the book took off in Quito in March 2013, a writing workshop held in Montreal a few months after and the process that followed. Within the ISSC we are particularly grateful to its executive director Heide Hackmann, and to Laura van Veenendaal, Mathieu Denis and Charles Ebikeme, for backing the whole process and for their dedication and support in bringing together a widely geographically distributed team of urban researchers from all over the world. To Sharon Verwoerd goes one of our biggest acknowledgments for her incredible endurance in pulling us together throughout the different stages of the book production and for her highly professional editing management. To Susan Curran goes our gratitude for the quality of her language editing and for her flexibility and responsiveness to endless adjustments to many of the chapters in this book. We are also grateful to Robert Langham from Routledge for his flexibility in all the contractual aspects underpinning the production of this book and for giving this project the chance to reach urban researchers and practitioners from all over the world.

A very warm thanks is reserved to the four coordinators – Ferne Edwards, John Harris, Philip Lawton and Dominik Reusser – who generously supported the early stages of drafting of each part of the book and who actively contributed to shaping its overall structure and narrative. Philip Lawton deserves a special mention for his significant contribution in the coordination and editing of Part III and for his sharp and thorough feedback to earlier versions of the introduction to this book. Finally, for their invaluable contributions and untamed thinking we would like to thank all the authors: Mauricio Dominguez Aguilar, Ferne Edwards, John Harris, Maarten A. Hajer, Gareth Haysom, Manase Kudzai Chiweshe, Taibat Lawanson, Philip Lawton, Moises Lino e Silva, Elvira Mateos, Chipo Plaxedes Mubaya , Jenia Mukherjee, Patience Mutopo, Mzime Ndebele-Murisa, Franklin Obeng-Odoom, Jorge Pacheco Castro, Jose Palma, Dominik Reusser, Natalie Rosales, Diego Rybski, Diana Sanchez Betancourt, Irene Sotiropoulou, Jorge Sequera, Anna-Lena Winz and Mintesnot Woldeamanuel.

Last but not least, our gratitude goes to our colleagues and students in Bogota, London and Stellenbosch for listening to our rants about untaming and untamed urbanisms over the last 18 months and to our partners and children for enduring the many weekends, holiday periods and long hours dedicated to this book, but above all for making life fun and instilling the feeling that untaming projects might be worthwhile, in any form they take.

Adriana Allen, Andrea Lampis and Mark Swilling

Introduction

Why Untamed Urbanisms?

Adriana Allen, Andrea Lampis and Mark Swilling

Cities can be understood as the product of multiple taming practices and strategies, ranging from the techno-infrastructural domestication of nature to secure key resources, to the sociopolitical disciplining of the relational and organizational structures and behaviours that shape everyday life in cities. But cities are also profoundly untameable because they are a complex and often unintelligible web of institutional and everyday practices that produce them in fundamentally political ways, whether intentionally or unintentionally.

The notion of 'untamed urbanisms' is a subtle theme that pervades many recent contributions to urban theory. It resonates with Harvey's (2012) reading of the untameability of capitalist urbanization; Brenner, Marcuse and Mayer's (2011) call to recentre critical urban theory on the production of cities for people, not for profit; Brenner's most recent Lefebvrian reading of the uneven implosions and explosions of planetary urbanization (2013); Edensor and Jayne's invitation to challenge the universal application of theories of Western cities to a world of cities (2012); Robinson's call to examine the heterogeneity of practices that make cities and urban life (2006); McFarlane's exploration of urban learning as a political and practical, yet neglected, domain and how different environments facilitate or inhibit learning (2011); and Tonkiss, who argues that the social life of cities is shaped by 'actors [who] engage creatively in the logistics and politics of urban life in ways that go beyond the masterplan, the design commission and the competition entry, and which confuse any easy distinction between the expert and the ordinary, the technical and the amateur, the formal and the informal' (2013: 10).

Building upon the aforementioned work and other recent trends in the urban studies literature (Bayat 2000; Inam 2014; McFarlane 2011; Myers 2011; Pieterse and Simone 2013; Pieterse 2008; Roy 2009; Watson 2009; Whittaker-Ferreira 2007) and some contributions to the *Routledge Handbook on Cities in the Global South* (Parnell and Oldfield 2014), this book invites readers to explore how ordinary citizens and planners seek to change the city, or perhaps more precisely the urban spaces in which they exist, live and work.

Following the acknowledgement that we now live in a fast-urbanizing world, cities and urban life have also become the central locus of developmental planning narratives and interventions, where undesirable trajectories of socio-economic and environmental change are to be addressed, though often under new guises that perpetuate and reproduce what is deemed as 'undesirable' in the first place. Yet, against all odds, cities continue to be untamed. That is, they are produced in ways that challenge the 'taming practices' associated most clearly with the dynamics of capitalist consumption and the domesticating practices of mainstream urban planning and governance, which so often prioritize the ongoing viability of capitalist property markets. Our intention throughout this book is not limited to an examination of what makes that possible, but rather to explore the untamed and the act of untaming as forms of producing the urban that are rarely acknowledged or recognized as productive pathways to rethink what makes and could make cities conduits of social and environmental justice.

Born out of the encounter of a group of urban researchers from many different parts of the world in Quito, Ecuador, in 2013, this book offers a heuristic platform to interrogate how ordinary citizens and planners make sense of the city, by either confronting or engaging critically with hegemonic narratives of what a city or being an urbanite should be. Our central contention is that, all too often, such hegemonic narratives and practices embody taming processes that reduce complexity, homogenize and exclude in the name of progress and over-riding imperatives, while quietening other ways of producing and learning the city. Our focus is therefore on a diversity of urban practices, experiences and imaginaries that either thrive within the interstices of domesticated and controlled urban development processes or are hardly tractable, and difficult to manage, assimilate and mould.

In this enterprise, the contributors to this book are not bounded geographically, thematically, theoretically or by discipline, but rather by a shared intellectual discomfort with contemporary grand narratives and normative prescriptions that often obscure, marginalize or foreclose other possibilities to experience and imagine ways of being in the city and of producing it. The authors are also united by a common approach to their interrogation of the city, from a perspective that is conversational and also explicit about our personal positionality. Together, the different chapters take the reader through an exploratory journey to discover, explain and evaluate critically the potential of taming and untaming accounts of contemporary urbanisms, what and who drives them, and why and with what consequences. Our ultimate hope is that this book contributes to the generation of productive disruptions in the way we approach and interrogate urban change, away from a concern to control and subordinate the 'other', whether such other is nature, certain kinds of spaces, women, the urban poor, or those who culturally and behaviourally are deemed not to fit into tamed or disciplined ways of being urban.

Throughout the following two sections, we offer a number of further reflections on what this enterprise involves and why it is needed. Adopting a systems theory perspective, we start by examining the long-term trajectories that help us to contextualize the advent of the 'Urban Antropocene' – literally the urbanized 'age of human-induced evolutionary change' – as the context in which different and often competing contentions coexist about the role of cities in shaping wider socio-technical transitions and supporting different speculations on what type of urban change is required. We then return to the notion of 'untamed urbanisms' to discuss what the act of untaming might tender as a heuristic device to provoke new reflections on the way we read and seek to change current and future urban trajectories, and finally offer an overview of the structure and content of the book.

Re-ordering the urban Anthropocene?

There is growing acceptance across a wide range of publics that 'modern society' is currently facing historically unprecedented challenges at precisely the moment when the majority of the world's population is living in cities. The advent of an urbanized 'Anthropocene' comes with an all-pervasive sense that global change pressures such as climate change, resource depletion, ecosystem breakdown and persistent poverty threaten the conditions of existence of human life as we know it (Crutzen 2002). The onset of the global economic crisis in 2007/08 has resulted in a realization that we may have come to the end of the post-Second World War long-term development cycle (Gore 2010), and there is little understanding of what will come next. The result is an interregnum that Edgar Morin has called the 'polycrisis' (Morin 1999: 73), in which the task of 're-ordering' a world full of things such as trees, pipes, water, and of course cities and urban lifestyles, appears to be the central subject of new unfolding narratives. It then becomes useful to borrow from systems theory to understand the historical cycles of order and crisis produced through contemporary contentions of how such things should hang together (Pieterse, 2008; Hodson and Marvin 2010a).

Following Gore and Perez (Gore 2010; Perez 2013; Perez 2002; Perez 2007), the economic history of the industrial era can be understood as a succession of five overlapping socio-technical revolutions, with each lasting around 40 to 60 years (Swilling 2013). Each wave has followed a recognizable trajectory of inception, innovation, crisis and then mature deployment of specific transformative clusters of coupled socio-technical innovations in the major infrastructure sectors, in particular energy, mobility and communications. Given that cities are the spatial manifestation of the constellations of power expressed in particular socio-technical systems in specific geographical contexts, it follows that these waves of socio-economic transformation have corresponded to the radical restructuring of the space-economy of each nation's hierarchy of cities and towns (Swilling and Annecke 2012; see also Chapter 5 in this volume). This certainly applies to the current urban polycrisis (Hodson and Marvin 2010b).

The above account of contemporary overlapping socio-technical revolutions shows that each successive age was characterized by a major economic crisis at its mid-point. Each subsequent long wave has been driven by innovation incentivized by finance capital (seeking capital gains) that has tended to over-invest in promising spatially configured fashionable energy, mobility and communication technologies, thus creating speculative financial bubbles (Harvey 2012). As economies and cities crashed when these bubbles burst, the governance of ordering/taming projects became renewed – specifically, by states' interventions to reorganize society around a new set of institutions appropriate to the emerging over-invested technologies (such as oil, electrification, highways and suburban sprawl after the 1929 crash). In the process, every ordering project attempted to impose new cultural norms on urban society, discipline the more pernicious excesses of finance capital, and prepare the way for productive (dividend-seeking) capital to take over as the primary investor in the 'proven' socio-technical innovations and the myriad goods and services that these new infrastructures made possible. As Harvey (2012) argued, cities were always the contested terrains of creative destruction that lay at the centre of these dramatic historical transformations, though their role in taming the global crises of capitalism is perhaps more pronounced today than ever before in modern history.

There are strong ecological, social and economic arguments to support a transition away from business as usual towards a more sustainable inclusive economy, but the force and speed of current trajectories tend to overload the strategic capacities for action at global and national levels, and vested interests remain in control of powerful information flows. These mask the looming threats of polluting, greenhouse gas-emitting, resource-intensive technologies and the systems of economic accumulation and socio-environmental subordination that reproduce them. As homes for the majority of the world's population and in light of the enormous complexities that paralyse the governance of global challenges, cities are currently being re-interpreted as potentially crucial spaces for sustainability-oriented innovations that could coalesce into alternative socio-technical regimes in future. As in previous socio-technical revolutions when global geographical and intra-urban spaces were restructured by the dynamics of particular patterns of accumulation (Harvey 2012; Swilling 2011), the focus now shifts to the forces shaping the urban Anthropocene and how they may be shaping the next long-term development cycle. On a parallel basis and outside the spotlight of international development conferences and summits, cities are also increasingly the crucial nodes where, backed by local institutions and actors, complex systems of global wealth accumulation and concentration produce brutal expulsions (Sassen 2014). Cities obviously do not exist in a vacuum or outside wider social, economic and environmental projects, but acknowledging this is different from approaching them as mere sites or instruments of wider transitions and transformations. The drivers and sources of urban change require in our view a more dialectical examination that consciously resists the construction of new essentialisms, whether these endorse the notion that cities are the new re-ordering sites of global problems and therefore of global solutions or of unconstrained agency. This book seeks to offer a simultaneous interrogation of the structuring discursive and material effects of the urban polycrisis described above and to track the pathways that materialize and challenge the consolidation of old and new ordering projects across grounded material practices and discourses on the past, present and future of cities.

On taming and untaming the city

As argued at the beginning, taming is a process that can take many forms across a rich diversity of urban contexts. It is, however, recognizable as a set of attempts by urban intermediaries to use visioning, planning, discourse-building, coalitioning and funding strategies to impose a certain order, logic and coherence on complex dynamics which are deemed to be too opaque, too seemingly directionless and therefore too uncontrollable to provide the basis for purposive outcomes aligned with the requirements of accumulation, rational urban planning, urban consumption and appropriate modes of cultural behaviour. Siemens, for example, recently published a report entitled *Investor Ready Cities: How Cities can Create and Deliver Infrastructure Value*, which explicitly argues that those cities that successfully tame these complex dynamics using the new ICTs will become the most attractive to investors (Siemens *et al* 2014).

Transforming cities into tamed domains of information-based accumulation will depend to a large extent on whether it will, in practice, be possible to simplify or reduce complexity in the name of 'progress'. In this book we seek to resist the 'taming' of urbanism by emphasizing the 'untameability' of the city in its various manifestations in the global North and South. The most lively and rich examples of urbanism tend in reality to be too complex, too diverse, too incompressible, too ever-changing to be so easily tamed. However, what really matters above all is what could (possibly unintentionally) be suppressed or even annihilated by the *process of taming*. Critically, it could be argued that attempts to tame the city could overthrow what drives the energy, entrepreneurialism, innovations, assemblages, networking, heterotopias, passions and dreams that ensure the survival of rich, creative, alive and open-ended urbanisms. In our view, the cognitive fusions and reformations that emerge from the frictions, struggles and contestations made possible by the messy unpredictable agglomerations and assimilations of the city need to be recognized and protected from the sanitized urban utopias currently punted by some powerful actors – in particular the global technology companies – who recognize the strategic significance of the city.

However, for us this is not a 'dualism'; it is not about a simplistic counterposition of the 'tamed' and the 'untamed'. These are interlocked processes that feed off and can potentially co-produce each other, with threats that lie at the extremes: from the sanitized lines of the overly 'tamed' technotopias being marketed today by some technology corporations, through to the endlessly messy assemblages of the seemingly directionless 'untamed' (which some like to romanticize). Instead, our central argument is that by examining the dialectical dynamics of taming and untaming we can recognize how the 'urban Anthropocene' is being made and unmade at multiple levels as diverse actors co-opt, reformulate and fuse together one or another rendition of their understanding of urbanism, the information age, economic crisis and environmental breakdown.

The bids to tame the city can take many forms, each expressed as a 'project' at the popular level and often underpinned by a particular body of scholarship and theory. A non-exhaustive list of globally constituted 'projects' of the city that reflect a wide range of perspectives include the re-emergence of a faith in 'big planning' underpinned by the science of modelling, as championed by the former Arup chief executive Peter Head's initiative 'The Urban Sequestration Trust', among others; the increasingly influential 'Resilience Perspective' – now adopted by the Rockefeller Foundation, with links to the Stockholm Resilience

Centre (SRC) and the International Council for Local Environmental Initiatives (ICLEI); UN-HABITAT's 'Urban patterns for a green economy' initiative (UN Habitat 2013); the UN Environment Programme's (UNEP's) Global Initiative for Resource Efficient Cities; the World Bank's Sustainable Infrastructure group focus on material flow analysis, socio-technical systems change, and the Eco2Cities initiative (Hoornweg and Freire 2013); the C40 Cities Climate Leadership Group's emphasis on the opportunities offered by the world's megacities to create resilient places for the business world to tackle climate risks and greenhouse emissions (CPD 2014); the Green Building movement and the rapidly growing 'Smart Cities' agenda (Komninos 2009; Townsend 2013) and associated calls for massive investments required to make cities smarter, among others.

The examples above are part of a rapidly solidifying global urbanism that approaches the urban Anthropocene as one world, while actively normalizing the production and reproduction of 'differential sustainability'; that is, the possibility 'of adjusting thresholds to meet the needs and wants of certain privileged social groups and territories at the expense of others' (Allen 2014: 523). At the same time, the 'polycrisis' is expressed most clearly in the widening of the range of a large number of globally produced but locally experienced risks. The legalization of the security state to provide a safe space for economic activity in the face of risk (Greenhouse, 2010) has implied at the local level the securitization of space and a peculiar type of bio-control over people and places. This entails detailed strategies to plan, monitor, securitize, protect and push – when needed – those actors, communities and processes that cannot be easily tamed or domesticated in zones of both social and physical exclusion.

By contrast, those that share a perspective that values the untameability of the city are on quite a wide continuum that encompasses multiple sites of social insurgency, everyday urbanism and engagement with urban governance. On one end you might find Shack Dwellers International (supported by organizations such as the International Institute for Environment and Development (IIED), London; the Bartlett Development Planning Unit (DPU), London; the African Centre for Cities (AAC), Cape Town; and the Sustainability Institute (SI) Stellenbosch, among others), who valorize the untamed collective agency of the poor in building the urban, while seeking to bridge their efforts with the transformations required to co-produce more just and sustainable urban trajectories with other urban actors (Allen 2012; Maricato 2009; Mitlin 2008; Mitlin and Satterthwaite 2013; Swilling *et al.* 2013). These perspectives run right through to, at the other end, the work of Mike Davis (2005), Malik Simone (2010) and Asef Bayat (2000), who read the production of cities as a permanent struggle against tameability. In an attempt to bridge the gap between everyday urbanism, resistance and engagement, a number of writers have explored the interactive and relational dynamics that transform urban systems. These thinkers include Marcuse *et al.* (2009), Guy *et al.* (2011), McFarlane (2011), (the new) Castells (2012), Parnell and Oldfield (2014), Allen *et al.* (forthcoming) and Swilling (forthcoming), among others. By recognizing that urban change cannot simply be derived from structural economic changes at the national and global levels or from grand planning frameworks, these writers insist on the importance of tracing the profound role played by specific configurations of urban actors who actively engage prevailing power relations to realize a wide range of future urban visions.

The contributions to this book engage these various traditions as articulated across both global North and global South contexts. Our message is clear: because cities do not provide a clean slate, we must all be careful about what we assume is actually going on or what is possible. What matters is how we comprehend and work with both taming and untaming dynamics. Undoubtedly, actions are necessary, but they must be informed by a nuanced understanding of these complex dynamics that may be conceptually distinct but in practice always manifest in relation to one another. Seeking action without critical reflection on the dialectics at play between taming and untaming runs the risk of producing and re-producing old and new unjust urban utopias. But equally, theorizing urban change without an axiological discussion of what type of action might be possible or desirable can be purposeless, confining our understanding to multiple readings of complexity while overwhelming any sense of what transformative change might mean or entail. This is, for example, the danger of the conceptually cluttered urban resilience framework.

Departing from the notion of a polycrisis unfolding under the urban Anthropocene could be read by many as yet another attempt at creating a single grand narrative. Throughout this book, however, we approach this diagnosis rather differently: navigating through this polycrisis opens in our view multiple sites of untamed speculation and action, as well as new opportunities to discuss strategic visions of transformative urban futures. In other words, departing from a critical and grounded reading of the urban polycrisis opens up the poly-reframing of contemporary urban trajectories, which in turn rejects the formulation of single-issue or single geography grand theories of change. As such, the concept of 'untamed urbanisms' is posed here to provoke new epistemological engagements not just with a diagnosis of the urban polycrisis but rather with the way in which actions to readdress such manifestations suggests the need for new framings of what is wrong in the first place. Such 'actions' range from those effected at the individual and household level to those institutionalized through planning framings.

Indeed, this might imply something deeply disturbing and problematic about the notion of the urban Anthropocene itself. If the notion of the Anthropocene is intended to suggest that humans have become the dominant geo-physical drivers of evolution, then the notion of the 'urban Anthropocene' implies that it is 'urban-based humans' in particular that have become this driver – a leitmotif that is now reflected in the frequently used notion of 'planetary urbanism' and in the notion that we therefore need 'Smart Cities' that are low carbon and resource efficient. The proliferation of modelling as a dominant research practice in sustainability science tends to reinforce this way of thinking. In effect, this suggests that cities have tamed global evolutionary dynamics in ways that endow these formations with a moral responsibility for ensuring the future survival of the entire web of life. At precisely the moment when the extra-ordinary powers of science and technology make possible the taming of natural evolution, these powers also effectively fail to provide the much longed-for panacea because of a tendency to rely on complex modelling tools that virtually without exception assume the rational – and therefore tameable – individual as the primary building block of the analysis. These models cannot come to terms with what is effectively 'unmodellable' – the dull compulsion of the untamed dynamics of the everyday urbanism of the world's most dynamic cities and the unfolding logics of long-term structural transitions beyond the direct control of human agency or 'management'.

In other words, by invoking the notion of a dialectic between taming and untaming dynamics, we are also raising questions about the kind of knowledge needed to address not only the *internal* nature of our cities, but also the relations *between* our cities and the ecosystem services produced by the non-urban hinterlands and waterbodies that are consumed within cities (with urban elites consuming the lion's share). Undoubtedly models have their uses, but the qualitative analyses that pervade many of the chapters in this book help surface realities that escape the modes of analysis that have hitherto informed recent narratives about anthropogenically determined outcomes. As a result we face the prospect that models will emerge that inform policy choices for 'managing' urban transitions that neglect a broad swathe of urban realities that cannot be tamed by increasingly sophisticated quantitative modelling tools aimed at validating huge expenditures on a wide range of technofixes.

This book engages with the politics of urban transitions, exploring the tensions and dialogues between hegemonic and non-hegemonic framings, and seeks productive disruptions in our understanding and capacity for radical pragmatism. As argued by Inam, '[t]he most fundamental shifts in transforming cities do not happen by tinkering around the edges, but by fundamentally rethinking processes, methods, and outcomes of urbanism' (2014: 18). At the same time we are mindful to avoid the dualism often found in urban studies between a normative, prescriptive or standardized pathway for urban development, and the much preferred desire to enjoy the city ironically through deconstruction and relativism. Thus, we are more interested in the interactive actions of taming and untaming as a way of knowing and acting upon the city, rather than the creation of another taxonomic system (the tamed and the untamed) to apprehend urban change.

Overview of the book

The rest of the book is structured in four parts, which are outlined below. Part I explores the wider socio-environmental transitions within which taming and untaming urbanisms operate, simultaneously examining how such transitions are either neglected or used to legitimize different courses of action and non-action. Part II digs critically into the plurality of experiences and everyday urbanisms that are often misrecognized forms of production of the city. Part III examines the capture of planning by mainstream narratives, and explores planning as a possible act of untaming, in an attempt to reframe its practice in a time of disciplinary crisis. Finally, Part IV works through the transformative potential and limits of different practices that consciously and unconsciously open new alternatives and bring to life suppressed imaginaries of cities – and what being in cities means – for a diverse range of actors that rarely become the focus of analysis. We conclude with a set of provocations that have implications for future research trajectories and transformative urban practices.

Part I: Trajectories of change in the urban Anthropocene

Cities are the emergent outcome of long historical cycles of seemingly interrelated socio-economic, spatial, institutional and ecological dynamics. How precisely these dynamics are connected depends on the conceptual lens used to comprehend them, with each lens phasing out of sight some of these key dynamics in favour of a particular dominant concern or interest. Long cycles of economic development transform the ecological systems within which they are embedded at local, regional and global scales. These long cycles and multiple scales interact in context-specific ways. Over the past century and a half, paradigms for reducing the complexity of the urban phenomenon have come and gone, but what remains is the irrepressibility and irreducibility of context. It is now time to find ways of grasping from different angles what it means to think about the trajectories of urban-ecological change in the era of the urban Anthropocene.

A world of cities disconnected from (real) natural systems was imagined in the nineteenth century and built in the twentieth century. Now that we know the negative consequences of this for all humanity and the wider web of life, we are confronted with the far from small task of fundamentally rethinking what urbanism would mean if the twenty-first century is to culminate in 6 billion living in cities by 2050 in a world of 9.5 billion without destroying the planet we inhabit. The chapters in Part I explore this challenge, while offering thought-provoking ways of reframing the way in which sustainable and just urban trajectories might be imagined and pursued.

Part II: The untamed everyday

The 'untamed everyday' section is framed by three major debates, all traditionally cast in the metaphorical scene of urban development polarities. The first one concerns the opposition between agency and structure (Giddens 1984). Albeit in different ways, all chapters place themselves within a tradition that focuses on the reflexive character of human conduct. To take this stand implies challenging the idea that human conduct is purely shaped by forces and actors that people neither govern nor comprehend. Thus the first key argument running through this section is that human agency interacts with the broader forces and pressures discussed in Part I, both playing a fundamental role in shaping them and providing a reason to think about their transformation.

Discourse is part of the dynamics of everyday life, as much as it is constitutive of development at large, and specific urban processes of a different kind and span. Thus, a second key theme is that through the political and cultural construction of discourses, language is not only spoken but also makes possible in different ways the exercise of power (Foucault 2002). This results in dominant discourses that are capable of excluding or including with terrible strength, at times supported by appalling violence, such as those on rational planning, urban growth and competitiveness, the smart city, the informal city, the slum city and so forth. This is also true of binary discourses such as formal/informal and poor/non-poor which often provide political, legal and policy justification for those who have the authority and capacity to rule over others. These discursive devices are needed not only by urban administrations but also, paradoxically, by those who claim ownership of the direction that urban transformation should be taking in order to save the urban from ecological collapse.

The third key argument running through the chapters challenges the fashionable idea that cities and people will inevitably adapt in fairly predictable ways to conditions of increasing socio-environmental uncertainty. Spanning a high degree of diversity – in terms of geographies, cultures and processes – all the chapters use case studies to challenge evolutionist readings of social change. Thus, to think of socio-environmental change, development and justice as an irreversible sequence of stages – while uncritically adopting concepts that originated in the natural sciences, such as adaptation and resilience – produces short-sighted and most often tautological explanations. The everyday is untamed inasmuch as the diverse pathways to greater social justice in the city reflect the range of interests and actors at play, regardless of different ways of thinking and building forms of urban living across geographies. However, it would also be incorrect to think that there is no connection at all among the dynamics of everyday life. In fact, as a repeating fractal across geographies, hegemonic models of market-driven cities have brought about a common pattern that apparently differs from place to place but, at the same time, preserves an unchanging pattern that repeats itself: this is the new role carved for the agency of individuals as self-protecting actors within the logic of commodification and securitization of private life often reinforced by a wider human rights discourse. Part II of the book argues that these emerging patterns raise questions about the discourses on the future city that claim that urban politics needs to look not only at macro-structures, but also at the processes that crystallise daily into social practices and inequalities that reinforce and ultimately shape the unfolding and ever-changing nature of these structures.

Part III: Disrupting hegemonic planning

Urban planning encompasses a set of processes that are often seen as engaging all elements of urban life while at the same time being treated as something that can be separated from the everyday activities taking place in the city. While this may seem a contradictory endeavour, it highlights the key issues regarding the urban question for the coming years: how can urban planning serve to influence the wide array of factors deemed necessary for a sustainable urban future? This part of the book invites an examination of what planning *is*, and what planning *does and could do* to become a truly democratic and inclusive process.

In the context of historical development, urban planning can to a large extent be seen as an 'ultimate taming' project and set of mechanisms. Discourses of planning are so bound up with hegemonic power structures that the power at work often becomes hidden or naturalized. In this regard, planning, with its mantra of 'common sense', is particularly suited to the neoliberal age. At its most extreme, this is evidenced in the ease with which large corporate entities have become embedded in public policy through the 'smart city' agenda or in the emergence of risk as an overarching organizing concept, for both private and public sector management of neuralgic spaces and resources often found within or administered from actors strategically positioned inside the city itself. At the other end, it can be witnessed through 'creative' projects, such as pop-up shops, meanwhile spaces and temporary parks, which have emerged with particular resonance since the economic crisis of 2008. When taken at face value, these give an indication that urban planning is a loose and open-ended process that manifests in context-specific ways. Yet these projects themselves are often at the mercy of wider structural factors, such as cycles of investment and disinvestment, thus limiting the possibility of significant shifts in urban planning practice.

In attempting to analyse the various processes at work, each of the chapters in Part III connects planning to the wider political and economic contexts in which they are embedded. The authors seek to get beyond the notion that planning is inherently 'tamed' and by definition always at the mercy of wider power structures. In a critical manner, they point towards the potential for alternative forms of planning practice. Each of the chapters is guided by a desire to re-infuse everyday practice with theoretical insights drawn from a range of sources, including the re-emphasis on engagement from the community and neighbourhood level to the level of supranational organizations such as UN-HABITAT.

The argument is reinforced by a plea for greater levels of control over public resources that have a direct impact on the ability of planning to become a more open and democratic process with respect, in particular, to the allocation of housing and land resources. When taken together, these chapters search with great urgency for urban planning to become less about technical fixes and more about promoting cities as more 'just' spaces where spatially embedded citizen interaction becomes a core element of urban planning practices that recognize the wider ecological and economic context of urban development processes.

Part IV: Liberating alternatives

This part on 'liberating alternatives' explores people's narratives of living and thus creating cities within and beyond the limits of the contemporary disciplining practices that produce the urban. Recognizing that alternatives exist in a variety of forms on many levels, the chapters in Part IV step away from social movement theory to investigate socio-environmental change in the urban everyday, depicting emerging narratives that challenge marginalization and re-invoke citizens' rights to the city while creating new spaces and tensions to bring about transformative change.

The central questions explored within this section are: How can we understand urban life and everyday practices beyond needs? What factors or qualities make practices 'alternatives' or 'untamed' from the perspective of the mainstream? What is the destabilizing capacity of such practices? What fractures emerge in the friction between everyday practices and social regulation? To what extent are 'alternatives' transformative? In exploring the answer to these questions, the concept of freedom is problematized to unveil the limits of both formal distributive norms and obligations, and people's individual choices and preferences. The authors examine instead how freedom is dialectically constructed in the city, by whom, under what circumstances and with what consequences. Here a thread connecting parts II and IV is the search for a narrative other than the hopeless one so poignantly described by Greenhouse (2010) and others in *Ethnographies of Neoliberalism* (Makhulu, 2010; Miyazakim, 2010). In this sense, to talk about untamed urbanisms means referring to the tensions produced by the encounter between the new grand narratives and the alternatives emanating from those being pushed towards the social and/or physical margins of the city. The latter is an untaming process that reveals those acts of exclusion as not just resistances but powerful lenses to disrupt the narrowing logic of the marketization and commodification of urban life.

Untaming here takes place through subtle readings of undisciplined everyday practices that are often subversive at an ontological and axiological level. However, the authors in this part refrain from offering a romanticized view of quotidian practices, and instead invite the reader to explore critically the freeing potential of alternative ways of learning and making the urban. Based on primary research conducted into lived, everyday experiences of 'the city' from around the world, the six chapters included in Part IV explore the richness, diversity and plethora of understandings and practices that challenge conventional, regulated governance approaches. They revisit the notion of freedom through themes such as food, work, money, bodies and public space.

Note to the Reader

Untamed Urbanisms offers a critical exploration of different strands in the production of the city, focusing in particular on those that celebrate diversity and progressive processes, fostering critical dreaming and strategic action. By drawing largely on original research by a new generation of urban researchers located in institutions and debating and planning circles across the global South and North, this book sheds new light on old debates and aims to stimulate and provoke fresh interrogations about sustainable urban development. The book has been entitled *Untamed Urbanisms* precisely because the chapters are linked by a shared concern to repoliticize the relationship between urban development, sustainability and justice, and to explore the tensions emerging under real circumstances, as well as their potential for transformative change. Furthermore, the contributors have the kinds of interdisciplinary backgrounds and working contexts that enable them to drift away from traditional disciplinary constraints and trajectories.

A distinctive appeal of the book, together with the cultural, disciplinary and geographical diversity of the contributors, is the variation of discursive rhythms. Not unlike the fusion style in jazz, the move from one chapter or major part to what follows is never flat, but provides continuously shifting planes and perspectives. From the global (Parts I and III) to more locally specific cases and reflections (Parts II and IV), and at the same time from the global South to the global North, the book itself cannot be constrained into a single style, line of argument or disciplinary logic.

As editors of this volume, we have passionately wrestled for decades with the challenging task of engaging with cities and urban change through our research, pedagogical approaches and engagement with action planning and political activism. As such, we are, like this book, equally troubled and inspired by the need for both more aspirational planning practice and actionable theory.

Like a triad of musical conductors, we have sought to produce music but not without dissonance. Dissonance might be perceived as unstable sound or noise interrupting the flow of melody and harmony. But dissonance is in fact the complement of consonance, the building up and releasing of tensions that contributes to what listeners perceive as beauty, emotion and expressiveness in music. In the same way, *Untamed Urbanisms* pulls the reader in various directions, but without dissonance, and recreated consonance there would not be music, just monotony.

In the concluding chapter we offer a cross-reading of the different contributions included in this volume and an evaluation of the epistemological, methodological and axiological consequences of such an enterprise. Meanwhile, we invite the reader to listen and enjoy the sound of the different chapters while embracing every dissonance encountered in the journey as a potential productive disruption to hegemonic thinking and action that aims to tame the untameable.

References

Allen, A. 2012. Water provision for and by the peri-urban poor: public partnerships or citizens co-production? In I. Vojnovic (ed.), *Sustainability: A Global Context*. East Lansing, MI: Michigan State University Press.

—— 2014. Peri-urbanization and the political ecology of differential sustainability. In S. Parnell and S. Oldfield (eds), *A Routledge Handbook on Cities of the Global South*. London: Routledge, pp. 522–38.

Allen, A., Griffin, L. and Johnson, C. Forthcoming. *Environmental Justice, Urbanization and Resilience in the Global South*. London: Palgrave Macmillan.

Bayat, A. 2000. From 'Dangerous classes' to 'quiet rebels': politics of the urban subaltern in the global South. *International Sociology*, 15(3): 533–57.

Brenner, N. 2013. Theses on urbanization. *Public Culture*, 25(1): 85–114.

Brenner, N., Marcuse, P. and Mayer, M. 2011. *Cities for People, Not for Profit*. New York and London: Routledge.

Castells, M. 2012. *Networks of Outrage and Hope*. Cambridge, UK: Polity.

CPD, C40 and AECOM. 2014. *Protecting our Capital: How Climate Adaptation in Cities Creates a Resilient Place for Business*. London: CDP.

Crutzen, P. J. 2002. The Anthropocene: geology and mankind. *Nature*, 415: 23.
Davis, M. 2005. *Planet of Slums*. London: Verso.
Edensor, T. and Jayne, M. 2012. *Beyond the West: A World of Cities*. London and New York: Routledge.
Foucault, M. 2002. *The Archaeology of Knowledge*. London and New York: Routledge.
Giddens, A. 1984. *The Constitution of Society*. Berkeley, CA: University of California Press.
Gore, C. 2010. Global recession of 2009 in a long-term development perspective. *Journal of International Development*, 22: 714–38.
Greenhouse, C. J. (ed.) (2010). *Ethnographies of Neoliberalism*. Philadelphia: University of Pennsylvania Press.
Guy, S., Marvin, S., Medd, W. and Moss, T. 2011. *Shaping Urban Infrastructures: Intermediaries and the Governance of Socio-Technical Networks*. London: Earthscan.
Harvey, D. 2012. *Rebel Cities: From the Right to the City to the Urban Revolution*. London and Brooklyn: Version.
Hodson, M. and Marvin, S. 2010a. Can cities shape socio-technical transitions and how would we know if they were? *Research Policy*, 39: 477–85
—— 2010b. Urbanism in the Anthropocene: ecological urbanism or premium ecological enclaves? *City*, 14(3): 299–313.
Hoornweg, D. and Freire, M. 2013. *Building Sustainability in an Urbanizing World*. Urban Development Series Report Number 17. Washington, DC: World Bank.
Inam, A. 2014. *Designing Urban Transformation*. New York and London: Routledge.
Komninos, N. 2009. Intelligent cities: towards interactive and global innovation. *International Journal of Innovation and Regional Development*, 1(4): 337–55.
Marcuse, P., Connolly, J., Novy, J., Olivo, I., Potter, C. and Steil, J. 2009. *Searching for the Just City*. London and New York: Routledge.
Maricato, E. 2009. Fighting for just cities in capitalism's periphery. In Marcuse, P., Connolly, J., Novy, I., Olivo, C., Potter and Steil, J. (eds), *Searching for the Just City*. New York and London: Routledge, pp. 72–88.
McFarlane, C. 2011. *Learning the City: Knowledge and Translocal Assemblage*. Oxford: Wiley Blackwell.
Makhulu, A. M. 2010. The question of freedom: post-emancipation South Africa in a neo-liberal age. In Greenhouse, C.J. (ed.), *Ethnographies of Neoliberalism*. Philadelphia: University of Pennsylvania Press.
Miyazaki, H. 2010. The temporality of no hope. In Greenhouse, C.J. (ed.), *Ethnographies of Neoliberalism*. Philadelphia: University of Pennsylvania Press.
Mitlin, D. 2008. With and beyond the state: co-production as a route to political influence, power and transformation for grassroots organizations. *Environment and Urbanization*, 20: 339–60.
Mitlin, D. and Satterthwaite, D. 2013. *Urban Poverty on the Global Scale: Scale and Nature*. New York and London: Routledge.
Morin, E. 1999. *Homeland Earth*. Cresskill, NJ: Hampton Press.
Myers, G. 2011. *African Cities: Alternative Visions of Urban Theory and Practice*. London: Zed Books.
Parnell, S. and Oldfield, S. 2014. *The Routledge Handbook on Cities of the Global South*. London and New York: Routledge.
Perez, C. 2002. *Technological Revolutions and Financial Capital: The Dynamics of Bubbles and Golden Ages*. Cheltenham, UK: Elgar.

—— 2007. *Great Surges of Development and Alternative Forms of Globalization*. Working Papers in Technology Governance and Economic Dynamics. Norway and Estonia: The Other Canon Foundation (Norway) and Tallinin University of Technology (Tallinin).

—— 2013. Unleashing a Golden Age after the financial collapse: drawing lessons from history. *Environmental Innovation and Societal Transitions*, 6: 9–23.

Pieterse, E. 2008. *City Futures: Confronting the Crisis of Urban Development*. Cape Town: UCT Press.

Pieterse, E. and Simone, A. M. 2013. *Rogue Urbanism: Emergent African Cities*. Johannesburg and Cape Town: Jacana.

Robinson, J. 2006. *Ordinary Cities: Between Modernity and Development*. London: Routledge.

Roy, A. 2009. The 21st-century metropolis: new geographies of theory. *Regional Studies*, 43(6): 819–830.

Sassen, S. 2014. *Expulsions: Brutality and Complexity in the Global Economy*. Harvard: Harvard University Press.

Siemens PwC and Berwin Leighton Paisner. 2014. *Investor Ready Cities: How Cities can Create and Deliver Infrastructure Value*. London: Siemens.

Simone, A. 2010. *City Life from Jakarta to Dakar: Movements at the Crossroads*. London: Routledge.

Simone, A. and Abouhani, A. 2005. *Urban Processes and Change in Africa*. London: Zed Press.

Swilling, M. Forthcoming. Ecocultural assemblages in the urbanizing global South. In J. Pretty (ed.), *Ecocultures: Blueprints for Sustainable Communities*. London: Routledge.

—— 2013. Economic crisis, long waves and the sustainability transition: an African perspective. *Environmental Innovations and Societal Transitions*, 6: 95–115.

—— 2011. Reconceptualising urbanism, ecology and networked infrastructures. *Social Dynamics*, 37(1): 78–95.

Swilling, M. and Annecke, E. 2012. *Just Transitions: Explorations of Sustainability in an Unfair World*. Cape Town and Tokyo: UCT Press & United Nations University Press.

Swilling, M., Tavener-Smith, L., Keller, A., von der Heyde, V. and Wessels, B. 2013. *Rethinking Incremental Urbanism: Co-Production of Incremental Informal Settlement Upgrading Strategies*. Just Transitions – International Sustainable Development Research Conference: Stellenbosch. 2–4 July 2013.

Tonkiss, F. 2013. *Cities by Design: The Social Life of Urban Form*. Cambridge, UK: Polity Press.

Townsend, A.M. 2013. *Smart Cities: Big Data, Civic Hackers, and the Quest for a New Utopia*. New York and London: W.W. Norton & Company.

UN Habitat. 2013. *Urban Patterns for a Green Economy*. Nairobi: UN Habitat.

Watson, V. 2009. Seeing from the South: refocusing urban planning on the globe's central urban issues. *Urban Studies*, 46: 2259–75.

Whittaker-Ferreira, J.S. 2007. *O Mito Da Cidade-Global: O Papel da Idologia na Producao do Espaco Urbano*. Sao Paulo: UNESP.

Part I

Trajectories of change in the urban Anthropocene

Written by researchers located in both the global North and South, the chapters in Part I discuss the general trajectories of urban change that have emerged in the urban Anthropocene.

Chapter 1 by Mark Swilling (South Africa) – entitled 'Towards sustainable urban infrastructures for the urban Anthropocene' – challenges the ecologically disembodied conception of urban modernity by introducing into urban analysis an understanding of metabolic flows of resources through urban systems. Urban modernity tamed nature by reducing it to flows conducted by urban infrastructures whose designs and governance have not changed much since the nineteenth century. In order to establish a way of reconfiguring urban infrastructures, Swilling argues for the need to re-embed urban systems within a wider conception of bioregional resource flows which contrasts with how these flows are taken for granted within the traditional conceptions of urban modernity. In a resource-limited world where the distribution of resources needs to be more equitable, this is no longer feasible.

It is argued that the dominant mode of urban infrastructure governance is already being challenged in a number of ways, three of which are discussed specifically. The first two aim to tame the potential threats of resource limitations: either reinvigorate public sector infrastructure governance with a systems theory approach that recognizes the limits to centralized management, or privatize infrastructure governance using the smart city solutions. The co-production of urban services by organized social movements and state agencies is presented as another response, but this time as a response to the limits of state capacity to meet the needs of rapidly expanding urban settlements in poor and middle-class areas.

Despite the paradigms of urban planning that have implicitly denied the ecological contextualization of cities, Chapter 2 by Jenia Mukherjee (India) – entitled 'Sustainable flows between Kolkata and its peri-urban interface: challenges and opportunities' – argues that cities have always been embedded within local ecosystems which have been shaped and reshaped to suit urban requirements in very specific ways. The case study of Kolkata reveals how key actors have consciously planned and acted over many decades to tame the ecosystems that the city depends on for crucial services, from sewage treatment to food production. However, in recent years the emphasis has shifted from taming to outright destruction to make way for property developments. This, in turn, has resulted in attacks on the livelihoods of many who depend on Kolkata's peri-urban ecosystems, and also new developmental challenges, as ecosystem services such as sewage treatment are eroded.

Adopting a Western perspective on urbanization and the history of urban planning, Chapter 3 by Maarten A. Hajer (The Netherlands) – entitled 'On being smart about cities: seven considerations for a new urban planning and design' – contends that the taming of the city to prepare for fundamental changes is a recurring theme in the history of urban development. He refers to the sanitation syndrome in the late 1800s and the highway boom in the mid-twentieth century as two of the most significant precedents. Today's smart city agenda is the contemporary expression of this approach to city-wide restructuring. The smart city agenda is the most dominant contemporary discourse for taming the urban by invoking an algorithmic urbanism that promises to finally deliver on the nineteenth-century dream of the city as a seamless paradise of 'lights, water, motion' for all. However, Hajer's conclusion is that this is a false promise delivered by some corporates at a time when governments have declared defeat when it comes to taming the city.

Titled 'Is big sustainable? Global comparison of city emissions', Chapter 4 by Dominik Reusser, Anna-Lena Winz and Diego Rybski (Germany) points out that while it is important to think of cities from a carbon perspective, this must be done by differentiating between different kinds of cities in the developed and developing world, since efficiencies and income growth have differential impacts in the two regions. Their evidence suggests that in the developed world larger cities are less carbon intensive per capita than smaller cities, but the opposite is the case in the developing world where larger cities tend to concentrate expanding numbers of people whose incomes are rising rapidly.

Chapter 5 by Gareth Haysom (South Africa) – entitled 'Urban-scale food system governance: an alternative response to the dominant paradigm?' – addresses the contested linkages between cities and globalized food systems in a changing global context of rising food prices and increasing concerns about the security of urban food supplies. These global food systems are crisis-ridden because they must find ever more efficient ways of taming ecologically and socially exploited food-producing regions around the world in order to deliver nutritionally poor foods to a rapidly expanding urban population. The emerging role of cities as actors in this space raises the potential for key city-based actors to contest this globalized taming of food-producing regions by securing and ensuring adequate and even higher-quality food supplies from local sustainably managed food bioregions.

1 Towards sustainable urban infrastructures for the urban Anthropocene

Mark Swilling

Introduction

In recent years there have been numerous institutional reports, academic analyses and networks that have articulated the idea that cities are well positioned to lead the way when it comes to transitioning to more sustainable modes of production and consumption (Hoornweg and Freire 2013; Kamal-Chaoui and Roberts 2009; LSE Cities, ICLEI and Global Green Growth Institute 2013; Suzuki *et al.* 2009; Swilling *et al.* 2013; UN-HABITAT 2009, 2012; UNEP 2010; WWF 2010). The most recent reports by the World Bank (Hoornweg and Freire 2013) and UNEP (Swilling *et al.* 2013) have taken this further by emphasizing the significant opportunities for innovation and transformation provided, in particular, by the rising level of investment in urban infrastructures.

In this chapter I hope to reconcile what have hitherto been between separate trajectories of my research over the past five years: on the one hand an interest in the dynamics of the global polycrisis using long-wave theory (Swilling 2013), and on the other an interest in urban infrastructure transitions using a synthesis of material flow analysis and transition theory (Swilling 2013; Swilling and Annecke 2012). Given that previous industrial cycles have required particular spatial configurations (Swilling and Annecke 2012, ch. 5), I am fascinated by what the contemporary reimagining of the future of our cities (primarily in the global South) can tell us about what may be unfolding on a global scale.

The point of departure for this chapter is the long-wave perspective expressed in the Introduction that the global polycrisis marks a key turning point that brings into focus the global significance of the current rising level of investment in urban infrastructure. However, because this time round there are resource limits to what is possible, it needs to be accepted that in order to secure more sustainable metabolic flows through decoupling, it will be necessary to reconfigure urban infrastructures. This is unlikely if prevailing approaches to infrastructure planning and governance persist. Hence, a new discussion has started within the engineering profession about alternatives to the nineteenth-century infrastructure governance paradigm that remains dominant today. Two direct threats to the nineteenth-century paradigm are then discussed: the smart city agenda propagated by global technology companies, and the 'co-production platforms' emerging from the social movements active in the informal settlements of cities in the global South.

Urban metabolism and transition

Projections for urban growth over the next 30 years are staggering, but they assume that the available supply of energy and materials will be sufficient to meet growing demand. Given that many of the energy and resource flows that cities currently depend on are finite and in some cases are already reaching their limits, it follows that achieving ever more prosperous urban lifestyles for more people will depend on whether it will be possible to do much more with limited resources than is currently the norm. A new literature on the metabolism of industrialized societies has emerged that establishes the linkages between socio-technical and socio-ecological systems (Baccini and Brunner 2012; Farrao and Fernandez 2013; Fischer-Kowalski and Haberl 2007; Giampietro, Mayumi and Sorman 2012).[1]

Although contested (Jackson 2009), the term 'decoupling' has come to be associated with efforts to break the causal link between economic prosperity and the depletion of finite resources or degradation of environments, and can be used as a lens through which to envision the reconciliation of human and environmental interests in rapidly growing cities (Fischer-Kowalski and Swilling 2011; Swilling *et al.* 2012).

Conventional approaches to delivering services to urban dwellers use gigantic networks of centrally controlled interlocked wires, pipes, roads and other infrastructures to manipulate the vast and varied flows of resources that enter into, circulate within and exit from cities in support of particular conceptions of city living (see Swilling and Annecke 2012, ch. 5). Industrial ecologists refer to the build-up of what they call 'socio-economic stocks' within the city, consisting of material stocks (such as buildings and infrastructural systems) and the flows of resources that go into maintaining and using these stocks (such as energy and water). Studying the patterns of matter and energy moving through and within cities is critical in finding solutions to optimize them in the pursuit of better resource management (Costa *et al.* 2004; Farrao and Fernandez 2013; Swilling *et al.* 2012) and decoupling.

Urbanists outside industrial ecology who are interested in sustainability have in recent years integrated the general concept of resource flows into their analyses of urban economies (Crane and Swilling 2008; Guy *et al.* 2001; Heynen *et al.* 2006; Hodson and Marvin 2009, 2010; Robinson *et al.* 2013; Swilling 2010a, 2010b).The application of material flow analysis (MFA) to the city scale provides a useful framework for understanding the complex empirical dynamics of these flows (for recent examples see Barles 2009, 2010; Costa *et al.* 2004; Farrao and Fernandez 2013; Fernandez 2007; Kennedy *et al.* 2007; Robinson *et al.* 2013; Weisz and Steinberger 2010). Policy-makers wishing to promote a more sustainable city can use this kind of research to enable them to make decisions about the building of new – or retrofitting of existing – urban infrastructures that take into account the long-term flows of strategic resources into and out of the city. (For three major recent reports on this see Hoornweg and Freire 2013; Suzuki *et al.* 2009; Swilling *et al.* 2013.)

Rethinking urban infrastructure planning and governance

Urban infrastructures hold the key because they are potentially the focus of fiscal expenditures and private investments to stimulate economic growth; key fiscal investments in poverty reduction/eradication; and as social-ecological-infrastructural systems, determinants of the future ecological sustainability of the city and, by extension, the global economy. A number of leading global consulting companies are already encouraging investors to focus on the long-term returns on investments in urban infrastructure, which they estimate could rise to over $40 trillion in the next 20 years (Airoldi *et al.* 2010; Doshi *et al.* 2007). The World Bank estimates that annual investments in basic urban infrastructures in the global South need to be doubled to achieve the $1–1.5 trillion annual investment levels that are needed to meet basic needs (Hoornweg and Freire 2013: 8). Following two major global reports that focused attention on the key role that urban infrastructures will have to play in the building of green economies (Hoornweg and Freire 2013; Swilling *et al.* 2013), the question is whether these investments in a new generation of (new and retrofitted) urban infrastructures – often with life spans of up to 100 years – will in reality equip cities to handle the linked challenges of increasingly complex and therefore largely unpredictable dynamics of resource depletion, climate change, eco-system restoration, economic development and social equity. In short, can long-term infrastructure planning and investment be reconciled with uncertainty?

There are obviously problematic implications for cities in the fact that the power to make these capital investment decisions lies with a small group of major investors. Besides this, much will depend on whether it will be possible to reconceptualize the governance of urban infrastructure transitions in ways that help overcome the obduracy of 'locked-in' socio-technical systems. Transition researchers have been paying attention to this issue for some years now (Guy *et al.* 2001; Maasen 2012). According to a group of professors from MIT's Engineering Systems Division, the core problem is that the institutions and socio-technical systems for managing infrastructures today were first developed in the nineteenth century, when there was little need to consider the complexities of resource limits, financial constraints, the roles of non-state actors and the demands of scale brought on by the second urbanization wave. Although they call for a 'dramatic transformation of the scope, scale, and institutional architecture of these infrastructures' (Hansman *et al.* 2006: 148), they admit that '[d]espite the importance of infrastructure', the engineering profession has

> no comprehensive theory for it, no best practice approaches for its design, management, and transformation. We lack rigorous methods for developing, evaluating, and evolving future infrastructure architectures that must incorporate legacy elements while also responding to new technologies, knowledge, and demands.
>
> (Hansman *et al.* 2006)

While the mainstream engineering professions continue, it is hoped, to deliberate on these profound challenges, two alternatives have emerged that explicitly critique the rigidities of the nineteenth-century model. The first is the smart city agenda propagated mainly by the global technology companies (GTCs) and realized largely via the neo-privatization of urban infrastructure governance, while the second can be referred to as the incremental urbanism that has emerged in the sprawling semi-serviced or unserviced sectors of the cities of the global South. Whereas the former is positioned as an accumulation strategy to resolve the global polycrisis on terms that suit the shareholders of the GTCs, the latter reflects incrementalist strategies articulated by movements of the urban poor with very different outcomes in mind.

Before considering these alternatives further, it is necessary to explore the arguments by two groups of engineering researchers – the MIT group referred to above, and the Zofnass Programme for Sustainable Infrastructure at Harvard University's Graduate School of Design.

The MIT group suggests that to rise to this challenge, infrastructure governance will need to be thoroughly transformed in three ways (Hansman *et al.* 2006):

- a broader 'systems approach with deep technical and social science perspectives' will be needed that can cope with 'dispersed decision making and myriad stakeholders'
- strengthened relationships between practice and research will be needed to stimulate innovations for 'effective transition'
- a common approach across 'different infrastructure domains' will need to replace the existing disciplinary fragmentation and specialization that characterizes, in particular, city-level governance of urban infrastructures.

For the MIT group, rapid shifts in technology, deregulation, demand fluctuations, natural and social 'threats to operations', unanticipated competition, the impact of information and communication technology (ICT), and changing societal needs raise the following key question: 'Can we continue to rely on incremental changes to our systems?' (Hansman *et al.* 2006: 148). To provide a theoretical foundation for a more transformational approach that addresses this question, the MIT group suggests 'it may be useful to develop a network-based theory of infrastructure' (Hansman *et al.* 2006: 154). In practice, they argue, this would entail the radical step of defining infrastructures as complex adaptive systems, including the notion that system change entails mastering new methods and capabilities for integrated infrastructure planning across domains, working with external and internal stakeholders, developing shared visions and plans, and negotiating the nature of change.

For Norton, this will entail a conception of integration that is not about more technological advances. Instead:

> integration will require extensive and detailed cross-disciplinary understanding of multiple issues, across multiple domains. This represents a paradigm shift in understanding, in that future planners and designers will be less

'subject matter experts' of each relevant domain and more 'multiple domain experts' across wide disciplines.

(Norton 2013: Kindle loc. 2958)

This is certainly radical stuff for a profession trained to manage 'large technical systems' by building organizational cultures that value above all the logics of technocratic rationality, quantification and specialization (Summerton 1994). It remains limited, however, because it assumes all this can happen outside the global logics of power and accumulation, which often depend on technocratic fragmentation and reductionism.

Responding to the fact that nearly all the sustainability rating systems in the built environment sector have focused on buildings rather than infrastructure, Harvard's Zofnass Programme for Sustainable Infrastructure (ZPSI) has developed a rating system called Envision which is explicitly designed to rate large-scale infrastructure projects.[2] It is claimed that this approach is supported by 25 of the largest engineering firms in the world, which, it is claimed, collectively generate '60–70% of all engineering revenues worldwide' (Hoornweg and Freire 2013: Kindle loc. 159).

The Envision tool is explicitly designed to fundamentally change the way infrastructure is designed, constructed, operated and decommissioned from a sustainability perspective. This is achieved by rating each of these phases of the lifecycle using criteria explicitly derived from systems theory and ecological urbanism (Mostafavi 2012). The four primary categories are 'Resource allocation', 'Natural world', 'Climate change' and 'Quality of life', with specific criteria for each category weighted according to the phase of the lifecycle being analysed. Most significantly, the overriding aim to integrate infrastructure planning across traditional sector domains (energy, water, waste and so on) is reflected in the explicit realization that

> synergies and overlays of infrastructure systems had a significant potential contribution to sustainability. It was not enough to study and optimize a given infrastructure within its typological confines; the analysis had to expand in a multi-layered approach in which infrastructure systems would be grouped based on their synergistic potentials.
>
> (Georgoulias and Allen 2012: Kindle loc. 5971–7)

Table 1.1 summarizes the main categories, subcategories and key questions assessed by the detailed Envision criteria.

Significantly, this framework of analysis goes beyond energy/climate issues to include resource flows and eco-system services; and it includes social criteria under the 'Quality of life' category. Equally significantly, despite pressure to the contrary from the engineering profession, the group has resisted incorporating into the Envision tool cost–benefit, cost-effectiveness and economic assessment tools, on the grounds that if they were incorporated the results would be skewed in favour of these financial/economic factors.

Table 1.1 Categories, subcategories and key questions

Category	Subcategories	Key questions
Resource allocation	• Materials: reduce/reuse/recycle • Energy: use less/use renewable • Water: use less/reuse onsite	What is the source? – choose local and renewable How is it used? – be efficient How is it disposed of? – recycle and reuse
Climate change	• Emissions: reduce CO_2 • Adaptability: prepare for the future	Are you reducing climate impact? – emit less CO_2 Are you prepared for climate change? – build with an eye on the future
Quality of life	• Health: safety and precautions • Education: promote sustainability • Community values: respect community input	Are you protecting the community? – ensure safety and security Are you involving the community? – respect the culture and listen Are you promoting sustainability? – educate and inform
Natural world	• Site selection: choose the best site • Habitat: preserve the environment	Where is it located? – choose sites with least impact Are you preserving the environment? – limit pollution to site Are you preserving the ecology? – don't disrupt natural processes

Although the ZPSI approach will undoubtedly influence the future design and implementation of infrastructures via projects developed by some of the world's largest consulting firms, it suffers from two drawbacks for the purposes of this discussion. First, it is focused on infrastructure *projects* and not on the ongoing planning and management of city-wide urban infrastructure *systems*. The MIT approach articulated by Hansman and colleagues (2006) is, in this respect, more useful. Second, both the ZPSI and the MIT approaches lack a sense of urbanism. This is, of course, unsurprising given that the remit of both is infrastructure in general. Nevertheless, by establishing an assessment framework rooted in sustainability and systems thinking, both provide potentially useful points of departure for reimagining publicly accountable city-level urban infrastructure governance regimes and practices. However, what both approaches lack (despite the emphasis on complexity) is an appreciation of the limitations of all design and planning tools when it comes to transforming cities. The untameability of the complex dynamics of urbanism across all contexts is a reality that lies way beyond what most engineers seem able to grasp.

Smart cities and co-production platforms: alternatives or building blocks of a synthesis?

As I have argued elsewhere, it is unsurprising that the GTCs have emerged from the global economic crisis as the key agents of productive capital, with utopian ambitions to drive the next accumulation wave (Swilling 2013). They have all projected their respective hegemonic projects by synthesizing selected elements of the three dominant narratives of the current conjuncture: the information age, the urban age and the environmental crisis. This discursive synthesis has generated promethean images of a more sustainable world that can be achieved via the algorithmic transformation of urban infrastructures (Townsend 2013). The GTCs promise what most city governments cannot deliver: new 'green-tech' solutions, large-scale long-term investments in urban infrastructures and new governance capabilities. What they want in return is the right to invest capital on scale into the infrastructures of the world's urban space-economies to shape on their own terms the conditions for the next long-term development cycle. As Hajer argues in Chapter 3, like the Light Water Motion revolution which fundamentally transformed cities from the mid-nineteenth to the early twentieth centuries, if implemented over the coming decades these investments could transform what urbanism means in equally fundamental ways.

Various labels are used to refer to quite a wide range of initiatives which I prefer to think of as *algorithmic urbanism*, with the smart city agenda being just one version of this broad trend (Hollands 2008). These include the 'knowledge city' (which focuses narrowly on business–academia relations); 'creative city' (which enlarges the knowledge city to include the creative professions, as discussed by Lawton in Chapter 14); 'smart city' (mainly about ICT in networked infrastructures); and the 'informational city' (following Castells 2009, combining elements of the knowledge and creative city with cognitive transformations – both progressive and elitist – wrought by the phenomenon of 'self-managed mass communications'). More recently, the 'green city' discourse has emerged in certain narratives as synonymous with the smart city (European Commission 2010), while some grassroots open-source 'low-tech' initiatives have attempted to appropriate the 'smart city' narrative for counter-hegemonic purposes (Townsend 2013).

But what specifically is the smart city agenda? In my view, this label should be used to refer quite specifically to initiatives mounted by the GTCs to strategically position themselves (after all, IBM does own the copyright for the term). These include the C40 League's Siemens-funded Smart City initiative, and the World Business Council for Sustainable Development's Urban Infrastructure Initiative. The latter brings together experts from numerous GTCs (including Acciona, Aecom, AGC, CEMEX, EDF, GDF, Suez, Honda, Nissan, Philips, Schneider Electric, Siemens, TNT, Toyota and UTC), and case study work is taking place in Philadelphia, Pa.; Rio, Brazil; Surabaya, Indonesia; Tilburg, Netherlands; Turku, Finland; and four cities in Gujarat, India (Hoornweg and Freire 2013: 118).

Individual companies have also mounted their own global programmes, including IBM, which is regarded as the biggest player in the European context (Smarter

Cities Programme); CISCO Systems (Internet Business Solutions Group); Veolia (Veolia Environment, focused on urban systems management in the water, energy, waste and transportation sectors); Philips (Livable Cities Programme); Alstrom (EMBIX initiative for carbon-neutral eco-cities); and Siemens (Infrastructure and Cities programme). Siemens could well emerge as the biggest player in developing country contexts because it does not only do information systems; it can also finance and build bespoke heavy infrastructures (railways, wind farms, telecommunications and so on).

Furthermore, a number of major city-wide (including 'new city') developments are under way with at least one GTC as a major partner. Songdo in South Korea, where CISCO is the primary technology partner, is now the poster-child of this generation of high-tech smart algorithmic urbanism. Others include Dongtan City (on Chongming Island near Shanghai), Sino-Singapore Tianjin Eco-City, Sino-Singapore Nanjing Eco-Tech Island, Meixu Lake District (Hunan Province), Masdar City in Abu Dhabi, Sitra Low2No in Finland and PlanIT Valley in Portugal. (For an overview of these initiatives see Alusi *et al.* 2012.)

From this brief overview of the actors and initiatives, it should be clear that collectively the smart city agenda does amount to a hegemonic project in the making. More than likely, it will reinforce what Graham and Marvin (2001) called 'splintered urbanism' – private sector investments in 'premium infrastructures' that favour highly mobile web-connected urban elites within urban enclaves that are increasingly disconnected from the urban dynamics of the city as a whole (Luque *et al.* 2013). They could also fail on their own terms for being expensive property developments that lack viable economic foundations (Alusi *et al.* 2012: Kindle loc. 7614); or, as Richard Sennett argues, this 'closed system urbanism' could engender 'stupefication' by reducing the complexities that give rise to the 'cognitive stimulation through trial and error' that drives innovation – in short, the very opposite of 'smart' (Sennett 2012).

However, for the Harvard group a new mode of infrastructure governance will depend on the effective deployment (and related institutional reorganization) of the smart city technologies (Alusi *et al.* 2012; Papanikolaou 2012). It is clear that no matter which infrastructure governance model is adopted by a given city government, it is hard to imagine this being done in a way that does not take advantage of available ICT. Besides the cost-driven choices about what systems are affordable, the most serious choice is not whether to digitize or not, but whether it is necessary to digitize by effectively surrendering public control over one or more urban infrastructures to one or more GTCs. Some cash-strapped rapidly expanding cities in the global South, however, may have very little choice. There is evidence, for example, that Siemens is giving undertakings to some of these cities that it can raise the funds for new smart-grid-controlled urban infrastructures (such as public transport) if it is granted long-term (25–50-year) concessions to control these infrastructures. Taken to its logical conclusion, the worst scenario here is premium infrastructures for the rising middle class managed by a GTC (such as the new heavily subsidized intra-city rail systems in Johannesburg/Pretoria and Bangkok) while the rest of the population are left dependent on services provided by increasingly unaccountable cash-strapped city governments. This new form of techno-apartheid should be avoided.

Top-down algorithmic urbanism delivered by public agencies, GTCs or public–private partnerships is not, however, the only alternative to the nineteenth-century infrastructure governance model. In the sprawling under-serviced and unserviced sectors of the urban global South, households and communities have started to develop their own institutional forms for managing access to ongoing supplies of basic urban services (in particular water). The underlying social processes can best be referred to as *incremental urbanism* because access to services is not determined via connections to formal networked infrastructures, although this can be the eventual outcome. Incremental urbanism is the (often precarious) emergent outcome of myriad socio-technical assemblages created by households and communities engaged in the quiet encroachments of everyday life that make survival possible. (For examples of this perspective see Bayat 2000; McFarlane 2011; Pieterse 2008; Simone 2004.)

The more mature community-based institutional forms that have emerged from incremental urbanism for managing access to services have begun to be referred to as 'co-production platforms' (CPs) (Allen 2013; Allen *et al.* forthcoming 2015; Mitlin 2008; Swilling *et al.* 2013). It is these CPs that are significant for this discussion, especially in light of the argument by Allen and colleagues that they may well be precursors for a new mode of 'polycentric governance' of urban infrastructures. This could be more appropriate for the governance of incremental urbanism than conventional approaches (Allen *et al.* forthcoming 2015).

One of the more significant examples of CPs is the community water boards (CWBs) that have emerged in Latin America.[3] Known collectively as the Justicia Hídrica (Water Justice) movement, it is estimated that there are around 80,000 CWBs in Latin America supplying 40 million people in both poor informal settlements and middle-class neighbourhoods. In both Cochabamba (Bolivia) and Caracas (Venezuela), official state recognition and sanction of these CWBs confirmed the argument that they could become viable platforms for co-producing water services. After the election of Evo Morales in 2006 the Ministry of Water and the Environment was established with an explicit mandate to force 'co-production partnerships' with the 28,000 community-based water provision institutions (only 27 of which were formally recognized). Only 48 per cent of Cochabamba was serviced by SEMAPA, the municipal provider. Between 500 and 600 Comités de Agua (CAs) met the needs of the rest mainly by accessing groundwater or, as the groundwater was depleted, by buying water in bulk from vendors. The first CAs emerged in informal settlements in the 1980s, spreading into other poor and middle-class areas later on. In 2006, 49 CAs federated into an association (ASICASUDD-EPSAS) for the purposes of co-managing water services with the state ('co-gestión'). The Morales government has since actively supported the CAs 'as part of a wider overhaul of the water sector'.

In Caracas the CPs were associated with the Mesas Técnicas de Agua (MTAs – technical water committees). With origins going back to temporary experiments in the early 1990s when the Caracas municipal government responded to water protests by establishing the MTAs, the election of Hugo Chavez in 1998 created the space for permanent institutionalized CPs in the water sector. The local MTAs were revitalized and then federated into district-level Consejos Communitarios de Agua (CCAs) for co-managing neighbourhood-wide and city-wide plans. The model became national policy in 2001 when the Organic Drinking Water and Sanitation Service Act (LOPSAS) was adopted. Since 2001 the national agency that coordinates water provision for 80 per cent of the population, Hidroven, has actively supported the MTA-CCA model. There are now 7,500 MTAs in Venezuela.

Although formal state recognition in Bolivia and Venezuela allowed CPs in the water sector to proliferate, there are also many examples from other parts of the world. These include the well-known Orangi Pilot Project in Karachi, Pakistan, and the Baan Mankong in Thailand (Boonyabancha 2009; Hasan 2006), plus numerous projects in Asia, Africa and Latin America initiated by slum-dweller federations associated with Shack Dwellers International (see www.sdinet.org). In South Africa, my own recent experience in establishing CPs in the energy sector (using solar power) in informal settlements has confirmed that it is necessary to pay attention to revenue streams to cover the ongoing cost of operations and maintenance. This was achieved by combining subsidies from government and fees paid by the 'customers' of the social enterprises that were set up as energy vendors (Swilling *et al.* 2013). This approach has now been applied to local sanitation systems, which include biogas production as a complementary revenue source.

Is a synthesis possible?

Although the socio-economic interests driving the smart city agenda and incremental urbanism could not be more different, it is not difficult to imagine how they could be complementary. Undoubtedly, at the moment they are far apart: it is impossible to imagine how top-down private or public delivery of expensive smart city solutions can be reconciled with the grassroots polycentric governance represented by the CPs. Nevertheless, from the South African experience it is clear that a reliable incorruptible flow of revenues from slum dwellers into social enterprises can be achieved by using the cellphone network for making and recording payments. Similarly, the providers of subsidies can be reassured with real-time information that the funds are going to the targeted 'beneficiaries'. This is an example not of a smart technology that surrenders control to a GTC, but rather of how a community-based approach can be reconciled with public resources (subsidies) by using cutting-edge ICT that reduces transaction costs and secures transparency. In this way a thoroughly new mode of infrastructure governance can be created that works with affordable digital systems, and could make possible a more inclusive urbanism than a smart city alternative delivered by a GTC.

Conclusion

To conclude, it has been argued that mounting investments in urban infrastructures will, more than likely, shape the dynamics of the second urbanization wave, and determine how a transition to more sustainable urban metabolic cycles is conceived and executed by key actors. By embedding the challenge of urban infrastructures within an understanding of urban metabolic flows, it becomes very clear that the prevailing nineteenth-century infrastructure governance paradigm needs to be replaced. However, the discussion about this problem and possible solutions influenced by network approaches is still very much at an early stage within the mainstream engineering professions. At the same time, the GTCs are marketing their smart city solutions, and in the cities of the global South 'co-production' platforms have started to emerge that could potentially herald new forms of polycentric urban governance.

Future research will need to explore the institutional hybrids that may emerge, as algorithmic and polycentric governance fuse together into what could become a new networked mode of infrastructure planning and governance. To this end, it will be necessary to incorporate urban metabolic flow analysis into the analytics of these new modes of networked governance in order to ensure that they express rather than ignore the challenge of sustainable resource use.

Notes

1 For a thorough contemporary review of the application of this approach to cities, see Robinson *et al.* (2013).
2 See www.sustainableinfrastructure.org/rating/
3 This and the next paragraph on Bolivia's and Venezuela's CPs are drawn from Allen *et al.* (2013).

References

Airoldi, M., Biscarini, L. and Saracina, V. 2010. *The Global Infrastructure Challenge: Top Priorities for the Public and Private Sectors*. Milan, Italy: Boston Consulting Group.
Allen, A. 2013. Water provision for and by the peri-urban poor: public-community partnerships or citizens co-production? In Vojnovic, I. (ed.), *Sustainability: A Global Urban Context*. East Lansing, MI: Michigan State University Press, pp. 309–40.
Allen, A., von Bertrab, E. and Walnycki, A. forthcoming 2015. The co-production of water justice in Latin American cities. In Allen, A., Griffin, L. and Johnson, C. (eds), *Environmental Justice, Urbanization and Resilience*. London: Palgrave.
Alusi, A., Eccles, R. G., Edmondson, A. C. and Zuzul, T. 2012. Sustainable cities: oxymoron or the shape of the future? In S. N. Pollalis *et al.* (eds), *Infrastructure Sustainability and Design*. London and New York: Routledge.
Baccini, P. and Brunner, P. H. 2012. *Metabolism of the Anthroposphere: Analysis, Evaluation, Design*. Cambridge, MA: MIT Press.
Barles, S. 2009. Urban metabolism of Paris and its region. *Journal of Industrial Ecology*, 13(6): 898–913.
—— 2010. Society, energy and materials: the contribution of urban metabolism studies to sustainable urban development issues. *Journal of Environmental Planning and Management*, 53(4): 439–55.
Bayat, A. 2000. From 'dangerous classes' to 'quiet rebels': politics of the urban subaltern in the global South. *International Sociology*, 15(3): 533–57.

Boonyabancha, S. 2009. Land for housing the poor – by the poor: experiences from the Baan Mankong Nationwide Slum Upgrading Programme in Thailand. *Environment and Urbanization*, 21(2): 309–29.

Castells, M. 2009. *Communication Power.* Oxford: Oxford University Press.

Costa, A., Marchettini, N. and Facchini, A. 2004. Developing the urban metabolism approach into a new urban metabolic model. In N. Marchettini *et al.* (eds), *The Sustainable City III.* London: WIT Press.

Crane, W. and Swilling, M. 2008. Environment, sustainable resource use and the Cape Town functional region – an overview. *Urban Forum*, 19: 263–87.

Doshi, V., Schulam, G. and Gabaldon, D. 2007. Lights! Water! Motion! *Strategy and Business*, 47: 39–53.

European Commission. 2010. *Europe 2020: A European Strategy for Smart, Sustainable and Inclusive Growth.* Brussels: European Commission.

Farrao, P. and Fernandez, J. E. 2013. *Sustainable Urban Metabolism.* Cambridge, MA: MIT Press.

Fernandez, J. 2007. Resource consumption of new urban construction in China. *Journal of Industrial Ecology*, 11(2): 99–115.

Fischer-Kowalski, M. and Haberl, H. 2007. *Socioecological Transitions and Global Change: Trajectories of Social Metabolism and Land Use.* Cheltenham, UK: Edward Elgar.

Fischer-Kowalski, M. and Swilling, M. 2011. *Decoupling Natural Resource Use and Environmental Impacts from Economic Growth.* Report for the International Resource Panel. Paris: United Nations Environment Programme.

Georgoulias, A. and Allen, J. 2012. The Zofnass rating system for infrastructure sustainability and decision making. In S. Pollalis *et al.* (eds), *Infrastructure Sustainability and Design.* London and New York: Routledge.

Giampietro, M., Mayumi, K. and Sorman, A. H. 2012. *Metabolic Pattern of Societies: Where Economists Fall Short.* Abingdon and New York: Routledge.

Graham, S. and Marvin, S. 2001. *Splintering Urbanism: Networked Infrastructures, Technological Mobilities and the Urban Condition.* London and New York: Routledge.

Guy, S., Marvin, S. and Moss, T. 2001. *Urban Infrastructure in Transition.* London: Earthscan.

Hansman, R. J., Magee, C., de Neufville, R., Robins, R. and Roos, D. 2006. Research agenda for an integrated approach to infrastructure planning, design and management. *International Journal of Critical Infrastructures*, 2(2/3): 146–59.

Hasan, A. 2006. Orangi Pilot Project: the expansion of work beyond Orangi and the mapping of informal settlements and infrastructure. *Environment and Urbanization*, 18(2): 451–80.

Heynen, N., Kaika, M. and Swyngedouw, E. 2006. *In the Nature of Cities: Urban Political Ecology and the Politics of Urban Metabolism.* London and New York: Routledge.

Hodson, M. and Marvin, S. 2009. Urban ecological security: a new urban paradigm? *International Journal of Urban and Regional Research*, 33(1): 193–215.

—— 2010. *World Cities and Climate Change: Producing Urban Ecological Security.* Maidenhead, UK: McGraw Hill.

Hollands, R. G. 2008. Will the real smart city please stand up? *City*, 12(3): 303–20.

Hoornweg, D. and Freire, M. 2013. *Building Sustainability in an Urbanizing World.* Urban Development Series Report no. 17. Washington, DC: World Bank.

Jackson, T. 2009. *Prosperity Without Growth? The Transition to a Sustainable Economy.* United Kingdom: Sustainable Development Commission.

Kamal-Chaoui, L. and Roberts, A. 2009. *Competitive Cities and Climate Change*. Paris: OECD.

Kennedy, C., Cuddihy, J. and Engel-Yan, J. 2007. The changing metabolism of cities. *Journal of Industrial Ecology*, 11(2): 43–59.

LSE Cities, ICLEI and Global Green Growth Institute. 2013. *Going Green: How Cities Are Leading the Next Economy*. London: London School of Economics and Political Science.

Luque, A., Marvin, S. and McFarlane, C. 2013. Smart urbanism: cities, grids and alternatives? In M. Hodson and S. Marvin (eds), *After Sustainable Cities?* London and New York: Routledge.

Maasen, A. 2012. Heterogeneity of lock-in and the role of strategic technological interventions in urban infrastructural transformations. *European Planning Studies*, 20(3): 441–60.

McFarlane, C. 2011. *Learning the City: Knowledge and Translocal Assemblage*. Oxford: Wiley Blackwell.

Mitlin, D. 2008. With and beyond the state: co-production as a route to political influence, power and transformation for grassroots organizations. *Environment and Urbanization*, 20: 339–60.

Mostafavi, M. 2012. Why ecological urbanism? Why now? In S. Pollalis *et al.* (eds), *Infrastructure Sustainability and Design*. London and New York: Routledge.

Norton, J. 2013. The evolution of urban water and energy infrastructure systems. In S. Pollalis *et al.* (eds), *Infrastructure Sustainability and Design*. New York and London: Routledge.

Papanikolaou, D. 2012. Intelligent infrastructures. In S. Pollalis *et al.* (eds), *Infrastructure Sustainability and Design*. London and New York: Routledge.

Pieterse, E. 2008. *City Futures*. Cape Town, South Africa: Juta.

Robinson, B., Musango, J., Swilling, M., Joss, S. and Mentz-Lagrange, S. 2013. *Urban Metabolism Assessment Tools for Resource Efficient Cities*. Stellenbosch, South Africa: Sustainability Institute.

Sennett, R. 2012. The stupefying smart city. In R. Burdett and P. Rhode (eds), *Urban Age: Electric City Conference*. London: LSE Cities.

Simone, A. 2004. *For the City Yet to Come: Changing African Life in Four Cities*. Durham, NC and London: Duke University Press.

Summerton, J. 1994. *Changing Large Technical Systems*. Boulder, CO: Westview Press.

Suzuki, H., Dastur, A., Moffatt, S. and Yabuki, N. 2009. *Eco2 Cities: Ecological Cities as Economic Cities*. Washington, DC: World Bank.

Swilling, M. 2010a. Sustainability, poverty and municipal services: the Case of Cape Town, South Africa. *Sustainable Development*, 18: 194–201.

—— 2010b. *Sustaining Cape Town: Imagining a Livable City*. Stellenbosch, South Africa: Sun Media.

—— 2013. Economic crisis, long waves and the sustainability transition: an African perspective. *Environmental Innovations and Societal Transitions*, 6: 95–115.

Swilling, M. and Annecke, E. 2012. *Just Transitions: Explorations of Sustainability in an Unfair World*. Cape Town and Tokyo: UCT Press and United Nations University Press.

Swilling, M., Robinson, B., Marvin, S. and Hodgson, M. 2012. Reshaping urban infrastructure: material flow analysis and transitions analysis in an urban context. *Journal of Industrial Ecology*, 16(6): 789–800.

—— 2013. *City-Level Decoupling: Urban Resource Flows and the Governance of Infrastructure Transitions*. Paris: United Nations Environment Programme.

Swilling, M., Tavener-Smith, L., Keller, A., von der Heyde, V. and Wessels, B. 2013. Rethinking incremental urbanism: co-production of incremental informal settlement upgrading strategies. Paper for Just Transitions – International Sustainable Development Research Conference, Stellenbosch, South Africa, 2–4 July 2013.

Townsend, A. M. 2013. *Smart Cities: Big Data, Civic Hackers, and the Quest for a New Utopia.* New York and London: W. W. Norton.

UN Environment Programme (UNEP). 2010. *UNEP Green Economy Report: Sustainable Cities*, draft 2. LSE Urban Age Project. London: London School of Economics.

UN-HABITAT 2009. *Planning Sustainable Cities: Policy Directions – Global Report on Human Settlements 2009.* London: Earthscan.

—— 2012. *State of the World's Cities 2012/2013: Prosperity of Cities.* Nairobi: United Nations Human Settlement Programme.

Weisz, H. and Steinberger, J. K. 2010. Reducing energy and materials flows in cities. *Current Opinion in Environmental Sustainability*, 2: 185–92.

World Wide Fund for Nature (WWF). 2010. *Reinventing the City: Three Prerequisites for Greening Urban Infrastructures.* Switzerland: WWF.

2 Sustainable flows between Kolkata and its peri-urban interface

Challenges and opportunities

Jenia Mukherjee

Introduction

That over half of humanity now lives in towns and cities is the most complex socio-economic phenomenon of the twenty-first century. In slightly over two decades, from 2010 to 2030, another 1.5 billion people will be added to the population of cities; by 2030 that fraction will be increased to 60 per cent.[1] Although urbanization has occurred since ancient times in human history, the most important ways in which the urbanization processes today are different from urban transformations of the past include the scale, the rate, and the shifting geography of urbanization (Seto *et al*. 2013: 4). Urban growth in the coming decades will take place primarily in Asia (China and India in particular) and Africa (especially Nigeria). The developing world has already entered into the high-growth, rapid-transition phase of the urbanization process, marked by numerous problems and challenges including the swelling of slums and squatter settlements; lack of city-wide infrastructures for services such as housing, health and sanitation; privatization and commercialization of infrastructures; city development plans based on the logic of foreign capital; the widening gap between the rich and the poor; and the changing nature of the rural–urban divide.

Scholars argue that one of the crucial aspects of the contemporary urbanization process in the developing world is the emergence of what is defined as the 'peri-urban' or semi-urban interface, where rural and urban features tend to coexist increasingly within cities and beyond their limits (Allen *et al*. 1999; Allen 2003, 2009; Shaw 2005). Various recommendations are being made to incorporate this new concept into both theory and practice (planning). These include the application of the urban–rural gradient paradigm as a powerful organizing tool for studying urban ecology and initiatives to come up with a specific approach to be applied in environmental planning and management (EPM) of these areas (Allen 2003: 147).

The peri-urban constitutes an 'uneasy' phenomenon, usually characterized by either the loss of 'rural' aspects (loss of fertile soil, agricultural land, natural landscape and so on) or the lack of 'urban' attributes (low density, lack of accessibility, lack of services and infrastructure, and so on) (Allen 2003: 136) and recent urban expansion or sprawl in the developing countries. Interestingly enough, if we look into the pages of history, we find that the sharp disconnect between the urban and the rural is only a recent occurrence, first appearing as late as the early twentieth century. Densely packed housing and central institutions within the defensive walls of the city, and residential settlement spreading far beyond that limit (a phenomenon that we might today call sprawl), was a pattern found frequently in the Near East, Asia and medieval Europe (Boone and Modarres 2006; Elmqvist *et al.* 2013). The layout of other ancient cities (like those of the Khmer of early medieval Cambodia, the classic Maya of Central America, and some pre-colonial African societies) was marked by a different type of sprawl or area spread, where residences were interspersed among agricultural plots in an extensive low-density continuum surrounding central institutional buildings and monuments (Evans *et al.* 2007; Scarborough *et al.* 2012; Simon 2008; Elmqvist *et al.* 2013). Ecosystem services, mainly in the form of agriculture, within these greater cities or broadly defined urban boundaries provided a major share of the city's subsistence.

The disconnect between the urban and the rural, or the urban infrastructures and the wider ecosystem of the city, was imagined in the nineteenth century and built in the twentieth century (see introduction), the Chicago School of urban sociology being one of the chief proponents. Cities came to be considered as separate entities detached from their peripheral areas; the interactions, flows, links and linkages between the two, which formed a vital component for the sustenance of both, were neglected and ignored.

To know, understand and consider the great variation of urban histories, rather than depend on and draw from mere generalizations and universal theories, it is relevant and beneficial to use a historical perspective across a large space–time scale. This approach prompts a researcher to take a case-study-based approach to exploring specific trajectories of urban development, the evolution of a particular urban space, the interaction between the city and its periphery, and the changing realities as history proceeds. I am a student of history and an inhabitant of Kolkata, one of the three megacities of India with a population of 10 million plus.[2] In this chapter, I explore the complex interactions between Kolkata and its peri-urban interface (PUI) since the days of their inception during colonial times. Considering primary historical sources, including official documents, reports, letters, extracts, maps and plans, I argue that the city and its PUI co-evolved as consciously constructed spaces following a hegemonic discourse of domination/subordination, the latter functioning as an output and input, produced and required by the city.

The British tamed its natural ecology (in the forms of creeks, swamps and marshes) into waterscapes (i.e. extensive canals connecting the city with its hinterland) to accomplish colonial capitalist motives of revenue generation, unintentionally giving birth to the eastern sewage-fed wetlands that in turn emerged as the space for the informal, 'untamed' practices of marginal peri-urban communities. Post-colonial urban planning narratives in the immediate post-independence period were strategically constructed to tame the untamed, legitimizing rapid urban sprawl at the cost of the peri-urban wetlands, for seeking capital/financial gains. With the popularization of 'sustainable development' followed by 'sustainable urbanization', like many other developing cities, its 'environment' had to be incorporated within the ambit of urban planning of Kolkata, paving the way for state/municipality-led 'urban environmentalism' that increasingly built upon capital-intensive beautification schemes and projects securing resources for capitalist restructuring within the neoliberal regime (Bose 2013), the untamed scapes and practices being rapidly tamed. However, state-led environmentalism received both acceptance and rejection from the middle class, whose vision sometimes collaborated with the authoritarian vision of the beautification and development of the city but also sharply collided against it, the Kolkata wetlands case being the strongest manifestation of this aspect. Though the city is being increasingly untamed by 'authoritarian environmentalism' validating mega-urbanization at the cost of wetlands and supporting ecosystem resources and affecting urban–peri-urban linkages, it is yet extremely important to understand the production of the city through these complex dynamics and dialectics of taming and untaming theories and practices embedded in the pluralities of Kolkata's environmentalisms.

Overview and objectives

The sustenance of Kolkata heavily depends upon its interaction with its PUI, mostly in the form of wetlands in the eastern part of the city[3] that act as a transitional zone, an urban–rural continuum for a rapidly urbanizing space. The proximity of the wetlands to the city and their interdependence is what sustains them. The East Kolkata Wetlands (EKW) are the world's largest resource recycling ecosystem, fully managed by local inhabitants using inter-generational knowledge. They recycle around 600 million litres of sewage and wastewater generated by the Kolkata Municipal Corporation (KMC) every day. The canals, artificially excavated during the colonial regime with the triple purpose of facilitating trade, transportation and drainage, carry and dump sewage water into the wetlands. The wetlands in turn provide ecosystem services and livelihood opportunities to the peri-urban poor, who sell their surplus produce in city markets. Most importantly, unlike most other populous cities Kolkata does not have a separate sewage treatment plant; the wetlands as a natural sink (often regarded as the 'natural kidney' of Kolkata) provide free services which would have otherwise cost the city around US$ 80 million per annum.

In spite of this, the PUI is significantly dwindling in size, heavily interrupting the ecological balance and threatening the socio-economic benefits for both wetlands and city. Kolkata has urbanized rapidly with an east-centric bias during the post-independent period,[4] at the cost of her wetlands. Initiatives from environmental scientists and civil society advocacy groups played a crucial role in having EKW put on the Ramsar list of Wetlands of International Importance (www. ramsar.org) in 2002, which has helped to protect the remaining 12,500 hectares of wetlands from further encroachment. Although the EKW enjoy legal protection through court orders, legislation and international conventions, conversions from wetlands to estates is still taking place. Over the last ten years there has been

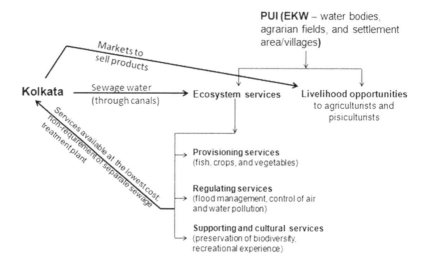

Figure 2.1 Sustainable flows between Kolkata and its PUI.

a sharp escalation of conversions, and a quarter of the surviving wetland area remains under severe threat. This spatial transformation through urban sprawl, disrupting the age-old urban/peri-urban interaction, implies catastrophic outcomes for the EKW and the urban systems that depend on it.

By going through expert and technical documents and from my own non-expert and non-technical repeated visits to the outskirts of the city (which made me nostalgic, since each time I went there I would notice and regret that a particular patch of green field or a water body had been replaced by concrete high-rise buildings), I identify the present challenges in the urban–peri-urban interrelationship, investigating factors behind their diminishing interdependence. The aim is to understand the whole issue within the politico-economic framework of urban planning in a developing city with a colonial heritage.

Urban and peri-urban: a colonial history of evolution and interdependence

Kolkata's natural ecology, with the Hooghly River on the west, the saltwater marshes on the east, and the Ganges and her numerous tributaries and distributaries intersecting the whole area, played a key role in the selection of the city as the seat of the imperial capital (Mukherjee 2009–10). The natural environment was gradually tamed, controlled and interfered with, keeping pace with the development of the universal laws of colonial hydraulics, to create an artificial system that facilitated both trade and transportation, and drainage and sanitation. The British project of urbanization implied the evolution and successful management of this complex hydraulic scheme.

The East India Company obtained a *Firman* (order) from the Mughal Emperor in 1677/78, which granted it rights and privileges to conduct trade freely in Bengal (the area of India in which Kolkata is located). There developed a brisk trade from 1680 onwards between the British, Dutch, Portuguese and French in the Hooghly region. The British wanted to establish an independent settlement in Bengal for appropriate exploitation of new trading opportunities (Roy 1982: 3). The three villages of Sutanuti, Kolkata (*Kalikata*) and Gobindapur, where Job Charnock had landed with a contingent of 30 troops on 24 August 1690, consisted of a narrow strip of land on the banks of the Hooghly, surrounded by swampy jungles and brackish lagoons on all sides. It was a place of mists, alligators and wild boars. Colonial reports and letters shed light on the unhealthy and deleterious environment of the area when the British first settled there (Chattopadhyay 1990: 6–8).

However, in spite of such disadvantages, the selection of the area was the result of a deliberate judgement on the part of the British, who realized the manifold ecological advantages that the place actually offered. The Hooghly River tapped the trade of the Ganges valley, and the settlement site was located at the highest point at which the river was navigable for seagoing vessels. The Ganges and its tributaries provided the foreign merchants with an opportunity to extend their trading operations inland over a wide area between Kolkata and other parts of Bengal, including Khulna, Faridpur, Backhergunj and Barishal. On the eastern side the site was protected from invasion by the presence of an extensive salt lake, the swamps and marshes of which made it invulnerable to the enemy. Moreover, the cost of land acquisition was less because of the marshy environment. Hence, the economic logic for the commercial development of the Ganges valley gathered momentum (Ghosh *et al.* 1972: 8), making way for Kolkata's urbanization.

Kolkata's urbanization occurred in parallel with canal construction and marsh reclamation. The colonial history of excavation of canals (which finally evolved into the city's Eastern Canal System: Inglis 1909: 1) and reclamation of marshes offers a unique insight into the growth of an expanding city. While the system emerged to make space for the colonial motive of interconnecting Kolkata with her hinterland, ensuring an unobstructed flow of raw materials and commodities to the city and the port, exploitation of economic opportunities was the most important factor behind Kolkata's expansion as one of India's largest urban centres. Inevitably, how to deal with the drainage and sewerage problem for the gradually expanding city became a major challenge. The Eastern Canal System, along with some additional cuts and excavations (which were then integrated into it), was built to drain the sewage into the saltwater marshes.

The first city drainage scheme directed waste water artificially into the River Hooghly (against the natural slope), and the river in turn provided drinking water to the city. This system failed in 1803, prompting the implementation of a new scheme. This involved an underground drainage system for disposing of sewage and stormwater through the same conduit into the saltwater swamps, which were then finally connected to the Bay of Bengal through the Bidyadhari River. The

Table 2.1 The Eastern Canal System: Excavated canals and the year of execution

Name of the excavated canal	Year of execution
Beleghata Canal	1810
Circular Canal	1831
New Cut Canal	1859
Bhangar Canal (canalized)	1897
Krishnapur Canal	1910

stormwater flow (SWF) and dry weather flow (DWF) canals were constructed following a combined drainage system designed by William Clark, a sanitary engineer and justice of the peace. The drainage scheme, comprising canals, sluices and bridges, and following the natural slope of the land,[5] was completed by 1884 (Ghosh and Sen 1987: 221; EKWMA 2010: 2).

It is important to note here that the Bidyadhari River acted as the outfall channel for the disposal of stormwater and sewage. The river rapidly showed signs of deterioration because the excavation and re-excavation of canals speeded up the process of silt deposition on the river bed. When it became absolutely defunct and was officially declared dead for both drainage and navigation in July 1928, a serious deadlock occurred in the city's drainage system. The immediate need was the implementation of an alternative outfall. The Kulti River seemed to be the only possible solution, and the Kulti Outfall Scheme was executed and commissioned in 1943. This led to a gradual transformation in the aquatic environment of the area from saline to non-saline; from saltwater marshes to sewage-fed freshwater wetlands. The Eastern Marshes were saline in nature, as the Bidyadhari River carried saline water from the Bay of Bengal and spilled over the low-lying area. The silting-up of the Bidyadhari River caused a decrease in the inflow of saline water. Moreover, with the decay of the river, sewage and stormwater came to be diverted into the saltwater lakes through canals, turning them into freshwater lakes. About 75 per cent of the total waste flows through the DWF and SWF channels from Bantala to Kulti (which is 22 km from Bantala); 15 per cent of the waste is carried from the northern part by the Bagjola Canal and Krishnapur Canal; and in the south, the Tolly's Canal carries 10 per cent of the additional discharge.

With this diversion in the discharge of the city, the salinity of the salt lakes dwindled from 800–1,200 to 500–600 parts per million. This turned the once profitable *nona bheris* (saltwater fisheries) into sewage-fed fisheries. The saltwater marshes that existed 200 years back between the Hooghly and Bidyadhari rivers gave rise to the present EKW (Gupta 2005: 24). When the Kulti Outfall Scheme was implemented, an adequate water-head was raised for supplying sewage to most of these fishponds by gravity, which resulted in the extension of wastewater fishponds further east and south-east for about 8,000 hectares (Ghosh 2005: 48).

The EKW lies between the levee of the Hooghly River on the west and the Kulti River on the east, and is distributed nearly equally between the two sides of the DWF channel that reaches the river. This serves as the PUI of the city and is, in turn, used as an output and an input, for material produced and required by Kolkata (Ghosh 2005: 43). In short, both the urban area and its PUI, and the inter-relationship and interdependence between the two, evolved as part of the colonial project of urbanization.

Free services versus colossal infrastructure: the recycling mechanism and present output from EKW

The EKW stretches over two districts, North and South 24 Parganas, and comprises 264 sewage-fed fisheries, agricultural land, garbage farms and some built-up area (Kundu *et al*. 2008: 868).

Following the pattern of land use, the EKW has been classified into two categories, the core and non-core wetlands areas. The core wetlands area includes water bodies and the garbage recycling area, and the non-core wetlands area includes agricultural land and settlement, spanning both rural and urban areas (EKWMA 2010: 7).

EKW generates various forms of ecosystem services including provisioning, regulating and cultural services. It has a long history of sewage-fed piscicultural and agricultural practices using local traditional knowledge. Informal aqua farming started in the late eighteenth century. After the decline of the Bidyadhari River, wastewater fishing, horticulture and agriculture were established as opportunities by private entrepreneurs. When the wetlands were transformed from brackish water lakes to sewage-fed fish farms with greater economic potential, large areas were also converted for settlements and agricultural development.

The most unique feature of EKW is the mechanism by which city sewage is treated and recycled into productive activities. The wetlands function as waste stabilization ponds (WSPs); sewage from the Kolkata Municipal Corporation (KMC) is treated in a series of contained pools in carefully managed conditions (Edwards 1992: 300). The canals function as anaerobic and facultative ponds and the fisheries act as maturation ponds. When the nutrient-rich effluent moves through the system, it is progressively cleaned and nutrients are redirected to the growth of algae or agricultural products grown along the pond edges. Solids are removed, composted and used to fertilize the surrounding fields. Algae and other aquatic plant materials are used to feed several fish species, which in turn create nitrogen and phosphorus-rich water to irrigate the adjacent rice fields (Jana 1998). Solar radiation is adequate for photosynthesis to occur. Solar energy is trapped by a dense population of plankton which is consumed by the fish. The fish not only maintain a proper balance of plankton population in the ponds but also convert the available nutrients in the wastewater into a readily consumable form (Kundu *et al*. 2008: 877). Here, nature and traditional knowledge mingle to create something unique and sustainable that could be applicable in other contexts. While

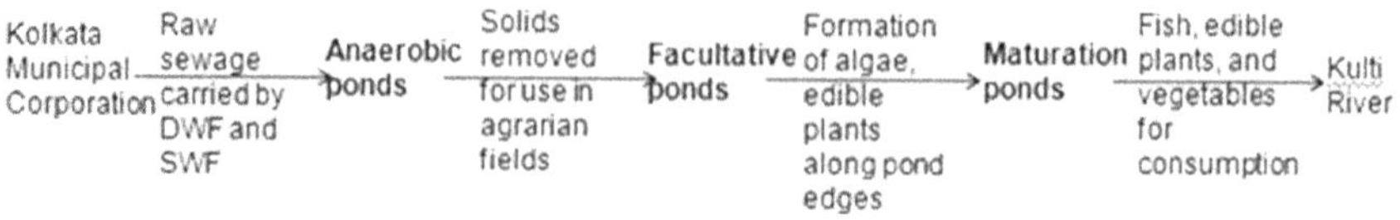

Kolkata Municipal Corporation → Raw sewage carried by DWF and SWF → Anaerobic ponds → Solids removed for use in agrarian fields → Facultative ponds → Formation of algae, edible plants along pond edges → Maturation ponds → Fish, edible plants, and vegetables for consumption → Kulti River

Figure 2.2 Waste recycling mechanism.

aquaculture can be described as a biological system, the wetlands function with additional inputs of fish seed, electricity, labour and a constant stream of waste-water and stormwater (Carlisle 2013).

The resource recovery mechanism has been developed and nurtured by indigenous peri-urban communities over many decades using low-cost technologies that run contrary to 'big technology' engineering and scientific waste management practices. Furthermore, the wetlands provide livelihood opportunities for these indigenous peri-urban communities. EKW is inhabited by 109 villages with a population of 150,000 (according to the household census of 2003). The fishers and farmers live on wetland produce and sell the surplus to city markets; 74 per cent of the working population draw their sustenance from fish farming, agriculture and horticulture (EKWMA 2010: 24). The city receives nearly one third of its daily fish requirement from EKW, which is about 11,000 metric tonnes per annum, and the area also produces 150 metric tonnes of vegetables each day.

The EKW provides not only free provisioning services (fish, crops and vegetables), but also regulatory and cultural services in the form of control of water and air pollution, groundwater recharge and flood control, preservation of biodiversity and habitat, and recreational spaces for the urban and peri-urban population.

Dwindling wetlands, diminishing flows: post-colonial urbanization and development

The interaction between Kolkata and her PUI is at stake as the wetlands face major challenges from innumerable factors. These include:

- Non-maintenance of water-bodies (*bheris*) and pollution: silting up of water bodies and canals, lack of infrastructure for aquaculture, lack of funds for maintenance of fisheries, irregular and insufficient water supply, lack of integrated aquatic resource utilization, insufficient sewerage supply (seasonal), and discharge of domestic and tannery effluent in the fish ponds.
- Non-availability of proper policies and legislation: unclear delineation of the wetland boundary, unclear land ownership, lack of development project assessment (environmental impact (EIA) and socio-economic), law and order problems, encroachment of water bodies leading to reduced employment, unscientific farming and harvesting because of union intervention, and lack of health and hygiene practices and education.

- Lack of awareness, abilities, rights and duties: absence of fishers' rights, lack of awareness among non-users and planners of the benefits, lack of coordination between the government, non-governmental organizations (NGOs) and locals, lack of work culture, limited ability of poor communities to fight encroachment, weakness of fishers' co-operatives, lack of recognition of fisheries as an industry.

However, a detailed investigation into these factors would show that mega-urbanization on the eastern part of the city since the post-independence period is the most severe threat to the wetlands, leading to shrinkage which in turn affects the urban/peri-urban interaction. This is the primary cause of the problem – all other problems flow from this.

West Bengal was flooded with a huge influx of people following Indian independence in 1947, which was accompanied by the partition of the country into two separate states, India and Pakistan. Kolkata, the capital of West Bengal, experienced the most population pressure, and this led the then chief minister, Bidhan Ray, to speak in favour of Kolkata's expansion through the rise of new townships. In 1956, it was proposed to establish the Salt Lake Township, at the cost of reclaiming the wetlands. In 1960, when 3.75 square miles of North Salt Lake was acquired, of the 58 fisheries of that area, 44 came to be sacrificed to meet the needs of the expanding city (*Master Plan* 1975). In the North Salt Lake area, 26 fisheries were taken over by the Salt Lake City housing complex alone, according to a report by the Kolkata Metropolitan Development Authority (KMDA) (KMDA 1976b). Between 1962 and 1967, 3,000 acres (approx.) of wetlands were filled up with silt from the Hooghly River to make way for major residential projects in Salt Lake City, and between 1967 and 1972 another 800 acres were converted for the expansion of the city (Kundu *et al.* 2008: 878). In the 1970s, 1,650 acres and 600 acres were reclaimed for the development of new projects and townships such as East Kolkata Township and Patuli respectively. In the 1980s, a part of the wetlands was encroached upon to make way for the construction of Eastern Metropolitan Bypass and Municipal Solid Waste Disposal Ground.

There were protests and petitions against this changing pattern of land use, typically displaying the nature of middle-class urban environmentalism in Kolkata. In 1991, city-based NGOs took up the cause of wetlands protection and conservation along with other environmentally minded bureaucrats. This was the first incidence of a movement that had an explicitly environmental goal in the metropolitan area. It forced the state government to take public opinion into account in its urban planning for the very first time. Several cases were fought in both the High Court and the Supreme Court to conserve the EKW (Dembowski 2001: 84–142). In 1992, a writ petition was filed by People United for Better Living in Calcutta (PUBLIC), as a lead NGO (joined by four other city-based NGOs) in the Calcutta High Court. The petition demanded that the State of West Bengal and its officers be legally bound to protect the wetlands in accordance with the West Bengal Town and Country Planning Act, 1979, section

46(1), Article 51A of the Indian constitution, which says that protection of the environment is one of the vital duties of the citizens of the country, and Article 21 of the constitution which implies the right to live in environmentally safe and pollution-free conditions.

The High Court delivered the verdict that '[t]here can't be any matter of doubt that the Calcutta Wetlands present a unique ecosystem apart from the materialistic benefit to the society at large' (Kundu *et al.* 2008: 879) and that no government or non-government body could reclaim any more wetlands. The Land Reforms Department and the Department of Environment, Government of West Bengal, identified 32 *mouzas* (local unit of land measurement) to be completely preserved as the waste recycling region of Kolkata. Following this, the land schedule and the report were sent to the Ramsar Convention, which then declared the EKW a Ramsar site (no. 1208) on 19 August 2002. A statutory authority called the East Kolkata Wetlands Management Authority (EKWMA), responsible for systematic implementation of wise use principles for the management of EKW, was set up under the East Kolkata Wetlands (Conservation and Management) Act in 2006.

But unfortunately, the Ramsar-designated 12,500 hectares, including 37 *mouzas* (five *mouzas* were later added), are also facing severe threats of rampant, unplanned urbanization. The EKW still suffers from ambiguous boundary definition and ownership. There is an immediate need to redraw the map of EKW, since no such effort has been made since 1985, and it is important to remove areas that have been urbanized, as this land-use change is irreversible (Niyogi and Ray 2013).

A *Times of India* (*TOI*) report said:

> Though the wetlands enjoy the protection of court orders, legislations and international conventions, there is no real shield on the ground. In the past 10 years, nearly 10 per cent of EKW has been converted into concrete. Another quarter of the wetlands are under threat. Land sharks use an old but ruthlessly effective method of walling up a part of the wetland and dumping tonnes of fly ash, concrete and garbage in the dead of night. Within weeks what was once a thriving *bheri* (fish pond) turns into dry land and the site for the next multi-storey.
>
> (Niyogi and Ray 2013)

The most threatened *mouzas* are Paschim Chowbaga, Chowbagha, Chak Kolar Khal, Kharki, Bhagabanpur, Karimpur, Jagatipota, Ranabhutia, Atghara, Mukundapur and Thakdari. Moreover, numerous water bodies have also been converted into paddy cultivation. The availability of sewage is not governed by the demands of fishers who are the primary users of it, but largely skewed in favour of the needs of the metropolis. During the monsoons, when there is significant waterlogging within the urban reaches of the city, the entire storm flows are flushed through the SWF to the Kulti River, leading to drastic declines in sewage flows by 60–80 per cent (EKWMA 2010: 21).

Table 2.2 List of *mouzas* in the Ramsar-designated EKW area

District	Police Station	Sl no.	Mouza	Status
South 24 Parganas	Tiljola	1	Dhapa	Part
		2	Chowbhaga*	Full
		3	Bonchtala	Part
		4	Dhalenda	Full
		5	Paschim Chowbhaga*	Full
	Sonarpur	6	Chak Kolar Khal*	Full
		7	Karimpur*	Full
		8	Jagatipota*	Full
		9	Mukundapur*	Full
		10	Atghara*	Full
		11	Ranabhutia*	Full
		12	Kantipota	Full
		13	Bhagabanpur*	Full
		14	Kharki*	Full
		15	Deara	Full
		16	Kheadaha	Full
		17	Khodahati	Full
		18	Goalpota	Full
		19	Kumarpukuria	Full
		20	Tardaha	Full
		21	Tihuria	Full
		22	Nayabad	Full
		23	Samukpota	Full
		24	Pratapnagar	Full
		25	Garal	Full
	Kolkata Leather Complex	26	Hatgaccha	Full
		27	Hadia	Full
		28	Dharmatala Pachuria	Full
		29	Kulberia	Full
		30	Beonta	Full
		31	Tardaha Kapashati	Full
North 24 Parganas	South Bidhannagar	32	Dhapa Manpur	Part
Added *Mouzas*				
South 24 Parganas	Purva Jadavpur	33	Kalikapur	Part
	Kolkata Leather Complex	34	Dakshin Dhapa Manpur	Full
	Tiljola	36	Nonadanga	Part
North 24 Parganas	Rajarhat	37	Thakdari*	Part

*Indicates the most threatened *mouzas*.

Beyond the consumption city? The polemics of urban planning and development

In the developing world, a serious loss of agricultural land, forest land and wetlands has taken place on urban fringes over the past few decades, occasioned by the tremendous growth of cities. Maintaining food production around urban areas is essential to the long-term survival of cities. Protecting these lands (and wetlands) from housing and industrial development and guaranteeing livelihood opportunities to the ecosystem-dependent communities are essential components in the development of successful strategies for urban food production (Furedy and Ghosh 1984). EKW is 'one of the rare examples of environmental protection and development management where a complex ecological process has been adopted by the local farmers for mastering the resource recovery activities' (Kundu *et al.* 2008: 869). But why did it face (and why is it still encountering) massive encroachment as a result of unplanned and uncontrolled urbanization on the eastern fringes of the city in spite of its tremendous importance? To understand this, it is imperative to look into the politico-economic forces that actually dictated the very pattern of Kolkata's urbanization and development in the post-colonial period, strongly influenced by local and global events.

To reiterate the point:

> The patterns and processes of urbanization in the developing world have been so strongly stamped by their colonial history that the contemporary reality cannot be properly understood without an analysis of the factors that were induced in the system during the colonial period to meet the requirements of imperialist exploitation.
>
> (Raza and Habeeb 1991: 49)

A three-stage model has been suggested for the economic and urban development of Kolkata (and also some other cities of India), characterized by distinct modes and relations of production and investment, policy and goals, and also distinct spatial forms. The stages are of a colonial economy during the first global period, a postcolonial (or command) economy during the nationalist period, and a post-command/reform economy during the second global period (Chakravorty 2000: 56–77).

Like many other port cities, Kolkata was created and colonized for colonial extraction and profit, to act as a point of trans-shipment of commodities and market for processed goods, and as a seat of administration. The urban layout and structure absolutely suited colonial needs and interests. As the main basis of the city was export trade, it was elaborately and inextricably connected and linked with Bengal and other parts of eastern India by canals, roads and railways. Urbanization was externally imposed to meet the needs of the colonial economy, 'delinked from the developments in the rural areas'; a 'colonially-induced urbanization . . . without roots' (Dasgupta 1987: 278). While Kolkata grew as a port city and administrative centre, the rest of Bengal remained backward, agrarian-based, and neglected. The population remained highly concentrated in Kolkata and its periphery (Dasgupta 1987: 279). In the immediate post-colonial nationalist phase 'development' as opposed to exploitation and extraction became predominant, with key ideas like import substitution, infant industry protection, balanced growth, self-sufficiency dominating the scene. In the present stage, like most of its 'developing' counterparts,

Kolkata has been reconnected to the global market following the failure of imports to substitute for industrialization in the south and the demand for new markets and production centres in the north (Chakravorty, 2000: 56–77).

Since the early 1990s India has followed the economic policies of the multilateral funding agencies, specifically structural adjustment programmes (SAPs) and associated privatization and commercialization of urban infrastructures (Mahadevia 2001: 242–59). Environmental programmes for making Indian cities, including Kolkata (along with Chennai, Hyderabad, Bangalore and Delhi), more sustainable have been undertaken. With the support of the UK Overseas Development Agency (ODA) (now known as the Department for International Development, DfID), the first Calcutta Environment Management Planning Strategy and Action Plan (CEMSAP) was initiated in 1995–6; the documents produced by CEMSAP were later used, at least partially, for improvement of the environment in the city. The Kolkata Environment Improvement Project (KEIP) was initiated in 2002 under the Sustainable City Programme (SCP), with the improvement of canals (including those carrying the sewage into the EKW) and solid waste management being important components of the project.[6] KEIP also stressed the treatment of sewage discharged into the DWF to increase the productivity of EKW fisheries. But in spite of the constant claims that it was a success story, most of its provisions have not been implemented, and of what has so far been implemented, the quality of implementation has been poor. This is an Asian Development Bank (ADB) funded project with an estimated cost of US$ 220 million. The external agencies have exerted a strong influence on official programmes and the city has fallen into a debt trap without any actual improvement of its urban infrastructure.

The duality and ambiguity in urban planning can be traced back to the formation of the KMDA in 1970 and the publication of the *Development Perspective Plan* in 1976, which emphasized a polycentric model of development along the east–west spatial growth axis of the city. This itself violated the earlier *Basic Development Plan* (BDP) of 1966, which focused on a bi-nodal strategy along a north–south urban development axis (KMPO 1966; KMDA 1976a). Since the implementation of DPP, the eastern periphery of Kolkata – the PUI – has become a space for real-estate speculation. The KMDA tried to attract private investment for projects aimed at the development of commercial complexes and market areas.[7] Although the next major plan of 1990, *Plan for Metropolitan Development 1990–2015*, generated warnings about the negative implications of the east-centric urban sprawl, development projects and urban expansion continued in the same manner at the cost of the city's wetlands (KMDA 1990). It is clear from the planning reports that the actual purpose of this pattern of urban expansion is to capitalize on the enormous development potential in the vast stretch of undeveloped land on the city's eastern fringes.

Conclusion

The dominant literature on urbanization and its present challenges focuses on the hardware of cities (built city infrastructure: transportation systems, housing, water works, sanitation, slums and so on). Scholars (especially urban sociologists) also seem to be concerned about the software of cities (as centres of creativity and lifestyle, involving culture and learning institutions and so on). But very little is written about the ecological infrastructure of cities which involves their wider ecosystems (Sukhdev 2013: v). A focus on the third aspect, reflecting more on the ecology 'of' cities rather than ecology 'in' cities (McDonnell 2011) can be an important approach to address the global discourse on urbanization and sustainability.

Urban places have to be studied as integrated components of long-term resilience. The urban includes much more than a particular density of people or area covered by built structures; it has to be considered as a complex socio-ecological system. Without such approach, important feedback mechanisms would remain invisible, misinforming policy and action. A redefinition of urban sustainability through the reintroduction of the social-ecological perspective would make invisible feedbacks and connections visible (Elmqvist *et al.* 2013: 14). The historical methodology (including historical analogy, forecasting, backcasting and so on) is extremely useful not only to identify the present challenges of urbanization (within the larger global context) but also to explore the potentials and opportunities for a particular city. Critical exploration and examination of the complexities of taming and untaming becomes essential to recognize and understand the complex making and remaking of the urban Anthropocene at multiple levels, including the different visions of the different actors in the social hierarchy regarding 'preservation', 'restoration' and most importantly 'improvement' of city and its natural environment.

When I look into the canals of Kolkata, which seem to be taking their last gasps, and visit the still remaining watery world of EKW in the midst of lush greenery, I deeply feel the need for sustenance for these lifelines of the city; the need for re-embedding the infrastructure of Kolkata within its wider ecosystems. As far as this particular case study is concerned, the survival of both the urban and the peri-urban completely depends on the continuation of their mutual interdependence through the proper functioning of sustainable flows between the city and its periphery.

Notes

1 Population Reference Bureau www.prb.org/Publications/Articles/2007/UrbanPopTo BecomeMajority.aspx (accessed 25 May 2014).
2 According to the latest census of India (2011), Greater Mumbai with a population of 18,414,288 continues to be India's biggest city, followed by Delhi (16,314,838) and Kolkata (14,112,536).
3 The wetlands are known as the East Kolkata Wetlands, and the nomenclature is owing to Dhrubajyoti Ghosh, an environmental engineer, who first discovered and documented the resource recovery features of the landscape.
4 India achieved independence on 15 August 1947.
5 The city had a natural eastwards elevation. The wetlands were nearly 8.5 ft (2.6 metres) below the highest point of the city.

6 www.keip.in/bl3/
7 It is important to mention here that in 1973 the International Development Association (IDA), a soft-loan associate of the World Bank, agreed to provide financial assistance for 44 out of 100 ongoing schemes under KMDA. The credit package amounted to US$ 35 million. IDA–I marked the beginning of a series of such credits for the development of Kolkata. The 278 crores rupees allocated for the Five-Year investment plan (1979–83) included World Bank assistance of US$ 87 million for a package of projects under IDA–II (Roy and Roy 1990).

References

Allen, A. 2003. Environmental planning and management of the peri-urban interface: perspectives on an emerging field. *Environment and Urbanization*, 15(1): 135–48.
—— 2009. Sustainable cities or sustainable urbanisation? *Palette* issue 1. Available at www.ucl.ac.uk/sustainable-cities (accessed 15 December 2013).
Allen, A., da Silva, N. L. A. and Corubolo, E. 1999. *Environmental Problems and Opportunities of the Peri-urban Interface and their Impact upon the Poor*. London: Peri-urban Research Project Team, Development Planning Unit, University College London. Available at http://discovery.ucl.ac.uk/37/1/DPU_PUI_Allen_Corubolo_daSilva_Environmental.pdf (accessed 26 May 2014).
Boone, C. G. and Modarres, A. 2006. *City and Environment*. Philadelphia, PA: Temple University Press.
Bose, P. 2013. Bourgeois environmentalism, leftist development and neoliberal urbanism in the city of joy. In T. Samara, S. He and G. Chen (eds), *Locating Right to the City in the Global South*. London: Routledge.
Carlisle, S. 2013. Productive filtration: living system infrastructure in Calcutta. *Landscape Urbanism*. Available at http://landscapeurbanism.com/article/productive-filtration-living-system-infrastructure-in-calcutta/ (accessed 15 September 2013).
Chakravorty, S. 2000. From colonial city to globalizing city? The far-from-complete spatial transformation of Calcutta. In P. Marcuse and R. V. Kempen (eds), *Globalizing Cities: A New Spatial Order?* Oxford: Blackwell.
Chattopadhyay, H. 1990. *From Marsh to Township East of Calcutta: A Tale of Salt Water Lake and Salt Lake*. Calcutta: K. P. Bagchi.
Dasgupta, B. 1987. Urbanisation and rural change in West Bengal. *Economic and Political Weekly*, 22(7): 276–87.
Dembowski, H. 2001. *Taking the State to Court: Public Interest Litigation and the Public Sphere in Metropolitan India*. New Delhi: Asia House. Available at www.asienhaus.de/public/archiv/taking_the_state_to_court.pdf (accessed 10 September 2008).
East Kolkata Wetlands Management Authority. 2010. *Conservation and Management Plan of East Kolkata Wetlands*. West Bengal: Dept. of Environment, Govt. of West Bengal. Available at www.ekwma.com/uploads/cmp_ekw.pdf (accessed 10 May 2012).
EKWMA and Wetlands International. 2010. *East Kolkata Wetlands Newsletter*. New Delhi: Print Shop. Available at www.wetlands.org (accessed 10 May 2012).
Edwards, P. 1992 *Reuse of Human Wastes in Aquaculture: A Technical Review*. Water and Sanitation Report No. 2. Washington, DC: World Bank.
Elmqvist, T., Redman, C. L., Barthel, S. and Costanza, R. 2013. History of urbanization and the missing ecology. In T. Elmqvist *et al.* (eds), *Urbanization, Biodiversity and Ecosystem Services: Challenges and Opportunities*. Dordrecht, Netherlands, Heidelberg, Germany, New York and London: Springer.

Evans, D., Pottier, C., Fletcher, R., Hensley, S., Tapley, I., Milne, A. and Barbetti, M. 2007. A comprehensive archaeological map of the world's largest preindustrial settlement complex at Angkor, Cambodia. *Proceedings of the National Academy of Sciences*, 104(36): 14277–82.

Furedy, C. and Ghosh, D. 1984. Resource-conserving traditions and waste disposal. *Conservation and Recycling*, 7(2–4): 159–65.

Ghosh, D. 2005. *Ecology and Traditional Wetland Practice: Lessons from Wastewater Utilisation in the East Calcutta Wetlands*. Calcutta: Worldview.

Ghosh, D. and Sen, S. 1987. Ecological history of Calcutta's wetlands conversion. *Environmental Conservation*, 14(3): 219–26.

Ghosh, M., Dutta, A. K. and Ray, B. 1972. *Calcutta: A Case Study in Urban Growth Dynamics*. Calcutta: Firma KLM.

Gupta, G. 2005. *Urban Wastewater: Livelihoods, Health and Environmental Impacts in India, The Case of the East Calcutta Wetlands*. New Delhi: Winrock International.

Inglis, W. A. 1909. *The Canals and Flood Banks of Bengal*. Calcutta: Bengal Secretariat Press.

Jana, B. B. 1998. Sewage-fed aquaculture: the Calcutta model. *Ecological Engineering*, 11: 73-85.

KMDA. 1976a. *Development Perspective Plan*. Kolkata, India: KMDA.

—— 1976b. *Area Development Strategy for Salt Lake Township (Bidhannagar)*, KMDA Report no. 6, Kolkata, India: Metropolitan Planning Circle, Directorate of Planning, KMDA.

—— 1990. *Plan for Metropolitan Development, 1990–2015*. Report no. 228. Kolkata, India: KMDA.

Kolkata Metropolitan Planning Organization (KMPO). 1966. *Basic Development Plan for the Calcutta Metropolitan District 1966–86*. Kolkata, India: Development and Planning Department, KMPO.

Kundu, N., Pal, M. and Saha, S. 2008. East Kolkata Wetlands: a resource recovery system through productive activities. *Proceedings of Taal 2007: The 12th World Lake Conference*: 868–81. Available at http://wldb.ilec.or.jp/data/ilec/wlc12/G%20-%20Pollution%20Abatement/G-1.pdf (accessed 23 March 2010).

McDonnell, M. J. 2011. The history of urban ecology: an ecologist's perspective. In J. Niemelä et al. (eds), *Urban Ecology: Patterns, Processes and Applications*. Oxford: Oxford University Press.

Mahadevia, D. 2001. Sustainable urban development in India: an inclusive perspective. *Development in Practice*, 1 (2–3): 242–59.

Master Plan for Fisheries Development. 1975. West Bengal: Part III.

Mukherjee, J. 2009–10. The victory of site over situation: exploring ecological dynamics behind Calcutta's selection as the seat of colonial capital. *Quarterly Review of Historical Studies*, 49 (3/4): 40–55.

Niyogi, S. and Ray, S. 2013. Wetland watchdog worries for Kolkata. *Times of India*, 13 July.

Raza, M. and Habeeb, A. 1991. Characteristics of colonial urbanization: a case study of the satellitic 'primacy' of Calcutta (1850–1921). In M .S. A. Rao, C. Bhat and L. N. Kadekar (eds), *Reader in Urban Sociology*. Hyderabad, India: Orient Longman.

Roy, B. 1982. *Marshes to Metropolis Calcutta (1481–1981)*. Calcutta, India: National Council of Education.

Roy, S. K. and Roy, K. 1990. Planning for action: the CMDA's involvement. In J. Racine (ed.), *Calcutta 1981: The City, its Crisis, and the Debate on Urban Planning and Development*. New Delhi: Concept.

Scarborough, V. L., Chase, A. F. and Chase, D. Z. 2012. Low-density urbanism, sustainability and IHOPE-Maya: Can the past provide more than history? *UGEC Viewpoints*, 8: 20–4.

Seto, K. C., Parnell, S. and Elmqvist, T. 2013. A global outlook on urbanization. In T. Elmqvist *et al.* (eds), *Urbanization, Biodiversity and Ecosystem Services: Challenges and Opportunities*. Dordrecht, Netherlands, Heidelberg, Germany, New York and London: Springer.

Shaw, A. 2005. Peri-urban interface of Indian cities: growth, governance and local initiatives. *Economic and Political Weekly*, 40(2): 129–36.

Simon, D. 2008. Urban environments: issues on the peri-urban fringe. *Annual Review of Environment and Resources*, 33: 167–85.

Sukhdev, P. 2013. Foreword. In T. Elmqvist *et al.* (eds), *Urbanization, Biodiversity and Ecosystem Services: Challenges and Opportunities*. Dordrecht, Netherlands, Heidelberg, Germany, New York and London: Springer.

3 On being smart about cities

Seven considerations for a new urban planning and design

Maarten A. Hajer

Smart cities or smart urbanism

Cities periodically experience transitions. There have been at least two in the past 200 years. In the nineteenth century, Western cities transitioned from medieval to industrial city structures. In Europe, motivated by taming discourses derived from the logic of industrialism, city planners tore down the city walls to make way for a new infrastructure of factories, railways and housing. They installed elaborate sanitary infrastructures to combat diseases. In the twentieth century, the invention of the car initiated a second transition. This time motivated by the taming potential of urban modernity, the resultant large-scale readjustments resulted in ring roads, high-rise tower blocks, central business districts and the 'suburb'. Today, there is a need, some argue, to re-tame the city by making a transition to eco-efficient city structures, or what some technology companies refer to as 'smart cities'.

The taming discourse of the 'smart city' promises an era of innovative urban planning. Information and communication technology (ICT) drives the discourse, aiming to make cities safer, cleaner and more efficient. Smart cities will then be able to 'sense' behaviour via 'big data' and use this feedback to manage urban dynamics. City planning will then become a continuous experiment, with cities serving as 'living labs' for new products and services. The optimism of this new taming discourse is captivating, but requires critical interrogation.

This chapter aims to assess whether this idea of smart cities possibly contributes to the quest for the sustainable and resilient urban system we need. It reflects on the motivations for and challenges of past transitions to appreciate the untameable complexity and multifaceted nature of urban transitions that the smart city discourse may be ignoring.

Urbanization is always the outcome of a process of discourse formation in which coalitions shape up and solidify around particular agendas, approaches and technologies. In that sense, studying smart cities is of paramount importance. It is a taming discourse that may well influence city development in the years to come.

What is new is that we now need to think about urbanization as a global phenomenon. Demographic calculations suggest that up to 70 per cent of people will live in cities by 2050, with most new urbanization taking place in Asia and sub-Saharan Africa. The reports of global consultancies such as the Boston

Consultancy Group agree with the World Bank's mind-boggling estimates of the US\$30 to \$50 *trillion* required in urban infrastructure investment over the next 20 years. This investment would extend infrastructure in the developing world and retrofit existing infrastructure in the developed world, some of which dates back to the nineteenth century.

While the consulting companies generate seemingly 'scientific' estimates of investment potential to activate the major financial institutions to participate in the new taming discourses aimed at modernizing rapid urbanisation, the smart city agenda suggests a way to spend this money. It proposes a digital upgrade to increase city efficiency without much reference to equity and social justice. It gives us a sense of déjà vu. The discourse of the modern, functional city that dominated twentieth-century planning promised a healthy urban life for all, with free-flowing traffic and electricity 'too cheap to meter', yet was not able to deliver. When it comes to smart cities, future possibilities look enticing but past failures are ignored because of the durability of suspect assumptions about how easily the city can be tamed.

The important debate on the future of cities deserves to be grounded in an understanding of the history of urbanism and the complexity of taming and untaming dynamics. This understanding can help frame a resilient and shared vision, without which investment is likely to flow into short-term agendas based on outdated twentieth-century urban planning practices.

Alternatively, if 'urban metabolism' is placed at the centre of the analysis, the potential for a harmonious transition becomes questionable. This chapter examines how we can infuse the smart city discourse with an understanding of the natural flows and particular histories of cities, their potential governance and institutional models, and the possibilities of organizing learning, both in and between cities. It argues that we need a 'smart urbanism' – a body of thought on urbanism that is powerful, integrative, action-oriented and sufficiently cognizant of the fact that there are severe limits to what can in fact be tamed in the rapidly expanding and transforming cities of the world.

The smart city as discourse

Urbanization is a crucial challenge for the twenty-first century. More people will urbanize in the next 40 to 50 years than in the last 200, according to the World Bank (Hoornweg and Freire 2013). This implies that in 'just 40 years cities will need to build the infrastructure for an additional 2.7 billion people' (2013: 125). China wants to rehouse 250 million people from rural areas to cities by 2030 (OECD 2013). The UN Department of Economic and Social Affairs (UNDESA) estimates that African cities will house an additional 800 million people by 2050 (OECD 2013: 33). This raises serious infrastructural challenges in terms of transportation, water and wastewater, solid waste and energy.

The notion of smart cities has emerged in this context from the major global technology companies as a logical way forward. According to the World Bank publication, applying smart city technologies could reduce carbon dioxide emissions by 7.8 gigatonnes by 2020 (Hoornweg and Freire 2013: 9). To put this figure in context, in 2012 US national emissions were 5,194 megatonnes and China's were 9,864 megatonnes (Olivier *et al.* 2013). However, while combining the full effects of applying smart technology looks impressive on paper, implementation faces political and physical challenges that the smart city discourse hardly ever recognizes.

In policy and politics, often smart cities are understood as a set of devices, proposals and instruments to be adopted, installed and operated. Policy-makers see this as a programme that opens up space for corporate entities to sell technological solutions. These solutions would address problems such as health, traffic congestion, energy supply, water supply, waste management and environmental quality. This top-down and centralized perspective is then typically criticized from a bottom-up perspective, which focuses on 'smart citizens' and open platforms (Townsend 2013; Greenfield and Kim 2013). The debate risks getting caught in a dichotomy where *a priori* value preferences ('small is beautiful' or 'big problems require integrated solutions') determine the stance of various actors.

Real change comes about through the emergence of a coalition of forces that creates the necessary persuasive power. Actors in the coalition agree on a strategic orientation and share a language for discussing cities. They do not necessarily agree on all the details. 'Smart cities' can be represented as such a discourse, as a way of seeing and talking that highlights some aspects of the urban reality while phasing out those realities that are inconvenient, in particular the affordability of the envisaged urban systems for those who are not formally employed.

Discourse is defined as 'an ensemble of notions, ideas, concepts and categorizations through which meaning is allocated to social and physical phenomena, and which is produced and reproduced in an identifiable set of practices' (Hajer 2009: 59–60). In this sense, Keynesianism or neoliberalism is a discourse, as both offer ways of seeing that became institutionalized into rules and routines. This is why discourse analysis postulates that language matters. Through language 'some issues are organized into politics while others are organized out' (Schattschneider 1960). In this way discourses become the tools for how the taming of the city is organised. Counter-hegemonic discourses, however, give expression to that which cannot be tamed by the process of 'organizing out' inconvenient truths.

When it comes to smart cities as a taming discourse, concepts such as 'smart grids', 'big data', 'efficiency', 'infrastructure', 'system' and 'information' dominate. This highlights the first key aspect of the smart cities discourse – it is a managerial project with a focus on using ICT to solve urban problems. This dominance of ICT leads urbanist Mark Swilling to view the 'smart city' discourse as a form of 'algorithmic urbanism' (see Chapter 2).

Second, smart cities are typically discussed in new, cross-over fora in which business, government and knowledge institutes find each other. These meetings are important, as this is where the imagination of the possible futures shapes up.

Third, smart cities are oriented to a particular organizational idea featuring public–private partnerships. This has implications for how consumers pay for their urban services. A 'pay per use' approach will replace 'public works' financed via taxation (Graham and Marvin 2001). While this provides an excellent private business proposition, the process neglects to examine how particular understandings of the 'smart city' relate to existing governance systems or civil society.

Fourth, smart city discourse approaches innovation primarily as a technological matter. It does not discuss the very *conditions* under which transition has to occur. The importance of looking at conditionalities has emerged strongly in one of the first comprehensive studies of a 'smart cities' partnership, the T-City in the German city of Friedrichshafen (Hatzelhoffer *et al.* 2012).

Fifth, smart city discourse is notably weak on the history of urbanism. Pointing at 'efficient' solutions is not new; the question is why technical solutions were often not seen as preferable and most had undesirable unintended consequences when implemented.

When it comes to cities, there can be no fixed solutions. The notion that the city is untameable suggests that urban politics is about making difficult choices, often after lengthy (often unpredictable) public consultation processes (Barber 1984; Hajer 2009). For the advocates of smart cities the challenge may lie in avoiding the dichotomy between the taming intent of 'big' tech solutions and the untaming dynamics of bottom-up participatory planning. What is undeniable is that we cannot continue to build cities on the default twentieth-century model that assumed centralized control via large public and private bureaucracies. Today, governments are also more vulnerable, and lack the authority, legitimacy and funding to 'bend the trend'. We may need to invent and define a mode of collaborative smart urbanism through debate that recognises that the city can only be tamed to a point, beyond which a much more complex world exists – this more so than ever before.

Previous city transitions

The sanitary reform movement

The problems faced by contemporary cities, while daunting, are not without precedent. The period from the mid-nineteenth century onwards is particularly instructive, as in this era cities began to install public infrastructure. The first sanitary survey of New York City took place in 1864:

> The inspectors wrote about overflowing privies, slime-covered streets filled with horse manure, and slaughterhouses and fat-boiling establishments dispersed among overcrowded tenements. One inspector reported that blood and liquid animal remains flowed for two blocks down 39th Street from a slaughterhouse to the river.
>
> (Pizzi 2002)

Cities such as London, Paris and Berlin faced similar consequences of slum life. To tame these cities, city governments cleared the slums, installed sewage systems and provided good drinking water. This eventually put an end to frequent epidemics of typically urban diseases in Western cities.

With hindsight, the installation of this infrastructure seems a coherent exercise. However, the process involved political conflict, resistance from vested interests and coalition-building. Social reformers such as Edwin Chadwick and Charles Booth put the issue on the agenda, and journalists spread the message to a wider audience. Governments began to investigate the challenge. Those with vested interests were only persuaded once comprehensive statistical work showed the need for sanitation infrastructure. In effect, infrastructural works on both sides of the Atlantic resulted from a 'sanitary movement' discourse coalition that combined the social issue of urban blight (ethical values) with installation of new infrastructure (technical considerations).

This new sanitation discourse inspired planners and designers to envision alternative city futures. People such as Frederick Law Olmsted, Ebenhezer Howard and Patrick Geddes responded to the call for more liveable cities, and each invented forms of city planning designed to reconnect the city to its natural environment in ways that effectively allowed cities to tame the ecosystems upon which they depended (see Chapter 2 for how this worked in Kolkata). The possibility of a more harmonious world inspired their designs. While their influence was never direct, their ideas became elements in the discourse. These elements were shaped further by political ideology, new technological inventions and choices of organizational form. For example, Howard's garden city idea paved the way for the suburb, but stripped it of his societal idealism.

The history of the sanitary movement of the nineteenth century illustrates that technological solutions cannot be isolated from the broader socio-political dynamics that shaped responses to the public problems of the day.

The modern city

The 'modern' movement dominated urban planning in the 1920s, epitomized in the work of the Swiss/French architect Le Corbusier and influenced by thinkers such as Siegfried Giedion, Walter Gropius, Bruno Taut and J. J. P. Oud. Planners and designers used new materials and methods of construction, such as steel, concrete and prefabricated materials, as well as modern styles, to create higher buildings. The modern movement continued to aspire to the 'garden city' notion and socially utopian ideals. By linking architecture to urban planning, the movement could use new materials to overcome public health problems and show ways to improve living conditions. There was an emphasis on differentiating spaces for working, living and leisure – each according to tightly defined codes aimed at effectively taming the unruly and (in certain parts of the world) potentially revolutionary popular classes. In modernist planning, nature was rigidly conceptualized so it could be ruthlessly tamed. Planning focused primarily on air quality and adequate lighting.

The possibilities of science provided the foundation for the modern movement, which proclaimed the 'functional city' as a solution to the urban problems of the day. The movement used survey and statistical analysis to find efficient solutions, with an emphasis on zoning, rather than detailed design. Cities, with some exceptions, have never taken up these solutions in their entirety.

Technological development and social critique outpaced modernist design. Prospects for the urban world also changed after the Second World War. The mass availability of the car created new transport issues in cities (see Berman 1983). Urban planners such as Robert Moses were active in a complicated discourse coalition that included real estate interests, mobility management concerns and bureaucratic strife between different agencies.

The modern movement relied on its strong ties to city governments, and employed a persuasive narrative linking the application of the latest technologies and the realization of political interests. Just as the dystopia of urban blight propelled the nineteenth-century sanitation movement, the utopian vision of a clean and dispersed car-based city captured the imagination of political elites. The imposition of this modernist format tamed cities in their very essence, diminishing them as untamed places of exchange, of inspiration and openness.

Following the Second World War, city planners restructured cities to accommodate the car. The emergence of the car as a means of mass transport extended the socio-spatial scope of modern planning projects. It was also at this time that planners conceived of highway systems. The mobility provided by the car allowed people to live further away from work. The car enabled the materialization of the 'suburb', which became a cornerstone of the 'American dream' promising a new way of life for the middle class that became an aspiration for people all over the world.

Europeans saw 'suburbanization' as urban sprawl, and attempted to guide the overflow into newly constructed cities, such as Milton Keynes in the United Kingdom. These new cities connected to the main urban centres through prioritized public transport systems. The regional scope of the city found its new expression.

The story of the modern city is told mostly through descriptions of organized housing and transport systems. However, most modern post-war cities were supplied by centralized, fossil fuel-based energy systems that generated electricity and delivered it to homes via a grid.

The transition to the modern city illustrates how twentieth-century urban development was the product of a discourse coalition in which planners and designers only played one part in the taming of the city. The idealism of the modernist planner must be seen in the context of continued economic growth, the motor industry's push to make cars consumer goods, and the emergence of a broadly shared sense of a good life related to suburban living. Resource use and waste were not taken into account, as much of this happened outside of city perimeters.

Cities in the Anthropocene

Until recently, nature has functioned as a useful hinterland for cities, providing the necessary building materials, fuels, water and food. Simultaneously, nature also functioned as a sink to clear away our waste and emissions. The nature–society nexus has now become dysfunctional.

Cities run on fossil energy, which causes global warming; they extract too much drinking water and do not recoup wastewater and nutrients; and they pile up waste in landfills. The modern system allows non-renewable resources, such as phosphorus and nitrogen, to flow into rivers and seas, causing environmental havoc, and throws away precious metals into landfills.

In the early 1990s, Nobel Laureate Paul Crutzen suggested that our industrial way of living had *geological* consequences. He coined the term 'the Anthropocene' to express this (Crutzen 2002). Subsequent work by Rockström, Steffen and others reinforced this claim. The human species is crossing planetary boundaries (Rockström *et al.* 2009; Steffen *et al.* 2004) in terms of climate change, biodiversity loss and the nitrogen cycle, and is at risk of crossing others. It is now important to rethink how cities function based on the acceptance of natural limits to the way they use resources.

The failure to conceptualize the relation between the city and the natural environment in metabolic terms was one of the tragedies of twentieth-century planning. While the early 1920s planner Patrick Geddes followed an integrated approach to the city and its hinterland, the subsequent modernist influence was oriented to growth and driven by a belief in the superiority of engineering and science. Most twentieth-century cities are locked into fossil fuel-based infrastructures, and this lock-in is institutionally embedded, making it difficult to transition to an ecologically benign metabolism. Scientists speak of 'nexus' problems in which issues around climate change, energy consumption, land use and biodiversity loss are fundamentally intertwined. A metabolic approach brings out those connections.

The tragedy is that urbanization patterns in the new cities of the global South are mostly following the default trajectory of the West. This is most apparent in the cities of China. The 'airpocalypse' in Beijing and other cities creates serious health hazards, affects agricultural production and negatively affects the economy (*Guardian* 2014). The decontextual high-rise developments in African and Asian cities follow this model more broadly.

Somehow the cities of the global South must find ways to leapfrog using available knowledge and technology and ways to reconfigure the urban metabolism of cities. Countries in the West introduced environmental protection and mitigation measures in the 1970s; however, the cities of the global South have not been allowed to leapfrog and they are now experiencing the same problems, but on a grander scale. For example, 3 billion people in the world still drink poor-quality water, and in India, only 160 out of 8,000 towns have both a sewerage system and a sewage treatment plant (Biswas and Brabeck 2014).

Smart urbanism: an agenda for planning and design

We are currently experiencing a discursive shift to create the new practices of twenty-first-century planning and design. In discourse analysis, we differentiate between 'discourse structuration' and 'discourse institutionalization' (Hajer 1995: 60–1).

Discourse structuration describes the process in which a particular way of understanding reality settles and becomes generally accepted. At this point, a particular sense of problems and solutions emerges. This discourse may become the new 'normal', and become institutionalized in new rules and routines, in laws, in new business models, in new roles for actors, and even in newly shared values.

Moments of discursive shift are moments of opportunity. The old institutionalized power relationships give way to debate. New actors often appear to discuss new issues in crossover fora. This is what is happening around the notion of a 'smart city'.

Let me share seven considerations that help smart city planning and design to break free from the assumption that it will be relatively easy and painless to tame the city.

'Decoupling' as the strategic orientation

In the next decades, we will need to decouple the rising prosperity of the city from ever-increasing resource use. For instance, we need to create our wealth using about a tenth of current greenhouse gas emissions. The UN Environment Programme (UNEP) International Resource Panel (IRP) *Decoupling Report* (UNEP 2013a) has brought this perspective into a wider urban agenda. Decoupling is a major break from the current 'urbanization by default' pattern, but if it is not achieved, cities will face increasing pollution, rising emissions, congestion and rising input costs, as prices absorb the downstream effects of resource depletion.

A persuasive story line about the future

Planning theorist James Throgmorton described planning as 'persuasive story telling about the future'. He argued that the essence of planning was not about ends and means, ordering and organization; rather, it was about a vision, a persuasive story with generative capacity. This persuasive story informs plan-making, restructuring, organizing and logistics (Throgmorton 1996) and confirms the central thesis of this book, namely that success today depends on ensuring that everyone is involved at all times.

We need new, persuasive ideas for the city that mobilize actors and resources, and that give city governors the confidence to make changes. The 'smart city' discourse mobilizes positive energy among elites, but it lacks a connection to the broader social reform agenda. Reconceptualizing the city must take into account the need for environmental sustainability, social justice and resilience to future shock. Smart technologies must enable cities to stay within a 'safe operating space' in terms of planetary boundaries; in addition, this space must be socially just (Raworth 2012). How to fuse these two 'spaces' is the heart of current debate on sustainable development goals. Creating separate goals for cities offers a way of linking urban development to the broader normative debate.

Smart cities are related to the concrete aspects of urban planning and policy-making, allowing for enhanced efficiency. This translates into the city being cheaper and easier to navigate, explore and exploit, as well as cheaper and easier to manage. Smart urbanism calls for a language that expresses more than efficiency and technology.

Urban metabolisms as a framework for strategic decision-making

Some aspects of good city life are very visible, while the metabolism of a city – the constant flow of inputs and outputs – is almost invisible. These metabolic flows comprise water, energy and food (UNEP 2013a; Ferrao and Fernandez 2013), building materials and wastes, among others. Inefficient metabolic systems will be vulnerable to the inevitable price effects of predicted resource scarcity, and they are likely to lead to negative feedback loops, such as smog.

Even the global North lacks statistics on its cities' inputs and outputs. Initiatives such as the Large Urban Areas Compendium by the World Bank and the Global City Indicators Facility are therefore timely (Hoornweg and Freire 2013; GCIF 2014).

Understanding urban metabolism calls for a focus on potential, on transformation and on transition, as well as on monitoring and evaluation. It is a multi- and trans-disciplinary effort involving designers, planners, scientists and policy-makers.

Focus on the default in infrastructure

Connecting smart city discourse to a sustainable urban metabolism provides the discourse with a purpose. The IRP identified the crucial role of urban infrastructure as 'to promote resource efficiency and decoupling at the city level, as well as well-being and access to services of their citizens' (UNEP 2013b: 7).

Infrastructure is a deeply problematic field from a governance point of view, as it is mostly sunk, covered and static. It is the result of decades, sometimes centuries, of cumulative investment. Maintaining and changing infrastructure is complex because it is used daily. However, existing infrastructure sets the default via the existing hardware of urban networks and via the software that determines how we use them. Smart technology can contribute to change via the latter, as it is easier to change the way we use, for example, the roads than the roads themselves.

Rules and ownership of infrastructure present challenges. Policy-makers need to reflect on the social consequences of the rules they adopt. For example, smart meters and smart grids might serve citizens, but privilege companies.

The days of blueprint urban planning and development are over. A large part of the predicted urbanization will take place in weak states with low regulatory capacity. Peer-to-peer learning could compensate for this lower capacity for strategic forward planning. Decoupling might be more about learning and copying than about elaborate bureaucratic planning.

Beyond the notion of a 'smart city from a box'

The idea of 'smart cities from a box' – generic concepts that are imposed on cities – will not work because cities are inherently untameable. Experimental cities such as Songdo in South Korea, Masdar in the United Arab Emirates and Dongtan in China have not lived up to their sustainability promises. They are the twenty-first-century equivalents to Brasilia, Abuja, Melbourne and Chandigarh, and clearly demonstrate what happens when governments plan for sustainability, but use outdated twentieth-century concepts (Kuecker 2013; Townsend 2013; Ferrao and Fernandez 2013: 131 ff.; Premalatha *et al.* 2013).

Engineers cannot decouple resource use and rates of economic growth in cities on their own, as technology and society are linked in complicated ways. For example, a car cannot be analysed as technology in isolation; it feeds into a broader system encompassing motorways, parking garages and out-of-town shopping malls to create the very idea of the commuter lifestyle. It is also central to a powerful industrial complex that creates jobs, generates knowledge and drives innovation. The importance of placing technologies in context cannot be overestimated. *Social innovations* can often bring about change. Examples of untamed technological innovations in the social sphere include community websites that organize sharing of tools in services.

It is most likely that a new blend of social innovations, new technologies and new business models will provide the disruptive force required to shift the dominant modern system.

A new open and collaborative politics

The notion that the twenty-first century will be shaped by 'decisive acts' by an elected city council is misguided. Innovation in the spheres of technology and social forms of organization outpaces the capacities of classical-modernist forms of government to implement taming strategies (cf. Hajer 2009, ch.1).

In *Seeing like a State* (1998), anthropologist James Scott studied the failure of schemes aimed at improving the human condition. He noted that when a state is overconfident in its reliance on science and technology and a civil society is too weak to raise questions or provide resistance, the state implements disconnected plans. These plans then place an undue burden on the state to execute the scheme, which often results in the adoption of authoritarian methods. This weakens the possibilities of joint implementation and learning.

Smart urbanism is about constant learning, inspiration, measuring, analysing and readjusting

It is necessary to rethink how public administrations operate within increasingly complex untameable environments. A well-educated civil society raises astute questions and demands, and the classical 'decide, announce, defend' model is vulnerable in a world of constant learning. ICT brings 'protoprofessionalization' within reach of many, and governments now face an 'energetic society' (Hajer 2011) that they can either embrace or antagonize. The art of urban planning must become the process of facilitating the untamed intelligence of a given city's citizens.

The ideas of John Dewey and the subsequent writings of Don Schon on learning, and the rethinking of public policy by authors like Majone and Wildavsky, who saw implementation as a phase of continuous learning (Pressman and Wildavsky 1984), align with the notion of an untamed 'energetic society' enhanced by access to and use of technology.

It is by no means obvious that cities will follow this track. The alternative option is that governments follow the established classical modernist model and aim for big contracts with a single party or a consortium of parties. It would then be easier to control upgrades of city infrastructure in terms of contract and performance measurement, but most likely far more difficult to learn and readjust.

Elsewhere I have argued for *radical incrementalism* in using the enhanced collective intelligence of cities to move towards a sustainable future without resorting to traditional tools to tame the city (Hajer 2011). This requires an open format to stimulate the entrepreneurial spirit. It assumes that infrastructure is conceived as a backbone to 'new' city life and that there are possibilities for continuous learning on that backbone. For example, open fibre-optic cable networks could facilitate entrepreneurs in providing new services.

It is important to consider the governance of infrastructure transitions. We need a strong coalition to make the transition; however, the organizations currently promoting smart cities are so powerful that they often exclude citizens from the process. Amsterdam's 'smart city' agenda provides an interesting blend of high-end, high-tech interventions and a scattered set of experiments that involve citizens, along with collaborative projects that implement decoupling at street level (ASC 2014).

Collaborative governance implies openness to different outcomes. It is not effective if viewed solely as a tool to facilitate the implementation of a fixed set of predetermined goals. True coalition-building allows participants a voice, which then leads to creative conceptualization and implementation. It may seem counterintuitive as the process adds complexity, but this allows collaborative governance to find the best solutions. This, in turn, reinvigorates the idea of local democracy and demonstrates how to work with rather than against the untamed dynamics of the city.

Create a globally networked urbanism

The task of the twenty-first century might be to recognize the inherent untameability of the city by bringing back the ideal of cities as places of exchange, inspiration, social mobility, enhanced quality of life, inclusion and connectedness to nature.

As stated previously, the twenty-first-century city cannot work from a linear blueprint model. We can now use complex learning networks to speed up the sharing of information. Examples of emerging horizontal networks include C40 Cities, ICLEI, UN Global Compact, Global Initiative for Resource Efficient Cities, and the International Human Dimensions Programme (IHDP) Sustainable Urbanization Initiative. But these fora need to spend more time on actual policy analysis showing *why* certain interventions worked and under what preconditions.

Given current challenges, cities need to be able to adapt, readjust, copy and add on to existing practices and knowledge. Modernist thinking relied on coordination, with a linear division between thinking (science), deciding (politics) and execution (implementation). In contrast, it is more likely that city-level decoupling will be achieved if key actors stage (creative) 'co-opetition', which would encourage cities to excel, but also encourage them to share experiences and knowledge.

A global networked urbanism requires the development of a science of 'transplantation'. This would help identify the conditions under which schemes such as smart grids, rapid bus transit systems and solid waste management systems are successful, and their potential for replication.

The exciting possibilities presented by big data can obscure the importance of political debate, urban conflict and the expression of interests. Deliberative policy-making (see Hajer and Wagenaar 2003) aims to connect these issues.

It is most likely that twenty-first-century planning will not be about figurehead personalities, but rather about networks. Smart city urbanism is most likely to succeed if, as a configuration, it can constantly change and adjust. In a sense, it should not be a top-down techno-fix but rather *a project of projects*, creating the conditions for ongoing learning, reflection and adjustment through analysis and knowledge-sharing.

Conclusion

City-level decoupling is arguably the task of the century. The sanitary reform movement of the nineteenth century provides a sense of what is required to bring about the required shift, as does twentieth-century urban modernism. Both involved coalition-building to achieve specific goals. The current transition will need a broad engagement, 'a social movement that enlists science, the humanities, and us all to address the challenges we face building a planet of cities that can survive' (Townsend 2013: 320). To achieve this, the smart city discourse needs to connect to a societal context and correct its current technocratic orientation by recognizing that there are severe limits to what can be tamed. While cities contribute the most to carbon dioxide emissions and resource use, they are also the most capable of innovation and change.

Acknowledgement

This is a much abbreviated and slightly amended version of the essay of the same title which appeared in Maarten Hajer and Ton Dassen (eds), *Smart about Cities: Visualizing the Challenge for 21st Century Urbanism*, Nai/010 Publishers, Rotterdam, 2014.

References

ASC (Amsterdam Smart City). 2014. http://amsterdamsmartcity.com (accessed 24 April 2014).

Barber, B. R. 1984. *Strong Democracy: Participatory Politics for a New Age.* Oakland, CA: University of California Press.

Berman, M. 1983. *All That Is Solid Melts into Air: The Experience of Modernity.* London: Verso.

Biswas, A. K. and Brabeck, L. P. 2014. The Third World's drinking problem, Project Syndicate, 23 February. Available at: www.project-syndicate.org.

Crutzen, P. J. 2002. Geology of mankind. *Nature*, 415(23) (3 January).

Ferrao, P. and Fernandez, J. E. 2013. *Sustainable Urban Metabolism.* Cambridge, MA: MIT Press.

Global Cities Indicator Facility (GCIF). 2014. www.cityindicators.org (accessed 6 June 2014).

Graham, S. and Marvin, S. 2001. *Splintering Urbanism: Networked Infrastructures, Technological Mobilities.* London and New York: Routledge.

Greenfield, A. and Kim, N. 2013. *Against the Smart City (The City Is Here for You To Use).* Kindle ebook.

Guardian. 2014. China's toxic air pollution resembles nuclear winter, say scientists. *Guardian*, 27 February. Available at: www.theguardian.com/world/2014/ feb/25/china-toxic-air-pollution-nuclear- winter-scientists (accessed 28 March 2014).

Hajer, M. A. 1995. *The Politics of Environmental Discourse, Ecological Modernization and the Policy Process.* Oxford: Oxford University Press.

—— 2009. *Policy Making in the Age of Mediatization.* Oxford: Oxford University Press.

—— 2011. *The Energetic Society.* The Hague, Netherlands: PBL Netherlands Environmental Assessment Agency.

Hajer, M. A. and Wagenaar, H. 2003. *Deliberative Policy Analysis: Understanding Governance in the Network Society.* Cambridge: Cambridge University Press.

Hatzelhoffer, L., Humboldt, K., Lobeck, M. and Wiegandt, C. C. 2012. *Smart City in Practice: Converting Innovative Ideas into Reality.* Berlin: Jovis Verlag.

Hoornweg, D. and Freire, M. 2013. Building sustainability in an urbanizing world. A Partnership Report, Urban Development Series Knowledge Papers no. 17. London: ALNAP.

Kuecker, G. D. 2013. Building the bridge to the future: New Songdo city from a critical urbanism perspective. Essay for SOAS, University of London Centre of Korean Studies Workshop New Songdo City and South Korea's Green Economy: An Uncertain Future, 5 June.

Organisation for Economic Co-Operation and Development (OECD). 2013.Urbanisation and green growth in China, Regional Development Working Paper 2013/07. Paris: OECD.

Olivier, J. G. J., Janssens-Maenhout, G., Muntean, M. and Peters, J. A. H. W. 2013. *Trends in Global CO2 Emissions, 2013 Report.* The Hague, Netherlands: PBL Netherlands Environmental Assessment Agency, and Joint Research Centre (JRC), Ispra.

Pizzi, A. 2002. Apostles of cleanliness: the 19th-century Sanitary Movement denied the germ theory of disease, yet created our public health infrastructure, MDD Modern Drug Discovery 5(may 2002) no. 5, pp. 51–5, available at: http://pubs.acs.org/subscribe/jour-nals/mdd/v05/i05/html/05ttl.html (accessed 3 March 2014).

Premalatha, S., Tauseef, M., Abbasi, T. and Abbasi, S. A. 2013. The promise and the performance of the world's first two zero carbon eco-cities. *Renewable and Sustainable Energy Reviews*, 25: 660–9.

Pressman, J. L. and Wildavsky, A. 1984. *Implementation*, 3rd expanded edn. Berkeley, CA: University of California Press.

Raworth, K. 2012. A safe and just space for humanity: can we live within the doughnut? Oxfam Discussion Paper.

Rockström, J., Steffen, W., Noone, K., Persson, Å., Chapin III, F. S., Lambin, E. F., Lenton, T. M., Scheffer, M., Folke, C., Schellnhuber, H. J., Nykvist, B., De Wit, C. A., Hughes, T., Van der Leeuw, S., Rodhe, H., Sörlin, S., Snyder, P. K., Costanza, R., Svedin, U., Falkenmark, M., Karlberg, L., Corell, R. W., Fabry, V. J., Hansen, J., Walker, B., Liverman, D., Richardson, K., Crutzen, P. and Foley, J. A. 2009. A safe operating space for humanity. *Nature*, 461: 472–5.

Schattschneider, E. 1960, *The Semisovereign People: A Realist's View of Democracy in America*. New York: Holt, Rinehart & Winston.

Scott, J. C. 1998. *Seeing Like a State: How Certain Schemes to Improve the Human Condition Have Failed*. New Haven, CT: Yale University Press.

Steffen, W., Sanderson, A., Tyson, P. D., Jäger, J., Matson, P. A., Moore III, B., Oldfield, F., Richardson, K., Schellnhuber, H. J., Turner, B. L. and Wasson, R. J. 2004. *Global Change and the Earth System: A Planet Under Pressure*. Berlin, Heidelberg, Germany and New York: Springer-Verlag.

Throgmorton, J. 1996. *Planning as Persuasive Storytelling: The Rhetorical Construction of Chicago's Electric Future*. Chicago, IL: University of Chicago Press.

Townsend, A. M. 2013. *Smart Cities: Big Data, Civic Hackers, and the Quest for a New Utopia*, New York: W. W. Norton.

United Nations Environment Programme (UNEP). 2013a. *City-Level Decoupling: Urban Resource Flows and the Governance of Infrastructure Transitions*. Full report by the Working Group on Cities of the International Resource Panel (M. Swilling, B. Robinson, S. Marvin and M. Hodson). Nairobi: UNEP.

—— 2013b. *City-Level Decoupling: Urban Resource Flows and the Governance of Infrastructure Transitions*. Summary by the Working Group on Cities of the International Resource Panel (M. Swilling, B. Robinson, S. Marvin and M. Hodson). Nairobi: UNEP.

4   Is big sustainable?

Global comparison of city emissions

*Dominik Reusser, Anna-Lena Winz
and Diego Rybski*

Introduction

Human activities have become an important driver of changes in the geochemical cycles of the earth, altering flows of water, nutrients and greenhouse gases (GHG). As discussed in the Introduction, the term *Anthropocene* has been proposed for this new geological age (Crutzen 2006). There is no doubt that these changes are unsustainable and are causing or will cause damage to the ecosystem and society. In fact, there have been calls for a reconfiguration because we are transgressing or have transgressed important boundaries (Rockström *et al.* 2009) and are utilizing more than one Earth for our current way of living (e.g. Wackernagel and Rees 2013). Furthermore, not only do the environmental limits indicate a need for change; the steadily increasing costs of most resources (Dobbs *et al.* 2011) also demonstrate the need for a transition to sustainability.

Urban living is well suited to address the necessary change for three main reasons. First, it can host sociocultural experiments that can act as a catalyst for innovation. Second, ever more people are living in cities. Third, in cities material flows are concentrated and energy intensity is high, so change is particularly important in this type of environment.

In view of the sustainability challenge,[1] we can ask whether larger cities are more efficient because of better utilization of infrastructure, shorter distances or created co-benefits (Dodman 2009). An alternative view is less commonly discussed: smaller cities could be considered more sustainable because of reduced pressure on local ecosystem services and less need to import products from distant places, leading to the conclusion that we should counteract city growth. For example, Marcotullio and colleagues (2013) find that urban emission levels can be higher than those in non-urban areas in developing countries.

In this chapter, we investigate the relationship between city size and environmental impact using the example of GHG emissions. Our motivation is rooted in a deep concern about our future and the conditions we leave to next generations. It is our belief that better understanding the mechanisms and basic relations of the global challenges constitutes an important first step to initiate a change to more sustainability. Thus, we look at the following questions by analysing data from a wide range of cities:

- Are large cities, in relative terms, responsible for greater or lesser emissions?
- What are the possible explanations?
- How consistent are the explanations with the observed data?

To address the topic, we give a very short introduction to GHG emissions and climate change, then go on to relate this to infrastructure and societal change. We find that for reduction potential, it is important to better understand how emissions are connected to lifestyles, to assess inventories and possible drivers. We are aware that this kind of analysis can substantiate the taming discourse of the SMART City agenda, but we also hope that this analysis reinforces those social movements calling for radical lifestyle changes for the billion or so overconsumers that predominate in the cities of the developed world and that constitute rapidly expanding enclaves in the growing cities of the developing world. Thus, we next briefly look at potential drivers at different scales, from the national to the individual.

We then present the core argument that in countries with high gross domestic product (GDP) per capita, an increase in city size results in declining GHG emissions per capita; while in countries with lower GDP per capita, an increasing size of cities tends to correlate with rising GHG per capita. We test different drivers identified earlier in the chapter as potential explanations. A final section summarizes and wraps up the discussion in a way that critically addresses these findings from the perspective of the main themes of this book.

Climate change

Among the processes of global change, global warming is often regarded as the most pressing question (see e.g. Randers 2012). It is challenging because of the high energy requirements of large parts of society and the economy. It has been agreed that anthropogenic GHG emissions are the major cause of climate change (IPCC 2013). Because of the complex causes and effects, it is difficult to coordinate action to counter climate change, especially in tightly structured and regulated cities geared to maintain high-consumption lifestyles. Nonetheless, global coordination is needed, but international negotiations have proved difficult at best (Kartha *et al.* 2012). Equity questions related to GHG budgets are difficult to solve because while mainly urban consumers in the global North have used the majority of the historic GHG budget, the impacts of climate change are often felt most strongly in the global South where livelihood-supporting ecosystems are under threat.

It was agreed by the Conference of Parties (COP) to the United Nations Framework Convention on Climate Change (UNFCCC) that global warming has to be limited to 2 °C. Various budget approaches have been proposed to share permission to produce GHG emissions at a level compatible with the 2 °C limit between different nations (Schellnhuber *et al.* 2009; Costa *et al.* 2011). So far, no agreement has been reached on how to achieve this goal (Kartha *et al.* 2012).

Even if there is a warming of 'only' 2 °C, various impacts are expected (Parry *et al.* 2008). One effect is that climate change causes modifications to or the loss of various ecosystem services. For example, a lack of climate stabilization can result in the urban heat islands effect (Zhou *et al.* 2013). Adaptation to climate change is becoming an ever more pressing issue. While mitigation must be coordinated globally, adaptation measures are often local or regional (Adger *et al.* 2007). This multi-scale nature of the measures required makes climate change even more difficult to coordinate.

An energy-hungry society

Societal form (such as hunters and gatherers, agrarian and industrial societies) appears closely interrelated with the type and quantity of energy use. For example Haberl and colleagues (2011) investigated the interrelation of societal forms and social metabolism. In order to manage material flows, a society needs the appropriate resources, knowledge and infrastructure. Often, a dominating socio-technical configuration exists in a society, what some refer to as the socio-technical regime (Geels 2011). It might be possible to imagine alternative configurations, but these would typically need different resources, and different knowledge and rules within particular niches (Geels 2011).

Because of the considerable investment in the current socio-technical regime, we often observe a technological lock-in that is reinforced by the prevailing planning and governance systems. For example, the current energy system in most parts of the global North is designed for a fossil fuel-based, centralized energy supply with large power plants and corresponding power grids, inefficient energy use and supply-side management of variations. There could be an alternative configuration with more decentralized interconnected local networks and increased efficiency, but that would be difficult to realize because it would disrupt prevailing socio-technical regimes that provide the infrastructural foundation for the global economic system as it is currently constituted.

Current configurations often assume that increasing (economic) activity is coupled with increasing throughput of energy and material. What is needed is a decoupling in order to satisfy a growing population with decreasing throughput (UNEP 2013). For this, it will be necessary to reconfigure urban infrastructures (UNEP 2013). However, there is no consensus on how to achieve this. Large technological companies have a taming agenda expressed via the SMART City agenda, while a large number of environmental and social justice movements insist on disruptions to existing modes of consumption and production. Looking at the example of GHG emissions, factors other than infrastructure are also important for a potential decoupling. For example, socio-economic and cultural factors have a strong influence on the size of emissions from our nutrition, travelling, water use and housing requirements, to name just a selection of our daily needs (Reusser *et al.* 2013). To replace the current regime, we need first to experiment with niche innovations, many of which have historically emerged from marginal societal actors inspired by a more ecologically sustainable vision of the future.

But which alternatives are most efficient in reducing GHG emissions? If we focus on the energy supply sector and more economic and technological solutions, computer simulations (which admittedly assume rational behaviour) help to assess the costs of the various solutions. According to these calculations, it seems feasible to convert the energy supply infrastructure in a way compatible with the 2° target at moderate cost if policy and implementation constraints are ignored (Edenhofer *et al.* 2012). However, the approach taken in such studies does not include decentralized solutions less consistent with taming technocratic approaches to a low-carbon transition. It considers the interactions with other aspects in the lives of citizens in a limited way. By considering these other factors affecting emissions, we can gain ideas on how to use energy and infrastructure more efficiently for more socially progressive purposes.

Identifying emission drivers

Gaining a good understanding of GHG emissions through consistent reporting is demanding. For example, the guidelines for reporting inventories to the UNFCCC are a thick manual filled with detailed technical descriptions (IPCC 2006). The basic idea of this accounting framework is to count GHG emissions at the location where they are produced (so-called production-based emissions). However, emissions may occur during the production of a certain good, while it is consumed in different places. Thus, through trade, virtual emissions are transferred around the globe.

To correct for such traded emissions, the concept of consumption-based emissions has been introduced (Peters 2008; Davis and Caldeira 2010). For consumption-based emissions, all the emissions generated during the production of a good or service are accounted for in the country where this good is consumed. However, the data required to estimate consumption-based emissions are still quite uncertain. For example data are missing for certain countries (Ahmad and Wyckoff 2003). Also, the data required to assess changes over time in a consistent way are not available in sufficient quality for cities globally (Walmsley *et al.* 2012; Minx *et al.* 2013). Because of limited data availability on consumption-based emissions, we focus on production-based emissions in the remaining part of the chapter. Keeping the problem of production- versus consumption-based emissions in mind, we can try to understand the main drivers at different levels of accounting.

Using the IPCC reporting schema, we find emissions inventories that are pollutant specific and sector specific. While, in general we find increasing emissions with increasing income (GDP) at the country level, the question of reconfiguration and decoupling mentioned earlier also arises on the country scale. For many pollutants, as development progresses, the concentration first increases as a result of increased economic activity, then reaches a maximum and starts to decrease because of more efficient technology and more restrictive regulations. This inverted U-shaped curve for pollutants is called the environmental Kuznets curve (Kornhuber *et al.* 2014; Stern 2004). Whether such an environmental Kuznets curve for GHG is observable for GHG emissions depends on how development is measured (Kornhuber *et al.* 2014; Galeotti *et al.* 2006). Growth of emissions has been reported to be largest for the energy supply sector, for direct emissions from transport, for industry, for change in land use and forestry (IPCC 2007).

While current policies for climate mitigation often are set at the country level and global negotiations are of the highest importance, it is often at the city level that concrete infrastructure measures are taken and change occurs. The analysis and understanding of emissions at the city level is a very active field of research. Emissions are analysed based on atmospheric measurements (e.g. Tollefson 2012), trade data (e.g. Minx *et al.* 2013) or inventories (e.g. Dodman 2009). These studies identify high-consumption lifestyles associated with high incomes (Dodman 2009; Minx *et al.* 2013), as well as the occurrence of industry, education, car ownership and decreasing household size (Minx *et al.* 2013) as important explanations for high emission levels. Agreements exist at the country level with drivers regarding industry, income and mobility.

Looking at a household level, a study conducted in the United Kingdom integrated results from different surveys to relate household characteristics to emissions (Hargreaves *et al.* 2013). The study used representative surveys making the results valid for the entire United Kingdom. Hargreaves and colleagues (2013) found that, in general, emissions are higher for larger households (in terms of space and inhabitants), in a rural environment, with a household representative person of age 45–55, and from a higher occupational and socio-economic class. A statistical method to determine the factors with most power to explain emissions (analysis of variance – ANOVA) used by Hargreaves and colleagues (2013) shows, unsurprisingly, that income and number of cars have the most explanatory power, followed by household size and composition, and then other socio-demographic and economic factors. Again, we find agreement for the drivers including income and mobility, while industry does not directly apply at this level.

When is big sustainable?

In Rybski and colleagues (2015) we investigate how per capita emissions change with city size (the scaling behaviour of city emissions). In Figure 4.1 we show normalized per capita emissions of the city against population.

Emissions are influenced by country-specific factors, such as for example density of cities, because the denser European and Japanese cities require less transportation than North American and Australian cities. In order to control for such factors that are fairly constant throughout a country and make data comparable between multiple countries, we divide the city per capita emissions by the average per capita emission for the relevant country. Thus, we only look at the effect of city size (and potentially other city-specific circumstances).

Assuming that city emissions have been reported correctly and consistently, we find some evidence for a dependence on the GDP per capita. In countries with higher GDP (mostly from the global North – Figure 4.1 last panels), larger cities are more efficient, because they have lower per capita emissions than smaller cities. In countries with low GDP (mostly from the global South – Figure 4.1 first panels), larger cities have higher per capita emissions than smaller cities. From the results, it appears that differences exist in how emissions increase depending on GDP.

In the previous section, we reported a number of possible explanations for the difference in emission intensity. For example, we found that income, the number

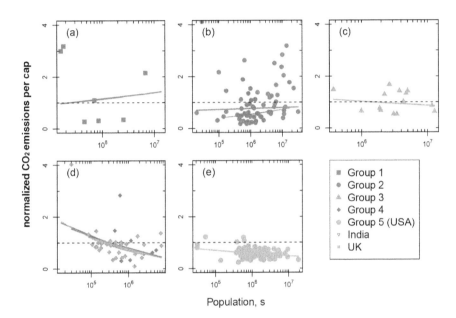

Figure 4.1 City efficiency in terms of carbon dioxide emissions. Per capita (annual) carbon dioxide emissions versus population. The emission values have been normalized by dividing by the country emissions per capita. The line indicates the regression line. City emission figures have been sorted and separated into groups according to the GDP per capita of the countries. (a) Group 1: Philippines (1), Bangladesh (4), Nepal (3). (b) Group 2: China (5), South Africa (1), Thailand (2), Greece (1), Sri Lanka (4), Slovenia (1), Czech Republic (1), Portugal (1), Spain (2), Mexico (1), Republic of Korea (2), Indonesia (1), Brazil (3), India (42), Bhutan (2) and India (42, brown open triangles). (c) Group 3: Germany (4), Italy (4), Singapore (1), Belgium (1), Finland (1), Japan (1), France (1), Sweden (1). (d) Group 4: United Kingdom (35), Netherlands (1), Canada (4), Australia (1), Switzerland (1), Norway (1) and United Kingdom (35, grey open squares). (e) Group 5: USA (122).

The United Kingdom and India appear twice, as part of a group and as individual countries.

Source of GDP data: World Bank: GDP per capita, PPP (current international dollar); World Bank, International Comparison Program database. http://data.worldbank.org/indicator/NY.GDP.PCAP. PP.CD (accessed December 2013).

of cars and transport emissions, household size, energy supply infrastructure, industry and land-use patterns can be used to estimate differences in GHG emissions. In this section, we want to test some of these factors for their potential to explain the dependency of per capita emissions on city size.

Income was identified as the most important predictor on a household scale in the United Kingdom, and was tested as the first potential explanation. Related to travel behaviour and land use patterns, we will look at how the distribution of facilities (such as for example hospitals, shops and restaurants) could relate to emissions. Finally, we also look at the importance of the industry sector as a third potential explanation.

Income in different cities was a factor in the investigations by Bettencourt and colleagues (2007). The authors found that the average per capita income in big cities was larger than in small cities. This finding can be combined with the finding that a person's emissions vary depending on their income. Hargreaves and colleagues (2013) reported that emissions increase with increasing income. Emissions increase fast with changes in low incomes and slowly with changes in high incomes (Chakravarty *et al.* 2009). We combined the observations by the Bettencourt 2007 and Chakravarty 2009 teams using simplifying assumptions about the distribution of the income in a particular city. This potential explanation leads to results consistent with larger per capita emissions in large cities, as observed for cities with low GDP. However, it is incompatible with the lower per capita emissions in large cities as observed for high GDP. If income is the basic mechanism affecting the scaling of emissions with city size, policies will have to limit the increase of emissions with increasing income for a decoupling to occur. However, in practice this will entail the implementation of quite fundamental socio-technical changes within highly complex urban environments where success depends on effective discourse coalitions rather than on technocratic solutions conceived by state planners.

Looking at travel behaviour and land use patterns as a potential explanation, we can make use of the findings of Um and colleagues (2009), who report that facilities are present in a denser form in areas with a denser population. However, population density increases faster than facility density. We checked different sets of assumptions to assess how per capita emissions change with city size. For every assumption we found that per capita emissions are smaller for big cities. Thus, using travel behaviour and land use patterns as an explanation is consistent with what we observe for cities with high GDP. If facilities and related travel behaviour create the basic mechanism affecting the scaling of emissions with city size, policies will have to ensure that there are short routes to facilities and that existing facilities are well utilized to make cities more sustainable. This could disrupt prevailing land-use and ownership patterns.

Finally, industry as a potential explanation can be assessed with data about the fraction of GDP produced from the industry sector, which is available from the World Bank database at a country level. It has been analysed and its dependence on the GDP per capita described by Lutz and colleagues (2013) at a country level. Based on a few assumptions, we find country-specific results on how per capita emissions change with city size. We find that per capita emissions increase more slowly with city size in countries with high GDP per capita than in countries with low GDP per capita, which partly reflects these observations. For some very dynamic economies where the share of the GDP from industries is quickly substituted by GDP from services, we find decreasing per capita emissions with increasing city size. However, such dynamic cases are rare (12 countries globally), and while Rybski and colleagues (2013) report such a behaviour for the United States, this is not the case based on our analysis.

If the importance of industry is the basic mechanism affecting the scaling of emissions with city size, policies will need to ensure emission-efficient industry and a tendency for more consumption of services rather than goods, to make cities more sustainable. Note that replacing local industry by imports to save emissions will not solve the problem on a global scale.

Overall, none of the explanations appears to be correct. Industry as a possible explanation seems most promising. However, in every case, we find that we can explain some of the observations, but not all. Most likely, all factors are important to a varying extent and each explanation has its limitations. Sufficient data for rigorous testing are currently lacking.

Discussion and conclusions

We started with the following question: 'Are large cities in relative terms responsible for greater or lesser emissions?', taking emissions as one example of interactions between nature and society. We reported on findings from a previous study by Rybski and colleagues (2013), where larger cities in countries with higher GDP (generally from the global North) have lower per capita emissions than smaller cities, and the reverse was observed for cities in countries with lower GDP. This puts into perspective the general rule that cities make it possible to deliver a good standard of living with reduced environmental impact. However, the rule may not be valid for all regions of the world.

We continued by looking for possible explanations and testing their consistency with the general tendencies observed in the data. We find, on the one hand, that the increasing per capita emissions with increasing city size that are characteristic of countries/cities with lower GDP per capita can be explained by both income distribution and the contribution of industry to the overall economy. On the other hand, the decreasing per capita emissions with increasing city size characteristic of countries/cities with higher GDP per capita are explained by the distribution of facilities and related travel behaviour. The contribution of industry to the overall economy also helps to explain a lower increase in per capita emissions in the case of higher GDP per capita, but normally not a decrease.

While none of the explanatory approaches is consistent with all the data, the findings are fairly plausible and not very surprising. In developed economies, average incomes increase slowly with city size (Bettencourt *et al.* 2007), but at the same time the efficiencies are greater in big cities due to agglomeration. In developing economies, moving to the city is often – for those with education and skills – about moving into the middle class. It will have to be tested whether income increases faster with city size for low-income countries. However, investments in the efficiencies of agglomeration in developing country cities are at an early stage. It therefore follows that size in developing country cities will correlate with rising carbon dioxide emissions per capita up to a certain point in the developmental trajectory.

Thus, we have not provided a general answer to the question whether larger cities are more efficient. Answers will have to be based on local experience. Policies to help move towards decoupling will need to include a mix of measures that are appropriate to the context.

Conclusion

Abstracting from the results presented in this study, the message to city managers is not to wait for a global agreement, but to begin now with a mixture of policies that are not derived from a global toolbox. Each city is different, and their contextual knowledge and learning should inform the way policies are formulated and implemented. This will allow the creative diversities of urban dynamics to shape policy options rather than be suppressed to accommodate taming discourses derived from the global policy elite that dominates major consulting firms and international financial institutions. In general, measures to increase the emission and energy efficiency of the energy supply are well suited to and may strengthen the local economy. All measures need to consider access and equity-related questions to also ensure social sustainability. In order to reduce travel-related emissions, strong policy measures are required to overcome lock-in effects, especially when these are vigorously defended by car-based middle-class elites whose interests are often represented in powerful political parties. A shift in mindset may help people to see urban life from a new perspective. For example, thinking of emissions along the entire product lifecycle is likely to shift priorities. Moreover, overcoming the scaling effects related to income probably requires specific approaches for different income levels: we need to start telling different stories of success and quality of life.

The basic underlying assumption in this chapter is that it is useful to identify general tendencies of how society functions and that this is possible using observations of the change in per capita emissions with city size. Some of the main limitations of the material presented include a systematic bias in the emission data reported which can not be excluded. For example, in a recent study Oliveira and colleagues (2014) report large US cities to be less carbon-efficient than small cities based on gridded emission data. Results from gridded emission data depend heavily on the algorithm used to distribute emission to grid cells. Furthermore, the data and analysis were based on production-based emissions, while consumption-based emissions compensate for virtual emission trade. The results would probably look different using consumption-based emissions.

An analysis of carbon footprints of municipalities in the United Kingdom found the footprints from a consumption-based approach to be normally higher and much more homogeneous than those using a production-based approach (Minx *et al.* 2013).

It was not possible to cover all explanatory approaches in our analysis, and the analysis could be extended. Moreover, questions related to distribution and equity have only been touched upon and deserve more attention. Despite the limitations, this chapter and the entire book are another step towards the urgently needed integrated analysis of nature–society interactions. Investigating how GHG emissions are scaled with city size is especially relevant because very fast urbanization is expected for the global South and it is essential to assess the consequences for future climate change. This analysis does not in and of itself reinforce a particular approach to the planning and governance of urban transitions to more sustainable modes of consumption and production. This data can be used to reinforce a taming SMART City agenda that tends to emphasize algorithmic technofixes focused exclusively on carbon reduction without affecting consumption levels. It can also be used to justify a more holistic approach to lifestyle change more consistent with untamed visions of future urban changes that tend to emanate from the environmental justice movements.

Note

1 At the same time as addressing environmental concerns, it is equally important not to forget about the equity question. How are environmental stresses and consequences distributed between the genders? This question must be posed, at both a local and a global scale.

References

Adger, W., Agrawala, S., Mirza, M., Conde, C., O'Brien, K., Pulhin, J., Pulwarty, R., Smit, B., and Takahashi, K. 2007. Assessment of adaptation practices, options, constraints and capacity, pp. 717–43. In M. Parry *et al.* (eds), *Climate Change 2007: Impacts, Adaptation and Vulnerability.* Contribution of Working Group II to the Fourth Assessment Report of the Intergovernmental Panel on Climate Change. Cambridge: Cambridge University Press.

Ahmad, N. and Wyckoff, A. 2003. Carbon dioxide emissions embodied in international trade of goods OECD Science, Technology and Industry Working Papers, 2003/15. Paris: OECD. http://dx.doi.org/10.1787/421482436815 (accessed 26 May 2014).

Bettencourt, L. M. A., Lobo, J., Helbing, D., Kühnert, C., and West, G. B. 2007. Growth, innovation, scaling, and the pace of life in cities. *Proceedings of the National Academy of Sciences*, 104(17): 7301–6.

Chakravarty, S., Chikkatur, A., Coninck, H. D., Pacala, S., Socolow, R., Tavoni, M. and de Coninck, H. 2009. Sharing global CO2 emission reductions among one billion high emitters. *Proceedings of the National Academy of Sciences*, 106(29): 11884–8.

Costa, L., Rybski, D. and Kropp, J. P. 2011. A human development framework for CO_2 reductions. *PLoS ONE*, 6(12): e29262.

Crutzen, P. 2006. The Anthropocene. In *Earth System Science in the Anthropocene.* Berlin and Heidelberg, Germany: Springer.

Davis, S. J. and Caldeira, K. 2010. Consumption-based accounting of CO_2 emissions. *Proceedings of the National Academy of Sciences*, 107(12): 5687–92.

Dobbs, R., Oppenheim, J., Thompson, F., Brinkman, M. and Zornes, M. 2011. Resource revolution: meeting the world's energy, materials, food, and water needs. Technical Report, November, McKinsey.

Dodman, D. 2009. Blaming cities for climate change? An analysis of urban greenhouse gas emissions inventories. *Environment and Urbanization*, 21(1): 185–201.

Edenhofer, O., Carraro, C. and Hourcade, J.-C. 2012. On the economics of decarbonization in an imperfect world. *Climatic Change*, 114(1): 1–8.

Galeotti, M., Lanza, A. and Pauli, F. 2006. Reassessing the environmental Kuznets curve for CO_2 emissions: a robustness exercise. *Ecological Economics*, 57(1): 152–63.

Geels, F. W. 2011. The multi-level perspective on sustainability transitions: responses to seven criticisms. *Environmental Innovation and Societal Transitions*, 1(1): 24–40.

Haberl, H., Fischer-Kowalski, M., Krausmann, F., Martinez-Alier, J. and Winiwarter, V. 2011. A socio-metabolic transition towards sustainability? Challenges for another Great Transformation. *Sustainable Development*, 19(1): 1–14.

Hargreaves, K., Preston, I., White, V. and Thumim, J. 2013. The distribution of household CO_2 emissions in Great Britain, 30 March. York, UK: Joseph Rowntree Foundation. Available at: www.jrf.org.uk/publications/household-co2-emissions (accessed 26 May 2014).

Intergovernmental Panel on Climate Change (IPCC). 2006. Overview, pp. 1–12 in *IPCC Guidelines for National Greenhouse Gas Inventories*. Japan: IPCC. Available at: www. ipcc-nggip.iges.or.jp/public/2006gl/ (accessed 26 May 2014).

—— 2007. Summary for policymakers. In B. Metz *et al.* (eds), *Climate Change 2007: Mitigation*. Contribution of Working Group III to the Fourth Assessment Report of the Intergovernmental Panel on Climate Change. Cambridge: Cambridge University Press.

—— 2013. Summary for policymakers. In T. Stocker *et al.* (eds), *Climate Change 2013: The Physical Science Basis*. Contribution of Working Group I to the Fifth Assessment Report of the Intergovernmental Panel on Climate Change. Cambridge and New York: Cambridge University Press.

Kartha, S., Athanasiou, T. and Baer, P. 2012. The North–South divide, equity and development: the need for trust-building for emergency mobilisation. In *What Next Volume III: Climate, Development and Equity*, pp. 47–75. Uppsala, Sweden: What Next Forum. Available at: www.whatnext.org/resources/Publications/Volume-III/Single-articles/wnv3_kartha-et-al_144.pdf (accessed 26 May 2014).

Kornhuber, K., Rybski, D., Costa, L., Reusser, D. E. and Kropp, J. P. 2014. Indication of environmental Kuznets curve in the relation between human development and CO2 emissions. Unpublished.

Lutz, R., Spies, M., Reusser, D. E., Kropp, J. P. and Rybski, D. 2013. Characterizing the development of sectoral gross domestic product composition. *Physical Review E*, 88(1): 012804.

Marcotullio, P. J., Sarzynski, A., Albrecht, J., Schulz, N. and Garcia, J. 2013. The geography of global urban greenhouse gas emissions: an exploratory analysis. *Climatic Change*, 121(4): 621–34.

Minx, J. C., Baiocchi, G., Wiedmann, T., Barrett, J., Creutzig, F., Feng, K., Förster, M., Pichler, P.-P., Weisz, H. and Hubacek, K. 2013. Carbon footprints of cities and other human settlements in the UK. *Environmental Research Letters*, 8(3): 035039.

Parry, M., Canziani, O., Palutikof, J., van Der Linden, P. and Hanson, C. (eds). 2008. *Climate Change 2007: Impacts, Adaptation and Vulnerability*. Contribution of Working Group II to the Fourth Assessment Report of the Intergovernmental Panel on Climate Change, vol. 37. Cambridge: Cambridge University Press.

Peters, G. 2008. From production-based to consumption-based national emission inventories. *Ecological Economics*, 65(1): 13–23.

Randers, J. 2012. 2052: A Global Forecast for the Next Forty Years. White River Jct., VT: Chelsea Green.

Reusser, D. E., Lissner, T. K., Pradhan, P., Holsten, A., Rybski, D. and Kropp, J. P. 2013. Relating climate compatible development and human livelihood. *Energy Procedia*, 40: 192–201.

Rockström, J., Steffen, W., Noone, K., Persson, A., Chapin, F. S., Lambin, E. F., Lenton, T. M., Scheffer, M., Folke, C., Schellnhuber, H. J., Nykvist, B., de Wit, C. A., Hughes, T., van der Leeuw, S., Rodhe, H., Sörlin, S., Snyder, P. K., Costanza, R., Svedin, U., Falkenmark, M., Karlberg, L., Corell, R. W., Fabry, V. J., Hansen, J., Walker, B., Liverman, D., Richardson, K., Crutzen, P. and Foley, J. A. 2009. A safe operating space for humanity. *Nature*, 461(7263): 472–5.

Rybski, D., Reusser, D.E., Winz, A.-L., Fichter, C., Sterzel, T.J., and Kropp, J.P. 2015. Cities as nuclei of sustainability? Environment and planning B: planning and design, under review. Available at http://arxiv.org/abs/1304.4406v2

Schellnhuber, H. J., Messner, D. and Leggewie, C. 2009. Solving the climate dilemma: the budget approach. Technical report. Berlin: German Advisory Council on Global Change (WBGU).

Stern, D. I. 2004. The rise and fall of the environmental Kuznets curve. *World Development*, 32(8): 1419–39.

Tollefson, J. 2012. Megacities move to track emissions. *Nature*, 492(7427): 20–1.

Um, J., Son, S.-W., Lee, S.-I., Jeong, H. and Kim, B. J. 2009. Scaling laws between population and facility densities. *Proceedings of the National Academy of Sciences*, 106(34): 14236–40.

United Nations Environment Programme (UNEP). 2013. City-level decoupling: urban resource flows and the governance of infrastructure transitions. Report of the Working Group on Cities of the International Resource Panel. Nairobi: UNEP.

Wackernagel, M. and Rees, W. 2013. *Our Ecological Footprint: Reducing Human Impact on the Earth*. Gabriola Island, BC, Canada: New Society.

Walmsley, T., Aguiar, A. and Narayanan, B. 2012. Introduction to the Global Trade Analysis Project and the GTAP Data Base. West Lafayette, IN: Ideas. Available at: http://ideas.repec.org/p/gta/workpp/3965.html (accessed 18 June 2014).

Zhou, B., Rybski, D. and Kropp, J. 2013 The statistics of urban heat island intensity. *Geophysical Research Letters*, 40(20): 5486–91. Available at: http://doi.wiley.com/10.1002/2013GL057320 (accessed 18 June 2014).

5 Urban-scale food system governance

An alternative response to the dominant paradigm?

Gareth Haysom

Food had a symbiotic relationship with cities for centuries. Food shaped cities. Food influenced the location, design, economies and politics of cities. For many cities their ability to ensure food availability determined their stature.[1] Recently, however, the relationship between food and the city has become increasingly opaque. Colonialism, industrialization and globalization have resulted in changes in food system functions. All of these changes have distanced cities from food production and changed the relationship between the city and food.

Defined in terms of the distribution of dietary energy supply, 868 million people around the world were considered chronically undernourished in 2013 (FAO 2013: ix). Crush and Frayne (2010) correctly argue that food insecurity is misleadingly regarded as an issue that only affects rural populations. African cities are expanding rapidly and are key centres of growth and development (UN-DESA 2012). For many urban residents, this growth and development is not translating into better livelihoods. Access to food is particularly problematic for poor people in African cities (Crush and Frayne 2010). In South African cities, where first apartheid and then prevailing policies have had a direct impact, urban food insecurity is high (Battersby 2011; SANHANES-1 2013). Current food system governance and policies perhaps even perpetuate urban food insecurity.

Urban food security and related consequences raise questions about the role of cities in the food system, and the processes that enable active city resident participation in the urban food system. It was these questions that precipitated my own enquiry into the nascent urban food system governance approaches and actions that I observed, both in my engagement with policy-makers and in practice.

The urban food system challenge forms part of a wider set of converging, mutually reinforcing transitions (Swilling and Annecke 2012). Four interconnected global, yet locally experienced, transitions are considered in this chapter. These include the second urban transition, the food system transition and the nutrition transition. Fourth, driven by the preceding transitions, is the emergence of alternative urban food governance innovations. These governance strategies are diverse. A collection of these emerging alternative food governance innovations are investigated, and provide a framework against which the South African urban food governance interventions are compared.

This chapter suggests that food insecurity in South African cities remains a pervasive and increasingly complex challenge. Addressing these complexities requires innovative governance approaches extending beyond the traditional remit of the city.

Mutually converging transitions

This book engages with the consequences of the polycrisis. The second urban transition is dealt with in Chapters 1 and 2. Linked to the untamed theme of the book, Pieterse (2013a: 21) highlights how descriptions of the developing world cities as 'endless vistas of shantytowns as the visible face of crisis' do not effectively capture the processes, networks and dynamics embedded within developing world cities. What the African city does reflect is an endless struggle for 'liveability', in which different forms of cityness emerge. The ability to participate in processes that enable the realization of the interests of urban residents is central to the notions of liveable urbanism (Swilling 2011: 90). This 'liveability' is observed in the changes that grassroots organizations have enacted through bottom-up agency (see Appadurai 2002).

A theme in the writings of Pieterse (2006, 2013b) is the question of participation, voice and, by implication, agency. Pieterse suggests that the role of communities in rebuilding the city is facilitated through the creation of '*homebru* strategies that emerge and flourish in a context of radical democratic politics that stretch across formal–informal, concrete–symbolic and consensual–conflictual binaries' (2006: 300).[2] Cities are in transition, particularly developing world cities. These transitions see different forms of agency and governance emerging. One area where this agency and governance is reflected is in how certain cities engage with food.

The food system transition process constitutes a broader set of interconnected transitions that reflect a number of attendant subtransitions. Friedmann and McMichael's (1989) food regime thesis focuses on the 'contradictory relations underlying the institutional and power structures across capitalist time, and at a particular conjuncture' (McMichael 2009: 292). Of interest here are the workings of the current food regime, the third or 'corporate' food regime, where the organizing principle is the market, not the empire (as it was in the first regime) or the state (the second regime) (McMichael 2009). I argue that one of the principal processes of the third food regime is a desire to tame. Taming is evident not only in how the retail market is structured, but also in how all points in the food system are being tamed. This taming reduces diversity and vibrancy within the food system. Problematically, this taming results in significant net losses – in farmers, health and, specifically, in food security, nutrition and voice. As discussed in the introduction, 'taming processes reduce complexity, homogenize and exclude'.

A number of food regime transitions have specific relevance to the urban food question. These transitions fall within the wider concept of what is termed the 'Big Food' transition (Stuckler and Nestle 2012; Monteiro and Cannon 2012). The Big Food phenomenon is evident in South Africa (Igumbor *et al.* 2012). Within the

Big Food transition, two sub-transitions are evident. One is the supermarket transition documented and theorized by Reardon and colleagues (see Weatherspoon and Reardon 2003; Reardon *et al.* 2012). The nutrition transition (Popkin 2002) is typified by adverse changes in diet, and is directly associated with urbanization (Mendez and Popkin 2004: 75).

Different groups are responding to the changes in the food system and the attendant consequences of the third food regime. While these groups are diverse, some are referred to as alternative food networks.

Alternative food geographies

The different responses to the current food system represent a maturing body of socio-spatial food theories under the umbrella of alternative food networks (AFNs) (Renting *et al.* 2003; Watts *et al.* 2005). AFNs are described as being:

> New rapidly mainstreaming spaces in the food economy defined by . . . the explosion of organic, Fair Trade, local, quality, and premium speciality foods. In these networks, it is claimed that the production and consumption of food are more closely tied together spatially, economically and socially.
>
> (Goodman and Goodman 2007: 2)

The same authors argue (with cynicism and truth) that these AFNs reflect a sense of 'upper class angst' (Goodman and Goodman 2007). As a result, the somewhat privileged view of AFNs requires the inclusion of wider food system-related discourses.

I have spent time working in different parts of the food system as a professional, and later as an academic and a researcher, trying to understand the system. My areas of interest include sustainable food and urban food issues. In this work, I have encountered proactive and valuable projects, processes and actors. However, these initiatives and actors often competed with one another, undermining the different approaches despite an overarching sustainability ethos. These experiences further support the need for the expansion of the concept of AFNs.

Borrowing from Wiskerke's (2009) term 'alternative food geographies', I build on the notions of an integrated and territorial agrifood paradigm to refer to AFNs and further expanded food system interventions as Differentiated Food Geographies (DFGs). This DFG approach seeks to categorize the different food system perspectives according to three areas of analysis: focus, scale, and ideology or politics. While a measure of overlap and duplication exists, this categorization highlights four different responses to food system challenges:

- A production focus – including the organic and other such movements, and reflecting a politics of land-based activism (see Altieri and Nichols 2005; Kate 2010).
- A green focus – still with a dominant production focus but seeking to validate green actions through labelling and certification. This reflects notions of

doing less harm and a politics of regulation (see Bennett 1997; Collins and Fairchild 2007).

• A justice focus – which considers issues such as food sovereignty and food justice but focuses predominantly on alternative market systems, displaying a politics of justice and culture (see Patel 2007).

• A spatial focus – which questions how specific scale-based domains engage with the broader food system and the levers and structures required to ensure wider benefit. Here the politics of equality and place-specific cohesion dominate (see Roberts 2001; Blay-Palmer 2009).

This chapter focuses on the spatial-specific responses in food system governance, as these reflect most directly the urban food governance trends and, I argue, hold potential for engagement with and validation of untamed urban food system actions.

International food governance analysis

A distinct spatial focus to food governance is emerging internationally. Belo Horizonte in Brazil has developed a number of city government-led pro-poor interventions (Barker 2007; Rocha and Lessa 2009). Other South American cities taking this type of approach include Bogotá and Medellín in Colombia. In North America, cities, counties and states are developing spatially bounded food governance initiatives. The Toronto Food Policy Council (TFPC), the designated custodian of the Toronto Food Charter, is aligned to, but outside, government (Friedmann 2007). Other examples of North American and European city food strategies reflect the need for local relevance, contextual knowledge and governance that generally extends beyond the current governance domain of the city.

While caution should be exercised and it is unwise to adopt uncritically any international trends in local food governance, some key themes within urban food governance are evident. These themes include a clearly articulated scalar boundary of operations, networked knowledge generation, participative governance, inter-ministerial engagement, a deliberate pro-poor orientation, and research-informed interventions used in the formulation of scale-specific food strategies.

This review has used data specific to two North American food governance sources. First are data from the Community Food Security Coalition (CFSC), a grouping of over 170 food policy councils (FPCs) (as of May 2012).[3] The data from these groups were drawn from CFSC sources, validated through online reviews and tested through key informant interviews. A report investigating Canadian place-specific food governance structures informed the second review. Here 64 organizations were investigated (MacRae and Donahue 2013).

The areas of focus of the CFSC initiatives offer insight into focus, mandate and need. Through a process of key word/phrase attribution, 12 areas of focus were identified and organized according to governance scale. Figure 5.1 reflects the frequency of focus at specific scales and highlights the dominance of a local-level focus. This focus offers insights into the changing role played by local entities in food governance. The focus on knowledge, policies and legal frameworks, and

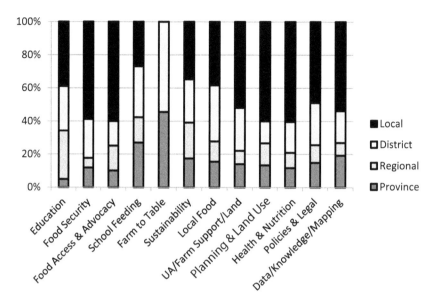

Figure 5.1 Area of focus by scale.

issues associated with planning highlighted at the local scale in Figure 5.1 reflects a local food systems trend (Dahlberg 1999; MacRae and Donahue 2013).

A key question that needs to be asked at this point is whether the formation of these scale-focused food governance structures possibly reflects a form of taming, even if this is as a counter to the taming associated with the third food regime?

The city of Belo Horizonte in Brazil has approached urban food system governance differently. In Brazil food is a right of citizenship (Barker 2007). A city government unit, the Secretariat for Food Policy and Supply (SMAAB), has engaged directly with urban food governance since 1993. Its actions have evolved into six main areas of focus: subsidized food sales, food and nutrition assistance, supply and regulation of food markets, support to urban agriculture, education for food consumption, and job and income generation (Rocha and Lessa 2009: 391). The case of Belo Horizonte is often described as a city-led initiative. However, one of the foundations of success in the Belo Horizonte case was the role and participation of civil society through the creation of the Municipal Council for Food Security at the start of the process. This provided a platform for social mobilization into policy and programmes (Rocha and Lessa 2009: 397).

It is important to stress that the local or city-scale focus does not imply self-sufficiency or the concept of localization (see Hopkins 2008). Local in this instance involves a focus on how food flows are governed in the interests of the local (Morgan and Sonnino 2009), taking care to avoid the so-called 'local trap' (Born and Purcell 2006). When the reviewed scale-specific food governance approaches are considered collectively, key operating principles can be deduced. These are described in Table 5.1.

Table 5.1 Scale-specific operating trends

Theme	Action
Governance	Governance that draws on multiple actors from within and outside government.
Management	The majority of cities play an indirect management role, using their convening authority to facilitate processes and actions as opposed to top-down management.
Knowledge/data	Recognition given to the knowledge and networks of multiple food systems actors, facilitating the equitable use and application of this knowledge. Considers immediate issues but also long-term trends.
Remit	Direct focus given to contextual issues pertinent to the specific locality. Broader issues are still considered but form the locality's perspective.
Interdisciplinarity	Focus on intersections between issues, breaking traditional governance silos. The interconnections between health, education, planning and environment dominate.
Ideology	A general alignment with an ethos of sustainability, but generally considered in a more integrative manner, beyond a sustainability-as-green focus.
Networking	Engagement with multiple food system actors and specifically other cities, sharing experiences, knowledge and challenges.

Source: own analysis

Many of the international city programmes emerged in the context of an urban food policy vacuum. Northern cities reflect a number of different governance approaches and motivations. In the South American city examples, the city governments drive processes but with embedded participatory processes. Recently new forms of food governance have emerged in certain South African cities.

South African urban food governance trends

South Africa has no urban-specific food policies, but general policies and legal frameworks that consider the challenges of food security are in place. These frameworks obligate all spheres of government to act. The two primary frameworks are the South African Constitution (Act 108 of 1996), specifically Section 27(1)b, the so-called 'Right to food clause' which compels organs of the state to ensure the progressive realization of the right to food. Second is the Integrated Food Security Strategy (IFSS) of 2002. The IFSS was formulated and housed within the National Department of Agriculture (now DAFF). Problematically, this focus perpetuates a rural, productionist view of food security and as a result effectively disregards urban food insecurity. A dominant focus on production may enable the desired positive food trade balance, argued as a determinant of food security in the National Development Plan (NDP 2012: 230), but this does not translate into food security at either the household or the city scale.

In the context of pervasive yet poorly understood urban food insecurity, it is necessary to reflect on the food security challenges in selected southern African cities. In 2008 the African Food Security Urban Network (AFSUN), focusing specifically on poor areas, found 77 per cent of people suffered from food insecurity in poor areas of the 11 southern African cities it surveyed. This trend was evident in the three South African cities within the AFSUN review. In Cape Town 80 per cent of those surveyed were found to be moderately or severely food insecure (Battersby 2011). More recently, the South African National Health and Nutrition Examination Survey (SANHANES) found 68 per cent food insecurity in urban informal areas (SANHANES-1 2013: 22), aligning with data from the 2012 General Household Survey reflecting food access constraints (StatsSA 2013).

Although other South African cities have engaged in forms of food system interventions, these remain locked in project and production-oriented interventionist paradigms. Stellenbosch and Cape Town, while in no way exemplars, reflect a new trend, one where more systemic approaches are emerging.

Through a partnership between the University of Stellenbosch and Stellenbosch Municipality, a food system study for Stellenbosch was carried out. As part of this process, a Draft Stellenbosch Food System Strategy (DSFSS)[4] was developed and adopted by the municipality in 2011. The DSFSS borrowed heavily from international urban food governance typologies in terms of governance and food security interventions. However, although formally approved, the strategy has not been implemented. Conceptual and process-related faults limited the uptake of the DSFSS. Enquiries into the stalling of the DSFSS revealed multiple challenges, highlighting the complexity of developing such governance structures. One of the key challenges reported was a disregard for food system agents and the argument that the top-down nature effectively excluded any untamed forms of food system agency.

Despite a long food history, Cape Town's current engagement in food system issues originates from the development of the Urban Agriculture Policy (UAP) of 2007 (CoCT 2007). The UAP implementation precipitated an ever-increasing engagement with wider food system issues (Visser 2012), which led to the realization that there was a need for a city-wide food strategy. This realization was reinforced by ongoing engagement with other cities, including Belo Horizonte and the TFPC in Toronto.

The nature of the emergent food system engagement precipitated a call for tenders to conduct a study into the food systems and food security in the City of Cape Town in 2013. This call sought to 'investigate [the] multi-faceted urban development challenge comprising of two inter-related aspects, namely 1) the components and effectiveness of Cape Town's food systems, and 2) the status of food insecurity in Cape Town' (CoCT 2013: 10). In May 2014 (at the time of writing) the study had been completed and was awaiting formal approval. The city now needs to determine how it will use the study findings and recommendations, which included detailed stakeholder reviews, to inform a city-wide food strategy.

Discussion

The Stellenbosch and Cape Town food strategy processes emerged in the contexts of an urban food policy vacuum, and of high, yet often unrecorded, levels of food insecurity and attendant dietary and nutritional challenges. Both urban areas eschewed traditional project-driven welfarist food system interventions. These nascent processes are argued to reflect the beginnings of a change.

One trend evident in Cape Town and Stellenbosch is an engagement with a far wider stakeholder group. Both the Stellenbosch and the Cape Town processes have actively sought to access knowledge networks at the community scale, where different actors are displaying agency, responding to and engaging in food system activities. These agency-type actions are a resource in food governance processes, a resource with essential knowledge about food system dynamics and faults. These agents are vital, even if they disagree with or contest government intervention in the food system. Such untamed epistemic communities offer valuable food system insights, and their inclusion in food system processes enables greater voice and agency in food strategy design.

Globalization and the associated neoliberal policies have prompted shifts in urban governance, altering the relationship between cities and the nation state. This shift has been described as a move from developmental Fordist-oriented approaches to liberalized entrepreneurialism (Harvey 1989: 4). Although some North American food governance structures (FGSs) reflect a form of urban food system entrepreneurialism, the general trends evident in FGSs reviewed avoid such liberal entrepreneurial governance. The international FGSs reflect neither a reversion to Fordist nor liberalized entrepreneurial governance approaches. The emergence of 'pluralistic' governance structures is driven by the absence of formal local food-focused governance initiatives (MacRae and Donahue 2013; Emanuel 2013), structures originally enabled through inclusive (Keynesian) local government. The liberalizing trend in local government has resulted in a food policy (and food-related remedial action) vacuum (Harper *et al.* 2009). Contextually focused FGSs are seeking greater levels of inclusivity and ways to counter inequalities in the food system (Harper *et al.* 2009). In many instances, the FGSs are created specifically because the trickle-down notion associated with liberal economic theory is not delivering the claimed food system benefit (Cook 2013).

It is clear from the international and South African cases that city government has a critical role to play in urban food system governance. Pieterse (2013c) posits that the city's governance role entails the city using its legitimate authority to convene divergent urban (food system) stakeholders. City governments have a unique ability to bring different groups together, through funding and their legal mandate, to ensure participatory processes. As the accountable entity (at the local government scale) for the progressive realization of the right to food, cities are explicitly required to play an active role in such processes. Additionally, if certain groups require greater attention (such as the vulnerable and food insecure), the city must direct additional attention to these areas, ensuring that the vision of any food governance process is aligned to wider city needs, while at the same time preventing capture by splintered ideological perspectives. Disparate views of the food system and food system outcomes are inevitable, as evidenced in the DFG. Informed by the city's dual roles of convener and custodian, cities need to play the role of facilitating food system processes and actively encouraging agent-style *homebru* and untamed actions. This represents a new and emergent form of place-specific, and in this case urban, food governance.

Conclusion

Urban food system actions are emerging. Many actors are active in urban food activities in the rapidly changing South African cities. City government and other food system stakeholders all have essential roles to play in urban food governance processes. The changing role of cities means that food system governance and food security interventions can no longer remain the domain of national government, focusing on rural areas where productionist responses dominate. Cities have a critical role to play in systemic governance interventions that seek to enable food availability as well as food access, appropriateness and agency.

This is not the exclusive responsibility of city government. Processes are necessary to facilitate the agency actions of a wider grouping of urban food system stakeholders. Such actions are emerging. There needs however to be a radical shift in how participation in urban governance processes is approached. Collaborative forms of urban food system governance offer potential pathways to improved food system governance. Accepting and embracing the untamed nature of many agency actions in the food system, and seeking out ways to include these agents or actors in food system processes, while retaining their untamed vibrancy, is argued to be an essential component of effective food system governance.

Notes

1 See Carolyn Steel's (2008) description of the first cities and how food influenced these for more on this point.
2 *Homebru* is a colloquial South African term used to describe emergent local actions, activities, responses or characteristics that reflect the local dynamics. This generally has positive connotations.
3 The CFSC was disbanded at the end of 2013.
4 For the full strategy see www.sustainabilityinstitute.net/assets/news_article_files/stel lenbosch_draft_food_strategy_july_2011.pdf

References

Altieri, M. and Nicholls, C. 2005. *Agrocecology and the Search for a Truly Sustainable Agriculture.* Mexico: United Nations Environment Programme.
Appadurai, A. 2002. Deep democracy: urban governmentality and the horizon of politics. *Public Culture*, 14(1): 21–47.
Barker, D. 2007. The rise and predictable fall of globalized industrial agriculture. International Forum on Globalization. San Francisco, CA.

Battersby, J. 2011. The state of urban food insecurity in Cape Town. *Urban Food Security Series*, No. 11. Kingston and Cape Town, South Africa: Queen's University and AFSUN.

Bennett, R. 1997. Farm animal welfare and food policy. *Food Policy*, 22(4): 281–8.

Blay-Palmer, A. 2009. The Canadian pioneer: the genesis of urban food policy in Toronto. *International Planning Studies*, 14(4): 401–16.

Born, B. and Purcell, M. 2006. Avoiding the local trap: scale and food systems in planning research. *Journal of Planning Education and Research*, 26(2): 195–207.

City of Cape Town (CoCT). 2007. *Urban Agriculture Policy for the City of Cape Town.* City of Cape Town.

—— 2013. Provision of a service provider: to conduct study on food systems and food security in the City of Cape Town. Tender number 414C/2012/13, Supply Chain Management. Version 4, pp. 1–58.

Collins, A. and Fairchild, R. 2007. Sustainable food consumption at a sub-national level: an ecological footprint, nutritional and economic analysis. *Journal of Environmental Policy and Planning*, 9(1): 5–30.

Community Food Security Coalition (CFSC). 2012. North American Food Policy Councils. Available at: www.foodsecurity.org (accessed 3 March 2013).

Cook, B. 2013. Interview, Toronto Food Policy Council Offices, Toronto, Canada, 9 May 2013.

Crush, J. and Frayne, B. 2010. The invisible crisis: urban food security in Southern Africa. *Urban Food Security in Southern Africa, Urban Food Security Series*, No. 1. African Food Security Network (AFSUN). Cape Town, South Africa: Unity Press.

Dahlberg, K. 1999. Local food systems: promoting sustainable local food systems in the United States. In M. Koc, R. MacRae, L. Mougeot and J. Welsh, *For Hunger-Proof Cities: Sustainable Urban Food Systems*, pp. 41–6. Ottawa: International Development Research Centre and Centre for Studies in Food Security.

Department of Agriculture (DOA). 2002. *The Integrated Food Security Strategy for South Africa.* Pretoria: Government Printer.

Draft Stellenbosch Food System Strategy (DSFSS). 2011. *The Stellenbosch Food System: Towards 2030, Draft Strategy Document.* Hope Project, Stellenbosch University.

Emanuel, B. 2013. Personal communication, Toronto Food Policy Council Offices, Toronto, Canada, 10 May 2013.

Food and Agriculture Organization of the United Nations (FAO). 2013. *The State of Food and Agriculture: 2013. Better Systems for Better Nutrition*. Rome: FAO.

Friedmann, H. 2007. Scaling up: bringing public institutions and food service corporations into the project for a local, sustainable food system in Ontario. *Agriculture and Human Values*, 24: 389–98.

Friedmann, H. and McMichael, P. 1989. Agriculture and the state system: the rise and decline of national agricultures, 1870 to present. *Sociologia Ruralis*, 29(2): 93–117.

Goodman, D. and Goodman, M. 2007. Alternative food networks. Draft entry for the Encyclopedia of Human Geography, 2 July.

Harper, A., Shattuck, A., Holt-Gimenez, E., Alkon, A. and Lambrick, F. 2009. *Food Policy Councils: Lessons Learnt*. Food First. Institute for Food and Development Policy.

Harvey, D. 1989. From managerialism to entrepreneurialism: the transformation in urban governance in late capitalism. *Geografiska Annaler. B, Human Geography*, 71(1): 3–17.

Hopkins, R. 2008. *The Transition Handbook: From Oil Dependence to Local Resilience.* Devon, UK: Green Books.

Igumbor, E., Sanders, D., Puoane, T., Tsolekile, L., Schwarz, C., Purdy, C., Swart, R., Durão, S. and Hawkes, C. 2012. 'Big food', the consumer food environment, health, and the policy response in South Africa. *PLoS Medicine*, 9(7): 1–7.

Kate, T. 2010. From industrial agriculture to agro ecological farming: a South African perspective. Working Paper Series no. 10. East London, South Africa: Eastern Cape Socio-Economic Consultative Council (ECSECC).

McMichael, P. 2009. A food regime analysis of the 'world food crisis'. *Agriculture and Human Values*, 26: 281–95.

MacRae, R. and Donahue, K. 2013. *Municipal Food Policy Entrepreneurs: A Preliminary Analysis of How Canadian Cities and Regional Districts Are Involved in Food System Change.* Toronto, Canada: Toronto Food Policy Council and Canadian Agri-Food Policy Institute.

Mendez, M. and Popkin, B. 2004. Globalization, urbanization and nutritional change in the developing world. In Globalization of food systems in developing countries: impact on food security and nutrition, Food and Nutrition Paper no. 83, pp. 55–80. Rome: FAO.

Monteiro, C. and Cannon, G. 2012. The impact of transnational 'big food' companies on the South: a view from Brazil. *PLoS Medicine*, 9(6): 1–5.

Morgan, K. and Sonnino, R. 2009. The urban foodscape: world cities and the new food equation. *Cambridge Journal of Regions, Economy and Society*, 3: 209–24.

National Development Plan (NDP) 2012. *National Development Plan: Vision for 2030, Our Future – Make It Work*. National Planning Commission. Pretoria: Government Printer.

Patel, R. 2007. *Stuffed and Starved*. New York: Melville House.

Pieterse, E. 2006. Building with ruins and dreams: some thoughts on realising integrated urban development in South Africa through crisis. *Urban Studies*, 43(2): 285–304.

—— 2013a. Grasping the unknowable: coming to grips with African urbanisms, pp. 19–37 in E. Pieterse and A. Simone (eds), *Rogue Urbanism: Emergent African Cities*. Auckland Park, South Africa: Jacana Media and Cape Town, South Africa: African Centre for Cities.

—— 2013b. City/University interplays amidst complexity. *Territorio*, 66: 26–32.

—— 2013c. Interview, Urban governance and participation, University of Cape Town, 20 June 2013.

Popkin, B. 2002. The shift in stages of the nutrition transition in the developing world differs from past experiences! *Public Health Nutrition*, 5(1A): 205–14.

Reardon, T., Chen, K., Minten, B. and Adriano, L. 2012. The quiet revolution in staple food value chains: enter the dragon, the elephant, and the tiger. Mandaluyong City, Philippines: Asian Development Bank and International Food Policy Research Institute.

Renting, H., Marsden, T. and Banks, J. 2003. Understanding alternative food networks: exploring the role of short food supply chains in rural development. *Environment and Planning A*, 35: 393–411.

Republic of South Africa (RSA). 1996. Constitution of the Republic of South Africa, No. 108 of 1996. Online: www.info.gov.za/documents/constitution/1996/a108-96.pdf (accessed 23 March 2011).

Roberts, W. 2001. The way to a city's heart is through its stomach: putting food security on the urban planning menu, Crackerbarrel Philosophy Series. Toronto, Canada: Toronto Food Policy Council.

Rocha, C and Lessa, I. 2009. Urban governance for food security: the alternative food system in Belo Horizonte, Brazil. *International Planning Studies*, 14(4): 389–400.

SANHANES-1. 2013. South African National Health and Nutrition Examination Survey Research Findings Presentation, 6 August 2013. Human Sciences Research Council and Medical Research Council of South Africa.

Statistics South Africa (StatsSA). 2013. *General Household Survey 2012.* Pretoria: StatsSA.

Steel, C. 2008. *Hungry City: How Food Shapes Our Lives.* London: Chatto & Windus.

Stuckler, D. and Nestle, M. 2012. Big food, food systems, and global health. *PLoS Medicine*, 9(6): 1–4.

Swilling, M. 2011. Reconceptualising urbanism, ecology and networked infrastructures. *Social Dynamics*, 37(1): 78–95.

Swilling, M. and Annecke, E. 2012. *Just Transitions: Explorations of Sustainability in an Unfair World.* Cape Town, South Africa: Juta.

United Nations Department of Economic and Social Affairs (UN DESA). 2008. *World Urbanisation Prospects: The 2007 Revision. Executive Summary.* Available at: www. un.org/esa/population/publications/wup2007/2007WUP_ExecSum_web.pdf (accessed 14 January 2011).

United Nations Department of Economic and Social Affairs (UN DESA). 2012. World Urbanization Prospects: The 2011 Revision.

Visser, S. 2012. Interview with head of Urban Agriculture Unit, Milnerton, Cape Town, 15 November 2012.

Watts, D., Ilbery, B. and Maye, D. 2005. Making reconnections in agro-food geography: alternative systems of food. *Progress in Human Geography*, 29(1): 22–40.

Weatherspoon, D. and Reardon, T. 2003. The rise of supermarkets in Africa: implications for agrifood systems and the rural poor. *Development Policy Review*, 21(3): 333–55.

Wiskerke, J. 2009. On places lost and places regained: reflections on the alternative food geography and sustainable regional development. *International Planning Studies*, 14(4): 369–87.

Part II

The untamed everyday

The chapters in Part II provide a set of case studies that engage with three major debates in urban studies, namely the polarity between agency and structure and how human and non-human living beings possess active agency within wider socio-ecological dynamics of change; the problematic implications of discursive narratives importing evolutionist assumptions about 'adaptation' into the social sciences from the eco-system sciences; and the simplifications implied by the state-versus-market dualism from the existing urban service delivery systems that proliferate in informalized cities of the global South. In doing so, the whole set of chapters enter into a productive dialogue with key themes of the book as far as its search for the 'untamed' and its intellectual operation of 'untaming' current urbanisms is concerned. Therefore the reader will find material for interesting reflection on at least four grounds: i) the contemporary production of injustice throughout the social production of space in the Fraserian terms of maldistribution, misrecognition and misrepresentation; ii) the presence of risk and vulnerability as constitutive part of every day life, especially of the poor but neither necessarily nor only them; iii) the 'de-territorialization' of the production of risk in contemporary urban settings of the global South in as much as risk is largely globally produced; and, finally, iv) the brutal forms of exclusion and expulsion that echo the recent and parallel reflection put forward by Saskia Sassen.

In Chapter 6, entitled 'Lost in translation: social protection and the search for security in Bogotá, Colombia', Andrea Lampis (Colombia) presents a set of case studies that question an increasingly common global trend in social protection: the so-called social floor and social investment paradigms. Urban areas in the global South are the testing ground for new social configurations of social protection, which are of great relevance for people and agency in general, not only for the poor. Although still formally administered by public bodies, these reconfigurations factually respond to the new logic of privatization and commodification of individual and collective security. Using the fractal metaphor, the case illustrates how women and men in both secure and insecure employment in Bogotá tend to escape the new hegemonic logic of social protection. The analysis underlines the contradiction between market-driven practices and the traditional welfare state-driven principles invoked to justify the implementation of these practices.

Entitled 'Potentials of the urban poor in shaping a sustainable Lagos metropolis', Chapter 7 by Taibat Lawanson (Nigeria) explores the responses of the poor to recombining socio-economic and environmental risks in Lagos, Nigeria. Familial patterns of collective action defined by others as 'informal' emerge as a structural feature of how the poor build their livelihoods in Lagos. Far away from the neoliberal celebration of the potential value of societies driven by market forces, the chapter's narrative guides the reader across a brutal landscape of complex economic agents and collective forms of solidarity. This sets in context the paradoxical claims of local government and local actors who strive to achieve the goal of making Lagos 'Africa's model megacity' by denying the existence of many layers of social exclusion and differential citizenry based on social status and economic purchasing power.

Chapter 8 by Mauricio Domínguez Aguilar and Jorge Pacheco Castro (Mexico), entitled 'Sustainability of what? The struggles of poor Mayan households with young breadwinners towards a better life in the peri-urban area of Merida, Yucatan, Mexico', presents a bottom-up reading of the social vulnerability of poor Mayan families for a better life in the peri-urban context of Merida city in the Yucatan peninsula, Mexico. The chapter shows how especially ethnicity, but also age and gender, shapes social vulnerability outcomes and deeply influences the struggle for more sustainable livelihoods. By bringing into focus these key dimensions of agency in the city, the case study challenges the straightforward use of the livelihood approach as well as of programmes aimed at poverty reduction, making the point that social and environmental sustainability are not only technical but profoundly political challenges because of the way ethnicity and lifecycle interact with asset ownership and land use in determining different forms of social vulnerability and exclusion.

Chapter 9 by Chipo Plaxedes Mubaya, Patience Mutopo and Mzime Ndebele-Murisa (Tanzania), entitled 'Local governance, climate risk and everyday vulnerability in Dar es Salaam', analyses the opportunities available to slum dwellers to deal with climate risk and vulnerability. Collective agency and action are hindered here by multiple causes of social vulnerability, including poor health, precarious employment, and little political voice or power. The study concludes that biophysical causes of vulnerability are not necessarily the main entry point for the analysis of vulnerability to climate risk. Within an already established scholarship on the 'double exposure' of the poor to critical environmental and economic events, the chapter provides a refreshing reminder about the need to look at the potential changes made possible by the collective agency of the poor, but without romanticizing what can be achieved given the limits imposed by structural constraints that originate in the recent and past history of the country.

Chapter 10 by John Harris (USA), entitled 'Accra's unregulated market-oriented sanitation strategy: problems and opportunity', explores how unregulated market-oriented sanitation strategies mount both problems and opportunities for local actors in Accra, Ghana. The author challenges the taming narratives of privatization, showing how one-size-fits-all schemes of privatized service provision do not reflect the complex thread of socio-technical configurations through which basic social needs and rights are expressed in Accra. Against a background where the plight of the urban poor regarding water and sanitation cannot be disentangled from widespread inequalities in terms of land and other resources, the chapter examines the governance of unregulated markets and political co-option, questioning how political interference affects the manner in which sanitation is provided for approximately 40 per cent of the city's population. Instead of taking a definitive stance for state-driven or market-oriented solutions, Harris problematizes the role of agency in the unregulated markets that characterize everyday life in settlements across thousands of cities in the global South.

6 Lost in translation

Social protection and the search for security in Bogotá, Colombia

Andrea Lampis

Introduction

The bail-out of the international financial system and international banks responsible for the ruin of entire economies and the life perspectives of hundreds of thousands of persons meant the decoupling of capitalism from any ethical pre-occupation with the consequences of the highly deterritorialized and financially driven model. The new social configurations of social protection, although still formally administered by public bodies, factually respond to the new logic of privatization and commodification of individual and collective security. In many cities of the world not only the urban poor but also the middle class increasingly face the daily task of having to reinvent again and again some fragile, often legally informal and nonetheless institutionalized (McFarlane 2012) form of security.

Based on fieldwork material from 2007, this chapter examines men and women workers' narratives about their ways of achieving and perceiving security and protection. In doing so it presents a case for a broadening of the conceptual approach on which rests the social protection reform led by international financial institutions in Colombia as in the global South at large.

Framing the debate on social protection in the twenty-first century

I have always been interested in the intersection between constraining social dynamics and the power of agency. I grew up, studied and later became an academic during an epochal shift that radically transformed the life goals and opportunities of my generation. Under the powerful push of globalizing dynamics and the power of remote agencies with the capacity to shape destinies, what was unthinkable only ten years before the beginning of the 1980s became reality. The world in which our generation believed they had grown up soon revealed a rather different sort of movie plot from the steady and comfortable picture of long-term job security and social welfare. New forms of vulnerability and risk emerged.

Thirty years later, right at the end of the year 2010, a decade marked by concerted global efforts to achieve the eradication of extreme poverty drew to a close in the midst of the most severe financial crisis since 1929. Between 2000 and 2010 multi-dimensional poverty and inequality deepened, and a recurring negative trend was also recorded in access to employment (Ocampo and Franco 2000). This reflected the direct impact of the negative economic cycle (Navarro 2009), as well as that over the last 30 years industrialization policies have been capital rather than labour intensive, and based on limited local or regional markets (Beall 2000).

In Latin America, De Mattos (2010) recalled how the majority of the political processes in the region were built on the aim of dominant local elites to achieve a significant leap forward in the construction of capitalist societies. An urban-territorial configuration was seen as a key piece of the entire project reflecting the need to combine the most rampant forms of land exploitation with the guarantee of a friendly market environment, avoiding social upheaval through concessions and tailored social safety nets (Vite-Pérez 2011).

Mainstream answers have remained rather blind to the implications of market-driven transformations. They have sought to figure out a way to reinvent highly institutionalized forms of state-led social policy to exercise a protective role especially for the most vulnerable through a combination of public and privately provided services.

In April 2014 the World Social Protection Report published by the International Labour Organization (ILO), in the face of a bold call for a new course of rights-based social protection strongly focused on social floors, after analysing the post-crisis measures undertaken worldwide after 2010 had to admit:

> As the crisis moved into its second phase from 2010 onwards, rising concerns over sovereign debt levels and fiscal deficits led governments to abandon fiscal stimuli and introduce fiscal consolidation measures. According to the IMF's projections of government expenditure in the World Economic Outlook database (October 2013), 106 of the 181 countries for which data were available moved to contract public spending in 2010.
>
> (ILO 2014: 121)

But the idea according to which state-led, substantially publicly provided social protection can be held as the solution for the crisis (Barrientos and Hulme 2010) also replicates a typical mistake of Western developmental thinking (Escobar 2008): of trying to accommodate a changing reality to its own ideals and principles, regardless of the disruptive power of economic global forces and national vested interests and politics.

It is on the basis of these considerations that I deem worth exploring the following argument, which I knowingly build from a minority position. As a result, it is off the map of mainstream thinking. By and large, the social policy literature – and most importantly the very politics that appropriated it – went through two major phases during the neoliberal era.

A first 'resistance phase', driven by the state-centred model, tried to tackle the problem most of us thought was central in the face of the mounting wave of neoliberal economics: 'how to protect'. As Ferguson (2010) put it in analysing the different uses and forms of comprehension of neoliberalism, this perspective led many scholars sensible to the issues of redistribution, inequality and justice to opt for a stance that was basically 'to be anti-something': for instance, anti-capitalism, anti-injustice or anti a growth-centred development model.

The second is the 'incorporation phase', driven by a market-centred model. This produced a conceptual framework in which even the 'anti' is gone and the simple fact of the market is the central axiom of the policy framework, which is based on the oxymorons of 'inclusive growth' or 'social investment'.

If this discussion is taken onto a more philosophical plane, we can see a link with Nagel's reflection on global justice:

> However imperfectly, the nation-state is the primary locus of political legitimacy and the pursuit of justice, and it is one of the advantages of domestic political theory that nation-states actually exist. But when we are presented with the need for collective action on a global scale, it is very unclear what, if anything, could play a comparable role.
>
> (Nagel 2005: 113–14)

He captures in a very lucid way an essential tension of our times: the defeat of the nation-state as the main agent providing a guarantee for social rights, and the parallel commodification of rights, and therefore of social protection too. I do not take this as an absolute truth, in order to prevent easy critiques from those who argue that the state still does play an important role in social protection. I agree, it does. However, it does so under the constraints of much more powerful economic and political actors, and most of all within the logic of the market itself.

Wood (2009) pointed out that in many poorer countries the problem for state actors is that power, authority and, more problematically, legitimacy lie significantly elsewhere. Saith noted that there must be something 'lost in translation' when we move from universal values to the Millennium Development Goals (MDGs). MDGs are well embedded in the neoliberal strategic agenda of having market goals and mechanisms. We are left to play the only game that is still in town, the 'Monopoly' of capitalism (Saith 2006).

As the 2009 bail-out of the international financial system and international banks responsible for the ruin of entire economies and the life perspectives of hundreds of thousands of persons showed, the above is not the case anymore. It symbolically and factually meant the decoupling of capitalism from any ethical preoccupation with the consequences of the highly deterritorialized and financially driven model. We need a view that is alternative to the map built by mainstream scholarship as far as agency and social protection are concerned, to refresh the understanding of how people build pathways to social protection in cities of the global South, and increasingly of the global North too.

Decoupling assistance from citizenship: the changing fractal in social protection

Social protection configurations tend to present different forms across time. However, each form preserves an inner structure, as a fractal. The repeating pattern across local differences in the case of the period after the Second World War was based on two axioms: first, the equality of citizens in terms of their right to receive protection in the face of risk; and second, the duty of the state to provide that protection for them on the basis of a social contract.

The second fractal emerged at the end of the 1990s, and is related to elements that characterize the recent trends in the financing of social protection. To further elaborate after Jenson (2013), the recurrent element within this second fractal is the new role carved for the agency of individuals as self-protecting actors within the logic of commodification and securitization of social protection. The transaction – as Jenson points out (2013) – is not a smooth one, and there is both continuity and discontinuity between the 'pro-poor growth' discourses of the 1990s and the 'social investment' discourses of the 2010s. There is continuity because 'pro-poor growth' visions consider market-driven development and sustained growth as central, and so does the 'social investment' perspective. The discontinuity lies in the fact that the domain within which human agency will try to achieve self-protection now is a market-oriented competitive constellation of formal and informal services and insurances.

From the socio-anthropological perspective this is by no means a new finding. Canclini (1995) had talked about 'citizen-consumers' almost 20 years ago. What deserves further research is both the lack of recognition of this shift within the discourse of international and national social development agencies, and how individual and collective agents seek, strive for and achieve security and protection.

As Jenson (2013) pointed out, the social investment perspective has achieved the status it enjoys nowadays because it encapsulates strategic elements that are needed to counteract the drivers of widening inequality gaps. However, the new element of the fractal is that the state is required to deal with the injustices generated by the market-centred development model. Jenson (2013) identifies three key elements in this new vision, expanding its fractal to both the global North and the global South:

- Learning and knowledge are the pillars of the economies and societies of the future.
- The future has to be assured before ameliorating the conditions of the present. (Emphasis on children and the reproduction of human capital.)
- Successful individuals enrich the common future.

Nonetheless, as Grassi (2014) has recently illustrated, even the return of democracy in Latin America, although it had the advantage of being broadly associated with a decline in political violence, represented a failure to redress long-standing 'social and welfare debts' or restore social justice. The recent literature on neo-extractivism by Latin American scholars has illustrated how both urban and rural spaces are nowadays only partially democratic spaces (Alimonda 2009; Escobar 2008).

From social risk management to social floors in Colombia

After the structural adjustment decade of the 1980s, Latin American countries have been reforming their social protection packages, first by the introduction of social safety nets, and later by conditional cash transfer (CCT) programmes. The social risk management (SRM) approach put forward at the end of the 1990s by the World Bank (2000) was used in Colombia after a major economic crisis in 1999 to inspire the CCT programme *Familias en Acción*.

From 2006 to 2008 the World Bank pursued an initiative in Colombia to delink health and pensions contributions from the type of employment. Its aim was to solve the problem of gaps in workers' contributions as well as the ambiguities of the legislation on informal employment. This was meant to create what has been called a 'social floor' (in Latin America labelled 'basic universalism'). The idea was promoted by both the World Bank (Perry *et al.* 2007) and the Inter-American Development Bank (Filgueira *et al.* 2006).

With the social floor and the social investment perspectives, the World Bank (Perry *et al.*, 2007) was trying to focus on what the institution has called the 'flip-side' of the informality coin, meaning its less researched side, and referring to the fact that traditionally the issue had been looked at from a structural perspective. There is, however, a danger that the result will be to blame workers' 'choices' and motivations for staying informal and not welcoming the new social protection packages derived from the 'basic universalism' paradigm.

The neoliberal argument, encapsulated by the International Financial Institutions' (IFIs') policies, was that privatization would lead to greater enterprise efficiency, and this would create benefits for the majority of countries. Instead, restrictive fiscal and monetary policies tended to limit production and employment, and all too often the labour market performed below the optimistically expected level (Sarmiento Palacio 2008: 252).

One of the main issues flagged up by recent World Bank-promoted research on a continental scale in Latin America is that weaknesses in the design and implementation of many programmes mean that in reality they exacerbate people's lack of access to protection and create further incentives for informality (Perry *et al.* 2007). In the long run, the goal behind this approach is to provide universal 'essential' health cover, delinked from the labour contract and financed by general taxation, along with 'poverty-prevention' pensions aimed at the elderly and the poor.

The hypothesis the World Bank and the government wanted to test to support a policy against social protection subsidies and in favour of a minimum but universal social floor was that subsidized workers were risk-averse and would not actively participate in a system oriented by the criteria of economic competition, quality and efficiency.

The case study

According to the Centre for Development Studies of the National University of Colombia (CID), from the 1990s onwards Colombia underwent a process of substitution of secure employment by precarious employment (CID 2004). The global participation rate increased from the beginning of the 1990s from 57 per cent to 62 per cent, as a reflection at the macro level of micro-social processes determined by critical vulnerability. Specifically, the loss of jobs by the main household earners prompted the entrance into the labour market of women, young people and the elderly. In 2009, the percentage of poor population by income in Colombia was 45.5 per cent and extreme poverty was 16.4 per cent, according to the National Planning Department (DNP 2011).

People's opportunities in cities so heavily marked by a greatly segmented labour market depend on income generation and the provision of public subsidies (Lampis 2010; Urrea 2010). Against this background, even the fragile economic recovery that the country recorded after 2002 did not resolve the crisis of the labour market, and the levels of inequality have remained basically unaffected from 1970 to 2010, showing how economic recovery did not manage to affect more structural inequalities in the country (Urrea 2010).

The study contacted the Secretariat for Social Integration of the city local administration and obtained a database of 4,000 workers classified in the System for the Identification of Potential Beneficiaries of Social Programmes (SISBEN).

The SISBEN index is the result of a multi-level analysis based partly on the standards of living approach and partly on the capability approach. The bottom three levels (SISBEN I, SISBEN II and SISBEN III) are considered eligible for a range of social programmes and subsidies. As the most multi-dimensionally poor, individuals who belong to households that rate as SISBEN I have so far been the most subsidized according to the methodology employed. The SISBEN system has been employed in the ranking of the population for the calculation of the contributions of individuals and households towards public health care insurance.

The Colombian Health Care System has to date been organized as a two-tier system. The subsidised tier (Régimen Subsidiado) provides significantly subsidized health care for those in SISBEN I and II and informal employment. The non-subsidized tier (Régimen Contributivo) provides health care insurance for the rest of the population, including those in SISBEN III. Because people rated as in SISBEN III are on the borderline between the two systems, they were a suitable control group.

Demographic data

The research surveyed 53 workers from Bogotá. The gender balance of this purposive sample was 39.6 per cent male and 60.4 per cent female. The workers ranged

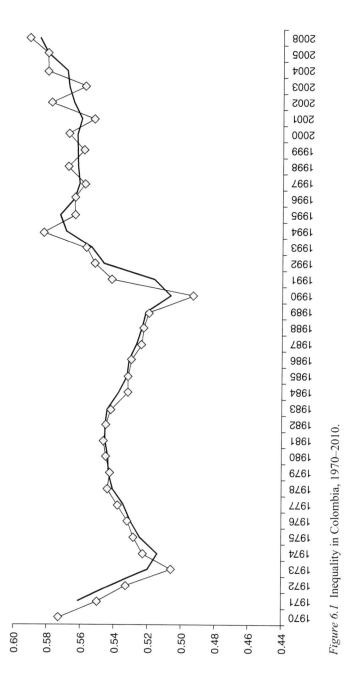

Figure 6.1 Inequality in Colombia, 1970–2010.

in age from 17 to 64, with a standard deviation (SD) of 10.47 from the mean of 36.5. General data on educational achievement reflect the fact that people's working perspectives and gains in quality of life are likely to be low or relatively low if they have not obtained a degree (see Table 6.1).

Workers were distributed along the following groups:

a   Informal sector workers classified as SISBEN I or II: in other words those eligible, at least in principle, for the Regimen Subsidiado, specifically:

    i   Male, self-employed/self-employed workers, categorized as SISBEN I or II

    ii   Female, self-employed/self-employed workers, categorized as SISBEN I or II

    iii   Male, informal salaried workers, categorized as SISBEN I or II

    iv   Female, informal salaried workers, categorized as SISBEN I or II.

b   Informal sector workers classified as SISBEN III, with males and females being analysed separately to act as comparator groups. Specifically:

    i   Male, informal workers categorized as SISBEN III

    ii   Female, informal workers categorized as SISBEN III.

Social vulnerability and its effect on work

The dynamics of vulnerability and the struggles of women and men to achieve more sustainable livelihoods seem to be factors that cannot be ruled out when analysing informality (Moser 1998). The vulnerability of people's lives changes over time, mostly because of critical life events involving the loss of resources, assets and capabilities that lead people to lose their entitlement to certain rights.[1] The study identified three typologies of life events related to people's tendency to enter either formal or informal employment.

First, there are life events that have an impact on people's opportunities to access education and training, which have an impact on endowments and assets, where the term 'assets' can be considered as referring to means to transform resources into capabilities (de la Rocha 2006; Lampis 2009, 2010; Moser 1998, 2009).

Table 6.1 Workers by highest educational attainment

Highest Educational Level	Frequency	%
None	2	3.8
Primary school (1–5)	9	17.0
Basic secondary school (6–9)	23	43.4
Upper secondary school (10–13)	14	26.4
Technical careers or training	2	3.8
University degree	2	3.8
Total	52	98.1
Missing	1	1.9

A second typology of events contributes to answering questions about what workers do in order to face unexpected and critical situations, and a third one consists of specifically employment-related life events that can be explained by the situations illustrated by the first two typologies.

The loss of a job is a very frequent experience. Here are quotes from two male workers from the group of self-employed males in SISBEN I and II, reflecting how these people are extremely concerned about their job security because of their role as the household's main breadwinner:

> Since there are no more jobs around we work for contracts in iron smelting. I have a lot of skills, but there is nothing to do. There were five or six of us but there was no job for anyone [after the crisis] with the exception of his [our boss's] cousin who had a contract. [This] contract, that was verbal and I had no social protection, no sir, nothing.
>
> (28 years old)

The study found a critical divide between informal and formal workers, both males and females, in terms of the relationships between critical life events having an impact on people's opportunities and both life and employment trajectories. This sheds light on the interlocking relationship between poverty and informality. The poor have limited access to formal employment, limited knowledge of social protection and low willingness to pay for formal benefits such as pensions, although they are more willing to pay for health as it has a more immediate impact on livelihoods security. McGrath and Keister (2008) showed that the effect of unemployment on asset accumulation is of the utmost importance for understanding informality.

Thus, when comparing the control (SISBEN III) and interest groups (SISBEN I and II), as well as comparing the two interest groups with each other, the study found gender differences in the magnitude of the impacts that critical life events had had on individuals. In both cases, among the most important critical life events were dropping out of school, and economic crises hitting the household and compelling young people to enter the job market at an early age.

Formal workers presented a completely different picture. Typically, their lives had been marked by greater security and stability, and the analysis of this dimension questions the idea that the motivation for being formal or informal depends on an individual's agency and personal preferences.

Labour history and workers' mobility

Only a handful of workers across the researched categories had at some point in their working lives had the chance to obtain health insurance and make pension contributions. Their mobility therefore tends to be between salaried informal jobs and petty self-employment, such as street selling. Self-employed women, particularly those female self-employed workers in SISBEN I and II, had had more precarious employment histories. One of the female self-employed workers in SISBEN I and II made these comments, which are typical of many we heard:

> While my dad was looking for a job I spent a while supporting the household, working as a live-in domestic servant. Because I was earning, I was the one who paid rent at home. This went on for a while. Later on, I was working and also receiving some help for my studies, and I used to help my brothers to pay for their studies. But then I had to dedicate myself to paid work.
>
> (40 years old, female)

On the whole, when we try to understand the complex effect produced by the intersections between self-employed work, informal work and precarious salaried jobs, we find that the search for security of income plays a major role. Women's working trajectories are different from those of men, largely because they tend to spend longer periods tied up with their productive and reproductive roles.

Self-employed male workers in SISBEN I and II are among the most interesting cases explored. All of them reported having experience and technical training which enabled them to keep working in the same activity for relatively long spells. Still, the case studies show that, depending on an individual's level of technical experience, age, gender and responsibility, for many individuals the best option was self-employed work. The following is a quote from one of these workers:

> So now as a self-employed worker the money is good, since at times you can earn the same as a salaried person . . . of course, there are also disadvantages, such as not having a pension or being able to pay for health insurance and at present I do not think there is enough money. Perhaps with time you could start to save for a pension.
>
> (36 years old, male)

A significantly different picture emerged from the analysis of the data gathered from female formal workers at SISBEN level III: that is, those just above the cut-off level for eligibility for the subsidized tier of the Colombian healthcare system. Most of them had had informal jobs in the initial years of their working lives, then went on to the lowest ranks of formal employment. For the majority of women in this group, this relative improvement in their working lives tended to alternate with moments in which their labour security swung backwards because of unemployment spells which harshly affected their households.

Male formal workers at level III of SISBEN also showed significant differences from male workers in the groups of interest, and also differences from women at the same SISBEN level. From the beginning of their working lives these men had had formal waged employment, although they had usually begun on the lowest rungs of the formal employment ladder.

Scholars such as Flórez (2002) and Portes and Haller (2004) have stressed the economic and institutional place of economic activities in society as a whole. They have questioned any purely dual vision and positioned the need to go beyond informal work to achieve a better grasp of the informal economy.

Employment conditions and quality of work

Under this dimension, the main finding was that a lack of formal written contracts, more than access to more complete packages of social protection, marks the difference between the six study groups and the two control groups of formal workers.

Female self-employed workers in SISBEN I and II work in conditions that tend to be very precarious both in terms of social protection and in other ways. This is shown by a quote from an informal salaried male worker:

> Where I work I am not insured. I arrive for a shift and they pay me. There is no pension, no severance pay, there is nothing . . . . So far so good. Since I work in a public business, a lot of people come there and the pay is good. The majority of the customers are people we know and nothing uncommon ever happens . . . no . . . it is good, I feel good about this job.
>
> (55 years old, male)

The differences between formal and informal employment are also stark because under formal arrangements workers have more voice and the state exerts more control than in the largely unregulated informal sector.

Motivation for being formal or informal

Women and men alike were not so much motivated to choose between formal or informal work per se, but which type of work they obtained was strongly influenced by their social and economic position. This was the factor that tended to determine whether they entered the labour market as self-employed or as informal salaried workers. However, despite this similarity, gender differences emerged quite clearly, as in the analysis of labour histories.

Both focus groups and in-depth interviews showed that women were more inclined than men to describe ambivalence and tensions brought about by their subjective life paths and identities around their working lives. For instance, they used the idea of flexibility versus stability to express the tension between having time for domestic obligations and time for income generation:

> Well, as a self-employed worker you manage your own time. But at the same time, you tend to become a slave to the job. To get some more money you do more work and leave the children alone and even the household chores.
>
> (40 years old)

Most women who said they preferred salaried work to self-employment generally did so because of access to a more regular income source, even if this was often low. None mentioned consumption smoothing in those words, but many underlined the problem of meeting monthly payments for public services and food.

Knowledge of social protection arrangements

In discussing social protection, and particularly health coverage for the low-paid there are three important points to be highlighted: affordability, security of provision and indirect assets protection.

On the whole, knowledge on health becomes increasingly precise as workers become more educated and better off: that is, when we go from SISBEN I and II workers to SISBEN III. Informal salaried workers know more than others in the first broad group. On pensions and other benefits, in the absence of active action by the state and the employers, knowledge is much higher among formal workers and is often acquired by means of mutual trust and solidarity.

The great majority (more than 80 per cent) of formal workers contribute to their pensions on a regular basis. However there are some cases of people who said they were making contributions but subsequently fell out of the system. Some workers who were in self-employed or informal work said they had made payments towards pensions in the month previous to the interview.

Willingness to pay for social protection

Willingness to pay for better and improved social protection is strongly related to lifecycle and household structure. The influence of these factors varies among groups and within groups. The main tension is between effective saving capacity over time and declared willingness to pay. While the latter could be relatively high, the former is often rather low.

Workers in SISBEN I and II are generally willing to pay for better health coverage, but the feedback that comes out from the comparison between the insights gathered about their knowledge of social protection mechanisms and motivation suggests it would be relevant to adopt a more flexible approach. They do value additional social protection and often state that they would like to have some access to programmes related to housing, leisure and training, but they cannot afford to make additional payments.

Self-employed workers, especially women in SISBEN III, are strongly conditioned by their low income levels. Women who are heads of households face particular pressures on their budgets. Also, their logic is to maximize security in the short run.

Their comments revealed the mistrust many typologies of workers have towards the public sector, providing elements to explain why self-help is so diffused in a country where labour stability is long gone.

Concluding reflections: The need for a renewed debate on agency and social protection

The findings from this case study also question the view of a straightforward relationship between a formal job and better social protection. The logic of poverty and vulnerability maximizing resources to provide for vital material and non-material needs is not driven by risk-aversion as much the fact that becoming 'more formal' is not only a cultural shift but entails the modification of structural conditions.

The old ways of thinking based on long-standing assumptions about social protection and social development which persisted through the twentieth century have been swiped away by institutional arrangements and social configurations that have deeply transformed ideas about the nature and role of the state, and the political role of public institutions.

The school of thought represented by Sen (1999), Nussbaum (2003) and Alkire and Foster (2007) among others, together with the strong institutional backing of the United Nations Development Programme (UNDP), produced a number of intellectually challenging and provocative insights. These ranged from the capabilities approach to the idea of human security (Ogata and Sen 2003) to the Human Development Index (UNDP 1990) and the Index for Multi-Dimensional Poverty Measurement (Alkire and Foster 2011). However, beyond the academic milieu or a few attempts like those by Colombia and Mexico with the Multi-Dimensional Poverty Index, the appropriation by local communities, by local administrators and – most of all – by the big transnational corporations and the private sector of all those elaborations is extremely low. These new approaches of the 1990s, which attempted to fill the post-1989 void, deserve nowadays a debate.

The point taken from scholars who adopt a critical stand here is that we are made to believe that these big international strategies are somehow the continuation of the original Western project of modernity centred on the universality of rights, and political and social citizenship.

Note

1 Examples of critical life events are loss of a job illness, and becoming a victim of violence (see Lampis 2009).

Bibliography

Alimonda, H. 2009. La colonialidad de la naturaleza. Una aproximación a la ecología política Latinoamericana. In H. Alimonda (ed.), *La Naturaleza Colonizada*, pp. 21–60. Buenos Aires: Consejo Latinoamericano de Ciencias Sociales (CLACSO).

Alkire, S. and Foster, J. 2007. Counting and multidimensional poverty measurement. Oxford Poverty and Human Development Initiative (OPHI) Working Paper No. 7. Oxford: OHDI.

2011. Counting and multidimensional poverty measurement. *Journal of Public Economics*, 95: 476–87. Paper No. 43. Oxford: OHDI.

Barrientos, A. and Hulme, D. 2010. *Social Protection for the Poor and the Poorest: Concepts, Policies and Politics*. London: Palgrave.

Beall, J. 2000. From the culture of poverty to inclusive cities: re-framing urban policy and politics. *Journal of International Development*, 12: 843–56.

Canclini, N. G. 1995. *Consumidores y ciudadanos. Conflictos multiculturales de la globalización*. Mexico, DF: Editorial Grijalbo.

106   *Andrea Lampis*

CID (Centro de Estudios sobre Desarrollo). 2004. *Bien-estar y macroeconomía: informe de coyuntura*. Bogotá: CID, UNAL and CGR.

DANE (Departamento Adminitrativo Nacional de Estadística). 2009. Principales indicadores del mercado laboral. Informalidad. Press release, 23 January. Available at: www.dane.gov.co (accessed 7 February 2009).

De la Rocha, M. (ed.) 2006. *Procesos Domésticos y Vulnerabilidad. Perspectivas antropológicas de los hogares con Oportunidades*. Mexico DF: CIESAS – Publicaciones de la Casa Chata.

De Mattos, C. A. 2010. *Globalización and metamorfosis urbana en América Latina*. Quito: Olacchi.

DNP (Departamento Nacional de Planeación). 2011. *Bases del Plan Nacional de Desarrollo 2010–2014: Prosperidad para Todos*. Bogotá, DC: Departamento Nacional de Planeación.

Escobar, A. 2008. Ecología política de la globalidad and de la diferencia. In H. Alimonda (ed.), *La Naturaleza Colonizada*, pp. 61–92. Buenos Aires: CLACSO.

Ferguson, J. 2010. The uses of neoliberalism. *Antipode*, 41(supp. s1): 166–84.

Filgueira, F., Molina, C. G., Papadópulos, J. and Tobar, F. 2006. Universalismo básico: una alternativa para mejorar las condiciones de vida en América Latina. Serie de Documentos de Trabajo I-57. Washington, DC: Inter-American Development Bank.

Flórez, C. E. 2002. The function of the urban informal sector in employment. Documento CEDE. Bogotá: Universidad de los Andes.

Gaviria, A. 2000. ¿Sobre quién ha recaído el peso de la crisis? *Coyuntura Social*, 23: 1–23.

Grassi, D. 2014. Democracy, social welfare and political violence: the case of Latin America. *Journal of International Relations and Development*, 17: 242–73.

International Labour Organization (ILO). 2014. *World Social Protection Report 2014/15: Building Economic Recovery, Inclusive Development and Social Justice*. Geneva: ILO.

Jenson, J. 2013. Broadening the frame: combining the social investment perspective and the inclusive growth approach. Paper for annual meeting of International Sociological Association Research Committee 19 on 'Poverty, Social Welfare and Social Policy', Budapest, 23–25 August.

Kalamanovitz, S. 2010. *Nueva Historia Económica de Colombia*. Bogotá: Tauros and Universidad Jorge Tadeo Lozano.

Lampis, A. 2009. Vulnerability and poverty: an assets, resources and capabilities impact study of low-income groups in Bogotá, Colombia. PhD thesis, London School of Economics and Political Science, Department of Social Policy.

—— 2010. ¿Qué de la vulnerabilidad social en Colombia? Conectar libertades instrumentales y fundamentales. *Sociedad y Economía*, 19: 229–61.

McFarlane, C. 2012. Rethinking informality: politics, crisis and the city. *Planning Theory and Practice*, 13(1): 89–108.

McGrath, D. and Keister, L. 2008. The effect of temporary employment on asset accumulation process. *Work and Occupations*, 35(2): 196–222.

Moser, C. 1998. The Asset Vulnerability Framework: reassessing urban poverty reduction strategies. *World Development*, 26(3): 1–19.

—— 2009. *Ordinary Families, Extraordinary Lives. Assets and Poverty Reduction in Guayaquil, 1978–2004*. Washington, DC: Brookings Institution Press.

Nagel, T. 2005. The problem of global justice. *Philosophy and Public Affairs*, 33(2): 113–47.

Navarro, L. 2009. Crisis y dinámica del empleo en América Latina. *Revista CEPAL*, 99: 25–41.

Nussbaum, M. 2003. Capabilities as fundamental entitlements: Sen and social justice. *Feminist Economics*, 9(2–3): 33–59.

Ocampo, J. A. and Franco, R. 2000. *The Equity Gap: Second Assessment*. Santiago de Chile: ECLAC.

Ogata, S. and Sen, A. K. 2003. *Human Security Now*. Washington, DC: UN Secretary General, Commission on Human Security.

Perry, G. E., Arias, O., Fajnzylber, P., Maloney, W. F., Mason, A. and Saavedra-Chanduvi, J. 2007. *Informality: Exit and Exclusion*. Washington, DC: World Bank.

Portes, A. and Haller, W. 2004. La economía informal. Serie de Políticas Sociales No. 100. Santiago de Chile: CEPAL.

Robinson, J. 2002. Global and world cities: a view off the map. *International Journal of Urban and Regional Research*, 26(3): 531–54.

Rodrik, D. 2002. After neoliberalism what? Paper presented at the Conference Alternatives to Neoliberalism, Coalition New Rules for Global Finance, 23–24 May, Harvard University, USA.

Saith, A. 2006. From universal values to Millennium Development Goals: lost in translation. *Development and Change*, 37(6): 1167–99.

Salama, P. 2003. Pobreza: la lucha contra las dos 'v', volatilidad and vulnerabilidad. Paper for International seminar on Poverty and Inequality in Colombia, Universidad Nacional de Colombia.

Sarmiento Palacio, E. 2008. *Economía and globalización*. Bogotá: Grupo Editorial Norma.

Sassen, S. 1994. *Cities in a World Economy*. Thousand Oaks, CA: Pine Forge.

—— 2001. *The Global City: New York, London, Tokyo*. Princeton, NJ: Princeton: University Press.

Sen, A. K. 1999. *Development as Freedom*, New York: Knopf.

Urrea, F. 2010. Dinámica de reestructuración productiva, cambios institucionales y políticos y procesos de desregulación de las relaciones asalariadas: el caso colombiano, in: E. de la Garza Toledo and J. C. Neffa (eds), *Trabajo and modelos productivos en América Latina: Argentina, Brasil, Colombia, México and Venezuela luego de la crisis del modo de desarrollo neoliberal*. Buenos Aires: CLACSO.

Vandenbroucke, F., Hemerijck, A. and Palier, B. 2011. The EU needs a Social Investment Pact. Observatoire Social Européen (OSE) Opinion Paper No. 5. Brussels: OSE.

Vite-Pérez, M. A. 2011. La territorialización de la política urbana and social: reflexiones generales desde el pensamiento sociológico. *Convergencia*, 18(57): 185–208.

Wood, G. 2009. Situating informal welfare within imperfect wellbeing regimes. Paper for International Conference of Politics of Non-State Welfare, Cambridge, MA, 8–9 May.

World Bank. 2000. *World Development Report: Attacking Poverty*. Washington, DC: World Bank.

—— 2012. Oxfam international response to the final draft of the World Bank's Social Protection and Labour Strategy 2012–2022: Resilience, Equity and Opportunity. Available at: http://siteresources.worldbank.org/SOCIALPROTECTION/Resources/280558-127 4453001167/7089867-1279223745454/7253917-1291314603217/7595300-1299088 294716/sp_strategy_final_review_oxfam_feedback.pdf (accessed 1 July 2014).

7 Potentials of the urban poor in shaping a sustainable Lagos metropolis

Taibat Lawanson

Introduction

The sustainability challenge for African cities includes how to respond to globalization issues and reconcile glaring socio-spatial inequality, while contending with climate change. However, many African governments seem ill-equipped to address these issues (Al-Zubaidi *et al.* 2012).

With a vision to be 'Africa's model megacity', the Lagos State Government is currently implementing various projects to overhaul the city infrastructure and attract foreign direct investment (FDI). These projects are often done without regard for the needs of the poor residents, who are constantly faced with institutional hostility, either through the declaration of their daily practices for making a living through informal economic activities as illegal, or the frequent threat of eviction from their homes, which are often located in informal settlements (Ahonsi 2002; Kamunyori 2007; Basinkski 2009).

In response, the urban poor in Lagos have made on-going adjustments in the face of social exclusion and rights denial in the city. These adjustments are achieved by their adopting different coping strategies within the multiple formal–informal interactions connecting them to the local formal economy and governmental projects in a way that can be compared to other urban realities of Africa and the global South at large (McFarlane 2012). The recurrent tensions in the urban space arising from a disconnect between the developmental policy thrust of policy-makers and the pursuit of survival of the population need to be understood, especially because this situation is emblematic of African urbanism (Watson 2014).

Recent studies, such as those of Gandy (2005), Sijuwade (2008), Adelekan (2010) and Aderogba (2012), have investigated the response of the poor to the threat of eviction, lack of access to social services and environmental hazards in Lagos. In line with the established tradition of urban vulnerability and livelihoods analysis of the nineties (Moser 1996; Beall and Kanji 1999), these studies all point to the fact that the urban poor seek to find alternative ways of coping with the challenges a megacity like Lagos poses for their livelihoods, seldom backed by institutional responses. They are doing so using innovative and unconventional methods, as had been affirmed by the works of Koolhaas in the Harvard Project on the City (2001) and Fourchard (2010), even though according to de Boeck (2007) the notion of poverty places too much stress on the weaknesses of the poor, and does not acknowledge the agency they possess.

Aligning with the belief that the key to effective poverty alleviation lies in identifying and harnessing the strengths in the familiar patterns and processes utilized by the urban poor, this chapter seeks to understand the strategies adopted by the urban poor in responding to the challenges of a twenty-first-century dynamic Lagos megacity. The chapter teases out the inherent potentials in informal systems currently being practised, and highlights the agency that can be recognized and adopted in Africa's distinct urban scenario. In doing so, the chapter enters into a dialogue with at least two bottom-line threads of the book as whole. On the one hand is the debate on the difficulty embedded in any attempt to easily tame local forms of slum urbanism, in as much as planning solutions most often tend to transform the physical space rather than the social and power dynamics of which the former is the real by-product. On the other hand is the debate on the co-production of the city, as most cities of the global South, and certainly Lagos among them, defy the very idea of co-production because deep forms of socio-political exclusion and misrecognition persist as the main articulators of the urban fabric there. These are explicitly analysed through the debate on formality/informality seen as an opposition between those who have the power to declare what is legal and those who are literally 'made' illegal by those political decisions and regulations. In this sense, the chapter might be considered as an agnostic piece within the book as a whole, especially in terms of the belief in the redemptive power of big planning discourses and overarching transformative paradigms.

The agency of the poor: literature overview

The need to recognize the resourcefulness of the poor and understand the extent to which they participate in urban economic and political life to achieve social, economic and political goals (de Soto 1989; Bayat 2000; de Boeck 2007), was highlighted as early as the 1990s in the works of Roberts (1995) and Beall and Kanji (1999). This position has been further reiterated by a more recent strand of literature (Mabogunje 2005; Hermanson 2010), and more recently in the submission of Khato (2012), who stated – as the voices denying it have not faded away – that the poor and oppressed do have agency and make both active and rational choices regarding survival within their limited resources.

A decade and a half ago, Carney and colleagues (1999) pointed out how livelihood-building processes comprise the capabilities, assets (including material and social resources) and activities required for making a living. While the Sustainable Livelihoods concept has been heavily criticized because it presents an overly optimistic view of how poor people organize their lives, by emphasizing more their opportunities and agency, rather than the impoverishment paradigm of earlier studies (de Haan 2012), the call it makes for recognition of how people knowledge is relevant for the crafting of more sustainable policies is important. For example, inclusive urban policies that guarantee for all 'the right to the city' can be produced by gleaning from alternative methods of urban living typified by the poor. This in itself is untaming the urban debate (see also Lawton, in Part III of this book).

One of the ways the agency of the urban poor in Lagos expresses itself is through the complex binds they develop with informal productive processes to access and accumulate assets (Tipple 2005). The strife for greater economic security within the uncertainties posed by city life results in a situation where as many revert to the informal sector for survival, depend on this sector strongly, and are usually unable to separate economic life from other aspects of social life such as culture, religion, kinship and lineage (Meikle 2002, Srinivas 2003; Satterthwaite 2006; Lawanson and Olanrewaju 2012). This is dominant in Lagos because according to the Lagos State Government (2012), about 93.7 per cent of business units in the state are located within the informal sector.

However, informality is often termed illegal, and various tiers of government continually strengthen policies that restrict the access of the poor to informal enterprises and housing (Charman *et al.* 2012). With informality being the dominant urban reality in many African countries, on the basis of my experience researching and working at the community level on health issues with the urban poor of Lagos, I therefore align with the submission of Satterthwaite and Hardoy (1993), that there must be something wrong with the law and attitude of government if the urban majority are forced to contravene laws daily in their quest for survival. A more recent study by McGranahan and Satterthwaite (2014) reveals that 21 years later the situation is yet to improve, as policy measures to control urbanization, especially in developing countries, still amplify inequality and tend to reduce the urban poor to precarious living conditions in fragile environments, ill-suited to habitation, and lacking access to basic public amenities and services. Hence, in a way that is closer to the elaboration of the urban ecology school of thought, this chapter reflects my uneasiness with the very idea of traditional technocratic planning as the more appropriate solution for the kind of urban contexts such as those of Lagos, where I live. This leaves me to wonder about what kind of new approach might provide an answer to the urge we feel for a renewed right-based and more inclusive planning approach for African cities (see Rosales, in Part III of this book).

In many instances, government's framing of formal–informal relationships contributes to the designation of informality in urban debates as a development problem, whereby the informal is devalued as not only legally illegitimate, but visually, socially and spatially illegitimate (McFarlane 2012). Many African policy-makers promote economic dualism and assume an autonomous relationship between the formal and informal sectors, hence rather than recognizing its potentially productive capacities (Harding and Jenkins 1989) they see the informal sector as an economic parasite which should be stifled to engender development (Gerxhani 2003). For example, despite accounting for 90.2 per cent of real estate assets in Lagos State, the informal economy is termed 'extra-legal'.

Informality and formality then become tools for negotiation, interaction and regulation in the city (Roy 2009). MacLeod and Jones (2011) highlight a typical scenario where some instances of informal land annexation or transformation such as squatting on vacant lots are designated as illegal and their inhabitants criminalized, while others manifesting as gentrification or change of use are seemingly formalized to enjoy state sanction (with fines for contravention of these developments) or even endorsed as practices of the state (rezoning). Forced evictions remain a common means by which land occupied predominantly by low-income groups is cleared for redevelopment in Lagos. The case of Maroko, which made way for highbrow Victoria Island Extension, was emblematic in the 1990s, resulting in the displacement of 300,000 low-income residents without compensation or relocation (Agbola and Jinadu, 1997). More recent evictions in Makoko, Odo-Iragunshi, Kuramo Village and Ijora Badiya have also resulted in loss of life and property for many more (Amnesty International 2013).

Another example is street vending, which is perceived as a manifestation of underdevelopment, rather than a clear display of urban resilience by the lowest cadre of society (Sassen 1997; Bromley and Mackie 2009; Cross and Morales 2007). As a result, there are multiple laws set up specifically to control and possibly eradicate street trading across the Lagos metropolis, with fines of up to $33 (N5,000) and imprisonment for up to six months for first-time offenders.

The agency of the urban poor of Lagos metropolis

Economic sustainability: informal livelihoods and finance networks

The informal economy is the highest employer in Lagos, attracting close to 75 per cent of the working-age population in diverse activities from street vending and roadside cottage industries to home-based enterprises (HBEs) (LASG, 2012). HBEs in particular have helped many a family overcome destitution through better access to income generation opportunities. At this stage, operators are usually unable to separate economic from other facets of life, and so combine the quantum of personal and domestic assets including living quarters, home appliances, vehicles and furniture for business, further corroborating the principles outlined in the sustainable livelihood framework.

A recent study across low-income communities in Lagos (Lawanson 2011) revealed that 82.5 per cent of the working population in these communities are engaged in some form of HBE, especially petty trade (51 per cent) and artisan services (38 per cent). The study further revealed that about 45 per cent of the respondents rely solely on home enterprises, with most households having multiple income earners (spouses 69 per cent, children 17.9 per cent and resident kinfolk 13.4 per cent). Across the Lagos Metropolis, the dominant business structure is the sole proprietorship (84 per cent); many have grown into larger enterprises (43 per cent), employing between one and four staff, with unpaid family workers making up only 8 per cent of staff strength

While HBEs are a basic means of survival for poor households, many who began HBEs for daily survival have transited to growth enterprises, employing kin and diversifying business activities, through funds raised from local financial aid networks similar to those modelled in the Grameen bank (Barua 2006). Micro, small and medium-scale enterprises (MSME) have been identified as the main thrust for economic development in developing countries (Charmes 1998; Mitullah 2004). It is interesting to note that prohibitive bank lending rates and collateral demands result in a situation where the majority of seed funding for small-scale enterprises comes from informal microfinance, the latter usually being a combination of pooled personal savings, proceeds of rotating credit schemes and informal lending schemes accessed through membership of cooperatives. Informal financial institutions have been identified as an avenue through which both the borderline and the absolute poor can access loans to become self-employed and escape poverty (Aryeetey 1998; Barua 2006; Karlan and Goldberg 2007; Iganiga 2008).

Informal financial networks in Lagos remain the dominant sources of finance for informal enterprises (Ijaiya 2010), and according to Birchall (2003) informal cooperative economic associations are a self-help invention of the poor. In the Lagos metropolis, the study of HBEs further revealed that about 90 per cent of respondents belong to either a neighbourhood-based cooperative thrift society or a rotating credit scheme (Lawanson and Oduwaye, 2014). Usually manifesting in social (neighbourhood, religious and ethnic) or economic (artisan or local market) groupings, their members rely heavily on these local fund-raising schemes for business expansion, capital asset acquisition and meeting household emergencies. As such, social capital is converted into assets as outlined in the sustainable livelihoods framework.

This communal engagement further highlights Simone's (2010) submission that people collaborate, using each other as infrastructure, in ways that may be unstable, tentative and temporary, but that also build a degree of economic security or opportunity, and a sense of the city. As de Soto (2001) outlined, when citizens in the informal sector need capital for housing or business, their only sources are people in their environment with whom they have a relation of mutual trust. Typical scenarios include pooling of resources for bulk purchase of items especially at festive periods and also for construction, cooperative society purchase of land for development, rotating credit schemes organized by residents of a building or street or members of a local church society, while community artisans such as tailors may organize into a thrift society in which the welfare of members is guaranteed and periodic levies and contributions collected from which individual members may borrow, should the need arise.

Environmental sustainability: urban vulnerability and informal governance networks

The Lagos metropolis is especially vulnerable to the vagaries of climate change because of its low-lying coastal location. In fact, McGranahan *et al.* (2007) and Spaargaren and Mol (2008), alongside the IPCC (2009), have predicted that Lagos is likely to be one of the worst-affected cities in Nigeria in the event of climate-change-induced hazards, particularly sea-level rise and flooding. Flooding had earlier been identified as a major obstacle to sustainable development in Lagos, especially among the urban poor (LASG 2004). According to French, Awosika and Ibe (2011), about 3 million people live in the low-lying areas of the Lagos metropolis, the vast majority of whom are additionally vulnerable because of their status as residents of informal communities characterized by extreme lack of infrastructure.

Typically, informal coastal communities in Lagos present a dire picture of environmental fragility. With many households having ten or more members, and with houses built mostly of locally available temporary materials, lack of neighbourhood infrastructure and poor drainage, the residents have faced various negative impacts of climate change in terms of health and productive assets, and are therefore thereby doubly exposed to biophysical and social vulnerability as described by O'Brien and Leichenko (2000).

Beyond individual and household vulnerabilities, urban poor residents of coastal communities in Lagos are also collectively vulnerable, as neighbourhood amenities destroyed during flooding incidents are seldom replaced or repaired promptly. The particular case of Ajegunle Ikorodu community was revealed in a study by Olajide and Lawanson (2014). The only secondary school was destroyed during the floods of October 2010. Students were relocated to other schools in the local government area, the nearest being at a distance of about 2 km across a busy ten-lane expressway. Although the school was reopened in 2011, the destroyed buildings were still under reconstruction in July 2013.

However, some communities are clearly proactive in their response to climate change vulnerability, in that rather than waiting for government aid they initiate self-help strategies to address local challenges. An example is Iwaya, an indigenous community and informal settlement located along the Lagos lagoon. Despite the constant threat of eviction by the Lagos State Government, residents of Iwaya have been able to harness the traditional leadership structure for community development and climate change mitigation and adaptation.

Most indigenous communities in Lagos are governed through a top-down structure, where the traditional leader (*Baale*) is the sole custodian and absolute ruler of the community, resulting often in exclusion on the basis of gender and other social indicators. However, Iwaya is governed through a decentralized hierarchical structure in which the *Baale* appointed community heads (chiefs) on each of the 32 streets in the community. These chiefs are responsible for coordinating environmental sanitation activities and ensuring the health, safety and welfare of the residents on their streets. They meet with the *Baale* on a weekly basis to chart the course of development of the community. A study by Nwokoro *et al.* (2014) revealed that 83.5 per cent of respondents in Iwaya were satisfied with this system of governance because it had resulted in cleaner surroundings and a reduction in sanitation-related illnesses (malaria and typhoid fever) as well as a reduction in flood-related accidents.

This atypical informal governance structure has enabled equitable representation of the people in the affairs of their community and engendered a stronger sense of community. The local organization structure, albeit informal, has been identified as a strategic asset which was leveraged to attract support and community development in Iwaya (AHI 2011). Iwaya is repeatedly selected for poverty alleviation projects because of this decentralized governance pattern as it offers a more viable platform for engagement with aid agencies. A non-governmental organization, Compass International, is embedded in the community, offering vocational training and basic health support, thereby assisting with improving livelihoods and reducing health vulnerabilities. A major achievement of this partnership was the establishment of a ten-bed primary health centre in the community. The land for the health centre was donated by the community, while construction was sponsored by the NGO, using local labour. The primary health centre is staffed by local indigenes who were sponsored for training in basic nursing and medical laboratory science.

Conclusion

In the midst of their varied vulnerabilities, the urban poor in Lagos have been able to develop certain adaptive traits which can be recognized, replicated and regulated for enhanced urban development. This chapter illustrates how socio-environmental security and resilience cannot be sought outside locally established cultural patterns. Therefore, its contribution to the wider debate on livelihoods and social vulnerability consists of a reminder about the difficulties that arise when scholars and policy-makers try to fit people's lives within any kind of normative framework, even those which are nominally progressive and anti-hegemonic (see the debate on 'slum urbanism and the quite encroachment of the untamed' in the conclusions of this book). One thread that runs through the responses of Lagos's urban poor to economic, environmental and social vulnerabilities is the strength of the informal networks. The various manifestations of informality in the Lagos metropolis are not dissimilar to those which have been espoused over the past four decades in the development literature. However, the cloak of illegality looms large over the sector. Rather than being 'institutionalised', informality should be recognized as an active response mechanism of poor citizens to the multiple vulnerabilities they are confronted with in the urban space. The poor have harnessed this strength by pooling resources, both tangible and intangible, to mitigate the effects of obvious challenges faced within their communities.

Simone's (2005) position is that any serious attempt to reinvent African urban centres must acknowledge and incorporate existing local knowledge that sustains and recreates informal urban economic social systems. It is important therefore to recognize that the poor, through the instrumentality of self-help efforts, are able to take the first step to escape destitution and transform their means of survival into viable means of sustenance. In the Lagos metropolis, livelihoods have been enhanced by home-based enterprises, and survivalist enterprises have been able to transit to growth enterprises, leveraging on informal financial networks. Cases of socio-environmental vulnerabilities have been mitigated by the activities of the informal governance networks. All these cases of self-help have employed largely non-monetary assets.

Though considered irrational and disordered by dominant powers, the truth is that informal networks are actually well ordered and governed by strict enforcement codes because, as De Soto (1989) stated, the informal community would rather develop its own laws and institutions to make up for lack of access than surrender to anarchy. Therefore, where effectively harnessed, these seemingly basic self-help structures can be utilized for engendering long-term development within the low-income communities and across the megacity.

Finally, rather than seeking to enforce complicated and widespread laws that usually disenfranchise the vulnerable, it is important that city governments aim for inclusiveness. Strategies for resolving the existing tensions between urban policy and urban realities are also necessary because local dynamics involved in the pursuit of livelihood security are an integral part of how cities evolve. It is important that the rhetoric go beyond formal–informal labels and the idea of informality as unacceptable within the urban fabric, towards a view of informality as a dynamic pointer to shifting urban relationships between the authorized and the unauthorized.

References

Action Health Incorporated (AHI). 2011. *Iwaya Community Asset Mapping Report.* Lagos: AHI.

Adelekan, A. 2010. Vulnerability of poor urban coastal communities to flooding in Lagos, Nigeria. *Environment and Urbanization*, 22(2): 433–50.

Aderogba, K. 2012. Global warming and challenges of floods in Lagos metropolis. *Academic Research International*, 2(1): 448–68.

Agbola, T. and Jinadu, A. 1997. Forced eviction and forced relocation in Nigeria: The experience of those evicted from Maroko in 1990. *Environment and Urbanisation* 9(2): 271–88

Ahonsi, B. A. 2002. Popular shaping of metropolitan forms and processes in Nigeria: glimpses and interpretations from an informed Lagosian. In O. Enwezor, C. Basualdo, U. M. Bauer *et al.* (eds), *Documenta11_Platform4. Under Siege: Four African Cities,* pp. 129–51 Freetown, Johannesburg, Kinshasa, Lagos and Ostfildern-Ruit: Hatje Cantz.

Al Zubaidi, L., Luckschelter, J. and Peter, C. 2012. What are sustainable cities? *Perspectives,* (12): 4–5.

Amnesty International. 2013. If you love your life, move out! Nigeria: forced eviction in Badia East, Lagos State. August 2013 Index: AfR 44/06/2013.

Aryeetey, E. 1998. Informal finance for private sector development in Africa. African Development Bank (ADB) Economic Research Paper no. 41. Côte d'Ivoire: ADB.

Barua, D. 2006. Five cents a day: innovative programs for reaching the destitute with microcredit, no-interest loans, and other instruments: the experience of Grameen Bank. *Global Microcredit Summit; Nova Scotia, Canada.* Nova Scotia, Canada.

Basinkski, S. 2009. *All Fingers Are Not Equal: A Report on Street Vendors in Lagos, Nigeria.* Lagos: CLEEN Foundation.

Bayat, A. 2000. From 'dangerous classes' to 'quiet rebels': politics of the urban subaltern in the global South. *International Sociology*, 15(3): 533–57.

Beall, J. and Kanji, N. 1999. Households, livelihoods and urban policy. Urban Governance, Partnership and Poverty Series, Theme Paper 3. Birmingham, UK: International Development Department, School of Public Policy, University of Birmingham.

Birchall, J. 2003. *Rediscovering the Co-operative Advantage: Poverty Reduction Through Selfhelp*. Geneva: International Labour Organization (ILO).

Bromley, R. and Mackie, P. 2009. Displacement and the new spaces for informal trade in the Latin American city centre. *Urban Studies*, 46(7): 1485–506.

Carney, D., Drinkwater, M., Rusinow, T., Neefjes, K., Wanmali, S. and Singh, N. 1999. *A Brief Comparison of the Livelihoods Approaches of the UK Department for International Development (DfID), CARE, Oxfam and the United Nations Development Programme (UNDP)*. London: DfID.

Castells, M. 1996. *The Information Age: Economy, Society and Culture. Vol. I: The Rise of the Network Society*. Oxford: Blackwell.

Charman, A., Petersen, L. and Piper, L. 2012. Informality disallowed? State restrictions on informal traders and micro-enterprises. Paper presented at the Towards Carnegie 3 Conference, Cape Town.

Charmes, J. 1998. *Street Vendors in Africa: Data and Methods*. New York: United Nations Statistical Division.

Cross, J. and Morales, A. 2007. Introduction: locating street markets in the modern/post-modern world. In J. Cross and A. Morales (eds), *Street Entrepreneurs: People, Place and Politics in Local and Global Perspective*, pp. 1–13. London: Routledge.

De Boeck, P. 2007. Recognition of urban agency beyond the notion of poverty. In S. Feys, A. Eijkelenburg and P. Verlé (eds), *The Urban Factor: Challenges Facing Sustainable Development* (proceedings of seminar in Brussels, 18–19 December 2007). Brussels: Belgium Technical Cooperation (BTC). Available at: https://wiki.uii.ac.id/images/archive/d/df/20110211121745!Tg_KOTA_urban_FACTOR_Challenges_facing_sustainable_urban_development(2).pdf (accessed 3 June 2014).

De Haan, L. 2012. The livelihood approach: a critical exploration. *Erdkunde*, 66(4): 345–57

De Soto, H. 1989. *The Other Path: The Invisible Revolution in the Third World*. New York: Harper & Row.

Fourchard, L. 2010. Lagos, Koolhaas and Partisan politics in Nigeria. *International Journal of Urban and Regional Research*, published online June 2010, and in 35(1): 40–56 (2011). Available at: http://onlinelibrary.wiley.com (accessed 3 June 2014).

French, G., Awosika, L. F. and Ibe, C. E. 2011. Sea-level rise and Nigeria: potential impacts and consequences. *Journal of Coastal Research*, 14: 224–42.

Gandy, M. 2005. Learning from Lagos. *New Left Review*, 33: 36–52.

Gerxhani, K. 2003. The Informal Sector in Developed and Less Developed Countries: A Literature Survey Discussion Paper TI-1999-083/2, University of Amsterdam

Harding, P. and Jenkins, R., 1989. *The Myth of the Hidden Economy: Towards a New Understanding of Informal Economic Activity*. Milton Keynes and Philadelphia: Open University Press.

Hermanson, J. 2010. Principles for realising the potential of urban slums, paper for International Housing Coalition. Available at: www.intlhc.org (accessed 11 July 2013).

Iganiga, B. O. 2008. Much ado about nothing: the case of the Nigerian microfinance policy measures, institutions and operations. *Journal of Social Sciences*, 17(2): 89–101.

Ijaiya, M. A. 2010. Impact of informal microfinance on economic activities of rural dwellers in Kwara South Senatorial district of Nigeria. Unpublished PhD thesis, Department of Accounting and Finance, University of Ilorin.

Intergovernmental Panel on Climate Change (IPCC). 2009. *Proceedings of Scoping Meeting for an IPCC Special Report on Extreme Events and Disasters: Managing the Risks on 23–26 March 2009 in Oslo, Norway*. Stanford, CA: IPCC.

Kamunyori, S. 2007. A growing space for dialogue: the case of street vending in Nairobi's Central business district. Unpublished MCP thesis, Massachusetts Institute of Technology, Boston, MA.

Karlan, D. and Goldberg, N. 2007. Impact evaluation for microfinance: review of methodological issues. Doing Impact Evaluation, no. 7. Washington, DC: World Bank.

Khato, C. 2012. We are here: a woman's journey of life in Kibera. *Perspectives*, 3(12): 41–5.

Lagos State Government (LASG). 2012. *The Lagos Policy Review*. Lagos: Lagos State Ministry of Economic Planning and Budget

Lagos State Government (LASG). 2004. *State of Lagos Megacity and Other Nigerian Cities: Report 2004*. Lagos: Lagos State Ministry of Economic Planning and Budget.

Lawanson T. 2011. Assessment of economic activities of home based enterprises in residential areas of the Lagos metropolis. Unpublished Ph.D thesis submitted to the Department of Urban and Regional Planning, Federal University of Technology, Akure, Nigeria.

Lawanson, T. and Oduwaye. L. 2014. Socio Economic Adaptation Strategies of the Urban Poor in the Lagos metropolis. *African Review of Economics and Finance*, 6(1): 140–60.

Lawanson, T. and Olanrewaju, D. 2012. The home as workplace: home based enterprises in low income settlements of the Lagos metropolis. *Ethiopian Journal of Environmental Studies and Management*, 5(4): 397–407.

Mabogunje, A. 2005. Global urban poverty research agenda: the African case. Paper for seminar on Global Urban Poverty: Setting the Research Agenda, Comparative Urban Studies Project, Woodrow Wilson International Center for Scholars, Washington, DC.

MacLeod, G. and Jones, M. 2011. Renewing urban politics, *Urban Studies*, 48(12): 2443–72.

McFarlane, C. 2012. Rethinking informality: politics, crisis and the city. *Planning Theory and Practice*,13(1): 89–108.

McGranahan, G., Balk, D. and Anderson, B. 2007. The rising tide: assessing the risks of climate change and human settlements in low elevation coastal zones. *Environment and Urbanization*, 19(1): 17–37.

McGranahan, G. and Satterthwaite, D. 2014.Urbanisation concepts and trends, IIED Working Paper. London: IIED. Available at: http://pubs.iied.org/10709IIED (accessed 1 July 2014).

Meikle, S. 2002. The urban context and poor people. In C. Rakodi and T. Lloyd-Jones (eds), *Urban Livelihoods: A People Centred Approach to Reducing Poverty*, pp. 37–51. London: Earthscan.

Mitullah, W. 2004. A review of street trade in Africa. Working paper commissioned by WIEGO/Kennedy School of Government, Harvard University, Cambridge, MA.

Moser, C. 1996. Confronting crisis: a comparative study of household responses to poverty and vulnerability in four urban communities. Environmentally Sustainable Development Studies and Monograph Series No. 8. Washington, DC: World Bank.

Nwokoro, I.,Lawanson, T., Ebuehi, O., Fadare, S., Agwu, J., and Soyinka, O. 2014. Neighbourhood-Environment Factors and Health Outcomes in Informal Communities of Lagos, Nigeria. Paper for University of Lagos Research Conference and Fair

O'Brien, K. and Leichenko, R. 2000. Double Exposure: assessing the impacts of climate change within the context of economic globalization. *Global Environmental Change*, 10: 221–32.

Olajide, O. and Lawanson, T. 2014. Climate change and livelihood vulnerabilities of low income coastal communities in Lagos, Nigeria. *International Journal of Urban Sustainable Development*, 6(1): 42–51.

Roberts, B. 1995. *The Making of Citizens: Cities of Peasants Revisited*. London: Arnold.

Roy, A. 2009. Strangely familiar: planning and the worlds of insurgence and informality. *Planning Theory*, 8(1): 7–11.

Sassen, S. 1997. Informalisation in advanced market economies. Issues in Development Discussion Paper 20. Geneva, Switzerland: ILO.

Satterthwaite, D. 2006. Humanitarian action in urban contexts. *Humanitarian Exchange*, 35: 1–45.

Satterthwaite, D. and Hardoy, J. 1993. Helping slum dwellers to help themselves. *Down to Earth*.

Sijuwade, P. 2008. Poverty, household strategies and coping with urban life: a look at the livelihood framework in Lagos, Nigeria. *Social Sciences*, 3(6): 467–72.

Simone, A. 2005. *For the City Yet to Come: Changing African Life in Four Cities*. Durham, NC: Duke University Press.

Spaargaren, G. and Mol, A. 2008. Greening global consumption: redefining politics and authority. *Global Environmental Change*, 18(3): 350–9.

Srinivas, H. 2003. Decision based model for identifying the informal sector. Kobe, Japan: Global Research Development Center. Available at: www.gdrc.org (accessed 1 December 2005).

Thoreaux, L. 2010. *Law and Disorder in Lagos*, BBC documentary. Available at: http://bit.ly/9VaX7g (accessed 11 June 2013).

Tipple, G. 2005. Employment and work conditions in home based enterprises in four developing countries: do they constitute decent work? *Work Employment and Society*, 19(4): 841–53.

Watson, V. 2014. African urban fantasies: dreams or nightmares. *Environment and Urbanisation*. 26(1): 213–29

Lagos State laws

Lagos State Environmental Sanitation Law, 2000.
Lagos State Road Traffic Administration Law, 2013.
Lagos State Street Trading and Illegal Markets (Prohibition) Law, 2003.
Lagos State Waste Management Authority Law, 2007.

8 Sustainability of what?

The struggles of poor Mayan households with young breadwinners towards a better life in the peri-urban area of Merida, Yucatan, Mexico

Mauricio Domínguez Aguilar and
Jorge Pacheco Castro

Introduction

Urbanization and globalization processes are transforming both the societies and the landscapes of the global South. Among the most relevant impacts generated by these global phenomena are those that directly or indirectly affect the livelihoods of poor households living in the peri-urban areas of southern cities (Rigg 2007; Potts 2013).[1] In their recent book on ethnicity and livelihoods in highlands China, Vietnam and Laos, Michaud and Forsyth (2013) posed the question of how these people, so diverse in ethnic terms, fashion their livelihoods after their homelands open to economic investment and political change.

In spite of being based on studies carried out in a different continent, this work shares with Michaud and Forsyth's two core ideas: a) particular ethnic groups within urban contexts develop quite specific patterns of social vulnerability; and b) sustainable livelihood studies have retained their relevance despite the critiques because they remain a useful lens for analysing how macro- and meso-social forces constrain individual agency and opportunities. From a consideration of the central role of young breadwinners in terms of the inter-generational reproduction of poverty,[2] this chapter analyses a particular ethnic group and the stage of the household cycle in order to better understand peri-urban livelihoods of Mayan families in a Mexican city. In so doing, it seeks to make a contribution to a renewed tradition of research on poor households' livelihoods from a perspective that values ethnic diversity as a key dimension of their social vulnerability.

The chapter opens a dialogue with one of the main threads of the books, the issue of social justice, in so far as it points out the importance of the ethnic dimension (being Mayan) and socio-demographic features (being a young adult) to understand how social exclusion and socio-spatial segregation are produced on the basis of forms of injustice that touch upon Fraser's (2009) three-tiered conceptualization of justice.

The sustainable livelihood approach and its critics

To recast the livelihoods debate in terms of the contemporary academic debate requires two caveats: risk and vulnerability are long since understood as produced throughout dynamics that intertwine global and local actors (see also Part II introduction and Chapter 6). Therefore the very search for development and well-being, even from a wholly humanist and freedom-based perspective (Sen 1999), cannot be framed without considering that the project of development is an integral part of what Beck (1992) defined as reflexive modernity. That is, the risks and the vulnerabilities affecting a local group like Mayan households in Merida cannot be understood by looking at the local urban and national contexts only. As pointed out by Sassen (2014), contemporary forms of exclusions are brutally produced by highly complex logic at multiple scales and enacted mostly in urban centres where economic and political power concentrate. These exclusions, we argue, once brought down to the local level reflect the misrepresentation of local communities and their rights and, following Fraser's main conceptual architecture, in turn generate injustices in the dimensions of redistribution and recognition (Fraser 2009).

In its early elaborations, the sustainable livelihood approach (SLA) considered households' livelihoods to be sustainable when they are able to cope with and recover from the impact of life events, as well as to maintain and increase the assets and capabilities they will use to face future risks and uncertainties (Chambers 1989; DFID 1999). The SLA framework was criticized over the past decade, often harshly. Nonetheless, it is an approach that has remained relevant despite the ambiguities of the term 'sustainable' and the vagueness of its methodological operationalization.

A critical issue related to the operationalization of the SLA into a useful framework for policy-making is that, even compared to more conceptually narrow monetarist approaches to poverty measurements (Ruggeri-Laderchi 2000), it does not specify what level of well-being is sufficient to lift a household out of poverty. The definition of well-being levels is controversial because any specific level of well-being is the result of the interaction of factors belonging to material, relational and subjective domains. Another issue is that only a few households make a living in a way that qualifies as sustainable in all the different dimensions of the concept (environmental, economic, social and institutional). Over time, competition for and depletion of assets are common features when households and social groups try to access the resources they need. The trade-offs involve impacts and risk transfers to other households and social groups, and should be better considered in the SLA (McGregor 2007; White and Ellison 2007; Marks and Thompson 2008; White 2009).

Merida's peri-urban area

Merida's peri-urban area is a recent formation, and one of the most visible territorial transformations that accompanied the development of Merida into a metropolitan city. This process started in the early 1970s and was characterized by the physical sprawl of Merida city, as well as the economic and functional integration of all the existing communities in its area of influence (Lapo 1983; Estébanez 1992; Ferrer 1992).

The peri-urban area extends across six municipalities and includes 270 communities (INEGI 2010; Domínguez 2011).[3] According to the 2010 census conducted by the Mexican National Institute on Statistics and Geography (INEGI), this peri-urban area has a total population of 101,601 inhabitants, who represent 10.73 per cent of the total population of the city.

Like any other peri-urban area, Merida has a complex typology of communities. We can highlight here the *pueblos* and *comisarias* (communities which existed before accelerated urbanization), irregular settlements, subdivisions (gated or open, vertical or horizontal, and scattered houses), as well as a wide range of land uses. Land ownership is concentrated in the hands of a few private owners, who control the growth of the city while speculating on future land prices.

According to data from the Evaluation National Council of Social Development Public Policy,[4] 29.4 per cent of the total population of Merida are poor, while 3.3 per cent are classified as in absolute poverty. Following UN-HABITAT's (2003a, 2003b, 2006) definition of slum, a recent study found that the highest rates of urban poverty can be found in the peri-urban communities of Merida city (Domínguez and Cabrera 2012).

Population and methods: identifying segregations and injustices

After a preliminary exploration, we selected the peri-urban communities of Chablekal and Dzitya for the study eventually carried out between October and November 2013. In Chablekal we surveyed 49 homes, and in Dzitya we surveyed 54 homes. We thus built two independent databases (one for each community) with all the information obtained from the surveys. From the final databases, we chose ten households with young adult members in Chablekal and another ten in Dzitya that met our criteria: they were poor and had Mayan ancestry.

Young adults' key characteristics were used to build the poor Mayan household typology which was utilized to carry out the analysis (see Table 8.1). This typology relates the households studied to household lifecycle stages.

Most of the poor Mayan households in general from Chablekal and Dzitya have nuclear household structures. They tend to have fewer children and a lower dependency ratio (Table 8.2) than earlier generations, and they also tend to live near their relatives.

A more detailed analysis of the household structures data, presented in Table 8.2, shows that 82 per cent of the total households in Chablekal and 80 per cent in Dzitya included young adult members. Over the last decades, adjustments in the households' composition and organization has helped them cope with the dramatic changes that the regional labour market has experienced.

Table 8.1 illustrates that 42.5 per cent of poor Mayan households with young adults in Chablekal and 48.8 per cent in Dzitya were in the conformation stage;

Table 8.1 Proposed typology for the poor Mayan households with young adult members considered in this study

Household lifecycle stages of the studied poor Mayan households	Young adults' key characteristics utilized to define these households lifecycle stages
Conformation	• Breadwinners of their nuclear households. • In their 20s. • Children still pre-adolescent, and some couples have no children yet.
Consolidation	• Breadwinners of their nuclear households. • In their 30s. • At least one child in adolescence.
Early dispersion	• Around half are single and without children, but the other half do have children. Some of those with children are married, but others are single parents. • All are still dependent in some way on their middle-aged parents' assets, since they are still living on their parents' housing plots. Among this particular sub-group of young adults are those that now have a partner and/or children (they represent the extended households of this study). • Almost all are working, a few work and study at the same time , while a significant number are continuing studies at higher levels (see Table 8.3), sometimes aided by scholarships.

Source: the authors.

25 per cent of these households in Chablekal and 23.3 per cent in Dzitya were in the consolidation stage; and 32.5 per cent of these households in Chablekal and 27.9 per cent in Dzitya were in the early dispersion stage. So in the majority of the poor households analysed, young adults were the main breadwinners (following the traditional pattern), although there is a growing trend within this social group to delay the dispersion (to start their own separate households) of young adults.

It is useful to begin analysing the dynamics of the early dispersion stage of the lifecycle of the studied households in Chablekal and Dzitya by dividing them into two typologies. The first one corresponds to extended households composed of young adults, their children and spouses (if any), and of course their parents (who are middle aged), as well as their brothers and sisters (if they are still living in the same house). The second typology consists of nuclear households where the middle-aged adults' children (that is to say, the young adults) are still single, and continue living with their parents.

The young adults in these two subgroups of early dispersion households tend to stay with their parents largely because of their need to develop strategies for accessing key livelihood assets (particularly housing and income savings), although this also depends on the specific conditions of their households. A few

Table 8.2 Selected demographic characteristics of poor Mayan households in general
from Chablekal and Dzitya

Selected demographic characteristics of poor Mayan households in general ([1])	% of all households in	
	Chablekal	Dzitya
Household structure Nuclear	61.22	57.41
Extended	18.37	22.22
Other	20.41	20.37
Number of children ≤ 2 children	81.63	77.78
≥ 3 children	18.37	22.22
Dependency ratio 0–50%	59.19	44.44
50–100%	26.53	33.33
> 100%	2.04	16.67
Households in this group with no one of working age([2])	12.24	5.56

Source: the authors using data from the surveys.
Notes:
(1) All data presented in this table refers to the total sample of the two independent survey databases generated for the research project. In other words this data refers to the entire population of both communities studied.
(2) These households are those integrated only by seniors.

work and study at the same time, while a significant number, some of whom have scholarships, continue studying at higher levels of education.

Out of the totality of the heads of households studied in the conformation and consolidation stages, most of the young adults had completed primary and secondary education, and some had studied up to the middle superior level.[5] Very few of those young adults had reached the superior educational level (Table 8.3).[6] Those with the lowest educational levels, and some of those who had reached the middle superior level, were found to have also acquired or been willing to acquire manual skills that would allow them to diversify their job opportunities, in spite of the low level of remuneration that in general is common in Mexico. As we have mentioned, a different trend was apparent among the poor households in the early dispersion stage: a significant number of their young adult members were concentrating on improving their education (Table 8.3).

Most poor households in the areas studied (regardless of their lifecycle stage and whether they have young adult members) have access to basic services, including electricity, piped water and mobile phones, though with limitations in their quality (Domínguez 2012; Domínguez and García 2012). Greater (geographic and socio-economic) challenges are faced when these households try to gain access to specialized health services, higher education, the internet and other facilities (Domínguez 2011).

Although it is true that in the majority of cases this new poverty (Sabatini *et al.* 2001) is not as extreme as to lead to extreme deprivations, it tends to be

Table 8.3 Education levels of young adults members of the studied poor Mayan households

Educational levels	Household lifecycle stages of the studied poor Mayan households					
	Conformation		Consolidation		Early dispersion	
	% Chablekal	% Dzitya	% Chablekal	% Dzitya	% Chablekal	% Dzitya
Primary	9.10	27.03	19.05	57.89	17.39	25.00
Secondary	42.42	45.94	47.62	21.07	39.13	18.75
Middle superior([1])	45.45	27.03	23.81	15.78	30.43	37.50
Superior([2])	3.03	0.00	0.00	5.26	13.05	18.75
No formal education	0.00	0.00	9.52	0.00	0.00	0.00

Source: the authors using data from the surveys.

Notes:
(1)   The middle superior level of education (known in Mexico as 'preparatory education') includes the three last levels of high school as well as the Anglo-Saxon collage level (which in Mexico in known as 'technical careers').
(2)   The superior level of education is equivalent to the Anglo-Saxon degree-level of professional qualifications (which in Mexico is known as '*licenciatura*').

significant enough to make these households permanently unable to fulfil their expectations of being able to live the kind of contemporary urban life that is promoted by the media and commercial advertising and is culturally accepted and sought within Chablkal and Dzitya as a model. As pointed out in the next section, these data, apparently so context specific, mirror a broader trend marked by social exclusion and socio-spatial segregation, characterised by broader opportunities for consumption but persisting inequality of access and social mobility and geographically concentrated disadvantages (Saraví 2004).

As in other Mexican urban geographies, the impoverishment context and social exclusion experienced by these (and other) families of the peri-urban area of Merida is closely related with the nature of the country's employment laws, as well as with the neoliberal adjustments that have accompanied Mexican globalization since the 1980s (Aparicio *et al.* 2009; Contreras and Contreras 2009; Cordera and Lomelí 2009; Marañón *et al.* 2009; Sánchez Almanza and de la Vega Estrada 2009; Urzúa and Brambila 2009). At the national scale, some of the most relevant and negative impacts that neoliberal adjustments have delivered on the livelihoods of the original populations living in the peri-urban areas of Mexican cities are possible due to the changes made in 1992 to the Mexican Agrarian Law. These changes took place at the constitutional level, in combination with the historic persistence of poverty in the region for Mayan households, the mediocre support that the government had given to them to cultivate their farmland and the insistence of the real estate industry push in the past two decades for the *ejidatario* groups of the area to sell their lands in a new liberalized land market.

As we discuss in the next section, these past actions meant a number of negative impacts that keep impinging on the present opportunities of Mayan households with young heads of household, as it is on the basis of this history of dispossession that most of these households do not any longer have access to these key liveli-hood assets (Pinkus Rendón *et al.* 2012).

Although the Mexican state has concentrated its poverty alleviation poli-cies during the last decade on ensuring that all the population are adequately fed, and its main institutional strategy on conditional cash transfers, it is not easy for poor households to access and stay on these programmes, particularly the conditional cash transfer programmes. The eligibility criteria for these are stiff, and the resources behind them are scarce. They lack financial sustainability because they are non-contributory. Two examples of cash transfer programmes are 'Opportunities' and 'Seniors'. Similar difficulties have being reported for other cities in Mexico and the global South (Lomnitz 1998; Mattos 2002; Entrena Duran 2006; Juárez Martínez 2006; Smets and Salman 2008).

The livelihoods of poor Mayan households with young adults

Traditional readings of inequality through the lenses of land and housing, long since recognized as key local productive assets for poor households (Moser and McIlwaine 1997), need to be re-read through a much broader lens. The broad-ening of income and non-income inequalities is a key feature that accompanies the opening up of Latin American economies from the early1980s until the mid-1990s, without a real reverse of that trend ever since (Cornia, 2004). Rakkonen, in a Mexican-based case study explicitly researching Merida, underlines the importance of overcoming the horizon of socio-economic segregation to include key racial and ethnic dimensions to understand socio-spatial segregation. Saraví (2004), reflecting on how Argentinian youth are affected by forms of spatial seg-regation that concern 'who they are', 'what they do' and the culture to which they belong, has brought forward a powerful argument to provide an innovative contribution to our case study. In fact, what seems to be happening in Mexican as in other Latin American cities is the production of multi-layered forms of socio-spatial segregation, which combine in a way that cannot be easily tamed the ele-ments of poor redistribution, misrecognition and misrepresentation.

These elements of social injustice are also historically produced as young Mayan adult members never belonged to the *ejidatario* groups which were given collective ownership rights over the farmland around Merida city under the for-mer Mexican Agrarian Law. When in 1992 this law was modified to permit the *ejidatario* groups to sell their lands, they sold them almost entirely to private individuals. This meant that their descendants (the young adults who are the focus of this study) had no opportunity to farm or give another use to their own lands in order to make a living.

Housing

Regarding housing, most of the studied households had been granted a portion of their parents' plots on which to build a house. However, the plots are now too small for further subdivision, and any spare land has often been sold to people from outside the communities (leading to a process of gentrification). When plots were sold, it was mostly for economic reasons.

Some young adults have salaried positions and others work freelance (Table 8.4), but in both cases most of their jobs are precarious and provide only a small income. Most young adults only have one job at a time, although if they lose this job they have some flexibility in finding a new one should they have a variety of manual skills (as many individuals do).

Since there are no large employers in Chablekal, most young adults commute to Merida city or to one of the few gated communities nearby, where they typically work in construction, as domestic servants or gardeners, or in retail (often in shopping malls in the case of Merida). All these occupations represent the new kind of job opportunities that the globalized labour market of the region preferentially offers to the members of this social group.

In contrast, there are some job opportunities in Dzitya, which has quarries and craft workshops. These occupations are dependent on global trade, since the products generated in the craft workshops are destined for the international market, because they are sold directly to the tourists either in Progreso beach or at other tourist attractions of Yucatan. In the case of the quarries, their production is exported mainly to the United State of America or to the Riviera Maya, where people from Canada and the USA spend their holidays. It is important to mention that in the craft workshops Dzitya's young adults work mainly as freelancers, while in the quarries they are employees. However, these enterprises employ only a proportion of Dzitya's young people, and others work in Merida, among other occupations as construction workers, electricians and in textile factories nearby, which are also manifestations of the economic globalization of the city.

Not all young adult women in the households studied had paid employment. Those with small children often did not work. A few received help from relatives to care for their children while they worked and others had nursery benefits. Women without children usually did seek employment. Many women preferred work with 'more freedom' such as domestic service, although those jobs do not offer them comparable benefits.

Health care insurance

There is a growing trend for employers to limit employee access to health benefits (IMSS), in order to lower their tax payments. In exchange for accepting a contract that excludes IMSS benefits, employers usually pay slightly more (in cash). Many of the studied households have no IMSS benefits, including those with no member in work and those whose workers are self-employed. Most of these vulnerable households have access to a government-promoted scheme known as 'Popular Insurance' (see Table 8.4). Although Popular Insurance is free, it provides only limited health coverage, and no pensions or social security payments for those unable to work or for their households. Those who find themselves in this position can face serious difficulties in meeting their basic living expenses.

Table 8.4 The most important assets and income-generating activities of the studied poor Mayan households

| Asset/activity | | Household lifecycle stages of the studied poor Mayan households | | | | | |
| | | Conformation | | Consolidation | | Early dispersion | |
		% Chablekal	% Dzitya	% Chablekal	% Dzitya	% Chablekal	% Dzitya
Labour							
Young adult members	Salaried	55.48	62.78	51.67	61.03	55.56	56.89
	Freelance	44.52	37.22	48.33	38.97	31.67	21.14
Other members[1]	Salaried	0.00	0.00	0.00	0.00	58.49	63.85
	Freelance	0.00	0.00	0.00	0.00	41.51	36.15
Health benefits	From IMSS[2]	54.55	34.78	44.44	36.84	51.35	48.15
	From the Popular Insurance[3]	36.36	26.09	33.33	14.82	43.24	7.41
	Without benefits	9.09	39.13	22.23	48.34	5.41	44.44
Activities to obtain goods or money	Micro-enterprise in dwelling[4]	23.52	9.52	10.00	29.00	15.38	16.66
	Gathering of products[5]	0.00	0.00	0.00	20.00	0.00	0.00
	Growing vegetables and husbandry	0.00	0.00	0.00	0.00	0.00	0.00
Other sources of money	Government cash transfer programmes[6]	11.76	9.52	Not available	15.37	Not available	16.67
	Credit from banks	5.88	0.00	0.00	0.00	7.69	0.00
	Pawning goods	0.00	0.00	0.00	0.00	7.69	0.00
	Remittances	0.00	0.00	0.00	0.00	0.00	0.00
	Family loans	0.00	0.00	10.00	0.00	7.69	0.00

Source: the authors using the survey data.

Notes:

(1) Other members include senior and middle adulthood members (in the case of the early dispersion households).

(2) IMSS is the Spanish initial for Mexican Institute of Social Security.

(3) Popular Insurance is a federal social programme that focuses on the health dimension of social security. This programme does not cover the whole variety of important risks that IMSS covers. This programme also lacks financial sustainability because it is non-contributory.

(4) Selling via catalogues, making handicrafts, etc.

(5) Recycled goods or natural materials.

(6) 'Seniors' and 'Opportunities' federal programmes.

Complementary income-generation activities

Our expectation prior to the field research was that the target households would gain a significant proportion of their livelihood from complementary activities such as growing their own food and some kind of small-scale income-generation like selling via catalogues or making food. However, this proved not to be the case. Only a few of the households studied performed these kinds of complementary activities (see Table 8.4).

As Table 8.4 shows, apart from their wages, the households studied had very little access to sources of money. As well as cash transfers from the government, potential sources were bank loans, household loans and pawning goods. Although remittances (from household members who have migrated for work) are significant in some contexts, they did not feature in this survey, since virtually no workers from this area migrate to other regions of the country or overseas.

Social assets

The most important social asset that these households have are their social networks, which support them in many ways, particularly at moments of greater difficulties (for instance, by lending them money: see Table 8.4). Nevertheless, the support available is limited because most households' social networks consist of other poor households whose ability to provide help is restricted (Gonzales de la Rocha 2006). Finally, it is important to mention that in moments of great difficulty these poor households usually get some support from the churches to which they belong or from charities.

Livelihoods sustainability of poor Mayan households with young breadwinners

The different vulnerability conditions that the studied poor Mayan households experience through the stages of their household lifecycle affect their capacity to cope with present and future problems. For those Mayan households in the conformation stage, an obvious problem is that they cannot easily send more members into the labour market. Another common problem is childhood sickness, which usually erodes their limited assets. Such households face their everyday problems through self-organization and cooperation with their social networks. These are resilience attributes (Quinlan 2003). Asset diversity (another resilience attribute) is manifested in these households not by the quantity of their assets, but by the combination of the limited assets they have to work with. Together with the willingness of breadwinners to change jobs as necessary, these poor households typically manage to remain in a reasonably stable state. This could perhaps be described as sustainability (although we are not so sure).

Poor Mayan households in the consolidation stage have the advantage that the wife is able to join the labour market once her children have a degree of independence. Older children typically also suffer less sickness, so these households usually have less frequent need to call on their limited assets. When these households manage to maintain their income over a reasonable period (usually more than three years), and they can depend on other factors such as self-organization, cooperation and asset diversity, they acquire a good degree of stability. Paradoxically, though, this stability rarely translates into significant improvements in their standard of living. This trend of apparent improvement in stability was usually higher for those classified as early dispersion households, because their young adult members take advantage of the available assets of their middle-age parents (see Table 8.1).

We did not find that the government programmes to fight poverty (particularly those providing cash transfers) had succeeded in helping the households we surveyed to develop long-term sustainable livelihood strategies or to make significant improvements to their standard of living. Payouts from such programmes naturally led to a temporary improvement in household incomes, but there is an obvious risk in creating dependency on such programmes, since they are not designed to (and do not) provide a long-term income supplement. The issue is not only to improve the services provided by these programmes but to protect households from fluctuations in the economic and political situation (Sandberg 2012; Sabates-Wheeler and Devereux 2013).

Conclusions

This research has shown the diversity and complexity of the ways in which poor Mayan households with young adult members make a living in Merida's peri-urban area. It also makes a contribution to the understanding of how these households' livelihoods interact with an urban context shaped by both global and local processes, as increasingly is the Mexican economy under economic liberalization. Nonetheless, as pointed out by several scholars analysing both Mexico and other countries of the region (Monkkonen 2012; Sabatini, Cáceres and Cerda, *et al.* 2001; Saraví, 2004), what we may still be calling 'the sustainability of people's livelihoods' cannot be easily tamed as there are subjective and cultural dimensions interacting with the processes of segregation. Depending on their social vulnerabilities, which are shaped by the ethnicity, age and gender of their members, specific households' structures and lifecycle stages, but also community aspirations and institutional action trajectories geared at securing assets ownership, their sustainability will differ.

Independently of the stage of their lifecycle, poor Mayan households with young adults typically have a certain degree of stability in their short-term income, allowing them to 'stay in the game' and move on after dealing with times of crisis. A key question here is whether this can truly be described as a sustainable livelihood. Although it is true that, in general, these households manage to keep their identities and function over time, it is also undeniable that they only achieve a very precarious standard of living. This is not enough to take them out of poverty. Over time, as they encounter different critical situations, their livelihoods are constantly under pressure and their capabilities and assets are eroded, thus the medium and long-term sustainability of their livelihoods remains at risk.

Research findings have practical and theoretical implications. Practically, this research should encourage us to make sure that governmental programmes and development opportunities are transformative and there is a more equal distribution of tangible assets (particularly land and housing) ownership among society.

The theoretical implication of this research is a set of questions about the usefulness of the classic literature on vulnerability and livelihoods that tends to focus on quantitative assets. This may result in a failure to capture the dynamics of inequality in a place-specific urbanization process. There is a need for a more in-depth analysis, not just of these Mayan households' livelihoods in Merida's peri-urban areas but also more widely across similar contexts, in order to develop an appropriate conceptualization of the livelihood strategies of poor households in the urban peripheries.

Acknowledgements

This chapter draws on information obtained from two research projects: 'The urban poor of Yucatan: Merida city case study' and 'The challenges that rural populations of northern Mérida are facing against the local impacts of economic globalization'. We are grateful to Oscar Batun and Yanine Cetina for their assistance in the statistical processing of the survey data.

Notes

1 A poor household is that experiencing a pronounced decrease in the well-being of its members, which is caused by their lack of control over those assets and capabilities needed for active participation in society. This definition was adapted from approaches by Haughton and Khandker (2009).
2 In this work young adults are defined as those aged between 20 and 40. However, a variety of definitions are used in different contexts, perhaps reflecting the fact that there are disagreements on the legal, occupational and emotional criteria that demarcate this group (Levinson 1986).
3 Merida's peri-urban area extends through the municipalities of Conkal, Kanasin, Merida, Progreso, Ucu and Uman.
4 Data available at: www.coneval.gob.mx/Medicion/Paginas/Medición/Anexo-estadístico-municipal-2010.aspx (accessed 10 June 2014).
5 The middle superior level of education (known in Mexico as preparatory education) includes the three highest levels of high school as well as the Anglo-Saxon college level (which in Mexico is known as technical careers).
6 The superior level of education is equivalent to the degree-level or professional qualifications (which in Mexico is known as *licenciatura*).

References

Aparicio, R., Villarespe, V. and Urzúa, C. M. 2009. Introducción. In R. Aparicio, V. Villarespe and C. M. Urzúa (eds), *Pobreza en México: Magnitud y perfiles*, pp. 13–17. Coneval, Universidad Nacional Autónoma de México, Instituto de Investigaciones Económicas, Instituto Tecnológico y de Estudios Superiores de Monterrey.

Beck, U. 1992. *Risk Society: Towards a New Modernity*. London: Sage.

Chambers, R. 1989. Vulnerability: How the poor cope. *IDS Bulletin*, 20(2).

Contreras, E. and Contreras, F. 2009. La pobreza de ingreso de los hogares y los cambios en el consumo físico de alimentos básicos. In R. Aparicio, V. Villarespe and C. M. Urzúa (eds), *Pobreza en México: magnitus y perfiles*, pp. 245–63. Coneval, Universidad Nacional Autónoma de México, Instituto de Investigaciones Económicas, Instituto Tecnológico y de Estudios Superiores de Monterrey.

Cordera, R. and Lomelí, L. 2009. Las concepciones de las élites políticas como determinantes de las políticas de combate contra la pobreza. In R. Aparicio, V. Villarespe and C. M. Urzúa (eds), *Pobreza en México: magnitud y perfiles*, pp. 265–91. Coneval, Universidad Nacional Autónoma de México, Instituto de Investigaciones Económicas, Instituto Tecnológico y de Estudios Superiores de Monterrey.

Cornia, G.A. 2004. *Inequality, Growth, and Poverty in an Era of Liberalization and Globalization*. Oxford and New York: UN-WIDER and Oxford University Press.

Department for International Development (UK) (DfID). 1999. Sustainable livelihoods guidance sheets. London: DfID.

Diario Oficial. 2012. Reglas de operación del Programa de Desarrollo Humano Oportunidades, para el ejercicio fiscal 2012. México City: Gobierno Federal.

Domínguez, 2011. Avances en el estudio de la estructura territorial de la Zona Metropolitana de Mérida, Yucatán. *Península*, 6: 185–99.

—— 2012. *Resultados Primera Encuesta Metropolitana Zona Metropolitana de Mérida.* Mérida, Mexico: Centro de Investigacion y de Estudios Avanzados del IPN.

Domínguez, M. and Cabrera, A. 2012. Precariedad de la vivienda. In M. Domínguez and A. García (eds), *Indicadores de Desarrollo Zona Metropolitana de Mérida Reporte 2012*, pp. 41–9. Mérida, Mexico: Centro de Investigación y de Estudios Avanzados del IPN.

Domínguez, M. and García, A. (eds). 2012. *Indicadores de Desarrollo Zona Metropolitana de Mérida Reporte 2012*. Mérida, Mexico: Centro de Investigación y de Estudios Avanzados del IPN.

Entrena Duran, F. 2006. Difusión urbana y cambio social en los territorial rurales. Un estudio de casos en la Provincia de Granada. *Revista de Estudios Regionales*, 77. Available at: www.redalyc.org/toc.oa?id=755&numero=10076 (accessed 4 June 2014).

Estébanez, J. 1992. Los espacios urbanos. In R. Puyul, J. Estébanez and R. Mendez (eds), *Geografía Humana*, pp. 357–84. Madrid: Ediciones Cátedra.

Ferrer, M. 1992. *Los sistemas urbanos: Los países industrializados de hemisferio norte e Iberoamérica.* Madrid: Editorial Síntesis.

Fraser, N. 2009. *Scales of Justice. Reimagining Political Space in a Globalizing World.* New York and Chichester (West Sussex): Columbia University Press.

Gonzáles de la Rocha, M. 2006. *Procesos Domésticos y Vulnerabilidad. Perspectivas antropológicas de los hogares con Oportunidades.* México: CIESAS.

Haughton, J. and Khandker, S. R. 2009. *Handbook on Poverty and Inequality*. Washington, DC: World Bank.

Juárez Martínez, M. L. 2006. Segregación urbana y sus implicaciones en las ciudades. Una aproximación teórica. *Palapa*, 1(2): 45–50.

Lampis, A. 2009. Vulnerability and poverty: an assets, resources and capabilities impact study of low income groups in Bogotá. Unpublished PhD dissertation, Social Policy Department, London School of Economics and Political Science.

—— 2010. ¿Qué ha pasado con la vulnerabilidad social en Colombia? Conectar libertades instrumentales y fundamentales. *Sociedad y economía*, 19: 229–61.

Lapo, G. M. 1983. *Geografía de las ciudades y fundamentos de urbanismo*. Moscow: URSS.

Levinson, D. 1986. A conception of adult development. *American Psychologist*, Jan.: 3–13.

Lomnitz, L. 1998. *Cómo sobreviven los marginados*. México: Siglo XXI.

Marañón, B., Sosa, A. P. and Villarespe, V. 2009. Producción y reproducción de la pobreza. De la 'marginalidad' a la exclusión. In R. Aparicio, V. Villarespe and C. M. Urzúa (eds), *Pobreza en México: magnitud y perfiles*, pp. 99–138. Coneval, Universidad Nacional Autónoma de México, Instituto de Investigaciones Económicas, Instituto Tecnológico y de Estudios Superiores de Monterrey.

Marks, N. and Thompson, S. 2008. Measuring well-being in policy: issues and applications. London: New Economics Foundation.

Mattos, C. 2002. Transformaciones de las ciudades latinoamericanas: ¿Impactos de la globalización?' EURE, 28(85).

McGregor, J. A. 2007. Research wellbeing: from concepts to methodology. In I. Gough and J. A. McGregor (eds), *Wellbeing in Developing Countries: From Theory to Research*, pp. 316–50. Cambridge: Cambridge University Press.

Michaud, Jean and Forsyth, T. (eds). 2013. Moving Mountains: Ethnicity and Livelihoods in Highland China, Vietnam and Laos. Vancouver: University of British Columbia Press.

Monkkonen, P. 2012. La segregación residencial en el México urbano. *EURE* 38(114): 125–46.

Moser, C. and McIlwaine, C. 1997. Household responses to poverty and vulnerability: confronting crisis in commonwealth, Metro Manila, the Philippines. Washington, DC: UN Development Programme, UN-HABITAT and World Bank.

Pinkus Rendón, M. J., *et al.* 2012. Las poblaciones rurales de Mérida y sus relaciones interétnicas con esta ciudad capital de la entidad yucateca de México. *Revista Pueblos y Fronteras*, 6(12): 236–67.

Potts, D. 2013. Urban livelihoods and urbanization trends in Africa: winners and losers? Environment, Politics and Development Working Paper Series, Department of Geography, King's College London, 30.

Quinlan, Allyson. 2003. Resilience and adaptive capacity: key components of sustainable social-ecological systems. *IHDP Update* (2): 4–5.

Rigg, J. 2007. *An Everyday Geography of the Global South*. New York, Routledge.

Ruggeri Laderchi, C. 2000. The monetary approach to poverty: a survey of concepts and methods. Queen's Elisabeth House, Working Paper N. 58: 1–18.

Sabates-Wheeler, R. and S. Devereux. 2013. Sustainable graduation from social protection programmes. *Development and Change* 44(4): 911–38.

Sabatini, F., *et al.* 2001. Segregación residencial en las principales ciudades chilenas: Tendencias en las tres últimas décadas y posibles cursos de acción. *Revista EURE* (82): 21–42.

Sánchez Almanza, A. and de la Vega Estrada, S. 2009. La medición excluyente de la pobreza y el crecimiento económico. In R. Aparicio, V. Villarespe and C. M. Urzúa (eds), *Pobreza en México: magnitud y perfiles*, pp. 165–243. Coneval, Universidad Nacional Autónoma de México, Instituto de Investigaciones Económicas, Instituto Tecnológico y de Estudios Superiores de Monterrey.

Sandberg, J. 2012. Conditional cash transfer and social mobility: the role of asymmetric structures and segmentation. *Development and Change*, 43(6): 1337–59.

Sabatini, F, Cáceres, G. and Cerda, J. 2001. Segregación residencial en las principales ciudades cilenas: Tendencias de las últimas tres décadas y posibles cursos de acción. *EURE*, 27(82): 1–34.

Saraví, G. A. 2004. Urban segregation and public space: young people. *CEPAL Review*, (83): 31–46.

Sassen, S. 2014. *Expulsions: Brutality and Complexity in the Global Economy*. Harvard: Harvard University Press.

Sen, A. 1999. *Commodities and Capabilities*. New York: Oxford University Press.

Smets, P. and Salman. T. 2008. Countering urban segregation: theoretical and policy innovations from around the globe. *Urban Studies*, 45(7): 1307–32.

UN-HABITAT. 2003a. *Slums of the World: Monitoring the Millennium Development Goal, Target 11*. Nairobi: UN-HABITAT.

—— 2003b. *Slums of the World: The Face of Urban Poverty in the New Millennium?* New York, UN-HABITAT.

—— 2006. *State of the World's Cities 2006/07. The Millennium Development Goals and Urban Sustainability: 30 Years of Shaping the Habitat Agenda*. Nairobi: UN-HABITAT.

Urzúa, C. M. and Brambila, C. 2009. Determinantes de la pobreza estatal. In R. Aparicio, V. Villarespe and C. M. Urzúa (eds), *Pobreza en México: magnitud y perfiles*, pp. 139–63. Coneval, Universidad Nacional Autónoma de México, Instituto de Investigaciones Económicas, Instituto Tecnológico y de Estudios Superiores de Monterrey.

White, S. 2009. Analysing wellbeing: a framework for development practice. Wellbeing in Developing Countries Working Paper 44. Bath, UK: University of Bath.

White, S. and Ellison, M. 2007. Wellbeing livelihoods and resources in social practice. In I. Gough and J. A. McGregor (eds), *Wellbeing in Developing Countries: New Approaches and Research Strategies*, pp. 157–75. Cambridge: Cambridge University Press.

9 Local governance, climate risk and everyday vulnerability in Dar es Salaam

Chipo Plaxedes Mubaya, Patience Mutopo and Mzime Regina Ndebele-Murisa

Introduction

Rapid urbanization in Africa is a contested issue due to the unreliability of census data from the 1970s onwards (Pott 2012). However, in those countries where data support a description of rapidly urbanizing realities (Dewan and Yamaguchi 2009; Taubenbock *et al.* 2009; United Nations 2008), cities face high concentrations of people who depend heavily on infrastructure systems including energy, water, communication and transport (Angel *et al.* 2005; Crush *et al.* 2011). The available literature shows how this high concentration makes these people vulnerable to a multiplicity of stressors, including climate change (Brückner 2012; Fay and Opal 2000; 2011; Ligeti *et al.* 2007; Mirzaie *et al.* 2007; Poelhekke 2011; World Bank 2010). Differential access to secure infrastructure and decent housing makes the urban poor more vulnerable than others to climate and weather extremes, increasing their exposure to the impacts of climate change, such as increased frequency and intensity of extreme climatic events, flooding from the projected rise in sea level, and water shortages (Ligeti *et al.* 2007; Heinrichs *et al.* 2011; World Bank 2010).

A taming narrative has been produced about Dar es Salaam's urban transformation. The city experienced a rapid rate of urbanization between 1988 and 2002 with a growth rate of 5 per cent compared to the 3 per cent of the national level, self-explaining concepts such as the considerable growth of population in unplanned settlements in the city (Gichere *et al.* 2011) and the limitations experienced by city planners to keep pace with the rapidly growing population (Casmiri 2009; Bull-Kamanga *et al.* 2003). Multilateral institutions have pointed out the obvious, expressing their serious concern for the implications population growth and limited planning capacity might have for the governance of the city. Not surprisingly, this helped justifying the approval of a World Bank project in 2013 with the following objective: 'To improve institutional performance for urban service delivery in program urban local government authorities' (World Bank 2014).

Following this mainstream and highly institutionalised approach to planning (see Rosales, Chapter 11 in this volume), the city's administration has tended to produce a normative view of inadequate planned developments in Dar es Salaam. According to this perspective, a high percentage (approximately 70 per cent) of the city's total population were living in informal settlements in 2001 (World Bank 2002), and this percentage is likely to have risen since, given that the population of the city has increased significantly since that time. About 8 per cent of these settlements are to be found in a low-elevation zone below the 10 metre contour line, making residents in this zone especially vulnerable to rises in sea level (Gichere *et al*. 2011). This gloomy picture for the urban poor is compounded by Dar es Salaam's vulnerability to a multiplicity of challenges including floods, sea-level rise and coastal erosion, water scarcity and major outbreaks of infectious diseases. However, evidence of response efforts in the city by the local populations point to the deconstruction of this normative view to begin to embrace an alternative narrative. Local people have long since begun the process of resisting political and institutional structures that limit the access to better opportunities and more secure livelihoods and, therefore, adaptation to climate risks. In the light of persisting social vulnerability across time, we consider the analysis of marginalized, asset-poor social groups a contribution to the key objective of this book, the untaming of key city processes. The persistence of different forms of poverty, exclusion and inequality tells a story that is not easily captured by views that reduce the complexity of city problems to a flat duality based on either the absence or the presence in excess of something, be that the bad planning of space, the weak governance or the uncontrollable population growth.

We, the authors, have lived in Africa all our lives and the lead author has lived and worked in Tanzania for the last four years. Our experiences with many African cities, Dar es Salaam included, are mainly those of squalor, poverty and inequality. In Dar es Salaam, we have noted that being poor means living in unbearable conditions, sub-standard housing with limited potable water system, limited access to electricity and only to a rudimentary sewage system. Poor communities are neglected by the government and the people with power, who have the capacity to care and provide some kind of assistance. The experiences that we have with Dar es Salaam and other African cities have prompted us to focus on the case study of Dar es Salaam, conducting a series of rapid assessments of the conditions affecting the urban poor in 2011. We sought to explore three core questions:

- What constitutes climate risk within the city?
- How does local governance interact with climate risk and social vulnerability?
- What are the opportunities for the urban poor to ameliorate their condition in the face of climate risk?

In this chapter, we discuss the findings from such research, which reiterate the need for a broader conceptualization of the urban poor and illustrate how local socio-political conditions influence the opportunities for response mechanisms available to poor women and men in African cities and the type and nature of multiple agency-oriented projects that residents employ to deal with challenges within a multiplicity of structural constraints. In this respect, we embrace the notion that acting in the face of shocks is an arduous task faced by poor households that tend to be constrained by structures and institutions within the political economy of the city and local-level initiatives that are regulated in the sphere of political and class structures that affect how people cope. Herein also lies the link of this chapter to the broader theme of the book as the poor men and women in the city embark on a journey to resist the urban planning conundrum, riddled with social exclusion tendencies, through self-help efforts that have the potential to lighten the challenges that these poor people face and initiate trajectories of change in the urban discourse.

People initiatives and the search for livelihood security in the contemporary urban African context

People's agency and initiative in the face of harsh critical situations has been studied for more than three decades now, and these studies highlight the duality of structure in shaping and being shaped by local-level agency (Chambers 1989; Giddens 1984, 1991, 1994, 2009). Group actions and considerations in developing projects for averting poverty and increasing livelihood options constitute an important element of how processes of social cohesion and innovation influence the way in which the urban poor cushion themselves against environmental, social, political and economic threats in a changing environment (Mutopo 2014). The idea of the poor as hopeless is part of a political and – at the same time – discursive construction, which is ultimately functional with dependence on donors and other external elements, and ignores people's own agency (Kithiia 2010). External support agencies often infuse targeted interventions with such narratives, meanings and inscriptions (Bank 2011: 30).

In the early nineties, Chambers and Conway proposed a then new framework for the analysis of rural livelihoods based on the concepts of capability, equity and sustainability. According to this seminal work, 'a livelihood comprises the capabilities, assets (stores, resources, claims and access) and activities required for a means of living' (Bank 2011: 6). Here it is important to address the trajectories of change experienced in the livelihoods approach over the past two decades, and why such an approach remains valid in understanding agency and the struggles of the different groups of the urban poor for a more decent living. Recent contributions from the literature on the dynamics of vulnerability (Moser 2009) reframe the debate on the livelihoods approach, placing it in a dialogic relationship with more specific vulnerability analysis that raises the political question of why and how people do or do not get access to assets. Lampis (2009) presents a chronological systematization of the vulnerability livelihoods literature, which examines the participatory rural approaches adopted in the 1970s all the way to current applied vulnerability analysis within the broader livelihoods approach. After these contributions, in our view, social vulnerability analysis is still relevant because within commoditized social spheres and social protection (see Chapter 6 in this book for a detailed discussion) access to assets and resources that are key to human, political and social rights, social vulnerability remain a concrete challenge as much as a political theme for debate.

Our central assumption is that societally inherent power dynamics influence the vulnerability of the urban poor and potentially constrain agency. Such assumption is situated within the roots of environmental politics and social formations (Savitch and Kantor 2002). Furthermore, factors such as class dynamics, normally perpetuated by city political governance systems, come into play as hindrances to dealing with social vulnerability. In spite of a widespread recognition of the limitations of traditional rational planning in African cities as the least equipped in terms of governance, infrastructure and economy to cope with staggering and compressed growth processes (Turok and Parnell 2009; Taylor and Peter 2014), studies carried out in other East African cities identified several important response measures and have kept calling on city planners to carry out a number of interventions ranging from strengthening urban infrastructure such as roads, culverts, bridges, drainage systems, and water and sewerage networks, to neighbourhood-scale adaptation in the form of livelihood-based measures to enable communities to build resilience (Douglas *et al.* 2008; Lwasa 2010). In the face of a straightforward call for greater institutional action, especially on urban infrastructure, the other side of the coin, clearly highlighted within the aforementioned literature, is that actions related to community-based adaptation tend not to exceed the level of making domestic energy briquettes from waste, supporting household consumption with urban agriculture or harvesting rainwater at the household level. In this regard, we call for alternative forms of governance, forms that empower local-level structures and institutions to play a greater role in enabling a conducive environment for the local voice to thrive in self-mobilization processes.

The influence of neoliberal thinking is evident in the average African city, where various projects involving ordinary citizens demonstrate the inability of the state to ensure clear rules of access and control over the distribution of services, in turn allowing different individuals and groups to open up markets in which public goods such as water are traded, leading to the commoditization of natural resources (Bank 2011). This state-versus-market dualism within current urban service delivery systems (see Harris, also in Part II of this volume) has mushroomed in peri-urban areas of cities of the global South, such as Bonde la Mpunga in Dar es Salaam, where this study is situated, giving way to asymmetric socio-technical configurations in access to services that represent key assets for livelihood security.

Bonde la Mpunga is an unplanned settlement close the Indian Ocean shore of Dar es Salaam (see figure 9.1). With another five areas that make up the Msasani ward, it is legally considered as an illegal settlement within the Kinondoni District. The characteristics of this area offer a very interesting scenario in which to research how low-income groups harness their agency in a typical flood-prone low-lying urban area, lending weight to and beginning to indirectly challenge the political systems that tend to perpetuate exclusion of the poor from city planning benefits. Hence the decision to focus our 2011 sampling on this settlement, using a two-stages procedure. First we selected the area on a purposive basis and, second, within that, a sample of 45 randomly selected households was intended to

520000

520000

9240000

9240000

Mbweni

Bunju

Kunduchi

Indian Ocean

Bonde la Mpunga

Goba

Kawe

Mbezi

KINONDONI DISTRICT

Mikocheni

Msasani

Nyarna

Kijito

Makumbusho

Ubungo

Sinza

Kinondoni

Mwananyamala

Manzese

Hananasif

Kimara

Makurumala

Ndugumbi

Makuburi

Mabibo

Mizimu

Magomeni

Mburahati

Kigogo

Kibamba

Dosi

N

0   3   6
Kilometers

TANZANIA

Kagera

Mara

Mwanza

Arusha

Shinyanga

Kilimatnjaro

Manyara

Kigoma

Tabora

Singida

Tanga

Rukwa

Dodema

Mbeya

Morogaro

Pwari

Kinga

Lindi

Ruvuma

Mtwara

Legend

Study Area

Ward Boundary

District Map

Indian Ocean_37

Figure 9.1 Location of the study area in Kinondoni District, Dar es Salaam, Tanzania.

provide a qualitatively representative sample of 10 per cent of the estimated 450 households in the study area.

Everyday vulnerability in Bonde la Mpunga

In the studied slum, households' vulnerability is characterized by exposure to climate and non-climate risks and shocks as well as a multiplicity of other challenges. A majority of respondents (68 per cent) highlighted that they had particularly noticed changes in rainfall patterns: fluctuating precipitation (60 per cent), and more frequent droughts (47 per cent) and floods (30 per cent). According to the concept of 'double exposure' to climate-change-related risks (O'Brien and Leichenko, 2000), biophysical stressors are not necessarily either the only or the main entry point for the analysis as – which we also contend – it is the interaction between biophysical risk and social vulnerability dynamics that generates both exposure to hazards and low resilience in the face of materializing vulnerabilities. Figure 9.3, presenting a ranking of non-mutually exclusive items related to the challenges faced by households in accessing services, reflects this mix of social and biophysical variables even in the perception of the interviewed heads of household.

In a guise that is not significantly different from what used to be considered common wisdom in the 1970s and 1980s (Chiotti and Johnson, 1995; Garcia and Escudero, 1981; Warrick and Bowden, 1981), local and national policymakers and politicians consider damage from climate-related events to happen because there is such a phenomenon as climate change. The notion that the biophysical component of climate change is the main driver of everyday vulnerability is contestable because, as pointed out by among others Adams (2009), it is functional to those approaches such as ecological modernization and market environmentalism, which promote both market- and engineering-based solutions while underplaying the relevance of the social construction of risk. They have been influential in lobbying with local administrations to frame responses to environmental problems in terms of technocratic interventions and capital investments, giving very little voice to communities or room for bottom-up approaches. Therefore, conceptualizing risk within a multiple stressor context promises to advance the notion of the 'untamed city' as opposed to designing solutions targeted largely at climate risk. In fact, as far as all adaptation is eventually a local process, there cannot be a normative, overarching model of adaptation valid everywhere and apt for conceptualization and operationalization in planning manuals.

As a case in point of the relation between social and environmental conditions, it is worth recalling how, already, some 16 million people a year contract malaria in Tanzania, and between 100,000 and 125,000 die every year from it (Jones *et al.* 2007). Bonde la Mpunga consists of tightly packed groups of small dwellings with no discernible streets, factors which heighten the sensitivity of the slum dwellers to floods and excessive rains. The majority (78 per cent) of the surveyed households in Bonde la Mpunga indicated that they had migrated from other areas to this settlement. We view this encroachment into illegal spaces by the poor as one of the 'weapons of the weak' in fighting the inherent urban inequalities that dominate the African city. This is coupled with low levels of education and often critical access to health care services. Lack of a sound drainage system and the high prevalence of stagnant water has led to the increase of breeding sites for mosquitoes and in turn to an increase in malaria and other water-borne diseases (see box 9.1), mirroring findings already presented by Tonnang and colleagues (Tonnang *et al.* 2013). The gloomy picture painted by the female respondent in box 9.1 highlights the social inequalities and exclusionary tendencies that are so deep rooted within the contemporary capitalism paradigm.

Box 9.1   Thoughts from a household member on multiple stressors

In our area, there is very poor infrastructure; there are no proper roads, there is no clean water, no dumping sites, no drainage system. Stagnant water is now bringing in mosquito breeding sites, leading to an increase in malaria cases. Because of the poverty in most families we have very few educated people in the area. We do not have access to clean water, we only depend on water vendors yet we are not sure whether the water they are selling is clean and safe for drinking or not. Our children also suffer from skin diseases because of the hot weather, lack of clean water and the dirty street surroundings. Our businesses are more heavily affected than anything else, which is problematic given the role that informal businesses play as a livelihood-supporting activity and way of generating income. This limits our opportunities to increase our income from informal trading and subsequently create a robust livelihood system as a form of adaptation to various challenges.

Respondent from survey, 2011

Social vulnerability and its interface with local governance in Bonde la Mpunga

While keeping in mind the already mentioned concept of the double exposure of the urban poor (O'Brien and Leichenko, 2000), it is now important to take the analysis down to some key insights produced by scholars analysing Africa at large and more specifically South Africa, who have provided valuable insights for the broadening of the analysis of the case presented in this chapter. Adequate provision of urban services potentially guarantees diminishing vulnerability levels (Leck and Simon 2012). They highlight that there is an 'emerging literature' on local governance and climate change agency and that their analysis of this discourse in South Africa is an effort in 'deploying insights from the limited existing literature' and drawing from empirical investigations undertaken in two neigh-bouring municipalities.

The Bonde la Mpunga residents' sensitivity to the impacts of floods is com-pounded by the crowded nature and lack of adequate planning of the settlement as indicated in the makeshift and poor construction of some of the housing in this location (see figure 9.2). The impacts from excessive rain are mostly felt through damaged infrastructure such as houses and roads (see figure 9.3). Rosales (2010) postulates that adequate planning must incorporate equitable, efficient and sustainable human settlements, including bringing on board the urban poor in the decision-making process, as a useful prerequisite for enhancing opportunities and the well-being of the people. This is within a framework where urban plan-ning has hitherto not addressed environmental issues such as climate change and related disasters, and ecological overshots (Rosales 2010). Our research reveals that local conditions determine the opportunities for response mechanisms and the type and nature of multiple agency-oriented projects that residents employ to deal with challenges.

There is evidence in Bonde la Mpunga of *self-help efforts* that are made by individual households to deal with both immediate and subsequent shocks and challenges. The self-help efforts are triggered by the general low-level contact of residents with government and little experience of receiving relief supplies.

Figure 9.2   Solid waste in dirty floodwater in Bonde la Mpunga, December 2011.

a

b

Figure 9.3 Transport woes during the recent floods in Msasani and swampy surroundings in Bonde la Mpunga, December 2011.

Selling household assets and borrowing food and cash appear to be inherent strategies that households employ as part of their survival efforts. Indeed, navigating the landscape of income generation as a response to climate risk has been shown to play a beneficial double role of providing food for the household and at the same time providing income to take care of other household needs (Drimie and van Zyl 2005; Thomas *et al.* 2007). Essentially, we suggest that the historical absence (or scant presence, at best) of state institutions in the spaces that the urban poor occupy,while having negative connotations, also contributes to the social construction of urban space as the result of the necessary action the urban poor have to undertake for their own livelihoods.

The case study of Bonde la Mpunga shows households engaging in small-scale businesses, such as youths acting as car mechanics, selling water and *Mama Ntilie* businesses for women.[1] Small garages and *Mama Ntilie* businesses are the kind of activities low-income people in the city can resort to in order to strengthen their livelihoods and on that basis try to find some viable response mechanisms to climate risk. Although these kinds of activities have been documented both in the past (Chambers 1989) and more recently (Moser 2009), we recast this conceptual framework as a way to challenge the hypocrisy of mainstream conceptual frameworks on climate change adaptation in African cities such as Dar es Salaam. Against the already described mainstream planning discourses and practices the agency of the poor is constrained, and only so much can be achieved given the limits imposed by structural constraints with livelihoods entrapped in a cycle of poverty (Leck and Simon 2012; Moser 2014).

The actual societal configurations show the great role played by market forces and the even greater state retreat (see box 9.2) from presenting a coping framework for the households studied as transitioning in the social dimension as indicated in studies carried out by Chambers (1989), Hendricks (2010); Pryer (2003), Moser (1998) and Lampis (2010), Kithiia (2010); Kithiia (2011), Nkurunziza (2007).

Box 9.2   Thoughts from a Bonde la Mpunga resident

My view is that serikali ya mtaaa *[the local government] tries to help in dealing with a lot of our problems but they cannot do more since they continuously report that they are underfunded. I have also noticed that they have been struggling to deal with the same problems for more than ten years now. We wish the government could provide funds to* serikali ya mtaaa *for them to be able to solve our problems regarding infrastructure such as sanitation facilities and storm water collectors. We would also appreciate it if they could respond to our calls on time as they usually take a long time to respond when we face problems.*

Respondent from survey, 2011

As in many other peri-urban areas of the global South, households use processes of communal help and rely on the agency of their members in averting crises, such as floods or outbreaks. In 1990 Cairncross *et al.*, referring to the relationship between urban administrations and local citizens in peripheral low-income areas, were already writing that

> in most cities, public investments in infrastructure do not benefit the poor majority since the settlements in which they live do not receive piped water, sewers and drains and benefit little (if at all) from investments in ports, airports, power stations and roads.
>
> (Cairncross, Hardoy and Satterthwaite, 1990: 13).

What is new or what has changed from 25 years ago? When we compare the analysis from the quote above with the fact that in Bonde la Mpunga, in the event of flooding, residents mobilize people to dig canals to direct water to the ocean and clean the neighbourhood, since flood water carries and deposits waste material, and still help each other in times of trouble by assisting neighbours with food and money to get household provisions, what can be added to the analysis of the often overlapping impacts of climate-related risk and everyday socio-economic vulnerability?

First, the very fact that, after a quarter of a century, many situations of deprivation have not been modified in any significant way cannot but generate astonishment and indignation. It is true that the argument that many cities in the global South have not been included in the dynamics and benefits of the global era is a long-standing one (Robinson, 2002), but it is nonetheless one worth reiterating. Second, the injustice attached to climate and social risks requires, as was recently put forward by Watson, a reconsideration of the importance of long-term planning for urbanizing Africa. However, cases such as Bonde la Mpunga reflect the gap still separating this goal from existing realities, as actual planning practices tend to overshadow the multi-causality of risk generation. And third, as discussed by Parnell and Pieterse, Africa's rapid urban transformation risks, among other things, generating the conditions for rapid, rent-seeking solutions closely bound to political and private interests (as reflected by the quote in box 9.2). Fourth, as urban Africa cannot just be considered the loci of crisis, war and social unrest, in the face of the many daily experiences of livelihood consolidation and struggle carried on by the organised civil society, a case study highlighting how this is reflected at the micro-level serves the purpose of contributing to the generation of a critical mass for future and more just scenarios.

Not only do local government institutional and policy efforts, in this case, do little to support the adaptation efforts by the slum dwellers. Time and resource limitations for players other than the individual households reduce these households' abilities to adapt to crises, and subsequently thwart their opportunities to enhance their livelihoods. The efforts to provide necessary amenities and help households in Bonde la Mpunga to deal with immediate shocks remain limited. This reiterates the notion of class and structural inequalities as couched in the contemporary capitalist realm, which tends to ignore the local-level capabilities of households to act for their own good.

Box 9.3 Reflections from a key informant

The growth of Bonde la Mpunga and developments in its vicinity has been fuelled by the proximity of the informal settlement to the city centre, which makes it very attractive to settlers, in the absence of deterrents for these settlers. In addition, investors disregard rules in order to acquire pieces of land that they use for their enterprises. In the same respect, the tempta- tion for city authorities to raise personal funds through clandestine deals is too high and contributes to this quagmire. These developments block the water channel and cause impacts of excessive rains and floods to intensify. Initially Bonde la Mpunga was designated for use for recreation, agricul- ture or restricted residential construction but [the settlement] has contin- ued to flourish since the 1980s.

Respondent from survey, 2011

The interplay between institutional and socio-economic dimensions branches out once more when considering how the conspicuous absence of local government institutions in Bonde la Mpunga enables migrants to continue to settle in undesig- nated areas (see boxes 9.2 and 9.3).

The inertia of African planning has been highlighted by Pieterse as the dominant response to the deepening crisis linked to urban growth and expan- sion. Key interviewed informants from local government and urban planning further highlighted that the lack of expertise and low capacity in terms of num- bers of city professional technical staff are among the reasons for the failure to fully implement interventions in slums in the city (see box 9.4). Meanwhile, the Tanzanian government is currently preparing another Master Plan, long after the original term of the previous one expired. Four master plans have to date been prepared for Dar es Salaam, with very little implementation of these plans (AAT 2009).

Box 9.4 Thoughts from a key informant

Our plans are rarely given full attention and remain on the shelves for sub- stantial periods of time. Moreover, lack of adequate funding limits us in implementing these plans. The national budget portion assigned to urban planning and development is meagre and we have therefore concluded that urban planning and development is not in the top ten government priorities. It is also important to address contradictions in salary scales for professional

(continued)

(continued)

technical staff doing similar jobs but from different ministries in order to avoid disincentives. Another major setback for us is that some of our policies for resettlement of squatters are against politicians' desire to maintain relations with the electorate.

Respondent from survey, 2011

The prevailing planning approach still tries nowadays to prevent the proliferation of slums through prohibitions and control, rather than by trying to widen the approach to understand the root causes and to work with different stakeholders towards alternative, more inclusive and just urban scenarios. For instance, during one of the interviews conducted, an urban planner claimed that issuance of permits and titles continue in areas such as Bonde la Mpunga, despite policies to the contrary (see box 9.4). This resonates with our assertion of class inequality as these permits are issued to the rich and elite in the city.

Box 9.5 Reflections from a key informant

There is little coordination between the Ministry of Lands and the Ministry of Local Government in the implementation of guidelines, which tend to overlap. There clearly are overlaps in the institutional frameworks in these ministries. We as urban planners in the Ministry of Lands usually find ourselves in conflicting situations with personnel from the Ministry of Local Government, yet it is clearly documented that these two ministries have distinct responsibilities. In addition, the inadequate urban planning in Dar es Salaam partly hinges on a degree of misinterpretation of development guidelines.

Respondent from survey, 2011

Conclusions

In this chapter, we have attempted to connect everyday vulnerability analysis, with an emphasis on how Dar es Salaam low-income settlements are affected by climate risk, with how environmental change is politically and socially constructed by traditional rational approaches to planning. Across the three following main findings we found a connection with a number of key cross-cutting issues of the whole book, in particular the need to re-conceptualize how exclusions are produced across scales that reach the domains of policy and culture behind the geographical limits of the built environment.

1   Vulnerability analysis and the political agenda originally set up by Chambers and Moser for rural and urban poverty are still relevant under new conditions

such as those created by neoliberalism in African cities like Dar es Salaam. Social vulnerability analysis should be the centrepiece within more recent elaborations on socio-environmental justice.

2   The concept of double exposure to both climate risk and socio-economic downturns seems a relevant entry point in order to contribute to the reframing of a discussion on everyday risks and livelihoods security in peri-urban contexts such as Bonde la Mpunga.

3   Within a broader discussion regarding how Africa urbanization is transforming the landscape, our case study contributes to reframing, in this case through a local lens, the broader question about the directionality of development practices and, specifically, of planning, which risks once more being controlled by politicians, planners and lobbyists, whereas local communities and households risk being excluded once more.

Note

1   *Mama Ntilie* is a name that has been given to the local small-scale businesses that have mushroomed, not just in the study area but across the city, in which mostly women, but also men, set up small restaurants and sell food.

References

Angel, S., Sheppard, S. and Civco, D. 2005. *The Dynamics of Global Urban Expansion.* Washington, DC: World Bank.

Architects Association of Tanzania (AAT). 2009. Heritage Conference. *Properties Magazine.*

Bank, L. 2011. *Home Spaces, Street Styles: Contesting Power and Identity in a South African City.* London: Pluto Press.

Bull-Kamanga, L., Diagne, K., Lavell, A., Leon, E., Lerise, F., MacGregor, H., Maskrey, A. *et al.* 2003. From everyday hazards to disasters: the accumulation of risk in urban areas. *Environment and Urbanization*, 15(1): 193–204.

Cairncross, S., Hardoy, J. E. and Satterthwaite, D. 1990. The urban context. In Cairncross, S., Hardoy, J.E. and Satterthwaite, D. (eds), *The Poor Die Young: Housing and Health in the Third World.* London: Earthscan.

Casmiri, D. 2009. Vulnerability of Dar es Salaam city to impacts of climatic change. Unpublished.

Chambers, R. 1989. Vulnerability: how the poor cope. *IDS Bulletin*, 20 (2).

Chiotti, Q. P., and Johnson, T., 1995. *Extending the Boundaries of Climate Change Research: A Discussion on Agriculture Journal of Rural Studies*, 11(3): 335–50.

Crush, J., Hovorka, A. and Tevera, D. 2011. Food security in Southern African cities: the place of urban agriculture. *Progress in Development Studies*, 11: 285.

Dewan, A. M. and Yamaguchi, Y. 2009. Land use and land cover change in greater Dhaka, Bangladesh: using remote sensing to promote sustainable urbanization. *Applied Geography*, 29: 390–401.

Douglas, I. *et al.* 2008. Unjust waters: climate change, flooding and the urban poor in Africa. *Environment and Urbanization*, 20(1): 187–205.

Drimie, S. and van Zyl, J. 2005. Human vulnerability to environmental change. Background Research Paper for the South Africa Environment Outlook report on behalf of the Department of Environmental Affairs and Tourism Human Sciences Research Council.

Fay, M. and Opal, C. 2000. Urbanization without growth: A not so uncommon phenomenon. Working Paper 2412. Washington, DC: World Bank.

Garcia, R. V., and Escudero, J. C., 1981. *Drought and Man: The Constant Catastrophe.* Volume 2. New York: Pergamon Press.

Gichere, S. K., Sikoyo, G. M. and Saidi, A. M. 2011. Climate change and its effect on cities of Eastern African countries. In B. Yuen and A. Kumssa (eds), *Climate Change and Sustainable Urban* 211 *Development in Africa and Asia.* New York: Springer Science.

Giddens, A. 1984. *The Constitution of Society.* Berkeley, CA: University of California Press.

—— 1991 *The Consequences of Modernity.* Cambridge: Polity Press.

—— 1994. Living in a post-traditional society. In U. Beck, A. Giddens and S. Lasch (eds), *Reflexive Modernization: Politics, Tradition and Aesthetics in the Modern Social Order.* Cambridge: Polity Press.

—— 2009. *Sociology.* Cambridge: Polity Press.

Heinrichs, D., Aggrawal, R., Barton, J., Bharucha, E., Butsch, C., Fragkias, M., Johnston, P., Kraas, F., Krellenberg, K., Lampis, A. and Ling, O.G. 2011. Adapting cities to climate change: opportunities and constraints. findings from eight cities. In Hoornweg, D., Freire, M., Lee, M., Bhada-Tata, P. and B. Yuen (eds), *Cities and Climate Change: An Urgent Agenda.* Washington, DC: World Bank.

Hendricks, B. 2010 City-wide governance networks in Nairobi: towards contributions to political rights, influence and service delivery for poor and middle-class citizens? *Habitat International,* 34(1): 59–77.

Jones, A. E., Uddenfelt Wort, U., Morse, A. P., Hastings, I. M. and Gagnon, A. S. 2007. Climate prediction of El Niño malaria epidemics in north-west Tanzania. *Malaria Journal,* 6:162.

Kithiia J. 2010. Old notion-new relevance: setting the stage for the use of social capital resource in adapting East African coastal cities to climate change. *International Journal of Urban Sustainable Development,* 1: 17–32.

Leck, H. and Simon, D. 2012. Fostering multiscalar collaboration and co-operation for effective governance of climate change adaptation. *Urban Studies,* 50(6): 1221–38 (published online 26 October 2012).

Ligeti, E., Penney, J. and Wieditz, I. 2007. Cities preparing for climate change: a study of six urban regions. Toronto, Canada: Clean Air Partnership. Available at: www.cleanair-partnership.org (accessed 10 November 2011).

Lwasa, S. 2010. Adapting urban areas in Africa to climate change: the case of Kampala. *Current Opinion in Environmental Sustainability,* 2: 166–71.

Mirzaie, M., Haghshenas, N. M., Moshfegh, M. and Javadkhani, H. 2007. Demographic dimensions of the urbanization process in selected African countries: new prospects and challenges. Paper for UAPS, 5 the African Population Conference, Arusha, Tanzania, 10–14 December 2007.

Moser, C. 1998. The asset vulnerability framework: reassessing urban poverty reduction strategies. *World Development,* 26(3): 1–19.

—— 2009. *Ordinary Families, Extraordinary Lives. Assets and Poverty Reduction in Guayaquil, 1978–2004.* Washington, DC: Brookings Institution Press.

—— 2014. Gender asset building and just cities. Background briefing document for WUF7 Networking Event.

Mutopo, P. 2014. *The Granary is Never Empty: Land Based Livelihoods and Female Transitory Mobility after Fast Track Land Reform in Mwenezi District, Zimbabwe.* Brill, Netherlands: Leiden Academic.

O'Brien, K. L., and Leichenko, R. M., 2000. Double exposure: assessing the impacts of climate change within the context of economic globalization. *Global Environmental Change*, 10: 221–32.

Poelhekke, S. 2011. Urban growth and uninsured rural risk: booming towns in bust times. *Journal of Development Economics*, 96(2): 461–75.

Pott, D. 2012. Challeging the myths of urban dynamics in Sub-Saharan Africa: the evidence from Nigeria. *World Development*, 40(7): 1382–93.

Pryer, J. 2003. *Poverty and Vulnerability in Dhaka Slums: The Urban Livelihoods Study.* Aldershot, UK: Ashgate.

Robinson, J. 2002. Global and world cities: a view off the map. *International Journal of Urban and Regional Research*, 26(3): 531–54.

Savitch, H. V. and Kantor, P. 2002. *Cities in the International Marketplace: The Political Economy of Urban Development in North America and Western Europe.* Princeton, NJ: Princeton University Press.

Taylor, A. and Peter, C. 2014. Strengthening Climate Change Resilience in African Cities: A Framework for Working with Informality. CDKN. Cape Town: African Centre for Cities.

Taubenbock, H., Wegmann, M., Roth, A., Mehl, H. and Dech, S. 2009. Urbanization in India: spatiotemporal analysis using remote sensing data. *Computers, Environment and Urban Systems*, 33: 179–88.

Thomas, D. S. G., Twyman, C., Osbahr, H. and Hewitson, B. 2007. Adaptation to climate change and variability: farmer responses to intra-seasonal precipitation trends in South Africa *Climatic Change*, 83: 301–22.

Tonnang, E. Z. H., Carhuapoma, P., Juarez, H., Gonzales, J. C., Sporleder, M., Simon, R. and Kroschel, J. 2013. ILCYM-Insect Life Cycle Modeling User Guide. A software package for developing temperature-based insect phenology models with applications for regional and global analysis of insect population and mapping. Lima: International Potato Center.

Turok, I. and Parnell, S. 2009. Reshaping cities, rebuilding nations: The role of national urban policies. *Urban Forum*, 20(2): 157–74.

United Nations. 2008. *Urbanization: A Global Perspective.* Proceedings of the Expert Group Meeting on Population Distribution, Urbanization, Internal Migration and Development, 21–23 January. New York: United Nations.

Warrick, R. A., and Bowden, M. J., 1981. The changing impacts of drought in the great plains. In Lawson, M. P., and Baker, J. C. (eds.), *The Great Plains: Perspectives and Prospects*, pp. 111–37. Centre for Great Plains Studies. Lincoln, Nebraska. University of Nebraska.

World Bank. 2002. Tanzania. Upgrading of Low-Income Settlements. Country Report. Washington, DC: World Bank. Available at http://web.mit.edu/urbanupgrading/upgrading/case-examples/overview-africa/country-assessments/reports/Tanzania-report.html (accessed 22 September 2014).

World Bank. 2010. *Cities and Climate Change: An Urgent Agenda.* December. Available at: http://web.worldbank.org/WBSITE/EXTERNAL/TOPICS/EXTURBANDEVELOPMENT/EXTUWM/ (accessed 9 June 2014).

World Bank, 2014. Tanzania – Urban Local Government Strengthening Program – P118152. Implementation Status Results Report, published 18/06/2014. Available at: http://documents.worldbank.org/curated/en/2014/08/20118711/tanzania-urban-local-government-strengthening-program-p118152-implementation-status-results-report-sequence-03 (accessed 22nd September 2014).

10 Accra's unregulated market-oriented sanitation strategy

Problems and opportunity

John Harris

The larger study from which this chapter is drawn was commissioned by Waste Enterprisers and sponsored by the Bill and Melinda Gates Foundation. Its original purpose was to investigate 'public toilet' sites in Accra, Ghana, articulating the maintenance and management practices of site operators in order to identify sanitation delivery challenges and potential strategies for future interventions aimed at expanding sanitation access in Accra. One of the assumptions tested was that toilet operators will forgo important maintenance tasks because of the cost, and that those decisions will directly impact on the availability of sanitation in the city. This fear was supported by the literature. When cost structure, management, lack of public participation or the socio-political context of toilet provision results in inadequate maintenance of sanitation facilities, serious problems emerge in community health, environmental degradation and constrained sanitation access (Burra 2003; Nance and Ortolano 2007; Schouten and Mathenge 2010).

In this chapter I attempt to diverge from the original purpose of the data collection. Here, the goal is to use the data to express how the everyday urban service provision arrangements in Accra and cities like it are far more messy and untidy things than the taming narratives of the privatization and critical frameworks would suggest. This way, the chapter speaks to overarching themes in this larger volume because it seeks to inform action through a nuanced understanding of complex dynamics, situating praxis between totalizing narratives on the one hand and the mundane realities of people's lives on the other. Accra is a context where an overall scheme of privatized service provision masks a diverse and contested everyday reality. The data provide an important case of market-oriented and unregulated sanitation schemes which both have problematic outcomes, and suggest space for improving access to sanitation and our conceptual approach to socio-ecological problem-solving.

Accra, the capital of Ghana and the country's largest city, has long struggled with sanitation. As Awortwi (2006) reports, by the mid-1980s approximately 60 per cent of the population relied on public toilets for their daily needs. These were large communal toilet blocks managed by local government. The facilities poorly served the city's population, which was effectively 'engulfed in filth' (2006: 227).

There are many reasons for this. The plight of the urban poor regarding water and sanitation cannot be disentangled from larger urbanization forces that resulted in widespread inequalities regarding land and other resources. The urbanization process in Accra has largely benefited colonial and post-colonial elites as a result of the manipulation of communal land institutions in urban and rural areas (Obeng-Odoom 2013). This contributed to poor rural migrants inhabiting increasingly dense urban neighbourhoods with insecure tenure. These communities were also largely neglected in terms of infrastructure investment and provision of urban services (Owusu 2010). Significant levels of ethnic segregation, particularly along socio-economic lines, exacerbated the underprovision of services (Owusu and Agyei-Mensah 2011). These factors all contributed to low levels of in-home sanitation and high reliance on public toilet facilities. The facilities were badly managed, staff were poorly paid or not paid, and users were unwilling to pay for bad services. All of these problems were made worse by public sector reforms that laid off staff at the sites in 1986 (Awortwi 2006).

In the 1990s a series of reforms introduced significant private sector involvement in the water and sanitation sectors in Ghana (Yeboah 2006; Awortwi 2006). By 2006, it was estimated that there were at least 90 small private contractors operating public toilets in Accra. These are loosely regulated enterprises operating toilet sites under several types of institutional arrangement with the Accra Metropolitan Assembly (AMA). While there has been some improvement in the sanitation sector relative to conditions prevalent in the 1980s, Accra continues to struggle. According to the *National Environmental Sanitation Strategy Action Plan 2010–2015* (Government of Ghana 2010), 39 per cent of Ghana's urban citizens depend on public toilets for their daily sanitation needs, and in the case of Accra, waste collected from public toilets is discharged into the ocean without treatment. Further, 11.5 per cent of Accra's population resort to open defecation. Fee-for-use management is ubiquitous, and one estimate suggests that in Ghana's urban population, toilet user fees could constitute as much as 10–15 per cent of a household's income for low wage earners (Korboe *et al.* 1999).[1]

As discussed above, this study was designed to evaluate management practices of public toilet sites operated by private enterprises. Forty-one public toilet owners or managers were interviewed in November and December 2012. Each respondent was asked to explain the day-to-day management of their toilet site. These included questions related to the following:

- maintenance tasks required to operate public toilet sites
- basic system technology and requirements
- the basic cost structure of the site
- public toilet strategies enlarging the customer base
- the relationship between individual sites, other public toilets and local government
- any challenges or bottlenecks experienced while providing the service.

Public toilet sites from 6 of the 11 submetro administrative units of Accra were included in the sample in order to vary the socio-economic status of catchment areas, keeping a primary focus on lower-income parts of the city. Site selection relied on the 'Slum Index' information created by San Diego State University for the Greater Accra region (Jankowska *et al.* 2012). The neighbourhoods were as follows:

- Jamestown, Asheidu Keteke Submetro, a lower-income area in one of the oldest parts of Accra
- Nima, Ayawaso East Submetro, a low-income neighbourhood that is highly contested by political parties
- Old Fadama, Ablekuma Central Submetro, a high-density neighbourhood where nearly all the residents have insecure tenure, and some of the worst socio-economic conditions in Accra are found
- Kaneshi, Okai Koi South Submetro, a neighbourhood in the vicinity of the Kaneshi Market, one of the largest public markets in West Africa, which is middle income, but with a significant presence of public toilets
- Alajo, Ayawaso Central Submetro, another moderate-income area with pockets of lower-income households and a significant presence of public toilets
- Osu, Osu Klottery Submetro: a mixed-income area containing high-income households including foreign expatriates and non-governmental organization (NGO) headquarters as well as many low-income households.

Figure 10.1 Submetro areas of Accra, Ghana.

Key informant interviews were also carried out with the following:

- the programme manager for a water, sanitation and health NGO operating in Accra
- the head environmental engineer for the Accra Metropolitan Assembly (AMA)
- a resident of Old Fadama and employee of the Ghana Federation of the Urban Poor
- the chair of a septic truck drivers' union
- a long-serving septic truck driver
- the secretary of the Alajo Development Committee
- the secretary of the Jamestown Public Toilet Owners Association
- a long-time resident and community leader in Nima.

Over the last several decades the question of who should provide urban services and infrastructure has been deeply explored. Mainstream development organizations (see e.g. World Bank 1993) increasingly argued that uncompetitive public monopolies were largely inadequate for the task of urban service provision, and asserted that if the government was the problem in infrastructure provision and service provision, then the answer was to cut the government out of the process. This belief was coupled with the assumption that the forms of centralized provision of urban services found in the developed world should be replicated as the only truly appropriate way to provide adequate services (Jaglin 2014). This neoliberal approach, particularly as applied to the water and sanitation sectors in the developing world, was widely utilized in urban development projects. This approach restructured and privatized service provision wherever possible, and brought a market logic to systems that were to remain publicly controlled.

This effort was significantly criticized for reasons involving access, quality and price (Zaki and Amin 2009). Other criticisms included the sequencing of implementation, the perceived abandonment of public utilities rather than attempts to provide more resources, and the condemnation of private provision on the ideological grounds that access to water and sanitation is a human right and such services should never be commoditized (Prasad 2006). Populations in the developing world resented higher charges for still largely inadequate services under privatized systems; considered much reform a veiled grab of power and profit (Mustafa and Reeder 2009); and found that the poor were still largely underserved, and that in some instances inequalities increased under reformist regimes (Castro 2007). The 'pro-poor sanitation' literature emerged as largely aimed at expanding the economic and social benefits of urban services through either more appropriate pro-poor technologies for sanitation, calling for urban governance changes that result in governments at multiple scales that are more responsive to the urban poor, or both (Nunan and Satterthwaite 2001; Cross and Morel 2005; Gutiérrez 2007; Paterson, Mara and Curtis 2007).

Many of these factors and others were included in a general reconsideration of certain liberalization policies (Rodrik 2006), with two divergent presumptions emerging about the role of private actors in the production of urban services:[2] either the push for privatization of urban services has run its course and we can expect increasing public control moving forward (Bel and Warner 2008; Prasad 2006) or there is a place for privatization in expanding the economic and social benefits of urban services, but privatization in its various manifestations can only be positive when deeply rooted in contextual appreciation and targeted in more specific and effective ways.

One of the problems with both the mainstream and critical scholarship cited above is that the narratives are often limited to large-scale monopolistic public, private or public–private partnership operations. In reality, many urban regions are served through 'other' private sector operators (Solo 1999). These are small private enterprises offering water, sanitation and other services for a fee. These enterprises are quite varied in type and quality, and are loosely regulated (Chenoweth 2004). These services are understood to be 'co-produced' by multiple agents in an attempt to meet the everyday needs of people in specific circumstances (Allen *et al.* 2008; Olivier de Sardan 2010). There is a growing realization that these types of decentralized approaches to sanitation have much to offer because of low comparable cost, flexible technologies, adaptability to varying physical and social constraints, and ease in facilitating wastewater reuse and recovery (Libralato *et al.* 2012). But because these systems are produced in local contexts impacted by specific technical, social and institutional realties, they defy easy categorization or generalization. As a result the neoliberal and critical taming narratives of water and sanitation are too often imposed from the outside and fail to connect to the reality of people's lives.

As Jaglin (2014) suggests, these other providers are the real way urban services are provided in many cities, and their diversity, vitality and innovativeness are too often missing from dialogue on urban services and the poor. Jaglin suggests that in every city there exist varied socio-technical 'dispositifs', or interactions between actors, technologies and institutions that co-produce service delivery configurations. This is also suggestive of Bourdieu's (1977) *habitus*, the understanding that the everyday norms that shape how citizens meet their daily needs are created in the interplay between social structures and individual agency. In a sense, this is the root of the untamed everyday of water and sanitation provision. In places like Accra, global debates about the role of governments and markets in the sector ebb and flow, but citizens as both 'other' providers and users of urban services bend systems to meet their own needs in ways that belie the prescriptions of the larger narratives.

In the context of Accra, the everyday reality of service provision maintains a market-oriented logic with little or no regulation. In Accra, 'public toilet' is a misnomer because public toilets are privately managed, or privately produced and managed. Services are provided in two ways. Every public toilet is either an 'AMA' toilet or a 'private toilet'. Accra Metropolitan Assembly (AMA) toilets, representing 41 per cent (N=17) of the sample, are toilets that were once run directly by local government, but have gone through a privatization process or which have been constructed since privatization. Awortwi (2006) established that there are several institutional arrangements for the operation of these toilets, including *affermage*, where all operation and maintenance is handed to a private entity for a period of time; *rehabilitate, operate and transfer (ROT)*, where a private enterprise is 'given' a defunct toilet to rehabilitate and operate for a time; *build, operate and transfer (BOT)*, where a private enterprise is allowed to build and operate a toilet until such time as the AMA takes it back; and *build, own and operate (BOO)*, where private enterprises are permitted to build and operate a toilet with payment obligations to the AMA.

Private toilets, representing 59 per cent (N=24) of the sample, are public toilet sites on privately controlled land. While the AMA still regulates these and collects revenues from their operation in the same manner as for AMA toilets, no contractual obligations exist between the AMA and the owner. While it is likely that it is the formal responsibility of the AMA to issue permits to all new and existing public toilets, this study finds no evidence that this is done systematically. Instead, the process described by respondents is that private toilets appear as the market demands them and entrepreneurs rise to meet that demand. After a private toilet site is established, the AMA will begin to collect revenue and provide an element of regulatory oversight.

In terms of regulation, the AMA submetro administrators frequently gather toilet owners together ostensibly to collect fees or to provide some kind of common use information about operating a toilet site. However, in some submetros, these meetings are expanded to include information on resource-sharing, problem-solving and other types of organizing.

The goal of the analysis that follows is to examine how the 'other' private sector operators in Accra function in an overtly market-oriented, unregulated way, showing this situation to be problematic for a number of reasons, but also using the case as an example of how large-scale taming narratives fail to grasp the everyday reality of the city, and how even in overtly problematic situations there is room to dig deeper into the everyday to find productive avenues forward. The three sections that follow discuss, first, how the unregulated market-oriented strategy opens space for the co-opting of sanitation services for political purposes to the detriment of urban citizens; second, how the unregulated market strategy tends to create conditions of too much competition between sanitation providers; and third, how a better understanding of the everyday provision of sanitation opens possibilities for socio-ecological problem-solving that can increase access to sanitation in Accra.

Unregulated markets and political co-option

All public toilets, both AMA and private locations, are managed at the submetro level as described above. For AMA locations, the contract between the local government and the owner is held at the submetro level. All decisions on granting or resending management contracts are made by submetro administrators. The process is quite political. Public toilets can be a good source of income, and contracts are often given as political patronage. It has long been the practice to hand over public toilets as the spoils of victory to political party 'footsoldiers' (Ayee and Crook 2003; Bob-Milliar 2012). If a contract holder is in the wrong party or someone else is owed a political favour, they might no longer be able to keep control of an AMA toilet. However, toilet sites are quite contested, and some are able to maintain control in the face of political change. For instance, Respondent FA, a long-time toilet manager in Alajo, described his experience as follows:

> The change of governments, when it [government] changes they will take it [management contracts] from you if you are not strong. When this government changed, they wanted to take it, but we did not agree. So I am still handling it. That is why they built this one [a new site next door] . . . so they have wanted to take it for political affiliation, but in Alajo, we don't allow that. We fought it and they could not take it . . . they are now putting new ones.

Respondent NJ described the plight of anyone who holds an AMA contract: 'You know in Ghana, when politics change, your business also change; your plans change, they collapse.'

Respondent FA also pointed out that sanitation in Accra must always be understood as a resource that actors will contest and vie to control. He stated: 'When money is involved, then they will come. Everyone fights for money. If you are not strong they will take it from you.'

As with any resource, there are many interested parties vying for control of public toilets. Local news accounts regularly report 'strong arm' tactics by party footsoldiers to gain or keep control of public toilets. In certain neighbourhoods, toilets are particularly connected to the political parties. Respondent TN, a manager of an AMA toilet in Nima, received his contract after the last change in political leadership. However, it was made clear to him that the toilet site must be used to meet the needs of the party. As he explained:

> When the people come in, normally most of the people in this community, they don't pay. They go in free. It is just [a few people] that pay. It is due to the party. The party colours. We have to maintain it in such a way that the party looks good. We have a problem then, you understand?

At TN's site, he suggests that only 30 per cent of his customers actually pay the user fee for the toilet. Other locations from other neighbourhoods in the study suggest that between 75 and 90 per cent of customers pay the required user fee, at least in part, because other sites are not as politically oriented and private locations are not as likely to be pressured through political parties to provide a free service to the community.

The socio-political context of sanitation causes problems for many toilet sites. Operators do not know whether or when they might lose control of the facility. The respondents often expressed the idea that they do not undertake investment because they fear losing control of their toilet site after having made an investment. Further, from the standpoint of public toilet managers, overt political intervention into the management of the sites leads many toilets to fall below the break-even point at which proprietors, even politically appointed proprietors, are able to maintain basic-level standards at the facilities and make a small profit. In the long run, this means less sanitary conditions for users and overall restricted access.

While the survey on which this data is based did not include questions on user satisfaction, other studies have looked at the link between political interference and public toilet user satisfaction in Accra. User satisfaction is higher where commercial operators are able to respond to user preferences without overt interference by local government (Awortwi 2006).

Here the everyday reality is juxtaposed with the narrative of market-oriented solutions. Many toilet sites remain controlled by political parties, and the struggle between providers, political actors and the preferences of individual users creates the context for everyday service access and the parameters guiding the evolution of those services. More will be said about this below.

Unregulated market competition among public toilet enterprises

According to the analysis, the average toilet site in the sample has an estimated annual profit of about US$8,000. Lower-performing sites, approximately 30 per cent of the sample, are estimated to be near the break-even point at an estimated US$300 annual profit; much higher performers exist and can bring in as much as US$16,000 per year. All the toilet sites in the sample use technologies that require human waste to be stored temporarily on-site in pits, tanks, buckets and the like. Removing that waste regularly through vacuum trucks or by hand is the most expensive, and probably the most important, aspect of site maintenance. If toilet sites cannot afford to do this basic activity they cannot function and they go out of commission. As discussed above, this was the prevailing conditions of public toilets in the 1980s. As an example, Respondent CJ recalled:

> There was a time, a few years back when [emptying the holding tanks] was not all that easy. All the AMA toilets were choked. The managers said they were not getting revenue to come and dislodge [empty the tanks] or to pay their workers, so you can't use the toilets. This is the reason why we started to privatize them to individuals.

Here it is important to note two things. First, cost recovery depends not just on the user fee rate, but on the volume of customers. More customers are required for profitability if the user fee is relatively low. Second, as the user fee rises, thereby enabling cost recovery, with each incremental price increase the price burden on customers also rises, and this is likely to constrain access to (effective demand for) sanitation. This is particularly true for children and women, who also bear the higher burdens of negative social impacts associated with restricted access to sanitation (Owusu 2010).

While it is conventional and intuitive to suggest that too many users at individual sites create unsanitary conditions and site maintenance problems, it is important to note that unregulated market mechanics are likely to have the adverse implications of there being too few users at a site. As Respondent KJ noted:

> When the first people started [to operate privatized toilet sites] the rumour went around that there was a lot of money in it, so people started to put up the public toilets, but it is not that good.

Respondent AB suggested the same: 'The customers are low, toilets are now too many. Previously it was not like this.'

This is important because although the average site is operating well above the break-even point, approximately 30 per cent of the sample reported being in potential danger of having to either raise user fees or dip below the revenue necessary to cover costs. This is a source of anxiety for these toilet owners, and is expressed in the sense that owners generally feel as though competition for toilet customers is rising. Respondent DA estimated that her customers were cut in half when a new toilet site opened very near hers. She expects she will have to raise her user fees soon if she is to remain in business. This underlines the political nature of many toilet sites, because it is common for respondents to describe how local party bosses will erect competing toilets near existing ones as a common form of political retribution when they are unable to evict a current toilet manager.

Currently the AMA does not regulate the location or distribution of public toilet facilities in an effective way. The narrative of the market suggests that under normal conditions we can presume that entrepreneurs will build new toilets as long as there are profits to be made. Eventually, it is thought, equilibrium will be reached, when there is an optimal number of sites at a cost users are satisfied with. Counter to the expectations of the market narrative, this situation is likely to continue to create considerable social costs. Approximately a third of the sample are performing poorly and in danger of dipping below the break-even point. Some 'weeding out' will be positive, as those with uncompetitive cost structures or poor management skills will exit the sector or more likely sell their sites to those who can run them more profitably. However, there is also the real possibility that increasing competition will apply downward pressure on the overall quality of service for these sites. We know from the above analysis that basic requirements should continue to be met by any site that remains open even with increasing competition; managers will have to perform basic maintenance such as emptying the waste holding tanks. However, under increasing competition, many could remain open while sacrificing the sanitary conditions required for public health, such as cleaning, offering hand-washing stations, or affording acceptable levels of privacy to users. This scenario would constrain access to sanitation because people who depend on public toilets would either have fewer options because of the rising costs, or the worsening conditions of the sites would encourage more open defecation.

Opportunities for innovation and improvement

The unregulated market-oriented context allows for too much political interference and simultaneously introduces unhelpful forms of competition into the provision of public toilets. These issues no doubt have negative impacts on the lives of the citizens of Accra. That said, the data also suggest that even in the current system there is room for improved outcomes. The key is in creating scenarios that better tie the provision of these services to the desires and preferences of citizen users. In other words, there is room within the existing service provision structure to amplify the decisions of urban citizens and their impact on the evolution of those structures through the exercise of choice.

The following exchange between the researcher and Respondent DO is informative:

JH: What then is the most important challenge [operating your public toilet site]?

DO: The most important challenge is when people come they will enter your toilet and see how it is. If it is clean then you will get more customers because nobody would like to go where there is smell. If a person comes here twice and sees your place is good – where he was going, he can stop it there. We also make our toilet so that you can't get any sickness.

JH: What are the things you have to do to make it a place where people want to come? What are people looking for?

DO: The spray [chemical disinfectants]; and that the workers are washing it; and that there are not rubbers [plastic bags full of faeces]; and that there is water to wash your hands.

Another respondent, NO, expressed a similar sentiment: 'If the place is not organized, the person can go in, see it, and go on to the next place.' Her comment was in the context of discussing common conditions at public toilets, and she euphemistically described faeces on the floor as being 'not organized'. If customers find such conditions, they can go to the next public toilet.

The preferences of the people described by the toilet managers are intuitive and likely to be universal. While these preferences should have important connections to the way businesses operate, currently these links are often quite weak. While the above interaction is indicative of toilet operators who are in a position to seek greater profits through an increase in user volume, the two forces of the unregulated market dynamics explored above undermine these connections considerably. That is, the current context has both too little market logic, whereby many sites are operated for political purposes to the detriment of the site's cost structure, and too much market logic, where increasing unregulated competition is likely to have pernicious effects. The preferences of users are lost among the din.

Innovative solutions are required to restore that link in the existing context. Mainstream development efforts have attempted to restore links by strengthening the 'long' and the 'short' route to improved services (World Bank 2003). This is a call for both improved client connections to service providers (short route) and citizen connections to those that create the policy context in which service providers operate (the long route). While these are worthy long-term goals, they are predicated on robust and transparent regulatory regimes in places that have had little such experience. Further, they are likely to reduce active citizenship to clientism. The pro-poor sanitation literature cited above is in some ways similar in its calls for more appropriate technology, the short route, and more responsive governance, the long route. These points are well taken, but neither camp's conception of the long or the short route will be successful if prescriptions include one-size-fits-all plans. Instead, service provision in contested contexts is far more likely to follow unpredictable or untamed paths guided by innumerable local negotiations, where individuals interact with social structures to co-create iterative change. The key is to amplify individual agency in these negotiations.

In Accra, the link to give individuals more power in iterative negotiations with service providers might come through certain types of specified intervention. These interventions must be careful not to interfere with the cost recovery logic or the need for owners to remain competitive by offering services customers want; this would ignore the everyday mechanics of toilet provision in the context. This rules out actively investing in new toilet sites without a deliberate spatial strategy. Also inappropriate are efforts to mandate a constant low rate or direct subsidy of the toilet owners' cost structure in order to keep fees low. Direct subsidies that do not connect sanitation provision to user preferences miss the point, and mandated fees below the cost recovery point would be self-defeating.

Instead, solutions could enable toilets to become more competitive by linking subsidies or in-kind solutions that are directly related to offering increasingly hygienic services where the cost of those services can remain stable for users. Experience has shown that regulatory bodies that might ostensibly oversee these activities are often weak or inept. Other ways are possible in this context because the sanitation crisis in Accra is in the midst of dynamic change, whereby the supply and demand aspects of sanitation are transforming. That human waste is seen as a valued resource means new revenue streams are available in the sanitation sector (Murray and Ray 2010). There is potential to use these new revenues to reinvest in toilet sites in a manner that is directly related to daily realities.

For instance, social enterprises that are currently profitably reusing effluent for fuel or fertilizer, whose mission it is to improve access to sanitation and promote sustainability, could reinvest in toilet sites in ways that increase the cleanliness and competitiveness of sites. This could be done, for example, through partnerships with cleaning supply companies, and by helping sites source consistent fresh water supplies. These might be subsidies, but they are connected to the ability of providers to provide services to users and not directly to the cost structure of a site, and therefore they are not capturable as profit without improving service provision.

An active civil society in neighbourhoods that rely on public toilets is an important force in the connection between the operation of public toilets and people's everyday desires for how they are provided. It is important to note that Old Fadama is the lowest-income neighbourhood from which the sample of toilet sites were drawn. The whole neighbourhood has insecure tenure, the area regularly floods, it is adjacent to the city landfill site, and it is largely untouched by the city's infrastructure. However, organizations such as the Federation of the Urban Poor, People's Dialogue on Human Settlements, and Slum Dwellers International are active there, and their activists are the community leaders and residents of Old Fadama. One of the key informants for this study was a resident of Old Fadama and an employee of the Federation of the Urban Poor. He described how in Old Fadama the group has had some success organizing to manage several toilets and bring pressure on the AMA for greater responsiveness in terms of toilet inspections and the provision of disinfectant services. Within the sample, toilet sites in Old Fadama reported much higher rates of AMA responsiveness. This type of social organization will be required to apply pressure to force the connection between new revenue streams for sanitation providers and improved services.

A coalition of social enterprises and civil society organizations could establish a 'toilet users' bill of rights', which acknowledges the profitability of public toilets and 'certifies' certain sites according to community standards and acceptable user fees, thereby making certified toilets more profitable through increased usage. This solution would work in conjunction with a social enterprise or a strictly for-profit entity as waste reuser. In either case, toilet sites would be likely to get new revenue streams and/or positive income effects, and it will require an engaged civil society along with customer demands that make sure profits are reinvested in ways that improve the user experience. It is possible that such action could help bring about the desired connection between user preferences and governance, for which the mainstream and pro-poor scholarship both call. A re-engaged public sector, after recognizing the potential in evolving systemic change, could tie new taxation opportunities to resources for better regulation of hygienic standards.

Conclusion

The manner in which sanitation is provided for approximately 40 per cent of Accra's population raises significant questions about its largely unregulated market-oriented strategy. It leaves too much room for political interference, which on the one hand lowers user fees at many sites below what is needed to maintain those sites at hygienic levels while also building new sites for patronage rewards that dilute the customer base of existing sites. Also, without a spatial strategy that requires submetro administrators to target where new private or AMA sites are located, how many sites overall are provided, and whom those sites are likely to serve, the cost structure of all sites is threatened, as are larger socio-ecological and public health goals. Taken together, basic sanitation service provision is unhelpfully disconnected from users' preferences, and the space for individual choices and collective agency to impact the structure and outcomes of service provision is too limited. This chapter has made suggestions about how to improve service provision in the midst of these challenges through tying future interventions directly to the competitive advantage of toilet sites based on user preferences.

The larger narratives surrounding sanitation in Accra and places like it seek to explain these situations through wide-angle and often tidy descriptions of how cities work. These narratives do not anticipate the complicated realities of daily life in real places (Scott 1998). This is true of the classic neoliberal approach as well as the critical response. The intent here is not to provide another set of one-size-fits-all recommendations. Instead, the suggestion is that in any socio-technical service provision configuration there are likely to be opportunities to amplify the voice of citizens through both individual choices and collective agency toward more equitable and sustainable outcomes. This requires a greater eye for detail and an appreciation for diversity and the messiness of innovative socio-ecological problem-solving.

Notes

1 Korboe *et al.* (1999) was a study of Kumasi, Ghana's second city. It is used here only to provide an estimate of the magnitude of sanitation user fees relative to household income.
2 For a more complete discussion of these debates see Allen, Hofmann and Griffiths (2008).

References

Allen, A. Hofmann, P. and Griffiths, H. 2008. Moving down the ladder: governance and sanitation that works for the urban poor. In *IRC Symposium: Sanitation for the Urban Poor Partnerships and Governance*, pp. 19–21. Delft, Netherlands: IRC.
Awortwi, N. 2006. Technology and institutional arrangements in the delivery of public sanitation and solid waste services in Ghanaian cities. *International Journal of Technology Management and Sustainable Development*, 5(3): 213–24.
Ayee, J. and Crook, R. 2003. 'Toilet wars': urban sanitation services and the politics of public-private partnerships in Ghana, Working Paper 213, Brighton, UK: Institute of Development Studies (IDS).
Bel, G. and Warner, M. 2008. Does privatization of solid waste and water services reduce costs? A review of empirical studies. *Resources, Conservation and Recycling*, 52(12): 1337–48.
Bob-Milliar, G. 2012. Political party activism in Ghana: factors influencing the decision of the politically active to join a political Party. *Democratization*, 19(4): 668–9.

Bourdieu, P. 1977 *Outline of a Theory of Practice*. Cambridge: Cambridge University Press.

Burra, S. 2003. Community-designed, built and managed toilet blocks in Indian cities. *Environment and Urbanization*, 15(2): 11–32.

Castro, J. 2007. Poverty and citizenship: sociological perspectives on water services and public–private participation. *Geoforum*, 38(5).

Chenoweth, J. 2004. Changing ownership structures in the water supply and sanitation sector. *Water International*, 29(2): 138–47.

Cross, P. and Morel, A. 2005. Pro-poor strategies for urban water supply and sanitation services delivery in Africa. *Water Science and Technology*, 51(8).

Government of Ghana. 2010. *National Environmental Sanitation Strategy Action Plan 2010–2015*. Accra: Government of Ghana.

Gutiérrez, E. 2007. Delivering pro-poor water and sanitation services: the technical and political challenges in Malawi and Zambia. *Geoforum*, 38(5): 886–900.

Jaglin, S. 2014. Regulating service delivery in Southern cities. In S. Parnell and S. Oldfield (eds), *The Routledge Handbook on Cities of the Global South*. New York and Abingdon, UK: Routledge.

Jankowska, M., Weeks, J. and Engstrom, R. 2012. Do the most vulnerable people live in the worst slums? A spatial analysis of Accra, Ghana. *Annals of GIS*, 17(4): 221–35.

Korboe, D. and Diaw, K. with Devas, N. 1999. Kumasi, Urban Governance, Partnership and Poverty Working Paper 10. Birmingham, UK: International Development Department, School of Public Policy, University of Birmingham.

Libralato, G., Ghirardini, A. and Avezzù, F. 2012. To centralise or to decentralise: an overview of the most recent trends in wastewater treatment management. *Journal of Environmental Management*, 94(1): 61–8.

Murray, A. and Ray, I. 2010. Commentary: back-end users: the unrecognized stakeholders in demand-driven sanitation. *Journal of Planning Education and Research*, 30(1): 94–102.

Mustafa, D. and Reeder, P. 2009. 'People is all that is left to privatize': water supply privatization, globalization and social justice in Belize City, Belize. *International Journal of Urban and Regional Research*, 33(3): 789–808.

Nance, E. and Ortolano, L. 2007. Community participation in urban sanitation: experiences in Northeastern Brazil. *Journal of Planning Education and Research*, 26(3): 284–300.

Nunan, F. and Satterthwaite, D. 2001. The influence of governance on the provision of urban environmental infrastructure and services for low-income groups. *International Planning Studies*, 6(4): 409–26.

Obeng-Odoom, F. 2013. *Governance for Pro-Poor Urban Development: Lessons from Ghana*. New York: Routledge.

Olivier de Sardan, J.-P. 2010. Local governance and public goods in Niger. APPP Working Paper no. 10. London: Overseas Development Institute (ODI).

Owusu, G. 2010. Social effects of poor sanitation and waste management on poor urban communities: a neighborhood-specific study of Sabon Zongo, Accra. *Journal of Urbanism*, 3(2): 145–60.

Owusu, G. and Agyei-Mensah, S. 2011. A comparative study of ethnic residential segregation in Ghana's two largest cities, Accra and Kumasi. *Population and Environment*, 32(4): 332–52.

Paterson, C., Mara, D. and Curtis, T. 2007. Pro-poor sanitation technologies. *Geoforum*, 38(5): 901–7.

Prasad, N. 2006. Privatisation results: private sector participation in water services after 15 years. *Development Policy Review*, 24(6): 669–92.

Rodrik, D. 2006. Goodbye Washington consensus; hello Washington confusion. *Journal of Economic Literature*, 44(4): 973–87.

Schouten, M. and Mathenge, R. 2010. Communal sanitation alternatives for slums: a case study of Kibera, Kenya. *Physics and Chemistry of the Earth, Parts A/B/C*, 35(13–14): 815–22.

Scott, J. 1998. *Seeing Like a State: How Certain Schemes to Improve the Human Condition Have Failed*. New Haven, CY: Yale University Press.

Solo, T. 1999. Small-scale entrepreneurs in the urban water and sanitation market. *Environment and Urbanization*, 11(1): 117–31.

World Bank. 1993. *World Development Report: 1994 Infrastructure for Development*. Washington, DC: World Bank.

—— 2003. *World Development Report 2004: Making Services Work for Poor People*. Washington, DC: World Bank.

—— 2010. *City of Accra, Ghana Consultative Citizens' Report Card*. Washington, DC: World Bank.

Yeboah, I. 2006. Subaltern strategies and development practice: urban water privatization in Ghana. *Geographical Journal*, 172(1): 50–65.

Zaki, S. and Amin, T. 2009. Does basic services privatisation benefit the urban poor? Some evidence from water supply privatisation in Thailand. *Urban Studies*, 46(11): 2301–27.

Part III
Disrupting hegemonic planning

Part III brings together a set of chapters that discuss from various perspectives the problematic and often contradictory role of urban planning processes and mechanisms within rapidly changing cities around the world.

Chapter 11 by Natalie Rosales (Mexico) – entitled 'Walking the path to urban sustainability: what is still missing in current urban planning models?' – examines the recent history of planning approaches, outlining conceptual shifts in contemporary urban planning. This includes the shift from technocratic approaches towards the emergence of a number of overlapping concepts which all promote a greater level of human engagement in the planning process, including 'advocacy planning', a greater focus on environmental issues, and a desire for more 'livable cities'. Drawing on a case study of Mexico City, the chapter explores the continued role of power and vested interests in the planning process, despite official shifts to more inclusive approaches. Rosales concludes by outlining the necessity of commitment by all actors to the promotion of sustainable urbanization.

Titled 'Are you really listening to me? Planning *with* the community in urban revitalization projects', Chapter 12 by Mintesnot Woldeamanuel (Ethiopia) and José Palma (USA) analyses the contradictions between urban planning as a process that promotes urban competitiveness, and the right to housing. The chapter draws on theories of public participation, such as 'community planning'. While recognizing the potential of such an approach, it also highlights the difficulty of promoting it in practice. This is outlined through examples from the global North and global South of large-scale evictions, which are often carried out in the name of the 'common good'. The authors conclude with a call for government to recognize the shortcomings of a neoliberal approach to urban planning practice.

Chapter 13 by Franklin Obeng-Odoom (Ghana) – entitled 'Sustainable urban development: a Georgist perspective' – examines the potential of applying such perspective to contemporary debates on land reform. Based on the work of nineteenth-century theorist Henry George, the chapter outlines the potential for land being returned to public use as a means of promoting sustainable urbanization. Although this is not to be achieved through the nationalization of land but through the taxation of land rent, land rent is seen as an interim solution, with the end-goal being the return of land for common usage through decommodification. While examining some of the potential pitfalls of such an approach, Obeng-Odoom argues that the Georgist notion that urban land should be shared by the commons has the potential to become a key element in the promotion of sustainable urban planning practice.

In Chapter 14 – entitled 'Beyond an imaginary of power? Governance, supranational organizations and "just" urbanization' – Philip Lawton (Ireland) examines framings of the 'just city' and the 'right to the city' in the context of policy frameworks advocated by supranational organizations such as UN-HABITAT and the European Commission. In examining the extent to which ideals of 'rights' and 'justice' are already central to such organizations, the chapter analyses both the potentials and the pitfalls of their incorporation into planned interventions. Lawton calls for a shift from imaging the ideal city based on imaginaries of fixed spatial outcomes (such as high-density living, transit-oriented planning and green landscapes) to a vision that focuses on just social processes and their impacts on people's everyday lives.

11 Walking the path to urban sustainability

What is still missing in current urban planning models?

Natalie Rosales

Theories, ideas and concepts around sustainable urban planning

Moving from planning theories to sustainability approaches

Our changing environment has increased the complexity of urban phenomena and the environment we inhabit. This means that urban planners are increasingly confronted with the challenge of how to deal with polycrisis: that is, a nested set of social, economic and environmental crises. That can take the form of rapid urbanization; shrinking and ageing cities; climate change and related disasters; sprawl and peri-urbanization, ecological overshots, poverty and informality among others (UN-Habitat 2009).

In this scenario, there are cities confronted with the redevelopment, regeneration and renewal of existing urban fabric which have suffered from abandonment and decay, while others are dealing with rapid urbanization processes that are creating vast areas growing inorganically with insufficient urban services and equipment.

Massive urban development projects, driven by government and private partnerships, have developed intelligent buildings, communication networks and sophisticated green infrastructure, creating isolated areas of prosperity and development. At the same time, local actors and communities are embarking on emergent projects that are less dependent on traditional planning interventions to improve urban conditions by transforming difficult sites, deprived zones and conflicted areas through alternative forms of delimiting and using spaces, often through unexpected and untamed actions and spontaneous uses.

It seems as if the aforementioned phenomenon of complex urban contexts in transition is squeezed in opposite directions. New answers are needed and indeed provided by new players, as traditional actors adapt their patterns, to respond to the mentioned challenges. So contrast, indeterminacy, multiplicity and simultaneity could be some of the notions that best describe the characteristics of these diverse, interconnected, ever-changing urban processes that occur at different scales, and worldwide.

In this context, the last three decades have seen a significant shift in planning theory. In broad terms, an important series of changes can be traced during a relatively short period: mainstream approaches to planning appeared to have shifted from a rational comprehensive perspective, to calls for 'advocacy planning', and more recently to a focus on collaborative and transformative planning. Such evolution has also been marked by the ascendance of the so-called 'sustainable development' paradigm (Ward 2002).

It is the aim of this chapter to contribute to the overall intention of the book by generating productive disruptions in the way we approach and interrogate urban change. While engaging with the notions of untamed urbanisms, the chapter examines how the implementation of hegemonic narratives of 'sustainability policy' through urban planning, are in effect taming the way in which the city is and should be produced. I argue that these narratives preclude possibilities to advance a strong sustainability perspective on cities that recognizes the vital role of environmental ethics, human rights, shared values, social responsibility and justice (Girard 2007).

Contrary to past planning models based on technical rationality as the grounding of knowledge, the examination of contemporary literature shows that planning theory has been re-conceptualized by ideas associated with the reframing of its processes, the analytical tools for decision-making, the role of planners, and planning practice as a means for social transformation (Friedman 1992; Fainstein 2000; Sandercock 1998; Ward 2002; Innes and Booher 2010). As a result, urban planning theories, in general, appear to be moving towards the promotion of solutions to achieve improvements in the quality of human life, while assuming conflict, instability, tension, uncertainty and imbalances as inextricable conditions of urban systems (Fainstein 2000).

Another pressing issue affecting urban planning in the last few decades has to do with the increasing recognition of the importance of degradation and pollution of the environment as a topic for discussion in social, political and economic scenarios, accompanied by the arrival of a new paradigm of development that encompasses economic, social and environmental aspects in a cross-generational perspective facing the urban Anthropocene.

In this context, the sustainable development debate has become a protagonist among new urban discourses, calling upon a more critical and reflexive attitude across all actors involved in the city fabric to generate both a new understanding of urban development, and different solutions on how to advance socio-environmental change.

Therefore, current debates on urban planning are increasingly being framed through the recognition of the interrelation between the emergence of new theoretical perspectives related to urban planning procedures, social transformations and the city as a liveable space (Lang 2000), as well as the importance of sustainable development, as a predominant discourse for socio-environmental change. This in turn has resulted on the propagation of conceptualizations linked to the notions of diversity, inclusion, equity, democracy, consensus-building, justice and environmental ethics throughout planning circles (Sandercock 1998).

As a Mexican researcher and practitioner participating in the contemporary dialogue of city-building, I have witnessed how this interrelation has shaped a new urban agenda for sustainable cities and a variety of urban planning policy packages both in my country and worldwide. However, the examination of recent planning practices in the context of Mexico City shows that these ideals may have had limited impact. This city, like many others, shows no evidence of becoming substantively more sustainable in social, ecological or economic terms. Therefore, planning still faces the challenge of doing more than merely coping with urban problems through land use regulations or enhanced market incentives. In practice, 'sustainable urban planning' has become activated via a series of stereotypical interventions that are still based on problem-solving and 'one-size-fits-all' blueprint thinking – all of which are collected in a set of new policies within outdated schemes that minimize and reduce their transformative potential towards an alternative and sustainable urbanism.

So, I consider that even when some sustainability narratives – defined as paradigms which anchor environmental sustainability issues with the physical form of cities and regions, because of the association between vehicular travel and mobility patterns with greenhouse gases, climate change and urban environmental quality – may be interrelated with planning for urban sustainability perspectives, they have not yet managed to transform urbanism. By the latter, I mean that we still face significant challenges in the way we conceptualize cities and the way we build them, in order to turn the existing urban environment into an enriched sustainable urban fabric. This specific question sets me off into an exploration on the shortcomings of current sustainable planning models.

With this aim in mind, this chapter reflects on the discrepancies between sustainable urban planning theory and development practice. Drawing from recent discussions on planning theories that critique mainstream planning, the chapter examines the divergences between professional discourses of planning and municipally adopted plans and the actions implemented to achieve these sustainability objectives and goals under real circumstances. In order to carry out this analysis I revised the main procedural documents and practices adopted at state level between 2007 and 2012, in which the Mexico City government introduced sustainable urban development values through the dissemination of planning concepts and new procedural instruments, with the view of creating a 'new urban order'.

Additionally, the chapter examines how the gap between theory and practice might be closed and outlines a new perspective to address the shortfalls of current sustainable urban planning.

Planning concepts and perspectives emerging from sustainability narratives

From the publication of the Brundtland Report in the 1980s, and the United Nations Conference on Environment and Development ('Rio Summit') in 1992, to the most recent Conference on Rio +20 in 2012, the debate about the role of cities in addressing global environmental problems, as well as their challenges and opportunities to achieve sustainable development, have been integral to urban policy discussions worldwide.

New approaches and perspectives going from the local to the global level, or from strong (biocentric, ecocentric) to weak sustainability (anthropocentric), have evolved since then (Archibuji and Nijkamp 1989; Pearce and Turner 1990), and new terms have certainly emerged and become rapidly popularized – such as 'eco urbanism', 'sustainable cities', 'eco villages', 'sustainable communities', 'resilient cities', 'green cities', 'eco cities', 'sustainable urbanization', 'sustainable urban development' and so on – all of which have contributed to disseminating the notion that planning and urban form are crucial to urban sustainability.

The pursuit of sustainability as a central aspect of contemporary urban planning has, then, revitalized urban and regional planning objectives to different extents worldwide, by introducing concepts like compact urban form and transit-oriented development, low carbon cities, food sensitive planning, urban resource efficiency, energy urban planning and planning for urban resilience, just to name a few (FAO 2000; Allen and You 2002; Morgan 2009; Jabareen 2006; UN Habitat 2007; Owens 1986; Polèse and Stren 2000; Davoudi 2012; Jenks *et al.* 2000; Bulkeley *et al.* 2010; Wheeler 2013; Pickett *et al.* 2004; Donovan *et al.* 2011; Birch and Wachter 2008).

In this context, the centrality gained in recent years by the notion of sustainable urban development, which has been endorsed by local, state and national government agencies in Mexican planning circles, has been influential in driving new concerns in planning exercises in Mexico City, such as citizen participation, a competitive and inclusive economy, urban environment, environmental protection, political reforms to impulse the right to the city, equity, security and justice, and a new urban order to address efficient services and quality of life for all (Gobierno del Distrito Federal 2001a). The debate around these matters has been a key factor to address environmental concerns, and has contributed – at least in appearance – to refreshing urban planning objectives, and to promoting different urban development schemes and more participatory ways of managing the city.

For example, this shift has triggered the emergence of new participatory spaces for governments, social groups, networks and organizations (the Mexico City Urban Sustainable Development Council, green forums, and sustainable development and inter sectorial commissions, among others) (Secretaria de Desarrollo Urbano y Vivienda 2009; Gobierno del Distrito Federal 2007c). These spaces have, in principle, opened the possibility to debate the challenges that cities and their populations within Mexico are facing on all fronts, how sustainability can be conceptualized within the city context and the growth potential of the city according to its ecological viability.

However, in practice, although Mexico City has adopted urban sustainability rhetoric in its policies and plans by adding the term 'sustainable' to a myriad of existing planning documents (e.g. urban sustainable development master plan, sustainable urban model, urban sustainable development, sustainable economic development, sustainable transportation planning), it is hard to find any evidence of what planning for sustainability might mean in concrete terms.

In contrast, planning models leading to plans and projects which could be implemented to bring sustainable changes have been reduced to strategies, often unwittingly, by the dominance of certain readings of sustainability such as the economic perspective which postulates growth, productivity in the use of resources, and competitiveness as the basis for prosperity of human and ecological systems in the city (World Bank 2000; OECD 1996); or the social, which emphasizes the role of management and urban governance to address poverty and environmental degradation and its impact on human health and quality of life (Stren 1995; UNHabitat 2002; Banister 2002; Hardoy *et al.* 1992). These approaches were favoured at the expense of the ecological perspective, in which sustainability is seen as feedback processes maintaining a dynamic equilibrium similar to the one on ecosystems (Tjallingii 1995; Girardet 1990; Bettini 1998; Rueda 1995).

In the context of Mexico City, programmes and planning instruments to guide urban development and land use have been only updated by integrating a limited extent of urban sustainability notions in the diagnosis, and some environmental sustainability objectives and strategic lines on ecological land use, liveability and public space, water, mobility, air, waste, energy and climate change (Gobierno del Distrito Federal 2007a, 2007b; Comisión Ambiental Metropolitana 2010) that have merely resulted on the 'greening' of urban planning.

So far, planning efforts in Mexico City to move towards sustainable urban planning, such as 'neighbourhood decision making' or 'pocket parks' are still deployed on the basis of outdated procedures and normative instruments embedded in routinized practices based on linear sequences, including integration of a thematic agenda, elaboration of diagnosis, image objective, strategy, the development of the plan, public consultation, shipping and approval of the plan by the general assembly, publishing, and the dissemination and application of the initiatives established.

Therefore, it can be argued that the actual practice of urban sustainable planning in Mexico City, as in other cities, still confronts surmountable challenges, such as how to integrate economic development, environmental protection and social justice domains, issues that usually overlap, in an usually extended Metropolitan area. As a result, planning officials tend to overlook complex urban phenomena, as a whole, disaggregating sectorial policies and actions for social exclusion, poverty, uncontrolled urban sprawl, pollution, and unsustainable consumption of land, water and other natural resources.

In order to scrutinize this argument, the sections that follow in this chapter examine the multidimensional forms in which theoretical debate on sustainability has been embedded in recent urban planning practices in Mexico City and their limitations.

Planning in Mexico City: understanding the shortcomings of sustainable urban planning

Drafting sustainability: Government discourse and planning documents

As mentioned before, in recent years Mexico City government has promoted urban sustainable development values through a range of projects aiming to create a 'new urban order', sustainable mobility and environmental protection and conservation. As we examine the discourse surrounding the 2006–12 General Development City Program, we find that planning documents advocate a more sustainable urban model by 'establishing a compact city, which facilitates mobility, strengthens the community, and improves the quality of urban life while respecting the regenerative capacity of ecosystems that guarantee sustainability' (Gobierno del Distrito Federal 2007c).

This discursive style for a sustainable city stated in planning instruments has served as a framework for urban policies, action, plans and investment projects for restructuring urban space. As such, it appears to be mainly aligned with an economic approach to sustainability and has been coupled with operative watchwords, such as reducing urban sprawl through the adoption of 'compact city' principles, low-carbon technologies, and the promotion of urban competitiveness.

As a result, to foster the city to a sustainable development path, actions which have been undertaken by Mexico City's government in recent years have involved the revitalization of economically depressed areas of the city, the recovery and renovation of public spaces, transport and infrastructure investments, and environmental protection.

These actions are based on the idea that promoting economic development and linking urban development patterns with environmental protection will make a more efficient use of economic, social and environmental resources. The City government considers these policies will reverse the processes that have affected the quality of life in Mexico City and will also make the city more competitive at regional and international levels (Gobierno del Distrito Federal 2007a). Even more, based on their applied notion of sustainability, policy officials are convinced of the policy impact on development and sustainability.

Consequently, implemented actions to create a 'new urban order' mostly focus on strategic economic projects to deploy urban revitalization, renewal and restoration of historic monuments, recovery of public spaces, pedestrianisation, green areas enhancement, street furniture and accessibility improvement (Gobierno del Distrito Federal 2007b).

The main objective of building 'a new urban order', through establishing the compact city, has been supported by some other multi-sectorial strategies to promote 'inclusive and sustainable mobility'. These strategies have mainly involved the promotion of environmentally friendly transport, which includes a bus rapid transit system (Metrobus system), a low carbon corridor, consisting of tram lines, and the replacement of taxis and mini buses by less polluting units; non-motorized mobility transport options (walking and cycling lanes, and an individual bicycling programme); and new road infrastructure that consist in building flyovers and freeways to double the road capacity (Gobierno del Distrito Federal 2010).

When it comes to actions to promote environmental sustainability, efforts have focused on three main activities: ecosystem protection and conservation; the aforementioned environmentally friendly transport initiatives, and environmental law enforcement. These included the ecological restoration of urban canyons and rivers that go across the city, policies for zero growth of informal settlements on ecological land use (Allen 2014), reinforced by a special environmental police body for the surveillance and closing down of illegal constructions in ecological areas, thus preventing the growth of informal settlements on ecological and rural land use, and to carry out routine patrols to monitor and prevent sites with the highest incidence of illegal logging and water pollution; and a myriad of monetary compensatory measures for environmental services intended to preserve ecological areas of the remaining agrarian communities around Mexico DF (ibid.).

Yet, while the effectiveness of the actions described in this section is still to be tested, in many ways they have illustrated a governmental recognition from the local to the national level of the need to transform planning through the adoption of more effective instruments for achieving sustainable urban development. This has led to renovated planning exercises and documents that claim that the approach implemented amounts to putting sustainable urban planning into practice, though the actions implemented to achieve sustainability objectives and goals remain elusive.

In many ways, it seems so far that sustainability has pushed professional organizations and other stakeholders to rethink practices, values, and methods of governing the city in a 'better' way that prioritises new policies which incorporate spatial frameworks and urban planning approaches for more sustainable urban form(s).

This is reinforced by the complexity of urban challenges Mexico City faces, such as informal settlements, urban sprawl, megalopolization, urban disorder and lawlessness, gentrification, pollution and unsustainable consumption of natural resources, ecological overshot, and decreased quality of life and liveability in the city, which combine aspects of environmental degradation, urban poverty, vulnerability, and inequalities in growth distribution and governance schemes. All these aspects suggest that urban sustainable planning should do better in evening up social, environmental, economic, territorial and institutional dimensions, and promote real possibilities for moving in progressive directions towards a sustainable development.

However, freeways construction to mitigate traffic congestion, environmental policing bodies to prevent the growth of informal settlements on ecological and rural land use, limited participation to promote new governance schemes, and planning process with little regard either to political conflict or to the specific character of the terrain on which it is working do not easily add up to a sustainable planning paradigm.

When examining the rhetoric of sustainable urban planning adopted by the government in the main planning documents produced to regulate the city's development, it is clear to me that some sustainable narratives have won the battle of public ideas and have contributed to creating some changes in Mexico City. However, it is less clear how the actions implemented have the capacity to address complex, rapidly changing socio-environmental problems resulting from interdependencies among socio-spatial imbalances and the uneven distribution of growth, while drawing communities into a transformative process that will address a common understanding, acceptance and ongoing commitment to make significant changes towards a sustainable future.

So far, I have considered the focus adopted by Mexico's governmental planning agencies towards sustainable urban planning, which has not led to a meaningful integration of sustainable development ideals into planning endeavours. First, sustainability notions still remain far from overcoming the limitations of mainstream planning models and perspectives to understand cities and regions not just as economic systems, or static inventories of natural resources, but also as socio-environmental systems.

Second, planning mechanisms (e.g. land use regulations, master plans, urban development programmes) have not moved towards more flexible procedural and contextual instruments to enable negotiated outcomes rather than just regulation. So even when planning processes have incorporated new instruments and existing procedural instruments have been embedded with sustainability objectives (e.g. Programa general de desarrollo del Distrito Federal, Programa de Desarrollo Urbano del Distrito Federal, Programas Delegacionales y Parciales de Desarrollo Urbano, Programa Sectorial de Medio Ambiente del Distrito Federal y el Programa sectorial de movilidad y transporte) they do not foster collaborative approaches that encompass integrative, transdisciplinary and inclusive perspectives of social actors and their contexts, or the appropriate means for launching sustainability priorities and integrating ordinary citizens in the city's development.

Example of the above are the policies for zero growth of informal settlements on ecological land use, already mentioned, or the attempts to green the planning process in Mexico City through a Green Forum held in 2007 to support a participatory planning exercise which presented possible measures to solve environmental problems facing the city. In this Forum, citizens inputs were limited to expressing their opinion about various policies and environmental measures that had already been approved and programmed.

Actually, some measures implemented in Mexico City caused distrust because of the lack of transparency, dialogue and consensus among many citizens with respect to the real priorities pursued by city authorities, and the fear of just being used to try to legitimize a city development model which serves, primarily, the interests of major developers, while sustainability is usually left behind or used as a background rhetoric. An example of this is an infrastructure project of a speed highway build in 2010 in the south-west of the city, which crosses six areas of environmental value and which was rejected by neighbours and social activists.

Even though Mexico City has an Urban Sustainable Development Council and inter-sectorial commissions to create a favourable institutional context for sustainable development, its government structures have not yet changed to enable horizontal and vertical coordination, and thus a more integrated way of understanding and managing the city. As a result, it can be concluded that implemented city actions adopt a narrow approach on environmental limits, urban–rural flows, socio-spatial segregation, inequality and social and environmental justice. Instead, they appear to focus on promoting the role of the market, to make up what is called a 'good business climate' (Domhoff 2005; Forester 1998) for attracting investment projects, and increasing productivity and competitiveness in a global economy (Harvey 2000), an approach that has clearly prevented a comprehensive analysis of the impact that growth strategies and investment have on the environment and on local communities.

The assessment of these policies and actions also confirms the persistence of planning approaches based on instrumental rationality, which have not transformed urban planning to a more flexible instrument for governance; nor do they offer solutions to the conflicting interests of the different stakeholders in the urban space, or even enable incremental changes that will set the ground to steer the city towards a sustainable development.

Planning for urban sustainability: bridging the gap between theory and practice

In this section, the discussion will focus on considering planning as an instrument for urban sustainability. According to Friedman (2011), the planning endeavour is about changing situations and societies to move towards conditions more likely to promote human flourishing within the environmental limits rather than the pursuit of material benefits for political and economic elites. This notion of planning is closely related to sustainable development values that embrace the ecological dimension of development, environmental protection, the satisfaction of human needs and aspirations, changes in the distribution of costs and benefits, and the notions of equity and diversity.

Beyond the traditional 'three-legged stool' model of sustainable development, this paradigm of development can provide us with a deeper appreciation of the complexity of urban issues and solutions. Moreover, sustainability knowledge can be a key contributor to reshape our understanding of and ability to act upon a rapidly urbanizing and increasingly unfair world, by embracing the ideas of interdependence, interconnection, integration, change and compromise.

So planning should not just be focused on the promotion of land use regulations, resulting in proposals and urban strategies composed of a large number of disjointed sub-projects, usually resulting in unintended, unanticipated, unsustainable and undemocratic consequences, as discussed in the case of Mexico City. Furthermore, planning should also imply a process: something practised and delivered (Riddel 2004). This endeavour should involve how to achieve transformative development (Sarkissian and Hurford 2010; Innes and Booher 2010; Friedman 2011). Therefore, planning for sustainability must foresee the potential of community building as an ongoing process of transforming the relations between society and nature, and work on alternative urbanism where cities become elements for educating and promoting biophilia (the love of living systems) (Wilson 1984; Beatley 2010) and sustainable values. This entails the broader idea that sustainable planning is not only related to greening cities, but also demands social and environmental justice as an ethical imperative.

Planning for sustainability should be, in sum, about changes in the current parameters of planning systems and structures; to move from being the ultimate taming project of simply rehabilitating, enhancing and maintaining cities' current conditions to an instrument with comprehensive opportunities for a complete integration of the sustainable development paradigm ideals. While the ambitious perspective outlined here could be interpreted as yet another imperative planning narrative, my central contention is that if planning is go beyond the shortfalls of current sustainable urban initiatives, its practice and theorization require a more explicit engagement with the ethical dimension of taming projects and with a reconsideration of the type of political processes that can enable incremental changes that will set the ground for complex transformations and might in turn make a difference between knowing the path and walking the path towards urban sustainability.

References

Allen, A. 2014. 'Peri-urbanization and the Political Ecology of Differential Sustainability.' In Parnell, S. and Oldfield, S. (eds), *A Routledge Handbook on Cities of the Global South*. London: Routledge, pp. 522–38.

Allen, A. and You, N. 2002. *Sustainable Urbanization: Bridging the Green and Brown Agenda*. London: DFID and UN-HABITAT.

Archibuji, F. and Nijkamp, P. 1989. *Economy and Ecology: Towards Sustainable Development*. Netherlands: Klumer Academic Publishers.

Banco Mundial. 2000. *Ciudades en Transición. Estrategia del Banco Mundial para los Gobiernos Urbanos y Locales*. Washington Banco Mundial Grupo de Infraestructuras y Desarrollo Urbano.

Banister, D. 2002. Urban sustainability. In Jeroen C. J. M. van den Bergh (ed.), *Handbook of Environmental and Resource Economics*. Cheltenham, UK: Edward Elgar.

Beatley, T. 2010. *Biophilic Cities: Integrating Nature into Urban Design and Planning*. Washington, DC: Island Press.

Bettini, V. 1998. *Elementos de Ecología Urbana*. Madrid: Trotta.

Birch, E. and Wachter, S. (eds). 2008. *Growing Greener Cities: Urban Sustainability in the Twenty-first Century*. Philadelphia, PA: University of Pennsylvania Press.

Bulkeley, H., CastánBroto, V., Hodson, M. and Marvin, S. (eds). 2010. *Cities and Low Carbon Transition*. New York: Routledge.

Campbell, S. 1996. Green cities, growing cities, just cities? Urban planning and the contradictions of sustainable development. *Journal of the American Planning Association*, 62 (3): 296–312.

Comisión Ambiental Metropolitana. 2010. *Agenda de Sustentabilidad Ambiental para la Zona Metropolitana del Valle de México*. Available at http://.www.sma.df.gob.mx/sma/links/download/archivos/asa_zmvm_version_completa.pdf (accessed: 8 February 2011)

Davoudi, S. 2012. Urban resilience: what does it mean in planning practice? *Planning Theory & Practice*, 13(2): 299–333.

Domhoff, W. 2005. *Power at the Local Level: Growth Coalition Theory*. Available at http://www2.ucsc.edu/whorulesamerica/local/growth_coalition_theory.html (accessed 22 April 2014).

Donovan, J., Larsen, K. and McWhinnie, J. 2011. *Food-sensitive Planning and Urban Design: A Conceptual Framework for Achieving a Sustainable and Healthy Food System*. Melbourne: Report commissioned by the National Heart Foundation of Australia (Victorian Division).

Fainstein, S. 2000. New directions in planning theory. *Urban Affairs Review*, 35(4): 451–78.

FAO. 2000. *Food for the Cities: A Briefing Guide for Mayors, City Executives and Urban Planners in Developing Countries and Countries in Transition.* Rome: FAO.

Forester, J. 1998. *Planning in the Face of Power.* Berkeley: University of California Press.

Friedman, F. 2011. *Insurgencies: Essays in Planning Theory.* London: Routledge.

Friedman, J. 1992. Planeación para el siglo XXI: el desafío del postmodernismo, *Revista EURE* 18 (55): 128–46.

Girard, F. *et al.* 2007, The human sustainable city: values, approaches and evaluative tools. In Deakin, M., Mitchell, G., Nijkamp, P. and Vreeker, R. (eds), *Sustainable Urban Development Volume 2: The Environmental Assessment Methods.* London: Routledge.

Girardet, H. 1990. *Creating Sustainable Cities.* London: Tilde.

Gobierno del Distrito Federal. 2001. *Programa General de Desarrollo del Distrito Federal 2000–2006.* México: Gaceta Oficial del Distrito Federal-Gobierno del Distrito Federal.

Gobierno del Distrito Federal. 2003. *Programa General de Desarrollo Urbano del Distrito Federal 2003.* México: Gaceta Oficial del Distrito Federal-Gobierno del Distrito Federal.

—— 2007a. *Plan de Acción Climática del Distrito Federal*, Gobierno del Distrito Federal, México,

—— 2007b. *Plan Verde. Acciones de Alto Impacto para una Ciudad con Futuro.* México: Gobierno del Distrito Federal.

—— 2007c. *Programa General de Desarrollo del Distrito Federal 2007–2012.* México: Gaceta Oficial del Distrito Federal-Gobierno del Distrito Federal.

—— 2010. *Programa Integral de Transportes y Vialidad 2010.* México: Gaceta Oficial del Distrito Federal-Gobierno del Distrito Federal.

Hardoy, J., Mitlin D. and Satterthwaire, D. 1992. *Environmental Problems in Third World Cities.* London: Earthscan.

Harvey, D. 2000. *Spaces of Hope.* Berkeley: University of California Press.

Innes, J. and Booher, D. 2010. *Planning with Complexity: An Introduction to Collaborative Rationality for Public Policy.* New York: Routledge.

Jabareen, Y. 2006. Sustainable Urban Forms. Their typologies, models, and concepts. *Journal of Planning Education and Research*, 26: 38–52.

Jenks, M., Burton, K. and Williams, K. (eds). 2000. *Compact Cities: Sustainable Urban Forms for Developing Countries.* New York: Spon Press.

Lang, J. 2000. Learning from the twentieth century urban design paradigms: lessons for the early twenty-first century. In Freestone, R., *Urban Planning in a Changing World: The Twentieth Century Experience.* London: Spon Press.

Morgan, K. 2009. Feeding the city: the challenge of urban food planning. *International Planning Studies*, 14(4): 341–8.

OECD. 1996. *Shaping the Urban Environment in the 21st Century.* Available at http://www.oecd.org/dataoecd/29/7/31621883.pdf (accessed: 12 March 2003).

Owens, S. 1986. *Energy, Planning and Urban Form.* London: Pion Ltd.

Pearce, D. W. and Turner, R. K. 1990. *Economics of Natural Resources and the Environment.* NewYork: Harvester Weathsheaf.

Pickett, S., Cadenasso, M. L. and Grove, J. M. 2004. Resilient cities: meaning, models, and metaphor for integrating the ecological, socio-economic, and planning realms. *Landscape and Urban Planning*, 69(4): 369–84.

Polèse, M. and Stren, R. 2000. *The Social Sustainability of Cities: Diversity and the Management of Change.* Toronto: University of Toronto Press.

Riddel, R. 2004. *Sustainable Urban Planning: Tipping the Balance*. London: Blackwell.

Rueda, S. 1995. *Ecología Urbana*. Barcelona: Beta.

Sandercock, L. 1998. *Towards Cosmopolis*. London: John Willey & Sons.

Sarkissian, W. and Hurford, D. 2010. *Creative Community Planning: Transformative Engagement Methods for Working at the Edge*. London: Earthscan.

Secretaría de Desarrollo Urbano y Vivienda. *Consejo para el Desarrollo Urbano Sustentable de la Ciudad de México*. Available at http://www.seduvi.df.gob.mx/portal/index.php/que-hacemos/planeacion-urbana/conduse/comite-del-conduse (accessed 18 September 2011).

Stren, R. 1995. *World Perspectives on the City, Urban Research in the Developing World*. Vol. 4. Toronto: Centre for Urban & Community Studies, University of Toronto.

Tjallingii, S. 1995. *Ecopolis: Strategies for Ecologically Sound Urban Development*. Leiden: Backhuys Publishers.

UN-HABITAT. 2002. *Sustainable Urbanization: Bridging the Green and Brown Agenda*. Nairobi: UN- Habitat.

——— 2007.*Global Report on Human Settlements 2007: Enhancing Urban Safety and Security*. Nairobi: Ed. UN- Hábitat.

——— 2009. *Global Report on Human Settlements 2009: Planning Sustainable Cities*. Nairobi: UN-Habitat.

Ward, S. V. 2002. *Planning the Twentieth-Century City. The Advanced Capitalist World*. London: John Wiley & Sons.

Wheeler, S. 2013. *Planning for Sustainability: Creating Livable, Equitable and Ecological Communities*, 2nd edn. New York: Routledge.

Wilson, E. 1984. *Biophilia*. Cambridge: Harvard University Press.

World Bank. 2000. *Cities in Transition: World Bank Urban and Local Government Strategy*. Washington, DC: World Bank Infrastructure Group.

12 Are you really listening to me?

Planning *with* the community in urban revitalization projects

Mintesnot Woldeamanuel and José Palma

Introduction

Increased urbanization creates a growing competition for cities to be attractive business destinations. As a result, several major cities are going through the process of urban revitalization, seeking to significantly transform formerly run-down or poor urban areas and create a better socio-economic and physical atmosphere. This approach has become an increasingly common practice in both the global North and the global South. Historical projects such as 'slum clearance in the USA' (Collins and Shester 2009) and current initiatives like 'Slum-Free Lagos'[1] and 'Slum-Free Mumbai' (see Gordon n.d.) are examples. The upshot of such projects has been to exclude the poor from the planning process, to name but one severe shortcoming of such an approach.

The mention of slum settlements means a problem for many cities that would like to be more attractive for businesses. So their local governments are designating land for business purposes without considering the concerns of the people who live on that land. They have focused on economic growth as their objective, claiming that growth-promoting policies result in greater good for the greater population (Fainstein 2010). This in reality is having enormous socio-economic effects on low-income and minority communities (Brunn, Williams and Zeigler 2003). This is a growing problem for many large cities where the majority of the populations are still in poverty (Davis 2007). There are also land-use policies that fail to address these issues, coupled with inconsistent governments failing to take action and to provide sustainable solutions to these issues (Aguilar and Santos 2011). Such land use policies not only fail to address the issues of slum and squatter settlements; in some places land use controls are the means by which community planning achieves social exclusion (Angotti 2008). In *New York for Sale*, Angotti (2008) argues that zoning and land use planning in the city have contributed to the segregation of neighbourhoods by race and class.

One of the severe effects of non-deliberative urban revitalization projects is eviction or displacement, which is common, for example, in Africa and South Asia. Despite several urban social movements that have opposed public and private projects that threaten to displace residents, in most cases displacement is the result of urban revitalization which affects low-income and racial minorities.

Those people evicted are poor, marginalized and have moved from their rural areas into the slums to locate hard-to-find jobs (Ocheje 2007). However, for city planners and managers, there is always a vision of a 'good city', and the vision focuses on easy flow of traffic and beautiful physical spaces. Moreover, these approaches often include the removal and displacement of poor people (Watson 2009a, 2009b).

Such planning ideology fails to recognize the rights of people to housing and a stable, healthy living environment that is free from threats of eviction and displacement (Angotti 2008). Conventional planning rather follows the ideas of neoliberalism, which focuses on market logic and competitive discipline (Purcell 2009). The planning process does not guarantee full participation to slum dwellers. Nevertheless, community involvement is very important in urban planning projects, especially in areas that are connected with urban renewal. It is important because case study after case study demonstrates how government policies, laws and regulations can impact the lives of so many people, particularly those who are forced out of their homes with no notice and no say in the planning process.

The concepts of community planning and public participation, as social justice and democratic processes, are well developed and have been debated for several decades (e.g. Lisk 1980; Arnstein 1969). However, in practice there are several social, economic, ethnic and most importantly political factors that challenge the inclusiveness and participatory nature of community planning. Ideas such as asset-based community development (ABCD) recognize that there are problems with planning agencies' connections with residents, and that real change in communities starts with communication between planners and local stakeholders (Kretzmann and McKnight 1996). The main stakeholders in urban revitalization projects are the people who live in the area being revitalized; therefore the communication must start from the community. The ideas of participatory and deliberative planning can be applied to many nations in which urban renewal projects are tied in with culture, religion, language, race and other factors that make it difficult to make large-scale change (Brunn *et al.* 2003; Stone 1989).

The growing gap between the planning process and the community does not really provide an opportunity for citizen participation. Many urban planners and local government officials seem to overlook the fact that they should be working *with* people, instead of working *for* people. Often, it seems that there is a neoliberal belief that in carrying out urban transformations, governments are helping the poor, and 'the invisible hand' of market decisions will determine economic outcomes that benefit all, including the poor and ethnic minorities (Purcell 2009).

In this chapter we explore the gap between the theories and the practices of participatory planning, focusing on the failure of urban revitalization programmes in the developing world, and gentrification processes in the developed world, to include the community as part of the planning process. Using case studies, we explore the socio-political and economic forces that are responsible for the characterization of people living in blighted areas as a problem to deal with rather than part of the planning process. We also examine the question of why urban upgrading practices have similar outcomes (marginalizing low-income groups and ethnic minorities) in both the developing and the developed world, and how creative and sustainable planning practices could be based on needs assessment, and tapping local resources and knowledge. The implication of participatory planning practices on sustainable urbanization is also highlighted in this chapter.

Public participation in planning: theory and practice

Numerous documents on public involvement agree that there are limited opportunities for the public to get involved in the planning process (e.g. Lane 2005; Munro-Clark 1992; Webber and Crooks 1996). Innes and Booher (2000) claim that, even if there are some opportunities for involvement, the traditional methods of public participation in planning simply do not work because they do not achieve genuine public involvement in planning or decisions, they do not satisfy members of the public that they are being heard, and they do not involve a broad spectrum of the public. These authors continue to argue that traditional public participation often antagonizes the members of the public who do try to work through these methods.

As public participation has become a rather ritualized practice, several scholars and activists keep asking a question: 'Does public participation serve any purpose?' (e.g. Sewell and Coppock 1977). Of course, the extent of public participation in planning is largely determined by the nature of the project, planning and policy. The definition of the planning problem, the kinds of knowledge used in planning practice and the conceptualization of the planning and decision-making context are the important determinants of the extent of participation offered to the public (Lane 2005). Beierle and Cayford state in *Democracy in Practice* that 'involving the public not only frequently produces decisions that are responsive to public values and substantively robust, but it also helps to resolve conflict, build trust, and educate and inform the public about the environment' (2002: 74).

Sherry Arnstein posed an important question in her famous piece 'A ladder of citizen participation' (1969): to what extent do efforts to involve the public make citizen participation meaningful? As Arnstein phrased it, 'there is a critical difference between going through the empty ritual of participation and having the real power needed to affect the outcomes of the process' (1969: 216). She strongly argued that if policy-makers and planners seek public participation, it is necessary that there be a redistribution of power. According to this view, unless citizens have a genuine opportunity to affect outcomes, participation is simply manipulation of participants (Arnstein 1969).

Many classic and contemporary planning concepts follow a non-participant approach. Like any rational comprehensive approach, the planning sequence involves a survey of the area, an analysis of the results and, finally, the development of the plan. However, by the late 1960s new models of planning began to emerge in response to criticisms of the rational-comprehensive approach. According to Innes and Booher (2000), planners and public officials found ways to test public opinion other than the traditional hearings or review-and-comment procedures. They increasingly relied on social science research methods such as public opinion polls, focus groups and other surveys. While these methods give public officials a more representative and accurate understanding of what the public want than the traditional procedures, they are criticized for being detached and scientific (Innes and Booher 2000). These approaches are being practised in several cities in developing nations, but cultural, racial and religious differences between groups in the planning area can make the practice rather difficult (Stone 1989).

A recent public participation approach seems to work better. This involves collaborative groups being set up at the local level in various forms to deal with everything from neighbourhood disputes to building infrastructure or developing a proposal for economic development (De Sousa Briggs 1998). Other types of collaboration have been introduced by public agencies, and engage not only professionals but also citizens in a joint effort to set the direction for their community. Many other initiatives have been started more spontaneously by players in a community (Ostrom 1990). These collaborative efforts involve organized interest groups, individual citizens and government agencies. Community workshops and visioning efforts engage dozens, even hundreds, of citizens in developing long-range aspirations for the community or identifying issues to which they want their elected officials to give priority. This is not to say that such deliberative and communicative planning is not without limitations, but the main limitation lies in lack of creative practices in bringing different perspectives and views to the table.

Practically speaking, in most developing nations, and arguably in some countries of the developed world, public participation is not yet at the level where the people are part of the entire planning process. Planning, in most places, is controlled by the elite who aim to shape the city in their own image (Yiftachel 1998). Researchers have documented the privileged position of the rich, and the deepening deprivation of the poor caused by urban and regional policies. David Harvey's revolutionary work, based mainly on structural analyses of American and British cities, has shown how the modern capitalist state in general, and urban planning in particular, is embedded in the facilitation of capital accumulation, and therefore in the repeated reproduction of class inequalities (Harvey 1973, 1985). This is especially manifested in projects related to urban upgrading and revitalization, where it is common to see a poorly managed planning process result in huge negative socio-economic consequences for the low-income population, including eviction and displacement. The predictable outcome of such practices is the unhealthy and unsustainable functioning of cities.

Blighted areas and urban upgrading: state of the eviction practice

Before discussing urban upgrading it is necessary to talk about what is to be upgraded: slums or blighted areas, sometimes formally designated for housing and sometimes informal. Slums, which are characterized by substandard housing and inadequate facilities, present some of the most pressing urban environmental problems in cities. Overcrowding and insanitary conditions increase the incidence of communicable diseases, such as diarrhoea, tapeworms and tuberculosis, and make infant mortality rates in slums almost as high as in rural areas (Takeuchi *et al.* 2008; Sclar *et al.* 2005). Water quality in slums tends to be poor, and community toilets often overflow. In inner cities of the developed world, blighted areas are characterized by an unappealing physical appearance, high levels of crime and economic disinvestment.

Slum improvement programmes in many countries were really little more than slum clearance – hardly a solution to the problem of lack of adequate affordable housing in cities. For example, in Title I of the National Housing Act of 1949, the US Congress launched an ambitious plan to rid American cities of their slums and to revitalize the economy of city centres. The goals were broad: to reduce 'substandard' housing, which was considered a breeding ground for crime and vice; to stem suburban migration; to invigorate downtown central business districts; to increase local tax revenues through gains in property values; and to encourage new private investment (Collins and Shester 2013; Groberg 1965; Teaford 2000). Over time, however, urban renewal efforts became increasingly controversial. Critics decried the disproportionate impact on poor residents, the use of eminent domain (the right of the government to acquire land for public use or public benefit) to trump private property rights, the destruction of cohesive neighbourhoods, the loss of historic buildings and the aesthetics of the new buildings (Collins and Shester 2013).

In some places the strategy shifted to one of improving and consolidating existing housing, often by providing slum dwellers with security of tenure, combined with the materials needed to upgrade their housing or – in areas where land was plentiful – to build new housing. These improvements might take the form of providing infrastructure services and other forms of physical capital, and also include efforts to foster community management, and access to health care and education. At the same time, some have called for replacing slums with multi-storey housing either on the site of the original slum or in an alternative location (Takeuchi *et al.* 2008).

Several cities in both the developing and the developed world are currently going through a slum clearance programme with the ambitious aim of becoming slum-free cities. The 'Slum-Free Lagos' programme in Nigeria is an ambitious plan to create a world-class Lagos as a competitive city by cleaning slum areas. However, the actions are not without collateral damage. Adam Nossiter wrote on a report in the *New York Times* on 1 May 2013:

> government backhoes came in to slum neighbourhoods on 23 February 2013 and ploughed through 1000 dwelling units, instantly making homeless perhaps 10,000 of Lagos's poorest residents and destroying a decades-old slum, Badia East. For days, residents wandered the chaotic rubble-strewn field, near prime Lagos real estate. They were dazed and angry. Small children slept on the muddy ground. Men climbed the mounds of rubble, searching. In intense heat, women, men and children said they were hungry and sleeping outside. The government had destroyed their present, they said, without making any provision for their future.

Making Lagos slum free, in physical terms, might seem a 'good' thing, but conventional and non-participatory practices of urban renewal have not only proved to be inappropriate to the realities of slum dwellers and of rapid urban growth and limited resources in Nigeria (and indeed in most African countries), but have also intensified the social problems. Slum clearance in Nigeria creates a vicious problem of housing shortage. Since demolition of housing must precede new construction in the project area, the existing stock of housing is decreased, forcing displaced people to seek shelter in the remaining housing in the city or erect squatter housing. This displaces the problem instead of solving it, sending slum conditions from area to area in a spiral process. The only solution is to build new dwelling units for displaced individuals before demolishing their present homes (Ocheje 2007).

In many instances in a variety of cities, forced evictions have taken place and the government has given those affected no compensation. 'Since 2000, over two million people have been forcibly evicted in Nigeria. The evictions have occurred in Lagos, Port Harcourt, and federal capital of Abuja' (Ocheje 2007). The political argument to justify these occurrences is that the aim is to achieve a 'common good' which will benefit the city, country or state as a whole. However, it certainly does not benefit those who live in slum areas if their dwellings are cleared away to make room for public improvement schemes such as new highways. The outcome of these urban revitalization projects is to push low-income groups beyond the city boundaries, and make sure that they do not return because they cannot afford to live in the replacement homes, which are typically designed for middle- and upper-class groups.

In addition, slum clearance creates psychological and environmental damage such as the break-up of social relationships and the upsetting of existing economic systems and opportunities (Dimuna and Omatsone 2010). This is a very good example of the lack of communicative planning and the notion that government and the market know better than the community.

As systematic and institutionalized as it is, there is also a noteworthy contemporary case of large-scale forced eviction in a US city. We are not talking here about the much publicized 1950s slum clearance programmes; it occurred in 2003 in Philadelphia. This destroys any notion that slum clearance ceased to be relevant in the developed world after the 1950s or 1960s. Gentrification – that is, a shift in urban areas toward wealthier residents and/or businesses as property values increase – is affecting many low-income and minority populations in several inner cities across America. The Philadelphia case was featured in a documentary, *All for the Taking* (McCullough, 2005). It described how the US Supreme Court ruled that local governments can use their power of eminent domain, based on the constitution, to forcibly appropriate private property and hand it over to another private owner for the 'public good'. This ruling furthered the widespread abuse of the eminent domain concept all over the country.

On 18 April 2001, the government of the City of Philadelphia approved a Neighbourhood Transformation Initiative (NTI). This project was intended to be one of the most ambitious urban renewal projects in recent Philadelphia history because of the amount of change that would take place in gentrifying blighted areas. The NTI was designed to reverse a 50-year pattern of population decline through urban renewal. By using eminent domain, the city authorized the acquisition of thousands of private homes in the areas designated for transformation, and built up a massive land bank. Many of these homes were owned or rented by the poor and the elderly, and most of them were inhabited by people of colour. Once it had acquired large blocks of land, the city turned to private developers to rebuild (and change) most of its historical neighbourhoods. However, many agree that this process was marked by a lack of communication with the property owners and renters.

One elderly African American homeowner interviewed in the documentary lived on Hoopes Street. She said that the City of Philadelphia started sending her notices in the mail telling her that her property was being appropriated and given to someone else. The idea of moving caused her great anxiety, and she struggled to find a new place to live. She described the area as a place whose community had deep roots, and where people were working together to fix problems that the city government simply ignored. The city did not make an effort to communicate with the community, and did not give it an adequate opportunity to debate the renewal plan. This is a good example of how planning processes can be used to exclude various segments and groups in the population from meaningful participation in decision-making, contributing to their marginalization and repression (Forester and Krumbholtz 1990).

Many of the Hispanic residents did not even get a notice in Spanish, and as a result they had even less awareness of what was to happen in their neighbourhood. The worst outcome was the psychological impact the development had on individuals who had lived in the area for many generations. According to Fullilove (2004), the people being pushed out had developed deep roots through living together. Disturbing this kind of community network is known as *root shock*. It is the same term as is used for a plant that is uprooted and transplanted, because the idea is the same. The plant reacts badly when it is ripped out of the soil, and it often fails to thrive in its new setting.

Of course, the local city government ensured that what happened complied with the letter of the law, and claimed it was for the good of the neighbourhood. Most of those who had to give up their homes were offered some compensation. However, few regarded this as adequate, let alone desirable. Many people were confused, regarded the development as an ordeal, and were not sure what to do for the best. They felt the city authorities were treating people as if they were commodities, not individuals. The elderly African American woman interviewed, who had worked hard for decades to improve her home, certainly did not see her enforced removal as an improvement. At the end of the documentary she had lost her home, and was ironically being fined in connection with its demolition. She struggled for two years to find another home, and meanwhile the community in which she had spent most of her life had been destroyed. These are all symptoms of a failed conventional non-participatory planning process.

The elephant in the room: the disconnect between local governments and residents

Slum clearance might be carried out with 'good intentions' from the economic and aesthetic points of view. What is often missing, however, is consideration of equity. If this is not part of the process, the planning might not be sustainable. Planning has its roots in modernist narratives that exclude certain groups of the society. Susan Fainstein discusses this issue in *The Just City* (2010). She criticizes city governments for imposing policies that favour downtown businesses and tourists but are disconnected from the needs of disadvantaged groups of residents such as those with low income, women and minority groups.

Many such beautification programmes fail to recognize that everyone in the city has a right to it, and that there is a need for more inclusionary planning. The poor and the marginalized need to be part of the problem-identification and planning process. They also need to be the primary beneficiaries of the redevelopment. Most revitalization programmes have 'others' in mind: investors, tourists, developers, upper-income elites and so on. Simply put, there is a gap between the local planning agencies and the very people the planning is supposed to benefit. This is a threat for sustainable urban development that seeks to ensure social equity and economic development.

A sustainable approach: communicative planning

Real community development starts with a community coming together and fixing the problem. It does not start with negative images of a neighbourhood from those who are not a part of its community. Better policies need to be focused on the capacities, skills and assets of the neighbourhoods that face economic challenges, since

> even the poorest neighbourhood is a place where individuals and organizations represent resources upon which they rebuild. The key to neighbourhood regeneration then is to locate all of the available local assets, meaning that before development can start there should be recognition of power with community involvement.
>
> (Kretzmann and McKnight 1996)

The very definition of progressive or sustainable community planning, according to Tom Angotti (2008), is planning that seeks to achieve local and global equity, social inclusion and environmental justice. Therefore, communicative, participatory and inclusive planning is vital to bring about a sustainable urban renewal with the goal of socio-economic justice.

To see how this can work, let us look at a community that faced its challenges not only through involving its members, but also by creating a support system that involved people of all ages, races and languages. Dudley Street is in Boston, Massachusetts, and its story was told in *Holding Ground*, a documentary by Lipman and Mahan (1996). It is an example that really generated interest in the issues of telling people's stories and ensuring their voices are heard. When this area was first settled its inhabitants were white immigrants, mostly Irish and Italian, working people who were strong on Catholic values. Over time a number of other ethnic groups moved into the neighbourhood. Some of the descendants of the original Irish and Italian settlers decided to move out, but they soon realized it had become difficult to sell a home or business in the area for a reasonable sum. Some chose instead to burn down their properties and claim against their insurance. This created a neighbourhood that was both run down and full of empty lots, some of which were used as garbage dumps. The neighbourhood was very clearly in decline.

In 1985 a meeting was held at St Patrick's Church on Dudley Street, and it was decided to form a group to change and rebuild the area. One African American woman raised her hand and asked, 'How many of you live in this neighbourhood?' None of those involved in the decision admitted to doing so. *One of the biggest mistakes that was made at this point was the failure to include the local residents in the conversation that would impact on the very place they called home.* The same woman commented later in the documentary, 'Planning never happens with the people who have to live with the result of whatever is built or designed. Residents need to be involved from the beginning.' So the residents decided to take charge. They set up a board, whose members were to be elected by the people every two years. Some of the seats were designated for representatives of local housing, social services and religious groups, and three were designated for representatives of the main ethnic groups in the area. The aim was for them to work together to revitalize their community.

Because the change was to be driven by the community, the board representatives wanted to start by hiring planners whom they could trust to not 'sell the community out'. In order to convey that message of unity, all members of the board found ways to communicate with the rest of the neighbourhood, for example by talking about the plans on the radio in different languages. The aim was to ensure that many people would come out in support and get involved in the planning process. The results were impressive: so many people attended the community meetings that the mayor of Boston asked to get in on the action. One early demand was that the vacant lots full of trash should be cleaned up. When nothing was done by the city government, community representatives went on television and demanded that the mayor keep his promise to act. This led to an agreement between the mayor and the local community: local people would lend a helping hand by clearing these the areas, then the council would ensure that the vacant lots were secured to prevent further dumping.

The planners were not left to plan in isolation: they were required to engage with the community, particularly involving the younger generations in the planning process. The aim was to ensure that they understood the importance of public policy and the impact that local people can have on their environment. People were coming together and dreaming of a better community. The debate did not revolve around the negative issues; instead, people were being encouraged to think for themselves and rely on the strengths already present to make their neighbourhood a more liveable place.

About a quarter of the land in the area was vacant and ripe for development. The problem was that most of it was owned privately. The community board asked the local council to use its powers of eminent domain to acquire the land for public good – *real public good.* As a result, 15 acres were acquired for which community-based plans for development could be made. There was a long battle to convince banks to invest in the community, but eventually financial backing was provided for house-building. People who had left Dudley Street began to come back to the area, because they had roots there and because they saw the positive change that the community had worked so hard to maintain.

This is a good example of Asset Based Community Development. This new approach genuinely empowers citizens and strengthens civil society, as the assets of communities are identified, connected and mobilized, and the abilities and insights of local residents become resources for solving a neighbourhood's own problems. This does not mean that troubled neighbourhoods do not need outside help, but rather that any genuine local revitalization project must in fact be citizen-led, with outside agencies acting in a support role (Russell 2009). There is the need for more inclusionary planning thought and practice. There is a need for an acknowledgement and celebration of difference. There are multiple threads within planning (such as advocacy planning, equity planning and communicative planning) that validate the need for communicative planning (Sandercock and Forsyth 1992).

Conclusion

If residents, as stakeholders, help make decisions at all stages of the project cycle, then development problems are more likely to be understood in their entirety, and solutions are likely to be more effective and sustainable (IADB 1997). However, many urban revitalization planning processes are disconnected from the very people whose neighbourhoods need to be revitalized. These often include low-income groups and ethnic minorities, who are not seen as having a 'right to the city' and the planning process. Community involvement is particularly important in urban planning, and should be a universal part of the planning system in both developing and developed nations. The government should be on the front line, ensuring that when businesses of any kind want to invest in a place, they listen to local people, including those who do not have a strong economic voice.

If local governments involved in urban transformation projects follow the neoliberal philosophy and leave projects to the market forces, the result will be both 'winners' and 'losers' from the project. Governments need to recognize that even under the neoliberal ethos there is a need for significant state intervention in order to facilitate public participation. Poor people are known to live in the shadows of cities, and often the elites do not want them to participate in decision-making, but governments must realize that these people do not only shape the characteristics of the city but are vital for its survival. That is why slums should not be cleared but improved for the benefit of their existing residents, in a way that avoids displacing any of them. Slum dwellers must have equal rights to the city, something that is the main objective of sustainable urban development. Sustainable planning needs to focus on assisting people to realize that they can create a route out of poverty. Pushing people out of their home environment not only affects individual families but has a tremendous impact on the community as a whole.

Governments (both local and national) must realize the importance of building communities from the inside, and understand that ensuring a stable economy is not only about bringing in corporate investors from outside and offering them land for economic developments. It is also necessary to ensure that the local community is heard and included in the economic development process. Sustainable urban development requires urban planners to work with people and listen to their needs. Its aim should be to ensure that everyone has a place to call home. Public participation needs to be meaningful so that people feel a sense of ownership and belonging.

Note

1 See *Welcome to Lagos*, a BBC documentary, 2010.

References

Aguilar, A. and Santos, C. 2011. Informal settlements' needs and environmental conservation in Mexico City: an unsolved challenge for land-use policy. *Land Use Policy*, 28(4): 649–62.

Angotti, T. 2008. *New York for Sale: Community Planning Confronts Global Real Estate.* Cambridge, MA: MIT Press.

Arnstein, S. R. 1969. A ladder of citizen participation. *Journal of the American Institute of Planners*, 35(4): 216–24.

Beierle, T. C. and Cayford, J. 2002. *Democracy in Practice: Public Participation in Environmental Decisions.* Washington, DC: RFF Press.

Brunn, S. D., Williams, J. F. and Zeigler, D. J. I. (eds). 2003. *Cities of the World: World Regional Urban Development.* Lanham, MD: Rowman & Littlefield.

Collins, W. J. and Shester, K. L. 2009. Slum clearance and urban renewal in the United States, 1949–1974. *American Economic Journal*, 5(1): 239–73.

Davis, M. 2007. *Planet of Slums.* New York: Verso.

De Sousa Briggs, X. 1998. Doing democracy up-close: culture, power, and communication in community building. *Journal of Planning Education and Research*, 18: 1–13.

Dimuna, K. O. and Omatsone, M. E. O. 2010. Regeneration in the Nigerian urban built environment. *Journal of Human Ecology*, 29(2): 141–9.

Fainstein, S. 2010. *The Just City.* Ithaca, NY: Cornell University Press.

Forester, J. and Krumbholtz, N. 1990. *Making Equity Planning Work.* Philadelphia, PA: Temple University Press.

Fullilove, M. 2004. *Root Shock: How Tearing Up City Neighbourhoods Hurts America and What We Can Do About It.* New York: Ballantine.

Gordon, D. n.d. 2020: India's imperfect vision. *Yale Globalist.* Available at: http://tyglobalist.org/in-the-magazine/features/2020-indias-imperfect-vision/ (accessed 28 May 2014).

Groberg, R. P. 1965. Urban renewal realistically reappraised. *Law and Contemporary Problems*, 30(1): 212–29.

Harvey, D. 1973. *Social Justice and the City.* London: Edward Arnold.

—— 1985. On planning the ideology of planning. In *The Urbanisation of Capital: Studies in the History and Theory of Capitalist Urbanization.* Baltimore, MD: Johns Hopkins University Press.

Innes, J. E. and Booher, D. E. 2000. Public participation in planning: new strategies for the 21st century. Paper for the annual conference of the Association of Collegiate Schools of Planning, 2–5 November.

Inter-American Development Bank (IADB). 1997. Why is participation important? In *Resource Book on Participation*. Washington, DC: IADB.

Kretzmann, J. and McKnight, J. P. 1996. Assets-based community development. *National Civic Review*, 85(4): 23–9.

Lane, M. B. 2005. Public participation in planning: an intellectual history. *Australian Geographer*, 36(3): 283–99.

Lipman, M. and Mahan, L. 1996. *Holding Ground: The Rebirth of Dudley Street* (documentary). New York.

Lisk, F. A. 1980. Popular participation in basic needs-oriented development planning. *Labour and Society*, 6(1): 3–14.

McCullough, G. (prod.) 2005. *All for the Taking: 21st Century Urban Renewal* (documentary). Berkeley, CA: Berkeley Media.

Munro-Clark, M. 1992. *Citizen Participation in Government*. Sydney, Australia: Hale & Ironmonger.

Nossiter, A. 2013. In Nigeria's largest city, homeless are paying the price of progress. *New York Times*, 1 May.

Ocheje, P. D. 2007. 'In the public interest': forced evictions, land rights and human development in Africa. *Journal of African Law*, 51(2): 173–214.

Ostrom, E. 1990. *Governing the Commons: The Evolution of Institutions for Collective Action*. Cambridge: Cambridge University Press.

Purcell, M. 2009. Resisting neoliberalization: communicative planning or radical democratic movements? *Planning Theory*, 8(2): 140–65.

Russell, C. 2009. Communities in control: developing assets. Carnegie Foundation report on the first European ABCD Summit.

Sandercock, L. and Forsyth, A. 1992. A gender agenda: new directions for planning theory. *Journal of the American Planning Association*, 58(1): 49–59.

Sclar, E. D., Garau, P. and Carolini, G. 2005. The 21st century health challenge of slums and cities. *Lancet*, 901–3.

Sewell, W. R. D. and Coppock, J. T. 1977. *Public Participation in Planning: An Alternative Democracy?* Chichester: John Wiley.

Stone, L. 1989. Cultural crossroads of community participation in development: a case from Nepal. *Human Organization*, 48(3): 206–13.

Takeuchi, A., Cropper, M. and Bento A. 2008. Measuring the welfare effects of slum improvement programs: the case of Mumbai. *Journal of Urban Economics*, 64: 65–84.

Teaford, J. C. 2000. Urban renewal and its aftermath. *Housing Policy Debate*, 11(2), 443–65.

Watson, V. 2009a. 'The planned city sweeps the poor away . . .' Urban planning and 21st century urbanization. *Progress in Planning*, 72(3): 151–93.

—— 2009b. Seeing from the south: refocusing urban planning on the globe's central urban issues. *Urban Studies*, 46(11): 2259–75.

Webber, M. and Crooks, M. L. (eds). 1996. *Putting the People Last: Government, Services and Rights in Victoria*. Melbourne, Australia: Hyland House.

Yiftachel, O. 1998. Planning and social control: exploring the 'dark side'. *Journal of Planning Literature*, 12(2): 395–406.

13 Sustainable urban development

A Georgist perspective

Franklin Obeng-Odoom

Introduction

The notion of urban sustainable development is in vogue, but how to attain this vision is a matter of rancorous debate. Approaches vary widely: should we look at cities in nature or nature in cities, strive for compact cities, or ask for green technology and recycling (Kos 2008)? Like the parent literature on sustainability generally (for a review, see Paton 2011 and other chapters in this book), concepts, meanings and approaches differ in what we might call 'urban ecologies'. Some borrow from 'ecological footprints' to stress the amount of land that is used up or degraded in the process of 'conspicuous consumption', to use a term coined by the institutional political economist Veblen, whereas others use ideas of 'urban sprawl' or urban expansion, and then of course there is the idea of 'urban ecosystem' used to stress the relationships between the city and nature as an interlocking whole (Rademacher and Sivaramakrishnam 2013: 1–3).

In these conceptions of urban sustainable development, however, the environment is typically decoupled from the environment–society–economy complex. The World Bank's official position on cities is stated in *Reshaping Economic Geography* (World Bank 2009), for example. The Bank makes a strong case for economic growth and the need to prioritize it over and above the environment, although it notes that the environment is important too (World Bank 2009: 34). The United Nations does much better in approaching the problem more holistically, but does not carefully theorize the structural connection between capitalism, nature, society, and economy, polity and institutions (Obeng-Odoom 2013).

Such is the nature of the neoliberal ideology. It takes hold of the spaces for possible progressive change, including urban planning – both as theory and practice. The structural links between planning and markets under neoliberalism and the tendency for planning to concentrate on form and ignore structure in order to ensure capitalist accumulation have long been theorized. For instance, in one of the seminal texts on neoliberalism, *The Road to Serfdom* (Hayek 1945), Austrian economist Friedrich Hayek argues that it is only planning for competition and profit that works under capitalism. The work of Campbell and her colleagues (Campbell *et al.* 2014), recently published in the *Journal of Planning Education and Research*, shows that such is evidently the state of planning today, prompting the researchers to make a passionate plea for new ways of planning generally.

In responding to this call and the more specific concern of this book – exploring ways of attaining 'untamed urbanisms' – this chapter introduces and outlines the benefits of a Georgist approach to urban sustainable development, previously overlooked in the literature. The approach emphasizes how social investment affects land values and rent, how surplus is generated, and how net income is distributed and impacts on sustainable urban development.

Although highly relevant in the current global political economy, the Georgist approach is rarely used in neoclassical resource economics, and these days scarcely used in heterodox urban political economy too (Stilwell and Jordan 2004; Stilwell 2011). This chapter presents Georgism as a challenge to existing discourses on sustainable development.

George's approach to sustainable development throws up complex distributional issues which are hardly acknowledged in the dominant discourses on sustainable development. The chapter argues that the primary emphasis on rent helps to show how the wrongful appropriation of nature tends to lead to speculation and profiteering which, in turn, lead to misuse and abuse of nature. Thus, under capitalist urban development, attaining 'sustainable urban development' *is* an oxymoron. Since emphasizing one segment of society neglects the other, and grafting 'everything' onto a grand approach buttered with markets generates further contradictions, the entire rentier basis of the capitalist system ought to be challenged. Henry George, however, did not provide a road map for moving from 'here' to 'there', and to this extent Georgism ought to be linked up with other green movements, an analysis of which is beyond the scope of this chapter.

The rest of the chapter is divided into three parts, dealing with a review of the dominant perspective of sustainability, Georgist analysis of sustainable urban development and its appraisal.

Sustainable development: a review of the dominant views

While various conceptions of sustainable development characterize the literature, it is the meaning of sustainability stated in *Our Common Future* (WCED 1987) that is the most widely used, as explained earlier in this book.

This view is often styled as the economic approach to sustainability, and is the dominant paradigm in the sustainability literature. It is characterized by the primary emphasis on the economic over the environment, and leads to conclusions such as eco-technological transformation of society, where cleaner and greener technology is encouraged to continue on a business-as-usual pro-growth path. It opposes state intervention, preferring instead to use market-based mechanisms such as emissions trading schemes for a clean environment (Paton 2011; Rosewarne *et al.* 2014). This approach is presented as being apolitical, pro-technocratic, and predominantly based on using modern technologies to 'save the planet' (Salleh 2011).

The history of modern technology generally has been documented elsewhere (e.g. Hård and Jamison 1998), so it is not repeated here, except the highlights of the relevant aspects of that scholarship to provide context for the subsequent discussion. Green technology first gained roots with the publication of the book

The Whole Earth Catalog. It made a strong case for individuals to change their lifestyles to save the planet. Accompanying such reforms was the need for quality technological change, leading to the founding of a new movement of 'appropriate technology' in the 1970s (Steinberg 2010). A highly influential person in the movement, the economist E. F. Schumacher, took a different view. He argued for structural change, as he saw the current system to be incapable of major changes to save the planet. Technology was important for him, but more important was the entire socio-ecological system in his days. With time, the movement slipped away from his ideals and instead got fixated on the notion of clean technology alone – without taking into account the political and systemic issues. This drift was part of a bigger issue of the loss of faith in the Keynesian state and the successful march of the neoclassical economics establishment and its generals, such as Milton Friedman, to establish that type of economics as the orthodox, the common and the dominant paradigm (Steinberg 2010).

In those countries in the periphery of the world system, the World Bank report *Environment and Development* (World Bank 1992) was the carrier-in-chief of the neoliberal case for sustainability. It announced its full support for the WCED Report and declared that 'continued, and even accelerated, economic and human development *is* sustainable and can be consistent with *improving* environmental conditions', based on two conditions (1992: iii). The first of these conditions is the aggressive pursuit of the links between more growth and effective environmental management. To achieve this outcome, the Bank preferred that all subsidies on natural resources such as water should be removed because they would tend to lead to overuse. Further, the Bank called for new technology to manage the environment.

Second is a call for institutions to voluntarily change their damaging practices towards the environment, so state corporations whose activities damage the environment ought to be made 'competitive'. A major step in that direction is to create property in land, as excluding others from the use of land is the only way to ensure that the land is put to its highest and best use. Further, the case is made for farmers to create property in land, as it is only private property that will encourage them to better invest in land (World Bank 1992: 1). In this approach, population growth is also blamed for causing poverty, and women in particular are blamed for being too fertile and hence in need of family planning (World Bank 1992: 23, 29, 173). Indeed, the World Bank report argued the case for prioritizing economic growth and voluntary change of behaviour. More recent analysis has been substantially influenced by this tradition. Dercon (2012), for instance, has noted that green growth is likely to be coupled with growing poverty. The growth fetishism has led to calls for limitless green growth (Squires 2013), anchored on an urban form that is green or typified by, among others, green gadgetry, green cars and green buildings (see, e.g., Emmanuel and Baker 2012).

In this literature, the notion of urban sustainable development is embraced, but in a reductionist way. The environment is typically decoupled from the environment–society–economy complex. The World Bank's report on cities, *Reshaping Economic Geography* (2009), makes clear the interest in economic growth and the need to prioritize it over and above the environment, although the Bank notes the importance of the environment (2009: 34). It is a classic case of the environmental Kuznets curve, positing that the environment and its sustainability can wait until such a time that income per capita has reached a certain level and the market, the sum total of disjointed individual actions, will ensure that the environment saves itself (for reviews see Acemoglu and Robinson 2002; Stern 2004).

The United Nations does much better in attacking the problem more holistically, but does not carefully theorize the structural connection between capitalism, nature, society, and economy, polity and culture. For cities in Africa, the guidance lies in the *State of African Cities Reports* (e.g., UN-HABITAT 2008, 2010). The predominant focus is local development, emphasizing green technology, without a fundamental shift. Rather, 'reducing energy use wherever possible; adding as much renewable energy as possible and offsetting any CO_2 emitted through purchasing carbon credits' (UN-HABITAT 2009: 41) are emphasized. The thrust 'is to find ways that cities can integrate these two agendas – to respect the natural environment and to improve the human environment, at the same time' (UN-HABITAT 2009: 40). Like other capitalist cities, therefore, the city in Africa is framed mainly as 'an engine of growth', with saving the environment understood as greener or cleaner energy (UN-HABITAT 2008: 89). In turn, the vision for the Nairobi 2030 plan is to obtain 'sustainable wealth' (UN-HABITAT 2008: 129).

This view of sustainability is part of a broader framing of it as attaining a 'green economy': continuing capital accumulation albeit with an ecological modernization twist. More explicitly, Africa is at the receiving end of polluting and degrading activities dispatched from the North to the South (Salleh 2012: 142). This is the green economy in Africa (Tandon 2011), anchored on the concept of 'green growth' or continuous growth at reduced environmental costs – greatly propagated by the OECD countries, especially during the Third Annual Meeting of the OECD Urban Roundtable (Hammer *et al.* 2011).

The politics, origins and connections between green growth and sustainable development have recently been documented (Cook *et al.* 2012), so no attempt is made to repeat that account here, except to stress that the idea is based on a premise that the inequities in society, economy and environment spring from human failings and lack of resources. With the problem so framed, there is now an emergent subfield of 'green jobs' in Africa (Charisma and Culhane 2013).

The orthodox view of sustainable development has been widely contested by heterodox political economists, but not from a Georgist perspective. Rosewarne and colleagues (2014) have provided a detailed review of critical approaches to sustainability, but the Georgist paradigm for sustainability is as yet undeveloped. Research on the role of land in critical political economy such as the Marxian perspective similarly sheds great light on the failings of the orthodox paradigms (see e.g. Munro 2013), but it does not do so from a Georgist ecological perspective. Little has been said about the Georgist perspective in current research on sustainable urban development (e.g. Stilwell 2011; Pullen 2013), so the rest of the chapter is devoted to an explication and critical appraisal of the Georgist paradigm.

The Georgist paradigm

One distinctive approach to the challenge of the orthodoxy is the one that Henry George developed in the nineteenth century. George's primary emphasis on the commodification of land as the source of all social and environmental crisis is unique. Unlike other heterodox approaches that emphasize corporate production in their critique of orthodoxy, George saw sustainable development first of all as returning land to common property.

George's ideas also stand in sharp contrast to orthodox theory which first regards land as capital, posits conservation or the management of land use as a way to make society sustainable, and claims that treating land as private property is the only way to attain its highest and best use (Hofmeister 2010: 143–58). To quote George:

> It is a delusion that land *must* be private property to be used effectively. It is a further delusion that making land common property – as it once was in the past – would destroy civilization and reduce us to barbarism. Lawmakers have done their best to expand this delusion [*sic*], while economists have generally consented to it.
>
> (George 2006: 219, emphasis in original)

So, contrary to the view that private property in land is necessary for sustainable land use, Georgists argue that it is private property in land that causes unsustainable land use and urban development. Besides, for George, land and water, oil and coal are all land, as is air – unlike the orthodox view that sees land as only the physical part of the earth (Hofmeister 2010: 158), nothing special and indeed substitutable (Gaffney 2008).

Although highly relevant and interesting, the ideas of George are as yet not very developed in the heterodox challenge to orthodox approaches to sustainability. George occupies a rather strange space in heterodox political economy. It is hard to place him, as his approach does not fit neatly into the left–right divide in the literature. In a 1992 address, the dissident philosopher R. V. Andelson described George as a heterodox who is willing to incorporate aspects of the capitalist logic into his fundamentally more socialist-leaning oeuvre, which spans the period from 1879, when he wrote his first book, to 1897, when he died. Twice George made an attempt at becoming a mayor, and therein lies the strength of his ideas for urban sustainable development.

Theory

George laid down his theory of natural resources and economic development (hereafter sustainable development) in his stimulating book *Progress and Poverty* (1879, republished 2006). He restated and reinforced the theory in *Social Problems* (1883), *A Perplexed Philosopher* (1892) and *The Science of Political Economy*

(1898), and some other publications. As with the Physiocrats and classical economists, George put land, labour and capital as the factors of production. He defined
land as all the free gifts of nature, labour as human exertion, and capital as stock
of wealth used for further production. To George, the factors of production are all
important, but not equally so. Labour initiates production, but cannot do so without land. Capital is important and enhances production, but without it, production
is still possible. Henry George argued that the source of growth is not capital,
but labour. This implied that, contrary to claims typically made by neoclassical
economists that developing countries ought to make conditions flexible in order
to allow capital to ooze in, it is rather labour, acting on land, that should be the
crucial driver of production.

He argued that all the factors of production worked well together, and it was
not their workings that caused 'poverty amid progress'. George argued that on
its own, capital was nothing. Labour creates capital, so the source of all progress
in society is labour. Nevertheless, capital has greatly expanded and enhanced the
exertions of labour, so capital is necessary and deserving of reward. The nature
of land, George argued, is rather different. Like labour and capital, it is crucial in
production, but unlike labour and capital it is not the creation of anyone. It is a
free gift of nature. In turn, the creation of exclusive ownership in land, and hence
the generation and subsequent appropriation of rent – which he defined as the
returns arising from the monopolization of natural resources – by a landowning
group is highly problematic, and indeed the source of the 'progress amid poverty'
problematique (George 2006).

Arguably, George's conception of sustainability is rooted in the notion
of 'equal rights in land'. Land, to George, encompasses the obvious – the
physical part of the earth. However, it goes beyond that to embrace all natural
resources.

The notion of equal rights, George argued, is not the same as joint or collective rights. For George these matters are merely secondary, and they arise only
when several people with equal rights want to use the same lot of land. But that
is different from suggesting that it is the collective or the society that confers
equal rights. To George it is nature itself, the existence of humankind, that leads
to the principle of equal rights. So, even when equal rights become transmogri-
fied into joint rights, the change is only one of limitation, not of abrogation, and
the right people have is not bestowed by others but by nature and the existence
of the human. The joint right is still an equal right because the limitation on it
is a similar right. There are two key implications of the limitation, according to
George:

> but (1) an absolute right to use any part of the earth as to which his use does
> not conflict with the equal rights of others (i.e., which no one else wants to
> use at the same time), and (2) a coequal right to the use of any part of the earth
> which he and others may want to use at the same time.
>
> (George 1892: 31)

It follows that the right is first, not springing from society or others, but the limitation – equality – does spring from societal considerations because there are others with like rights. To uphold these principles, to George, will be sustainable development. Holding exclusive right to property in land, on the other hand, is unsustainable.

In the Georgist conception of sustainability, as private property is created in land, rent begins to accrue. Public investments, technological advancement and population growth, among other factors, contribute to the increase in rent. Speculation enters the equation, as hoarding land from the public becomes highly lucrative, and the margin of production – the point beyond which production will not take place – gradually extends (George 2006). The process intensifies with rent skyrocketing: land is channelled into uses that are not satisfying of human need, but are intended to generate rent for landlords. Gentrifiers move into the city, as do investors, developers and residents intending to even further expedite the process, for example through gating (Obeng-Odoom 2014). The poor are forced or spat out to marginal lands on the periphery, the outskirts, the sprawling areas. There is no longer a compact city. Sustainable urbanism becomes an oxymoron as land uses are dictated not by human need but by the desire to extract more and more economic rent. Prime land is held out of the market for speculative reasons, while the poor hopelessly till poor lands. But private property is a contrivance. As it causes rent to increase, the cost of living generally to go up, and the system to become inflationary as a rise in rent tends to affect all production, it forces down wages and interest, not necessarily as an amount, but as a quantity, according to George.

Labour cannot forever surrender its wages to landlords as rent. It will tend to become discouraged at some point and hence will reduce production. And that is when the system can be thrown into a tail spin: a fall in production leads to a fall in wealth, and can lead to the suspension of the production process and hence of the engagement of labour, which in turn can lead to further falls in purchases. A system of crises ensues locally, nationally and globally. So creating private property in land cannot be sustainable.

Critique of existing approaches

From this perspective, Georgists question the neoclassical approach to sustainability. To Georgists, the neoclassical approach to sustainability emphasizing eco-technology and gadgetry and low population is highly problematic because more technology means more demand, and more demand suggests more production, which in turn further exerts pressure on nature (Stilwell and Jordan 2004). George's theory, then, is a direct challenge to the existing orthodox theory.

An extension in the demand for land suggests more rent may arise. Orthodox policies for attaining sustainable urban development have similar effects. The Clean Development Mechanism is a case in point. It entails the purchase of private land for the development of lots. Sequestration is the same. They both intensify the demand for land, they both endorse and extend private property in land, and hence they both intensify the rent–speculation–social problems dynamics. Other policies such as cap and trade and emissions trading schemes are praised by orthodox economists for their efficiency, but, for George, with greater efficiency there is more likelihood for increased rent. Hence these policies will set in motion the vicious cycle of unsustainable urban development.

To the left, too, George was critical. He spoke, for instance, against nationalization, contending that government property infringes the equal rights to land principle, and to the extent that it does not abolish rent, is ineffective. Further, he contended that nationalization risks collusion, corruption, bureaucracy and hence inefficiency. Thus rather than create another public outlet, he saw the taxation of rent as a way back to the land (George 2006: 224). Redistribution was also not favoured by George. According to him, land redistribution could work but only for a while. As population grows, there are two options. First, land will become concentrated in the hands of the original population that benefited from redistribution, and that population will become a new class of landlords extracting rent and causing pressure on labour, capital and the environment generally. Alternatively, if land continues to be redistributed, since there is a fixed quantity of it, the amount to any individual would become so small that it would be practically useless. In turn, there would be pressures for richer people to buy out smallholders and combine their lots. Finally, George was against the public purchase of all private land, for the reason that it is inefficient and ineffective.

Thus, in his analysis of sustainable urban development, it is hard to place George as either a 'right' or 'left' -wing social reformer. He was critical of both. However, to the extent that he claimed he believed in socialism, was against the privatization of the commons and against the treatment of 'land' as an ordinary factor of production, George was a radical or heterodox thinker. Aside from his heterodox diagnosis of sustainable development, his preferred solution was heterodox too.

George's solution

George preferred that all land be made common land to which all citizens have equal rights and access. That is different from government land which is bureaucratically managed by government functionaries. George offered a two-point process for reaching the goal. First, he recommended that all non-land-based taxes be abolished, because they penalize human exertion, discourage industry and kill initiatives. Also he believed revenue from land tax would be enough to support the state. Second, he recommended the taxation of rent arising from the use of land. Common land where rent is not generated at all is George's end goal, but to get there he recommended a single tax on land or site value. To him, this capture of the rent from land is a way to reconcile the individual and the collective, and possibly return to the situation where there is common land for the common person.

Some readers of George make the mistake of thinking that George's cardinal solution to the crises in sustainability was to use taxation, which is also a market-based approach (O'Sullivan 2012), but in fact George's preferred solution was to return land to common property. Land tax, to George, was an intermediate solution, a way to try to save land from its status as private property before returning it to common property. In his words, 'Nothing short of making land common property can permanently relieve poverty' (George 2006: xvii). He recommended the taxation of all nature, including the taxation of monopolies. 'The profit of monopoly', according to George, 'is in itself a tax on production. Taxing it would simply divert into public coffers what producers must pay anyway' (George 2006: 228). Also, the idea of a profit tax on rent extracted by the mining and oil complexes would be consistent with George's theory of sustainable urban development.

Appraisal

George's ideas have been widely criticized. O'Sullivan (2012), for example, has offered three criticisms. First, confiscating rent is a disincentive for landlords to effectively manage land. Second, it is unjust to dispossess landowners of their land. Finally, it is extremely difficult to accurately determine land rent. Neither George's recommendation for a tax regime based only on land nor the abolition of all other taxes has had much global acceptance. Indeed, even Georgists have suggested that this view is an exaggeration (Stilwell and Jordan 2004). Other reasons have been offered for why the land tax idea is best considered as only one of many tools. First is the capacity of the state and its institutions such as land use and urban planning authorities. What makes George so sure that the state that can be corrupt in doing land redistribution will be above board while extracting taxation? Besides, there are questions about capacity to design and collect rent, issues about whether the electorate is ready to pay, and questions about the adequacy of existing infrastructure, such as property address systems to do a land valuation and taxation exercise.

Georgists have tried to respond to some of these issues. The Henry George schools around the world, for instance, argue that reserving 5–10 per cent of rent to compensate landlords for their estate management services will simultaneously provide the needed incentive for management and offer society the rent it collectively creates. George himself dealt with the issue of the seeming injustice in dispossessing landlords of 'their' land. He argued that as the land is not the private property of landlords, there can be no injustice in restoring land to the status of common good. But George insisted that any improvements by landlords should not be confiscated (2006). While in poorer countries especially, logistical and institutional capacity can be a barrier to the estimation of rental value, and hence critics of George do have a case, modern land economists have developed sophisticated and practical approaches that can be used to overcome this concern with taxation capacity (Obeng-Odoom 2014). So while there are important challenges in applying George's ideas, most of them are surmountable.

Henry George's ideas have an enduring relevance to contemporary society. They have been applied to the analysis of urban development in Australia (Stilwell and Jordan 2004; Stilwell 2011) and China (Cui 2011). Efforts to apply Georgism to cities in Africa have been limited, but recent work (Obeng-Odoom 2012a, 2014) has tried to do so. However, this casts some doubts on aspects of the work of George, such as the claim that 'once the assessment [of tax] is made, nothing but a receiver is required for collection' (2006: 230). Of course, George had in mind the state in the advanced countries, whereas the work on Africa deals with the state in relatively ill-resourced countries, so this appraisal ought to be understood within historical and geographical contexts. There are those who argue that George did not take into account global forces, and a few who worry about the ambiguity in George's taxation design laws, but these matters can be overcome given efforts to show how the Georgist approach anticipated the recent global crises (Gaffney 2009).

George's own contribution was looked upon suspiciously by heterodox political economists, some of whom regard his attempt at fusing together elements of individualism into collectivism as compromising with orthodoxy. However, this argument against George is unfounded, as George tried to reconcile and synthesize rather than compromise. Indeed, the concerted attack waged by the neoclassical economics cabal with the aim of undoing George's work (Gaffney 1994), sometimes calling him an unscientific thinker (Pullen 2012: 119), and mocking his ideas in the mainstream *Wall Street Journal* (*Georgist Journal* 2013: 12–14), should assuage fears that George was mainstream. The lack of concrete analysis of how to move from the present frame of thinking to the Georgist ideal is clearly a weakness in the Georgist paradigm of sustainable urban development, but it is simultaneously an opportunity to provide a bridge between Georgism and other progressive perspectives that better theorize movements not just for any policy, but for just policy.

Conclusion

Urban planning has much to gain from embracing Georgist ecological thinking in breaking away from the hegemony of neoliberal ecological planning. A Georgist approach to sustainable urbanism is unique among the existing shades of opinion on the drivers and possible solutions to the sustainable urban development problematique. To George, the structural cause of the environmental, social and economic pillars of sustainable urban development is the turning of land into private property. Contrary to the view that private property in land brings about the highest and best use, George demonstrates that it is property in land that causes land to be put the least and worst use, and the environment to be subjected to destructive uses.

'Private land', George argued, is not intended for human need; it is typically available for use as a vehicle for speculation, investment and profiteering. While labour tills unproductive land under degrading and harsh conditions, private land lies waste, waiting to accumulate profit. In turn, under a regime of private land ownership, the price of land rises dramatically and the poor are driven out of high-priced areas into dehumanizing ghettoes. Land that could have been used for effective production, for example of food, is used for profit-making ventures that might not directly lead to satisfying pressing human needs. Increasing land values dwarf the wages of labour and interest on capital, and in the end tend to discourage production. The corollary is a general global depression followed by a boom, and then a bust again.

So, apart from enclosures of land being morally unjust because land is a free gift of nature, and hence people should not exert private ownership over land as though they produced it, George contends that the outcomes of creating private property in land are also unsustainable. This view differs markedly from the liberal-labour ghost that haunts the sustainability literature, and in which urban planning is deeply steeped. From a Georgist perspective, capitalist cities can never be sustainable and so reformist planning ideas about greater efficiency will only compound the problem. It is, George argued, only cities with common landownership systems that can be sustainable.

Common tenure itself can be attained via numerous ways – primarily public purchase, public confiscation and redistribution – but George did not find these avenues viable. He recommended taxing the net income from land and reinvesting the resulting revenues in social development, even though in practice some institutions may not have the capacity to implement this. Abolishing all taxation other than land tax is another part of the Georgist strategy, but this approach is widely contested even among Georgists. However, George's diagnosis is persuasive, as is his ultimate proposal of returning land to common property. It is the interim steps that require further analysis, and that provide urban planning with a window of hope, of taking control, of 'untamed urbanisms'.

References

Acemoglu, D. and Robinson, J. A. 2002. Political economy of the Kuznets curve. *Review of Development Economics*, 6(2): 183–203.

Andelson, R. V. 1992. Henry George and the reconstruction of capitalism, address to the American Institute for Economic Research (AIER) fellows, staff and guests, Great Barrington, 9 July. Available at: http://schalkenbach.org/rsf-1/on-line-library/works-by-robert-v-andelson/henry-george-and-the-reconstruction-of-capitalism/ (accessed 10 August 2013).

Campbell, H., Tait, M. and Watkins, C. 2014. Is there space for better planning in a neo-liberal world? Implications for planning practice and theory. *Journal of Planning Education and Research*, 34 (1): 45–59.

Charisma, S. A. and Culhane, T. H. 2013. Green jobs, livelihoods and the post-carbon economy in African cities. *Local Environment*, DOI:10.1080/13549839.2012.752801.

Cook, S., Smith, K. and Utting, P. 2012. Green economy or green society? Contestation and policies for a fair transition. Occasional Paper 10, Social Dimensions of Green Economy and Sustainable Development, November. Geneva, Switzerland: United Nations Research Institute for Social Development (UNRISD).

Cui, Z. 2011. Partial intimations of the coming whole: the Chongqing experiment in light of the theories of Henry George, James Meade, and Antonio Gramsci. *Modern China*, 37(6): 646–60.

Dercon, S. 2012. Is green growth good for the poor? Research Paper 6231. Washington, DC: World Bank.

Emmanuel, R. and Baker, K. 2012. *Carbon Management in the Built Environment.* London: Routledge.

Gaffney, M. 1994. Neo-classical economics as a stratagem against Henry George. In F. Harrison (ed.), *The Corruption of Economics*. London: Shepheard-Walwyn.

—— 2008. Keeping land in capital theory: Ricardo, Faustmann, and George. *American Journal of Economics and Sociology*, 67(1): 119–42.

—— 2009. *After the Crash: Designing a Depression-Free Economy.* London: Wiley-Blackwell.

George, H. [1879] 2006. *Progress and Poverty.* New York: Robert Schalkenbach Foundation.

—— 1883. *Social Problems.* New York: Robert Schalkenbach Foundation.

—— 1892. *A Perplexed Philosopher*, digitized 2006 by P. Møller Andersen. Available at: www.grundskyld.dk

—— 1898. *The Science of Political Economy.* London: Kegan Paul, Trench, Trumber & Co.

Georgist Journal. 2013. *The Wall Street Journal*, 122 (Spring): 12–14.

Hammer, S., Kamal-Chaoui, L., Robert, A. and Plouin, M. 2011. Cities and green growth: a conceptual framework, OECD Regional Development Working Papers 2011/08. Paris: OECD.

Hård, M. and Jamison, A. (eds). 1998. *The Intellectual Appropriation of Technology: Discourse on Modernity, 1900–1939.* Cambridge, MA: MIT Press.

Hayek, A. F. 1945. *The Road to Serfdom with the Intellectuals and Socialism.* London: Institute of Economic Affairs.

Hofmeister, J. 2010. *Why We Hate the Oil Companies: Straight Talk from an Energy Insider.* New York: Palgrave Macmillan.

Kos, D. 2008. Nature in the city or the city in nature? *Urbani Izziv*, 19(2): 129–32.

Munro, D. 2013. Land and capital. *Journal of Australian Political Economy*, 70 (Summer): 214–32.

O'Sullivan, A. 2012. *Urban Economics.* Boston, MA: McGraw-Hill Irwin.

Obeng-Odoom, F. 2012a. The mystery of capital or the mystification of capital? *Review of Social Economy*, http://dx.doi.org/10.1080/00346764.2012.761758

—— 2012b. Good property valuation in emerging real estate markets? Evidence from Ghana. *Surveying and Built Environment*, 22 (Nov.): 37–60.

—— 2013. The state of African cities 2010: governance, inequality, and urban land markets. *Cities*, 31 (April): 425–9.

—— 2014. *Oiling the Urban Economy: Land, Labour, Capital, and the State in Sekondi-Takoradi, Ghana.* London: Routledge.

Paton, G. J. 2011. *Seeking Sustainability: On the Prospect of an Ecological Liberalism.* London: Routledge.

Pullen, J. 2012. Henry George on property rights in land and land value: equal and private, or common and public? In T. Aspromourgos and J. Lodewijks (eds), *History and Political: Essays in Honour of P.D. Groenewegen.* London and New York: Routledge.

—— 2013. An essay on distributive justice and the equal ownership of natural resources. *American Journal of Economics and Sociology*, 72(5): 1044–74.

Rademacher, A. and Sivaramakrishnam, K. 2013. Introduction: ecologies of urbanism in India. In A. Rademacher and K. Sivaramakrishnam (eds), *Ecologies of Urbanism in India*, pp. 1–41. Hong Kong: Hong Kong University Press.

Rosewarne, S., Goodman, J. and Pearce, R. 2014. *Climate Action Upsurge: The Ethnography of Climate Movement Politics*. New York: Routledge.

Salleh, A. 2011. Climate strategy: making the choice between ecological modernisation or living well. *Journal of Australian Political Economy*, 66: 124–49.

—— 2012. Green economy or green utopia? Rio+20 and the reproductive labor class. *Journal of World Systems Research*, 18(2): 141–5.

Squires, G. 2013. *Urban and Environmental Economics: An Introduction*. London: Routledge.

Steinberg, T. 2010. Can capitalism save the planet? *Radical History Review*, 107 (Spring): 7–24.

Stern, D. I. 2004. The rise and fall of the environmental Kuznets curve. *World Development*, 32(8): 141–39.

Stilwell, F. 2011. The condition of labour, capital and land. Paper presented at the Conference of the Association for Good Government, Sydney, Australia, 16 July.

Stilwell, F. and Jordan, K. 2004. The political economy of land: putting Henry George in his place. *Journal of Australian Political Economy*, 54 (Dec.): 119–34.

Tandon, Y. 2011. Kleptocratic capitalism, climate finance, and the green economy in Africa. *Capitalism Nature Socialism*, 22(4): 136–44.

UN-HABITAT. 2008. *State of African Cities Report*. Nairobi: UN-HABITAT.

—— 2009. *Planning Sustainable Cities: Policy Directions – Global Report on Human Settlements*. London: Earthscan.

—— 2010. *The State of African Cities 2010: Governance, Inequality and Urban Land Markets*. Nairobi: UN-HABITAT.

World Bank. 1992. *World Development Report: Development and the Environment*. New York: Oxford University Press.

—— 2009. *World Development Report 2009: Reshaping Economic Geography*. Washington, DC: World Bank.

World Commission on Environment and Development (WCED). 1987. *Our Common Future (the Brundtland Report)*. Oxford: Oxford University Press.

14 Beyond an imaginary of power?

Governance, supranational organizations and 'just' urbanization

Philip Lawton

Introduction

Throughout the last decade, there has been renewed interest in notions of justice and human rights in an urban context. Indeed, in the aftermath of the economic crisis of 2008, these issues have become particularly salient. Following from the work of Lefebvre (1996), much of this has revolved around the notion of the 'right to the city' (Mayer 2009; Marcuse 2009a). Similarly, albeit with a more direct focus upon urban planning, the notion of the 'just city' has received attention through the work of authors such as Fainstein (2010) and Uitermark (2010). This chapter seeks to analyse the potentials and pitfalls of the notions of the 'just city' and the 'right to the city' in the context of existing political-economic circumstances (Fainstein 2010, 2014; Novy and Mayer 2009). In keeping with the theme of this volume, the chapter begins with the presumption that sustainable urbanization can only be achieved through the integration of notions of equity (Fainstein 2010) and governance (Jessop 2002).

The chapter is the outcome of a convergence of two fields of research, which, although overlapping, have formed somewhat distinct elements of my writing. The first of these is a focus on the 'creative city', and the second is an analysis of public space, with a particular focus on the ideal of the 'European city' (see Lawton and Punch 2014). While each of these subfields draws upon a different research trajectory, there are some points of convergence, which have led me to the examination of the 'just city' (Fainstein 2010, 2014) and the 'right to the city' (Harvey 2008).

A significant amount of attention has been paid to the notion of the 'creative city', particularly since the publication of Richard Florida's (2002) *The Rise of the Creative Class*. In building on core areas of related research, the analysis I have carried out in this field has sought to focus on a number of key elements. First, it has highlighted the extent to which the 'creative class' is something that can be seen as both globally and locally constituted. This part of my research has been particularly engaged with the extent to which the notion of the 'creative class' can be seen as a form of mobile policy (Lawton *et al.* 2010; Bontje and Lawton 2013). Second, I have analysed the relationship between residential choices and the 'creative class' (Lawton *et al.* 2013), examining the relationship between the lifecycle and residential preferences among members of the 'creative class'. Critically, following from the work of Peck (2005), the research has argued that the popularity of the 'creative class' within policy stems from its ability to repackage and further already existing approaches which themselves are highly entrepreneurial.

The second field of research, which is focused on analysing the 'European city', has engaged critically with the European city as an ideal form of urban environment. In particular, and in drawing on cities such as Dublin and Amsterdam, my work has aimed to engage in the wider dynamics of urban development beyond the rhetoric of the ideal 'European city'. Moreover, the discourse surrounding much European urban development has sought to promote ideals of the city which promote entrepreneurship over wealth distribution (Novy and Mayer 2009). The emerging urban image is thus of an ideal of unproblematic interaction within public space that is focused on consumption amid a transformed and modernized historic European city centre of squares, boulevards, upmarket shopping and café culture. With a focus on these factors, previous work examining Dublin (Lawton and Punch 2014) illustrates the manner in which the 'European city' became representative of the increased desire to remodel the city along neoliberal lines:

> Overall, it can be argued that academic narratives such as the 'European city', though flawed and open to criticism in themselves, can sometimes offer a seductive ideological 'new suit of clothes' for planning. The 'European city' narrative can also be seen as a discursive hook in the business of competing for status internationally and selling the city as dynamic, interesting and different, yet quintessentially 'European'.
>
> (Lawton and Punch 2014: 881)

While I have treated these topics somewhat separately within the various associated publications, there are overlaps between the 'European city' ideal and the 'creative class'. As is evidenced in the Dublin case study (Lawton and Punch 2014), and in cities such as Amsterdam (Bontje and Lawton 2013; Novy and Mayer 2009), the entrepreneurial dynamics of the 'European city' and the promotion of the 'creative class' have become increasingly integrated into urban policies throughout Europe. When taken in combination, the analysis of the various ideals and the extent to which they neglect much of the realities of urban processes has led me to a greater interest in questions surrounding the 'right to the city' and 'justice' in an urban context.

As a means of investigating the connections between ideals of justice and equity and the urban question, this chapter analyses the approach of international bodies, including UN-HABITAT, and various European bodies, including the Council of Europe and the European Commission. In the context of this book, the chapter picks up on the question of 'scale'. It is posited that the above-mentioned bodies are key actors in the emergence and transmission of policies and ideals that often seek to 'tame' the city. Moreover, as will be critically examined throughout the chapter, these bodies play a central role in the promotion of different urban forms as encapsulating certain principles that, at least at face value, are supposed to promote a 'better' urban future. The chapter concludes by suggesting a movement beyond the association of 'rights' and 'justice' with particular urban forms, and instead seeks an approach to the urban that is more process-oriented. It advocates a form of planning which moves beyond a domination by highly visually oriented ideals of city building, and instead seeks to untangle the way in which neoliberalism naturalizes highly unequal forms of urban development (Jessop 2002). Crucially, in terms of connecting this chapter with the wider themes of the book, it is argued that addressing this scale of engagement offers an important strand in discussing the notion of 'untamed urbanisms'.

Governance and the 'competitive city'

Throughout the last few decades, through the influence of neoliberalism (Jessop 2002; Brenner and Theodore 2002) cities have been caught in a maelstrom of urban competitiveness. This shift, which can be traced back to the 1970s, can, at least in 'western cities', be viewed in the context of the increased pressure on the welfare state. It has resulted in the transformation of urban governance from a focus on 'managerial' factors, such as housing provision, infrastructure development and other forms of provision, to a more 'entrepreneurial' approach. This entrepreneurial approach is instead focused on the promotion of business interests and the attraction of increasingly footloose industry (Harvey 1989).

This transformation has included the wholesale remodelling of central city areas, as a means of both attracting residents and promoting the city to tourists. Indeed, in so doing, this approach to urban development has often brought together notions associated with sustainability, such as higher-density living and walkable neighbourhoods, with increasingly entrepreneurial and neoliberal ideals of city-making (Lawton and Punch 2014). When these concepts are taken together, cities are increasingly promoted as visually alluring places to live and work in, and to visit. Indeed, this discourse has become such a dominant feature of contemporary urbanization that municipalities now take very seriously the various global rankings about 'quality of life' and the attraction of wealthy residents, such as are produced by organizations such as Mercer and *Monocle* lifestyle magazine.[1]

These shifts, and their influence on urban governance, cannot be perceived as simple or linear in their development. They involve a vast and complex set of processes and actors who engage in largely differing ways. In order to understand these shifts, it is therefore important to look at the wide array of actors engaged within the social and spatial dimensions of 'governance'. It is important here that while we recognize the extreme shifts of recent years, we do not overstretch the role of 'neoliberalism'. The development of cities has historically been influenced by a set of actors and institutions that hold a disproportionate amount of power. As Molotch commented, 'The people who participate with their energies, and particularly their fortunes, in local affairs are the sort of persons who – at least in vast disproportion to their representation in the population – have the most to gain or lose in land-use decisions' (1976: 314). With increasing resonance over the last few decades, governance has come to be understood as a set of processes which involve different agencies and actors coming together to influence decision-making in cities and city regions. Harvey commented, in decrying the focus on government alone:

> the real power to reorganize urban life so often lies elsewhere or at least within a broader coalition of forces within which urban government and administration have only a facilitative and coordinating role to play. The power to organize space derives from a whole complex of forces mobilized by diverse social agents. It is a conflictual process, the more so in the ecological spaces of highly variegated social density.
>
> (Harvey 1989: 6)

Harvey (1989) also highlighted that it is essential to understand the role of cities within wider social processes. Indeed, when examining cities, it becomes necessary to understand the manner in which, from a dialectical perspective, the highly differentiated spaces of contemporary cities are produced by, and serve to reproduce, a diverse range of social forces (Harvey 1996; Lefebvre 1991).

Pointedly, the city often becomes simultaneously something that is seen as solving various social problems, and a separate entity that can stand alone without regard to the forces that would be necessary to produce such a reality. On the one hand, cities become what Peck *et al.* (2013) refer to as 'over-responsibilized', meaning that there is an expectation that city authorities have to solve various urban problems, including environmental issues, unemployment and poverty. Yet at the same time the city becomes representative of promoting a utopian ideal of society, without any meaningful outline of how this will become a reality.

Indeed, notions of the 'good city' tend to emerge as a common means of representing the idea of the urban across time and space (Amin 2006). A striking example is twentieth-century modernism, which for all its failings espoused a city that promoted the needs of people from a wide cross-section of society. However, as Amin elaborates with reference to the present period, 'Utopia has lost its logos, meaning, appeal and organising force, as meanings of the good life shift to immediate, temporary, private and hedonistic projects' (2006).

Much of the current phase – which is manifest in different guises in different locations – espouses a notion of a city that is targeted most particularly at the consumption habits of wealthy and middle-class citizens. Yet at the same time such an image is naturalized as representing a city that is somehow better for 'everyone', even if it is organized in a highly unequal manner.

Much of the recent approach to urban development, particularly in a European and North American context, has focused on the reappraisal of historic city centre areas. Such spaces are often presented through a geographical imaginary of higher densities with a mixture of uses predominantly focused on consumption-oriented practices and gentrification (Smith 2002; Zukin 2009, 2010; Lawton and Punch 2014). Pointedly, the image of gentrification can often fit directly into what is presented as a form of sustainability framework: the reappropriation of historic buildings within walkable (socially mixed) communities. This 'gentrification as policy' approach revolves around somewhat seductive urban environments – harmonious street interaction (Jacobs 1961) in restored historic buildings (Zukin 1982) or hi-tech apartment developments offering a 'better way of life' – but in reality it promotes one-sided ideals of urban life which result in exclusionary outcomes (Lees *et al.* 2008; Smith 2002).

When combined with the significant amount of attention to Richard Florida's (2002) 'creative class', this urban ideal has become a key point of reference among planners and policy makers (see Lawton *et al.* 2013) as representative of the 'good city'. Yet in reality there is a mismatch between the need to promote sustainable urbanization and a city that is increasingly oriented towards neoliberal ideals associated with gentrification (Smith 2002), while also tending to hide or downplay social inequalities and tensions between different social groups (Lees *et al.* 2008).

Pointedly, one of the key features of contemporary approaches to the city is the assumption that there is a direct link between social cohesion and urban competitiveness (Fainstein 2001). While this perspective is contradicted by much literature in urban studies from the 1970s onwards, as Fainstein also pointed out (2001), it has become a dominant means of promoting an increasingly entrepreneurial approach towards urban development. Here, the perspective is that social cohesion is a necessity and an outcome of an urban competitiveness agenda (Fainstein 2001). Thus, while urban governance has been dominated by the naturalization of an entrepreneurial (neoliberal) approach, it often draws upon ideals of cohesion, tolerance (Florida 2002) and 'inclusive' means of planning as a form of justification of such processes.

Rights, justice and governance

While much urban discourse has been dominated by critical accounts of neoliberalism, recent years have also witnessed the emergence of a significant amount of debate about the future shape of cities in relation to potentials and limitations of democratic engagement, particularly through planning practices that are set up as open and deliberative. Purcell (2007) summarized how much of this debate has revolved around ideals of 'communicative planning'. Drawing extensively from Habermasian theories of communicative democracy, 'communicative planning' promotes the notion that all actors have an equal stake in planning processes. Advocates thus promote communicative approaches to planning on the basis that they neutralize power and produce a fairer outcome. Pointedly, with direct relationship to the European scale, these notions have emerged within key documents and agreements among various bodies that seek to promote more socially balanced and sustainable cities. For example, such elements were a dominant theme in the 1994 Aalborg Charter (European Commission 1994). This is emphasized in Aalborg +10, which sought to re-emphasize the original commitments through the evocation of 'participatory democracy' and a commitment to five key principles, which are summarized as:

1   Further develop a commonly shared long-term vision for a sustainable city or a town;
2   Build participation and sustainable development capacity in the local community and municipal administration;
3   Invite all sectors of local society to participate effectively in decision-making;
4   Make our decisions open, accountable and transparent;
5   Cooperate effectively and in partnership with adjoining municipalities, other cities and towns, and other spheres of Government.

(European Commission 2004)

Notions of 'inclusion' and participation are placed as central features of approaches to governance at the European scale, and fit within the remit of the wider dynamics of urban transformation that are espoused by various supranational European bodies. However, as Purcell (2007) commented, communicative planning seeks to promote consensus among a population around a common theme, rather than inclusion in the decision-making process. It can therefore be critiqued on the basis of not so much challenging a set of processes, as becoming wholly embedded in them and merely seeking some form of deliberative outcome.

The difficulty of this approach is often highlighted in respect to its failure to challenge already existing inequalities within cities. Thus, communicative planning, while seeming at face value at least to promote democratic engagement, is held to be naïve about the structures of power in society. Critics such as Purcell (2007) therefore state that, as an approach, communicative planning can become too easily subsumed within a neoliberal agenda. Fainstein outlines this critique as follows:

Much of this critique is in my view appropriate but the remedy proposed – a more open, more democratic process – fails to confront adequately the initial discrepancy of power, offers few clues to overcoming co-optation or resistance to reform, does not sufficiently address some of the major weaknesses of democratic theory, and diverts discussion from the substance of policy.

(Fainstein 2010: 24)

From this perspective, approaches to the restructuring of urban governance must therefore seek to challenge the inherent inequalities, rather than assume that different groups can have an equal say in how cities change.

In drawing on the notion of equity, Fainstein (2010, 2014) argues for balanced inclusion in decision-making, with the interests of different groups represented (2014). She is at particular pains to stress the need for a shift in the discourse from a focus on notions of efficiency and competitiveness to a focus on equity and justice. In opposing forms of utopianism, she instead seeks out the potential for change in the context of the existing political and economic structure (Fainstein 2010; Novy and Mayer 2009). As a means of illustrating this, she draws on the example of Amsterdam – due to her perception of its balance of equity, diversity, tolerance and sustainability.

Fainstein's formulation of justice in the city has, however, not been without its critics. Novy and Mayer (2009), for example, critique her idealization of Amsterdam and her treatise on the 'just city' more generally. This is based both on the actually existing evolution of Amsterdam to a more 'competitive city' agenda and on what they perceive as the problematique of promoting a Eurocentric notion of the 'just city'. Moreover, in questioning the forms of negotiation and debate that might be possible within Fainstein's framing of the 'just city', Harvey and Potter (2009: 46) are somewhat disparaging: 'Certainly her proposal incorporates disagreement and debate, but these differences are ultimately to be harmoniously resolved, so to speak, over a cup of cappuccino at a sidewalk café.' Critical scholars, such as David Harvey and Peter Marcuse, have thus sought to challenge the potential of a 'just city' in the context of the existing political and economic structures.

In the context of a desire to move beyond 'justice' (Marcuse 2009b), much scholarship has evoked Lefebvre's (1996) dictum of the 'right to the city' (Harvey 2008). This work has been at pains to stress the importance of particular social movements and what they can offer towards a democracy in the city (Marcuse 2009a, 2009b; Mayer 2009; Purcell 2007). This has been particularly salient since 2008, with the emergence of various groups such as Occupy claiming a right to be heard through invoking a right to the city. However, it has also emerged as a key element in organizations such as UNESCO (see Mayer 2009) and UN-HABITAT (2008), as a means of pointing to the current problems with globalized processes of urbanization. There is potential within the approach to bring notions that are often discussed at the level of academic discussion and operationalized in various social movements to the level of broader structures of governance. Much of this ideal is expressed through a rights-based approach to the city:

> The 'right to the city' has evolved over the past 50 years as a challenge to the exclusionary development, selective benefit-sharing, marginalization and discrimination that are rampant in cities today. More than a new legalistic device, the right to the city is the expression of the deep yearnings of urban dwellers for effective recognition of their various human rights.
>
> (UN-HABITAT 2008: XVII)

However, this institutionalization of the 'right to the city' is not without its shortcomings and associated critiques. Thus, with direct reference to the use of the ideal of the 'right to the city' in the *World Charter for the Right to the City* by UNESCO and UN-HABITAT, Mayer states that

> unlike the Lefebvrian notion of the right to the city, this institutionalized set of rights boils down to claims for inclusion in the current system as it exists, it does not aim at transforming the existing system – and in that process ourselves.
>
> (Mayer 2009: 369)[2]

Thus, as furthered by Mayer (2009), such a vision aims at challenging severe urban problems, such as poverty, availability of shelter and so on, yet it does not seek to challenge the structures that produce them. While organizations such as UN-HABITAT recognize the key elements that might symbolize sustainable urbanization, there is often a disjuncture between ideal and reality. For example, in a recent report, UN-HABITAT said, 'Municipal authorities can prioritize expenditures on social security nets, local/regional infrastructure and other types of development, with a view to securing longer-term growth while stimulating consumption and/or employment in the short term' (2013: 8). Here, in following from Mayer (2009), there is a necessity to recognize the structures that in the first place lead to urban inequalities, and second, could be altered in order to address them.

Formulations of rights have also become evident in various supranational bodies at the European scale. Through the development of various charters and policy documents, each of these points to the desire for a sustainable urban future. For example, the *European Urban Charter* of 1992 sets out the vision of cities as follows:

> The charter is guided by the belief that citizens have basic urban rights: the right to protection from aggression; from pollution; from a difficult and disturbing urban environment; the right to exercise democratic control of their local community; the right to decent housing, health, cultural opportunity and mobility.
>
> (Council of Europe, 1992: 7)

The city is presented as something that can stand for, and at the same time produce, the essential elements of a balanced urban existence, where democracy and rights are central elements of everyday life. Yet the contradictions between the processes outlining how such scenarios will become a reality are absent from such formulations. At various levels of engagement, the discourse around urban development in Europe in recent decades has thus been dominated by ideals of integration, through for example social mix, without any significant focus on redistribution (Novy and Mayer 2009).

On the ground, as discussed earlier in this chapter, European cities have to greater or lesser extents been subjected to what Brenner and Theodore (2002) refer to as the forces of 'actually existing neoliberalism' (Novy and Mayer 2009; Lawton and Punch 2014). Thus while the idealization of European cities revolved around the balancing of economic progress, alongside policies that supported some form of redistribution, such as social housing, the reality has been vastly different. By 2008, this reality was becoming apparent and undeniable. Following from the 1992 *European Urban Charter*, a second *Urban Charter* was agreed in 2008. In this the Council of Europe commented:

> We are particularly alarmed by spatial disparity processes that are leading to gentrification of certain urban areas, by the uncontrollable rise in land

prices in our urban centres and its parallel phenomena of ghetto formation in peri-urban areas and by the appearance in certain places of 'gated communities' that encourage a spatial segregation which is breaking up our towns and cities.

(Council of Europe 2008)

Such a synopsis at least acknowledges much of the critique of the contemporary European city that has been central to critical urban studies of recent decades (Jessop 2002). Moreover, it also acknowledges, at least implicitly, the sheer power of forces at work in influencing the daily reality of contemporary cities.

A core challenge for the future of cities is to develop policies that promote ways to challenge the normative assumptions about cities as economic engines. As Purcell commented, 'Urban scholars have analyzed in detail how neoliberal globalization has negatively impacted cities and city-regions. What we require now is an active search for creative and progressive alternatives to the current situation' (2007: 197). Questions might thus be asked about in what way supranational organizations such as UN-HABITAT frame notions of 'rights' and the origins of such notions. Outlining a set of 'rights' seems at most to promote an ideal of engagement of different social groups, but does little to challenge the structures that serve to produce inequalities in the first place. As well as challenging the spatial manifestation of injustices, there is a need to challenge the structures that serve to produce such in the first place.

Discussion: a governance of recognition?

It is evident in the various documents of organizations such as UN-HABITAT and the European Commission mentioned above that there is at least some form of desire to incorporate formulations of urban justice and rights into urban governance. One of the key challenges that emerges is how to make this a reality. Such an ideal already exists, at least at the level of rhetoric:

> The right to the city can provide municipal authorities with the platform they need for a wide range of policies and initiatives that promote an 'inclusive' urban environment. The right to the city calls for a holistic, balanced and multicultural type of urban development. Therefore, it must pervade all policy areas, including land use, planning, management and reform, and it must do so in close cooperation with government agencies and civil society.
>
> (UN-HABITAT 2008: 127)

Such a perspective holds out the possibility that notions of justice, equity and rights could become central to urban governance. Yet in such a formulation there is the assumption that governance itself can be altered in a manner that recognizes the imbalances in power structures and seeks to address them. If it could exist under the current system, as Fainstein (2014) perceived, a formulation would put forward a form of governance in which normalization, or structures that place actors such as property interests, overlapping political interests and land owner-ship at the centre of governance, are dismantled through what Purcell (2009: 158) calls a 'de-hegemonizing' of political life. This formulation would seek to iden-tify those who gain disproportionately from political decisions (Molotch 1976; Harvey 1989).

The state, and particularly the manner in which it operates at the level of the city or city-region, is of key importance here. Such a perspective is highlighted by Fainstein as follows:

> We thus need to return to the concept of the enabling state rather than simply the entrepreneurial state and recognize that overemphasis on participation and decentralization evades the issue of just distribution, which may be sub-sumed by a capabilities approach to social justice but nevertheless is a neces-sary condition.
>
> (Fainstein 2001: 888)

Such a formulation would necessitate that governance be restructured through a recognition of the need to offer a greater level of opportunity to those groups for whom it is most necessary. In thinking through what such a formulation might look like, it is important to promote the inclusion of a wide array of social actors, including the disadvantaged, the poor and the homeless, not just in the forms of 'inclusive' communicative planning processes, but in a manner that tackles the reproduction of injustice in the first place. Such recognition should also be mind-ful of the factors that serve to increase the powers of particular interests, and of the need for active engagement with seeking to challenge them.

From the clearance of informal settlements in various cities throughout the global South, to the wholesale selling-off of lands in Western European con-texts, the negative impacts of contemporary capitalism (Peck *et al.* 2013) become clear. In order to address the approach to urban governance in favor of 'justice' and 'rights', there needs to be a clear recognition of the manner in which these processes actually impact on cities, over and above the dominance of an urban-competitiveness mantra. Indeed, there are evidently within current debates some challenges around notions of the 'untamed' itself. While hegemonic planning seeks certain levels of 'order', it also leaves in its wake, an untamed urban envi-ronment. Thus, the desire, as is outlined within this book, for cities to become somewhat 'untamed' does so in a manner that would allow for better urban futures to emerge in the wake of processes that themselves are so often unstable and contradictory.

To return to the subtitle of this chapter; 'Beyond an imaginary of power', the necessary shifts would require a refocus on the actual impacts of urban processes over and above the dominance of particular spatial ideals of the city. Much of the discourse around justice and rights in the city rejects spatial utopianism. While Fainstein disputes its use in the context of actually existing political-economic circumstances, Harvey perceives utopian ideals of city-making as repressive (Harvey and Potter 2009). Yet, in espousing the potential of less rigid forms of planning – or the 'untamed' – there is perhaps a form of utopianism emerging. This is a form of utopianism that seeks for a fairer, more inclusive city.

Notes

1 See: http://monocle.com/magazine/issues/15/the-worlds-top-25-most-liveable-cities/ and: www.mercer.com/articles/quality-of-living-survey-report-2011
2 For more on the World Charter for the Right to the City, see: www.urbanreinventors. net/3/wsf.pdf (accessed 25 June 2014).

References

Amin, A. 2006. The good city, *Urban Studies*, 43(5/6): 1009–23.
Bontje, M. and Lawton, P. 2013. Mobile policies and shifting contexts: city regional competitiveness strategies in Amsterdam and Dublin. *Tijdschrift voor Economische en Sociale Geografie (TESG)*, 104(4): 397–409.
Brenner, N. and Schmid, C. 2014. The 'urban age' in question. *International Journal of Urban and Regional Research*, 38(3): 731–55.
Brenner, N. and Theodore, N. 2002. Cities and the geographies of 'actually existing neoliberalism'. *Antipode*, 34(3): 349–79.Council of Europe. 1992. *Standing Conference of Local and Regional Authorities of Europe: European Urban Charter.* Brussels: Council of Europe.
—— 2008. *European Urban Charter II: Manifesto for a New Urbanity.* Brussels: Council of Europe.
European Commission. 1994. *Aalborg Charter.* Brussels: European Commission.
Fainstein, S. 2001. Competitiveness, cohesion, and governance: their implications for social justice. *International Journal of Urban and Regional Research*, 24: 884–8.
—— 2010. *The Just City.* Ithaca, NY: Cornell University Press.
—— 2014. The just city. *International Journal of Urban Sciences*, 18(1): 1–18.
Florida, R. 2002. *The Rise of the Creative Class: And How It's Transforming Work, Leisure, Community, and Everyday Life.* New York: Basic Books.
Harvey, D. 1989. From managerialism to entrepreneurialism: the transformation in urban governance in late capitalism. *Geografiska Annaler*, 41(1): 3–17.
——1996. *Justice, Nature and the Geography of Difference*, Malden, MA: Blackwell.
——2008. 'The right to the city', *New Left Review*, 53: 23–40.
Harvey, D. and Potter, C. 2009. The right to the just city. In P. Marcuse, J. Connolly, J. Novy, I. Olivo, C. Potter and J. Steil (eds), *Searching for the Just City: Debates in Urban Theory and Practice.* London: Routledge.
Jacobs, J. 1961. *The Death and Life of Great American Cities.* New York: Random House.
Jessop, B. 2002. Liberalism, neoliberalism and urban governance: a state-theoretical perspective. *Antipode*, 34(3): 452–72.
Lawton, P. and Punch, M. 2014. Urban governance and the 'European city': ideals and realities in Dublin, Ireland. *International Journal of Urban and Regional Research*.
Lawton, P., Murphy, E. and Redmond, D. 2010. The role of 'creative class' ideas in urban and economic policy formation: the case of Dublin, Ireland. *International Journal of Knowledge-Based Development*, 1(4): 267–86.
—— 2013. Residential preferences of the creative class? *Cities*, 31: 47–56.
Lees, L., Slater, T. and Wyly, E. 2008. *Gentrification.* New York: Routledge.

Lefebvre, H. 1991. *The Production of Space*, trans. D. Nicholson Smith. Malden, MA: Blackwell.

——1996. The right to the city. In E. Kofman and E. Lebas (eds), *Writings on Cities*. Malden, MA: Blackwell.

Marcuse, P. 2009a. From critical urban theory to the right to the city. *City*, 13(2–3): 185–97.

——2009b. Beyond the just city to the right to the city. In P. Marcuse, J. Connolly, J. Novy, I. Olivo, C. Potter and J. Steil (eds), *Searching for the Just City: Debates in Urban Theory and Practice*. London: Routledge.

Mayer, M. 2009. Shifting mottos of urban social movements. *City*, 13(2–3): 362–74.

Molotch, H. 1976. The city as a growth machine: toward a political economy of place. *American Journal of Sociology*, 82(2): 309–32.

Novy, J. and Mayer, M. 2009. As 'just' as it gets? The European city in 'just city' discourse. In P. Marcuse, J. Connolly, J. Novy, I. Olivo, C. Potter and J. Steil (eds), *Searching for the Just City: Debates in Urban Theory and Practice*. London: Routledge.

Peck, J. 2005. Struggling with the creative class. *International Journal of Urban and Regional Research*, 29: 740–70.

Peck J., Theodore, N. and Brenner, N. 2013. Neoliberal urbanism redux? *International Journal of Urban and Regional Research*, 37(3): 1091–9.

Purcell, M. 2007. City-regions, neoliberal globalization and democracy: a research agenda. *International Journal of Urban and Regional Research*, 31(1): 197–206.

——2008. Resisting noeliberalization: communicative planning or counter-hegemonic movements? *Planning Theory*, 8: 140–65.

Smith, N. 2002. New globalism, new urbanism: gentrification as global urban strategy. *Antipode*, 34(3): 427–50.

Uitermark, J. 2010. An in memoriam for the just city of Amsterdam. *City*, 13(2–3): 347–61.

UN-HABITAT. 2008. *The State of the World's Cities 2010–2011*. London: Earthscan.

——2013. *The State of the World's Cities 2012–2013*. New York@: UN-HABITAT/ Routledge.

Zukin, S. 1982. Loft living as 'historic compromise' in the urban core: the New York experience. *International Journal of Urban and Regional Research*, 6(2): 256–67.

——2009. Changing landscapes of power: opulence and the urge for authenticity. *International Journal of Urban and Regional Research*, 33(2): 543–53.

——2010. *Naked City: The Death and Life of Authentic Urban Places*. New York: Oxford University Press.

Part IV

Liberating alternatives

Part IV on 'liberating alternatives' contains chapters that explore the narratives developed by people living in – and thus creating – cities beyond the limits of the contemporary disciplining practices that produce and shape urban development processes.

Engaging with the re-politicization of intersectional analysis, in Chapter 15 – entitled 'Negotiating and creating urban spaces in everyday practices: experiences of women in Harare, Zimbabwe' – Manase Kudzai Chiweshe (Zimbabwe) explores the negotiation and contestation of urban spaces by four women in this city. Instead of simply gesturing towards the way in which class, gender, ethnicity and age operate in the city, the author applies a portraiture method to substantiate empirically the lived experiences and interconnected identifications of the four women's narratives, as they carve out ways to be in a city where bodies and public spaces are tightly controlled under a hegemonic masculinity order.

Chapter 16 by Moises Lino e Silva (Brazil) – entitled 'A conversation in a dentist's chair: employment, marginality and freedom on the borders of a Brazilian favela' – also takes an ethnographic approach but this time to examine the untamed practices of those who claim time freedom over the dictates of formal work, the latter explored as a deeply embedded and naturalized requirement to be included in the city. Offering an immersion into the lives of various women and men in Rocinha, a favela in Rio de Janeiro, Brazil, the author reveals the freeing potential of everyday practices that escape the otherwise seemingly unavoidable urban social order that portrays formal employment as the only way for the poor to have a legitimate place in the city.

The following two contributions revisit the question of gentrified and reclaimed public spaces. Cities have been the central sites of class struggles over who controls urban resources and life and the locus of potentially radical urbanisms since well before the emergence of the Occupy Movement. Entitled 'Contested taming spatialities: the micro-resistance of everyday life in Buenos Aires', Chapter 17 by Jorge Sequera and Elvira Mateos (Spain) explores the tensions unfolding between the gentrification of Costanera Sur – a downtown area in Buenos Aires city, Argentina – and the micro-resistance of everyday life practices that every weekend continue to reclaim this area through popular street barbecues, informal markets, music and dance. The authors examine the clash between the mutually encroaching practices and aspirations of real estate developers, upper- and middle-class urbanites, working-class women and men, and slum dwellers.

In Chapter 18 – titled 'Public spaces and transformative urban practices in Cape Town' – Diana Sanchez Betancourt (Colombia) also focuses on the micro-practices of re-appropriation of public spaces, this time in Cape Town, South Africa. The chapter scrutinizes the transformative potential of a diversity of social experimentations that playfully seek to overcome the material and narrative Apartheid legacy of fragmentation and segregation. The author offers a new map of the city constructed through organic forms of citizen action and engagement that expand urban agency through social media and networking.

Chapter 19 by Irene Sotiropoulou (Greece) – entitled 'Everyday practices in Greece in the shadow of property: urban domination subverted?' – takes a refreshing and theoretically risky path, adopting a Jungian approach and a feminist critique of property to explore the subversive potential of everyday practices operating outside the rule of monetary exchange and obligatory (re)payment in two Greek cities. Here the appropriation of public space through practices that escape the taming power of capitalism is treated as a vehicle to examine the tensions confronting collective efforts to supersede scarcity and greed as two fundamental conditions underpinning the reproduction of capitalist patriarchy in the city.

Also in the realm of alternative – non-monetary – economies, Chapter 20 by Ferne Edwards (Australia) – entitled 'Free-ing foods? Social food economies towards secure and sustainable food systems' – takes the reader through a deep exploration of social food economies in Sydney, Australia. Stepping outside the prevailing industrial food system, the author looks into the practices of gleaning, growing and gifting food in the urban context. The chapter offers a critical examination of the untaming potential of these food procurement options by scrutinizing them through the lens of different forms of autonomy: autonomy of money, autonomy of thought and autonomy from the system.

15 Negotiating and creating urban spaces in everyday practices

Experiences of women in Harare, Zimbabwe

Manase Kudzai Chiweshe

Introduction

Women in Zimbabwean urban spaces are located at varying intersections of class, citizenship, background and race. This chapter examines how women experience urban spaces using the case of Harare in Zimbabwe. It focuses on how everyday practices can question and challenge hegemonic ideas about the urban. It uses a portraiture approach to weave an intricate outline of how four purposively selected women have experienced the city. The chapter shows how gender as a practice intersects with issues of urban life to create gendered spaces.

Connell (2005) argues that gender is not who we are but rather what we practise. Urban spaces define and impact on this practice in multiple ways. The chapter uses the concept of hegemonic masculinity to outline how women are controlled and contained in specific urban spaces, yet find ways and means to negotiate and create space. Women respond to interlocked oppressive structures within the city by continuously finding spaces to survive. For the women in this chapter, space is intrinsically linked with their livelihoods. Access to urban spaces, especially to the streets, is critical for income generation, as will be highlighted by their stories.

The work outlined in this chapter was inspired by my own experience of growing up in one of the poorest suburbs of Harare. When I was born my father was unemployed and had spent years being jobless. I am the fifth of seven children, and our survival for most of my childhood was dependent on my mother's street-vending enterprise. Her experiences of the city, while unique, highlight the varied stories of trial, struggle, sacrifice and negotiation within an often anti-female space. My mother's experiences motivated my choice of research and the methodology utilized, which concentrated on storytelling. The stories of four women used in this chapter reflect the many spatial and temporal tensions involved in the gendering of bodies within urban spaces. Through the stories an emerging pattern can be ascertained which helps in understanding the experience of women in urban Zimbabwe.

Colonial Harare and gendered spaces

Under colonial rule, Harare was known as Salisbury, the capital of Rhodesia. Barnes (1992) argues that the hallmark of colonial governance in Rhodesia was denying certain spaces to certain groups. From its foundation, the city was built on the basis of exclusion, especially of African women. As Vambe (1976) notes, 'Originally Harare was not intended for respectably married people, but for that type of 'native' who kept his wife and kids somewhere in the reserve of his birth' (cited in Ruzivo 2005:1). Such colonial construction of respectability

> was characterised by the same notions of respectability that had existed during pre-colonial times. At that time, respectable women were those who were fertile, who rejected any methods of controlling their fertility (through abortion, for instance), and who participated in laborious agricultural activities and other duties for their natal and matrimonial families.
>
> (Hungwe 2006:34)

The city was a male space, and the 'native' woman had no place in it. Gaidzanwa (1995) notes how women who defied this were often branded prostitutes and 'unrespectable women'. This colonial and patriarchal concern with women's respectability is part of an ongoing struggle over the control of women's bodies within urban spaces.

This marginalization of black women from the cities was not only perpetrated by white colonialists but rather found congruence with African patriarchy. Gaidzanwa (1992) explores this marriage of convenience based on the need to control the movement and operation of women's bodies. The colonial government wanted women to provide free social reproductive roles in the rural areas by caring for the old and injured workers without any cost to the government, while bearing more children. African males wanted their wives to remain in rural areas to secure their land claims. Respectable women thus stayed behind when their men folk went to the city, caring for their family in rural areas. Ruzivo (2005:2) adds:

> Older men, chiefs and colonial officials colluded to control women's mobility to the cities. In 1927 several chiefs and headmen called upon the colonial authorities to enact a pass system for any female who entered either mining towns, farms or any city. Ordinance 16 of 1901 was to be amended so that women who sought employment in the city would be required to obtain permits from senior administrative officials.

Hungwe (2006) also points out that colonial government thought it cheaper to provide bachelor accommodation for black workers, and also paid lower wages as the men were living alone. Having children and wives was seen as distracting, and black women were often accused of brewing and selling illicit beer. In colonial times alternative income-generating activities for women were often criminalized.

In the later years of colonization there was a steady increase in the number of women living in urban centres. Wells (2003) argues that the bulk of research on women during colonial times depicts their primary form of resistance as moving from rural to urban areas. Through this movement they played an active role in undermining patriarchal customs, which they experienced as oppressive. Yet the colonial construction of women as rural folk has continued after independence. The colonial practice of segregating spaces was continued for example in 2013, when the police started a programme of arresting women walking alone in the city centre at night. The implication is that only 'prostitutes' and 'unrespectable women' (Hungwe 2006) walk alone at night. The city at night is thus out of bounds for women.

Conceptual framework

In understanding the gendered dimensions of urban areas, I outline how the urban experience is based on the construction of hegemonic ideas of masculinities and femininities in such spaces. The articulation of masculinities and femininities affects access to and control of certain spaces. According to Connell (2000:46), hegemonic masculinity refers to a dominant form of masculinity that embodies, organizes and legitimizes men's domination in the world gender order as a whole. Hegemony shapes the way gender is performed in the context of regulation of actions through prohibition and taboo, and its performance iteratively shapes the ideals, values and cultural norms that inform and shape hegemonic masculinity (Butler 1990). Since masculine and feminine norms are defined and shaped by power relations that exist in material contexts (Datta 2008), revealing the spatially embedded and obscured performed patterns of hegemonic masculinity is important for understanding, for instance, the subordinate position of female cooperative recyclers. Since gender is a word used to describe everyday social practice and ordering of space (Connell 2005), it is necessary to focus on physical spaces such as the home and the work place to understand the production of masculine and feminine identities (Datta 2008).

Massey (1994) explores the pervasive and deeply embedded nature of gender throughout space, between cultures, classes, races and taking place over time. She argues that spaces and places in every aspect are thoroughly gendered. Hegemonic masculinity, in many cases, has a significant role in shaping gendered space. Urban areas, like all spaces and places, have a distinct spatial order. Datta (2008:191) confirms this notion by arguing that spaces are interpreted through 'representative aspects' that communicate 'natural' hierarchies among bodies within the spaces they occupy. Within urban spaces there are distinct performed gender roles, discourses and rituals of space that help to configure these hierarchies. Spatial practices, everyday understandings of gendered space, demeanour and attire are just a few examples of the deep-seated indications of a gendered social order among women in urban spaces.

To better understand how women experience the city, the chapter also utilizes Crenshaw's (1991) intersectionality theory. Urban women in Zimbabwe are found at the intersection of multiple and mutually reinforcing systems of oppression such as capitalism, racism and patriarchy. Thus, to understand how women are affected by urban life we need to understand where they are situated, and that they are affected by an intersection of factors besides gender, which include class, ethnicity, race and nationality. Crenshaw (1991) provides a theoretical orientation that explains the interplay of various factors defining an individual's position. The theoretical basis of the intersectionality approach involves viewing societal knowledge as being located within an individual's specific geographic and social location. This theory also analyses how various social and culturally constructed categories interact on multiple levels to become manifest as inequalities in society, as race, gender and class mutually shape forms of oppression in society.

To reduce the analysis of women's lives to gender alone is to strip them of the racial and class historical antecedents which characterize their marginal position in most African societies. The intersectionality approach is that difficulties arise because of the many complexities involved in making multi-dimensional conceptualizations that explain the way in which socially constructed categories of differentiation interact to create a social hierarchy. For example, intersectionality holds that knowing a woman lives in a sexist society is insufficient information to describe her experience; instead, it is also necessary to know her race, sexual orientation and class, as well as her society's attitude toward each of these memberships. It is only through analysing how these complex concepts intertwine and interlink that we are able to understand the gendered experiences of both men and women in different contexts.

Methodology: portraiture and narratives of urban women

The study utilized a qualitative approach based on Sara Lawrence-Lightfoot's (1983) portraiture method. Sandoval (2000) argues that portraiture provides in-depth analytical tools to better understand the experiences of marginalized persons. Women's lives in urban Harare can be understood from the standpoint of every vignette that defines their everyday existence. To provide a critical analysis of their struggles and relationship to the city, it was important for me to seek a method that brought out their voices. The city in its physical element and urban studies in general has a tendency to drown out the voices of marginalized and poor women. In explaining the advantages of the portraiture method, Lawrence-Lightfoot and Davis (1997:3) note:

> Portraiture seeks to combine systematic, empirical description with aesthetic expression, blending art and science, humanistic sensibilities and scientific rigor. The portraits are designed to capture the richness, complexity and dimensionality of the people who are negotiating those experiences. The portraits are shaped through dialogue between the portraitist and the subject. The encounter between the two is rich with meaning and resonance and is crucial to the success and authenticity of the rendered piece.

Because the intensity of the methodology makes it time-consuming, although all women have a distinctive history, it was important for me to be selective in the number and nature of women interviewed. I selected four women from diverse social contexts in an urban setting to highlight the varied experiences of gender and urban life. While the four cases are unique and context-specific, they provide a basis for analysis. The small sample provided rich exploratory data and allowed for the full participation of the storytellers. I selected one young woman living on the street to highlight the construction around gender, dislocation, poverty and homelessness. The second woman involved in informal trading and the third woman involved in sex work were selected to provide insights into alternative livelihood options in urban spaces, and a woman formally employed in a nightclub was chosen to highlight how urban livelihoods intersect with gender.

These participants – the sex worker, the street trader, the working woman and the girl living on the streets – ranged in age from 17 to 34. Their diverse backgrounds highlight how various factors intersect to influence how women experience the city. The interviews and stories were in Shona, which is the local language. They were later transcribed and translated into English using a language expert. This was done to ensure consistency of meaning and context. No names are given, as a way of protecting the research participants who were kind enough to share their lives and time.

The portraiture method allowed for a critical approach to analysing the everyday lives of these women. The women in the study became storytellers and not respondents, who through sharing their stories were creating a way of seeing the city as providing African spaces. Such a method promotes creativity in research while being empirical and rigorous. It demands that the researcher be an active listener and learner. It is an enriching process geared towards the emancipation of the participants. In the context of this research, portraiture was useful in deconstructing my own views about the women in the city. Rather than simplifying their existence as mere victims of urbanized patriarchy, they emerged as active agents who against the odds create spaces for survival in an environment full of intersecting oppressions and exclusion.

Findings

Portrait one: Living on the streets: the intersection of age, class and gender

The experiences of girls living on the streets provide an interesting insight into how age, class and gender intersect. Here is the story of one girl who has lived on the streets since she was born, which shows how these young women are actively creating space in difficult circumstances:

> The streets have been my home for the past twelve years. I was born on the streets and my mother was blind. It means that my life has been in and around the central business district. I know these streets like the back of my hand. My existence is difficult and living on the streets has taught me how to survive serious hardships. Girls on the street suffer various forms of abuse which

are mostly sexual. You learn about sex at a very young age, and sex is an important part of surviving the streets. People call us 'streets kids' and make us outcasts. No one trusts us and everyone shuns us. It is a lonely existence having never had a family. As a young girl, my whole life has been a struggle yet I have survived by sleeping in backstreets and dark allies, begging and even stealing. I have at times used my body to earn money. On the streets there is little protection from the police. On the contrary, I have experienced harassment at the hands of the police. There is no way to report so we suffer in silence. Clothes and food are at times hard to come by. Also living in the street you begin to abuse intoxicating substances. Despite all these challenges, I am here on the streets surviving.

Portrait two: Negotiating informal trading on the streets of Harare

Street trading in Harare has been dominated by women since colonial times. Under colonization, certain spaces (especially in the central business district) were not open to black people. Street trading is often conceptualized as 'informal trade', as a way of differentiating it from legal and mainstream business activities (Mupedziswa and Gumbo 2001). Such conceptualization leaves most women and men trading on the streets outside the realm of legitimate business enterprises. This stigma is at the heart of the tendency for city authorities to be discriminatory and abusive towards female traders. Their lived experiences are littered with running battles with council officials who are mandated to rid the city of illegal traders. Moyo (2013) narrates the story of one female trader in Zimbabwe:

> Mollin Siyanda, 46, a single mother of three from Harare's low-income suburb of Hatcliffe, is scared of being arrested by the council police as she sells fruit, vegetables and second-hand clothes on the pavement of the city centre without a permit. 'I take the [fruit and clothes] to the city centre to resell on the street pavements during evenings at peak hours as people are rushing back home,' she says of the goods she purchases every day at Mbare Musika, a major market in Harare. 'But I'm always operating under constant fear of council cops who often accuse me of being an illegal vendor.'

In post-colonial Zimbabwe women are being denied certain spaces on class and gender lines, yet for most women their livelihoods are directly connected to the streets. With an economy that went through several shocks after 2000, Zimbabwe finds itself with unemployment in the formal sector as high as 84 per cent (Moyo 2013). The street has thus become an important space for survival as traders compete against each other and council officials.

The post-2000 traumatic crisis, which peaked in 2008, was characterized by high inflation, food shortages, the breakdown of social services and high unemployment. The informal sector became the biggest employer, as people survived by setting up various small enterprises to eke out a living. Access to space thus became an important survival commodity, as people required places to do their trade. For most women, buying and selling in the streets has become an important source of income. I focus on these specific traders because they epitomize the battle for the city and its intersection with the gendered dimensions of urban livelihoods. The story below outlines the everyday battles for survival, belonging and making a living that these women have to face, and the difficult choices they have to make. Urban streets, constructed under the guise of urban planning, have remained highly patriarchal and exclusionary.

> Selling on the streets has become an important part of my survival and that of my family. I concentrate on selling vegetables such as tomatoes, onions, rape and *tsunga* [a green leafy vegetable] because they are bought very quickly. I cannot afford the asking price for a seller's licence which is US$20. My husband works in the informal sector where he sometimes does not get paid. It is up to me to ensure that my three kids eat. I wake up every morning at 4 am and leave for Mbare market where I buy most of my produce. There are also farmers coming from nearby plots who are selling produce at cheap prices. Selling on the streets is difficult mainly because of the city council officials. They are in plain clothes and everyday they keep confiscating our goods and arresting us. We are constantly running away from these people. Nowadays we only have a few vegetables on display to avoid losing our goods. We are told that it is illegal to sell on the streets, so we need to apply for licences and get market stalls. It is difficult to access a stall if you are not well connected. What do they want us to do? Maybe if we all become thieves. We are simply looking for survival in a difficult context. Despite these challenges we are devising ways to ensure our continued presence on the streets. We will not stop trading because that is the only thing keeping our families going.

Portrait three: Working women and the city

Women are employed in Harare in a variety of industries and positions. In this chapter I focus on a formally employed woman working in a nightclub to highlight how she navigates this male domain. This gives an insight into both the experience of working in the city at night, and being an income earner. The story illuminates how work within certain spaces in urban areas poses serious gendered challenges for women who do these jobs every day. The nature and experience of work is based on commonly held stereotypes of women. Women who work in nightclubs often face a societal backlash with accusations of being 'loose':

> I am a young woman of 24 years and still single. I passed my O level exams but could not afford to continue to A level. Without any skills employment is difficult to come by, so I have to make do with any work I can get. I started working in a nightclub two years ago but the most difficult part is working the nightshifts. Nightshifts are difficult because the patrons can be rowdy when drunk. Waitresses suffer various forms of sexual abuse including fondling

our breasts, being pinched on our buttocks and vulgar language. Almost all men think that we are easy, and they are always proposing to have sex with us. Another problem is the police who at times arrest us for 'loitering' or suspect us of being sex workers when we leave work late. The police are constantly arresting women walking alone at night, and this is very frustrating for those of us who work at night. Our club has bouncers who at least try to help us get taxis home and protect us from violent patrons. I have very little choice but to continue with this job despite the problems I am facing. What is also difficult is how people in the community where you live perceive you when they hear you work in a nightclub. You are labelled a prostitute and it is difficult to have meaningful romantic relationships without your work becoming an issue. I have had to lie about my work to some of my relatives but that is just part of what I have to do to survive.

Portrait four: The morality of making a living and the everyday struggle of sex workers

The struggles in the urban streets can be understood from the everyday experiences of sex workers in Harare's central business district. Sex work is illegal in Zimbabwe yet only the women providing these services are arrested and imprisoned. The male clients are left alone, which makes this an important issue of understanding how women negotiate spaces in urban centres. The illegality of sex work rests on the argument of maintaining the national moral fibre, yet if you unmask the true intentions it is clear how patriarchy has continuously used state institutions to police and control women's sexuality. In this section I outline the experiences of a sex worker who has been working in the Avenues area of Harare for the past five years. Her story, although elements of it are unique, is representative of the many and varied experiences of sex workers who work under harsh conditions without any protection from the state:

> I started working on the streets at the end of 2008. Working on the streets was not an easy decision but life forces you to be where you never thought you could be. Sex work is difficult especially when you operate from the streets waiting for clients night after night. You face so many challenges including clients who do not want to pay, police raids and at times thieves. I have been a victim of robbery while working on the streets, and without much protection we are vulnerable to all sorts of dangers. You cannot tell anyone in your family you do this type of work. It is a secret but I have a child who lives with my mother and feeding her requires money. The police are always having operations aimed at removing us from the streets yet we keep coming back. Arrests do not deter us from work, and with the number of girls increasing it is becoming more difficult to make money working the streets. When we get arrested at times we pay the police through sex to be released. We just pay fines or some girls without money spend a week or two in jail and finally get released. Society judges what we do as immoral yet in the past I have been

picked up by very rich and influential people including prominent church pastors. Every week younger and younger girls are joining the streets, so sex workers will always be there. It will continue even with the serious dangers associated with it.

Discussion

It is important to highlight the emerging issues from the stories of these four women in Harare. While the choice of methodology sought to provide first-hand storytelling of everyday experiences, there is scope to analyse how the stories speak to the notion of 'untamed urbanisms'. Through careful analysis, I shall highlight both the theoretical and the practical implications of these stories for our understanding of how women experience, survive, challenge, subvert and recreate space in male-dominated places.

Hegemonic masculinities and space in urban Harare

The stories outlined above highlight how gender constructs shared expectations and norms within urban spaces about male and female behaviour, characteristics and roles. Urban areas thus have their own unique imprints on how gender is performed. The existence of hegemonic masculinities as forms of gendered identities in urban areas maps out appropriate styles of being a man or woman, which are exhibited in institutional patterns, behaviours, experiences, appearances and practices. Masculinities and femininities are configurations of practice that are accomplished in social action, and therefore can differ according to the gender relations in a particular social setting (Connell and Messerschmidt 2005: 836). The stories have shown the context-defined space and practice of women in Harare. For example, the sex worker, informal trader, working girl and girl living on the streets all respond differently to their situation using their gendered experiences.

Masculinities and femininities are society-specific, multifaceted and multi-dimensional, and entail having the power to define what is 'normal' or 'ordinary' male or female behaviour. In urban areas, the normal definitions of masculinities have been challenged by women who continuously redefine what women can or cannot do. This is contrary to the mainstream conceptualization of the private–public debate in which women are expected to be economic 'children', dependent on the breadwinning capacities of men who are in various social relationships with them. While these everyday practices do not challenge the foundations of patriarchy, they are part of subversive actions questioning the hegemony of certain masculinities.

Women as active agents in urban spaces

While it is important to analyse the structural constraints facing women in accessing space in urban areas, it is equally important to highlight that women are active agents. In everyday practices they defy spatial boundaries and exclusion. They are continuously negotiating and renegotiating space and ways of making a living under difficult conditions. The urban experiences in this way thus involve control over women's physical bodies and their location within 'acceptable' spaces. Hungwe (2006) has shown that in Zimbabwe this process of naming and shaming women as a means of controlling their movement has colonial roots. Women have, however, always found ways to challenge these controls. Occupying the streets and male spaces, women are defying gendered norms about space and belonging. They are normalizing the presence of women in all spaces, and thereby slowly subverting hegemonic masculinities and femininities. Women are actively questioning gender hierarchies and exclusion from certain spaces as regulated by patriarchy through various institutions including the police.

The existence of patriarchy in many societies in Africa is not disputed, and that it subjugates women and relegates them to the private sphere is well documented. Yet from the stories above we can see how women are constantly negotiating their positions. The stories told highlight the various fascinating modes of identity which are constantly being created and recreated by active agents in urban women's everyday lives. Stories from urban Zimbabwe have shown that gender should be viewed as a product of location, negotiated by women and men with discursive and performative vocabularies that they deploy but do not command into existence. Urban spaces therefore shape and are in turn shaped by gender practices. What women and men do each day configures gender in specific ways. The everyday experience of women in diverse urban spaces is thus important in reconfiguring the spaced nature of gender and deconstructing certain ways of viewing women in urban areas.

Women in the city are found at the intersection of different oppressive systems. They have a specific age, class and race, and come from different backgrounds. The theoretical basis of the intersectionality approach involves viewing societal knowledge as being located within an individual's specific geographic and social location. The stories of women outlined in this chapter highlight how various social and culturally constructed categories interact on multiple levels to manifest themselves as inequalities within the city. To reduce analysis of women's lives to gender alone is to strip them of the racial and class historical antecedents that characterize their marginal position in most African cities. Intersectionality is of the view that difficulties arise because of the many complexities involved in making multi-dimensional conceptualizations that explain the way in which socially constructed categories of differentiation interact to create a social hierarchy.

What do the stories say?

While I do not seek to generalize the stories of the four women shared above, they illustrate how women are constantly negotiating space within a highly patriarchal and male-dominated space (see Sotiropoulou, Chapter 19 of this volume, for a more nuanced discussion of urban life and capitalist patriarchy). The stories are an important reflection of how women in various contexts are challenging the dominant narratives about space and bodies in urban areas. Through various activities these women are opening up space and enhancing their livelihoods in the face of harsh treatment from police and other social agents of surveillance. From the stories it is clear how public spaces are highly surveyed and women who dare engage in non-feminine activities are often subjected to harassment. This is particularly true in the third story, where a woman walking alone at night is regularly censured by the police.

The fight for space is not only about physical space but also about livelihoods, belonging and identity. Women are often relegated to the periphery of the city, and kept within the bounds of domesticity, yet they are continuously faced with the need to feed their families. Access to space is intrinsically linked with the ability to earn a living. Portraits two and four highlight two women who engage in different ways of earning a living, but both face a constant struggle to 'own' the space they work in.

The stories also speak about how women in urban spaces are found at the intersection of interlocked oppressions. The first portrait, for example, shows how gender, age, class, lack of education, race and family background intersect to leave young women living on the street vulnerable to poverty and abuse. Yet women are constantly struggling with these interlocked oppressive systems as active agents. Through their actions they are 'untaming urban spaces' by disrupting the status quo and challenging hegemonic patriarchal structures in urban areas. Such disruptions occur in the everyday practices of women who resist subjugation and redefine access to the city. Women are involved in everyday struggles that continuously increase their access to space within cities. Urban spaces are often built around dominant ideas about how people must and should conduct themselves. Going against expected norms is seen as deviant. The concept of untamed urbanisms thus speaks to these subversive actions that question the norms of urban life, such as at what times women may walk in the city centre, or from which spaces they can sell their wares.

Concluding remarks

Urban spaces in Zimbabwe were built on colonial systems of exclusion which have evolved within the post-colonial state. What is clear from the Zimbabwean cases outlined above is how hegemonic masculinities dominate and define space in gendered ways. Women in Zimbabwe, through their everyday practices in different contexts, are challenging these ideas and carving out spaces for survival. The city is gendered in complex ways, yet this process evolves over time as people negotiate and renegotiate meaning in interactions. The chapter has shown how everyday practices can become important in recreating and subverting dominant ideas about gender and space in urban settings. I used stories of four women in diverse contexts and with differing experiences to highlight how the underlying assumptions of space as gendered influence everyday life in urban areas. The chapter shows that women are not mere victims of urban processes, but rather are creative agents using limited tools at their disposal to create space and livelihoods.

They are continuously negotiating and creating space within urban spaces dominated by hegemonic masculinities.

The four portraits highlight unique experiences of women in urban settings. Every story is different, yet gender remains the most important identifier. How gender plays out for women in urban spaces remains highly situational. This highlights the importance of situatedness, which rejects generalizing tendencies that seek to universalize women as a monolithic group. The differences in ways of making a living, age, marital status, educational level and parenthood highlight how patriarchy is not itself homogenous in how it impacts on women. Through the intersectionality approach it was possible to note how patriarchy polices space and limits women from diverse backgrounds in specific ways depending on their location. For example, women working as vendors on the street face resistance from authority in a different way from women who work in nightclubs. Intersectionality shows that all women have a distinct story which is largely influenced by their own distinct position. The context and history in each case above shows how the individual's specific geographic and social location is important in determining how they experience the city. The stories show that women confront and are confronted by multiple practices encountered through urban life, but they do so differently depending on their social position. Thus, an intersectionality perspective allows us to capture how their positionality is negotiated in the interstices between the tamed and the untamed.

References

Barnes, T. A. 1992. The fight for control of African women's mobility in colonial Zimbabwe, 1900–1939. *Signs*, 17(3): 586–608.

Butler, J. 1990. *Gender Trouble: Feminism and the Subversion of Identity*. New York: Routledge.

Connell, R. W. 2000. *The Men and the Boys*. Sydney, Australia: Allen & Unwin; Cambridge, UK: Polity Press; Berkeley, CA: University of California Press.

—— 2005. Globalization, imperialism and masculinities. In M. Kimmel, J. Hearn and R. W. Connell (eds), *Handbook on Studies of Men and Masculinities*. London: Sage.

Connell, R. W. and Messerschmidt, J. W. 2005. Hegemonic masculinity: rethinking the concept. *Gender and Society*, 19: 829–59.

Crenshaw, K. W. 1991. Mapping the margins: intersectionality, identity politics and violence against women of color. *Stanford Law Review*, 43(6): 1241–99.

Datta, A. 2008. *Spatialising performance: masculinities and femininities in a 'fragmented' field. Gender, Place and Culture*, 1 (2): 189–204.

Gaidzanwa, R. 1992. Bourgeois theories of gender and feminism and their shortcomings with reference to Southern Africa. In R. Meena (ed.), *Gender in Southern Africa: Conceptual and Theoretical Issues*. Harare: Sapes.

—— 1995. Women, democratisation and violence in Southern African experience. Paper presented at a seminar on Women and the Democratisation Process in Africa, University of Pretoria, South Africa, 7–11 April.

Hungwe, C. 2006. Putting them in their place: 'respectable' and 'unrespectable' women in Zimbabwean gender struggles, *Feminist Africa*, no. 6. Available at http://agi.ac.za/sites/agi.ac.za/files/fa_6_feature_article_3.pdf (accessed 13 August 2013).

Lawrence-Lightfoot, S. 1983. *The Good High School: Portraits of Character and Culture.* New York: Basic Books.

—— 2005. Reflections on portraiture: a dialogue between art and science. *Qualitative Inquiry, 11:* 3–15.

Lawrence-Lightfoot, S. and Davis, J. H. 1997. *The Art and Science of Portraiture.* San Francisco, CA: Jossey-Bass.

Massey, D. 1994. *Space, Place and Gender.* Minneapolis, MN: University of Minnesota Press.

Moyo, J. 2013. Giving women in Zimbabwe's informal sector rights. Available at www. ipsnews.net/2013/05/giving-women-in-zimbabwes-informal-sector-rights/ (accessed 17 August 2013).

Mupedziswa, R. and Gumbo, P. 2001. Women informal traders in Harare and the struggle for survival in an environment of economic reforms. Research Report no.117. Uppsala, Sweden:NordiskaAfrikainstitutet.

Ruzivo, M. 2005. Elizabeth Musodzi: the Catholic woman agent of the gospel in Harare. *Studio Historiae Ecclesiastice*, 31(2): 63–75. Available at http://uir.unisa.ac.za/bit-stream/handle/10500/4354/Ruzivo.pdf?sequence=1 (accessed 23 July 2013).

Sandoval, C. 2000. *Methodology of the Oppressed*, Minneapolis, MN: University of Minnesota Press.

Vambe, L. 1976. *From Rhodesia to Zimbabwe.* London: Heinemann.

Wells, J. C. 2003. The sabotage of patriarchy in colonial Rhodesia: rural African women's living legacy to their daughters. *Feminist Review*, 75:101–17.

16 A conversation in a dentist's chair
Employment, marginality and freedom on the borders of a Brazilian favela

Moises Lino e Silva

The broken filling

During the many months when I conducted ethnographic research in Favela da Rocinha (Rio de Janeiro, Brazil), a favourite pastime was to eat at one of the many food stalls near the place I was renting in the favela. Unlike the better-known Brazilian '*açai na tigela*', the açai berry smoothie consumed in Rocinha was usually sold in flimsy plastic cups and not in bowls. These cheap cups could often be seen floating in large quantities in the open sewers of the favela. The smoothies came with a variety of sweet toppings, including chocolate syrup, condensed milk and *jujuba*, which is a gelatinous sweet at room temperature. Mixed in a cold smoothie, it becomes as hard as ice. While I was eating an açai smoothie in early 2010, I broke a filling on one of those colourful *jujubas*.

The next morning I set about finding a dentist. A neighbour recommended a clinic in the upper-middle-class area just across the street from Rocinha, called São Conrado. The clinic was located near the large supermarket where most favela dwellers did their grocery shopping. The dentist I found had short hair, light skin and a few wrinkles; she was not more than 40, but looked tired, with deep dark circles under her eyes. She offered to make a full assessment of all my teeth, which she did with the help of a small mirror and a strong light that bothered my eyes. She chatted while she worked, telling me what was wrong with my teeth, and asking where I lived and worked. It was difficult to answer with my mouth open, but during pauses in the examination I told her I lived in Rocinha and was an anthropologist, a researcher.

She then inquired about the theme of my research. With her hands in my mouth, I could only say the word 'freedom'. 'Freedom? How so?' I felt like laughing: it was a really difficult conversation for many reasons. At the next opportunity I explained that I was interested in learning more about how freedom was lived by Rocinha's residents.

She nodded and said, 'I am very interested in this question of freedom too! Do you know why? Because there is something about Rocinha that I do not understand myself.' I was curious. The dentist added:

> I am the owner of this clinic. Most workers here come from Rocinha, right? It turns out that none of these workers are interested in full-time long-term

employment. They work for a little while and then they want to leave. People do not want to work. Seriously, they prefer to stay out of formal work in order to have more free time! Do you understand that?

I was amazed by the way this dentist had engaged with my research topic. She went on, 'This is a big problem here at the clinic. We need maids, secretaries and security people – but no one stays for too long. They all want an easy life. Nobody wants to work hard like me!' I told her I was very interested in the questions she was raising, and in return she said she would like to read my work if it was ever published.

Alternatives to the alternative

How can we understand why many favela residents are not looking for formal job opportunities in Rio de Janeiro? How can we explain that while a middle-class dentist feels that she needs to work full-time, others across the street from her clinic, with much lower levels of education and work opportunities, choose to live from *bico* (temporary informal jobs)? What does this difficult conversation between the favela and the formal city, fostered by life in a metropolis, tell us regarding the issue of labour and the wider urban dynamics in Rio de Janeiro?

In an essay on the theme of 'Work and unemployment', Winefield and colleagues (2002: 2) come to this conclusion:

> Clearly, we need some different ways of understanding and thinking about work. We are entering a millennium in which work may become a less central part of who and what people are. We need to better accommodate new cultural understandings of personhood and connections, and of meaning and self-fulfilment.

My conversation at the clinic suggests that many favela dwellers are rethinking their commitment to the established work market. However, it is also clear that this fact comes as a surprise to the middle and upper classes in Rio de Janeiro. My dentist perhaps reflects a more general attitude: that in the city of Rio de Janeiro, and perhaps on a broader scale, people do not really expect the changes in the labour market in the new millennium to be pushed forward by favela dwellers. They do not see the future involving the poor refusing to engage in formal (often full-time) work. They continue to think that the more formal work is available for the poor, the better. Businesses operating in the neighbourhood of São Conrado still expect that there will be cheap labour available for their supermarkets, their clinics and their offices, so they can continue to make profits in this new century.

A couple of centuries ago, European elites were already expressing a great concern regarding similar issues. In 1862 Henry Mayhew tackled the situation of the urban poor in London who refused to work. *Those That Will Not Work* is the title of Volume 4 in a series of books called *London Labour and the London Poor*. The series provided important contributions to the understanding of metropolitan life during Victorian times. Particularly, 'the middle class readers of Mayhew may have learned for the first time how the other half lived' (Lyons and Lyons 2004: 44). Regarding the issue of metropolitan life and labour, Mayhew (1862: 3) argued:

> All society would appear to arrange itself into four different classes:
>
> I   Those that will work.
>
> II   Those that cannot work.
>
> III   Those that will not work.
>
> IV   Those that need not work.

Within the wider Victorian framework that legally divided the poor into two categories – the 'deserving' and the 'undeserving' poor – all those Londoners who occupied class III in the structure above were presented by Mayhew (1862) not just as deserving their poverty, but also as thieves, beggars and/or prostitutes. We have to wonder how pervasive similar narratives about the urban poor continue to be in metropolitan life today, and why resistance to engaging in certain types of work relations still seems to shock the elites in Rio de Janeiro almost as much as it shocked the elite in London a century and a half ago.

Over many other conversations I had during my fieldwork in Rio de Janeiro in 2009 and 2010, I heard from different people that the poor who did not want to work could only be rogues. Alba Zaluar (2002) also debates this point of view in her book *The Machine and Revolt*, which is based on fieldwork in the infamous City of God, a favela in the west zone of Rio de Janeiro. The rationale for this attitude could be summarized like this: the poor who do not wish to engage in serious work can only make a living through activity that is illegal, or at best marginal. How else could they do so? The rich can choose not to work because, by definition, they have already accumulated resources on which they can draw, but that is not true of the poor. According to this view, the very need to have a job is part of what defines a poor person: in other words, to be poor is to need to work to survive. In this sense, the poor are not supposed to be in a position to break the rules of how a capitalist society operates.

In this chapter I expose some problems associated with this argument. I explore the employment situation of specific slum dwellers, and try to understand the complexity of the topic from the point of view of those who live in Rocinha. I suggest it is necessary to produce a deeper critical analysis of both the current social arrangements in our cities and the existing alternatives to those arrangements. The critique of the alternatives already imagined and already established in the daily life of our cities, especially those alternatives that tend to be seen as unavoidable, can unleash a whole new set of possibilities for urbanism.

Making a living in the city

In Rio de Janeiro, slums have historically existed as urban reservoirs of cheap labour, mainly for employers in the most privileged parts of the city. Slum dwellers who do not meet this social function are seen as anomalies. In the 'script' of daily life in Rio, the alternative established for the urban poor who do not engage in formal employment (especially for young people who do not have formal work) is to become rogues. I argue that we need to better understand the variety of alternatives that exist to the social arrangements that prevail in our cities nowadays, so that we can better exploit the possibilities and potentials of untamed urbanisms.

The one-bedroom house that I rented belonged to a couple who were preparing to move out of the favela. My landlord, Laertes, owned a small stationery shop in Rocinha, a single-door business, but apparently profitable. In the house just above mine lived a couple of migrants from the north-east. Neither of them had a permanent job on a full-time basis. Ferreira did the kind of *bico* I mentioned earlier – working occasionally, without a legal contract. He had one regular commitment, helping a friend to sell pork in the Sunday market. Ana, Ferreira's wife, worked as a cleaner, again not on a fixed contract. Sometimes she worked three days a week, some weeks she decided not to work at all. Everything depended on the availability of work and also on her own willingness to work on a certain day. In spite of this lack of formal work commitments, Ana and Ferreira had successfully raised two children. Not without difficulties, they used to say, both their boy and their girl were independent grown-ups already. The parents were very proud of them.

Navigating the favela was not an easy task. There was a complex network of alleyways crisscrossing the place, but not many wide streets. Near the alleyway where I lived was the home of a photographer called Adriano. During the weekdays, Adriano was always at home or else helping as a volunteer in a school across from his house. It was mainly over the weekends that he did paid work. He was hired to photograph big parties which mostly took place at the weekend. I often joked with Adriano that while most people that I knew worked from Monday to Friday and rested over the weekends, Adriano did the opposite. He used to laugh too, saying he was doing very well that way.

Gustavo, one of Adriano's neighbours, was barely out of his teens but had already worked in a wide variety of jobs both inside and outside the favela. He never stayed long-term in any of them. Sometimes he worked for a single day and never returned. In other cases, it took him a few months to quit. In any case, Gustavo always found an excuse to leave both permanent and temporary jobs. Gustavo's family worried about him: not exactly about his lack of permanent employment, but more about why he did not seem to like any work at all. Had he simply become accustomed to depending on financial support from his family? Or had he found illicit work in the favela?

'The worker and the bandit'

The literature on how different groups of people relate to work around the world is vast and diverse, varying from the analysis of very specific industries to the implications of globalization for the question of labour and employment in general (Mintz 1960; Applebaum 1981; Ong 1987; Fine 1996). Winefield and colleagues (2002) remind us that in the United States and Australia, work is a central element in the constitution of people's lives, identity and sense of well-being. It is not by accident that in English it is common to ask, 'What do you do for a living?' People ask this in daily conversation because they try to infer from people's type of work not just their earnings, but also their class status and other aspects of their personhood. Nevertheless, in other countries and other social groups, work, income and personhood are seen as much more distinct categories. As a contribution to the body of literature on employment, this chapter does not focus on the very local or the very global scale of analysis. It considers the specific dynamics of employment at an urban scale, in a large Brazilian city, even if some prefer to consider it a fractured city (see Koonings and Krujit 2007).

As explained by Zaluar (2002), in Rio slum dwellers tend to use the term 'worker' to define a certain identity that is essentially different from the identity of the 'bandit'. In this sense, being a 'worker' does not mean precisely that someone has a formal job, or necessarily that they do more work than others. It is important to keep in mind that in this context, calling someone a 'criminal' does not mean they do not work. Quite the contrary: people in Rocinha often remarked on how hard many bandits worked, especially those in the lower ranks of drug trafficking. Therefore, the concept of a 'worker' in the favela was not necessarily related to how much people worked, but to the type of work that they engaged in. In order to be a 'worker', work did not need to be a priority in the life of a person either. In this context, to refer to someone as a 'worker' was to indicate that they made a living through activities considered somehow morally superior (even if only in the eyes of the police) to those such as drug trafficking, robbery, begging and prostitution.

The use of these two categories to refer to ways of living in the favela can be linked to broader historical dimensions in the relationship between the asphalt (the so-called formal city) and the favela (the so-called informal city). In the wider context of urban life in Rio de Janeiro, the 'informal' parts of the city are, on a deeper level, frequently associated with the image of 'illegality'. In this context, favelas end up being perceived as morally inferior urban spaces, by virtue of their very origins as illegal urban settlements. As I discuss elsewhere in greater detail (Doherty and Lino e Silva 2011), the understanding of favelas as informal (and illegal) areas of the city has very practical consequences in the life of favela dwellers, who seem to be blamed constantly for the lack of affordable housing options in Rio de Janeiro, and end up having to deal with the stigma of 'illegality' regardless of their individual conduct and life histories.

A very tangible consequence of perceiving favela dwellers as bandits *in general* is the second-class treatment granted to Rocinha dwellers by the police. During the time I lived in Rocinha, it was not uncommon for the police to break into private houses without warrants, for example. During periods of confrontation between police and drug traffickers, the situation got even worse, with police helicopters indiscriminately shooting from the air, without a precise target other than the boundaries of the favela. It is in the particular context, with favela dwellers trying to protect themselves from violent indiscriminate treatment by the police, that the distinction between 'workers' and 'bandits' becomes vital to improve the prospects of survival in a shantytown. To describe a person as a 'worker' highlights the fact that they are not a legitimate target for police violence. Only a tiny proportion of Rocinha's residents were involved in drug trafficking. Therefore, in this context, using the categories 'worker' and 'criminal' could be understood partly as an attempt to protect people from police abuse in the so-called 'illegal' parts of the city.

Mary, Adriano, Laertes and Ana were all considered to be 'workers' in Rocinha, despite not having the type of formal employment that my dentist might wish them to have. Gustavo, however, showed a deep lack of interest in any form of employment that would be considered legitimate in the favela. He could hardly claim to be a 'worker'. Nobody called him so, but nobody openly called him a 'bandit' either. In fact, it seemed to me that great anxiety, gossip and curiosity resulted from the fact that no one knew exactly how to classify Gustavo. Many simply called him lazy. He would reply that he was not lazy, he was simply too smart to sacrifice his time in working.

Alternative moral judgements

From my conversation in the dentist's chair in São Conrado, I derived a clear sense that many people living outside the favelas do not think of favela dwellers who do not have a formal job as 'workers', in contrast with what happens on the favela side of the story. In the view of many people in Rio de Janeiro, the poor only achieve the status of 'worker' if they fulfil certain legal requirements: most of all, if they have a legal contract officially stamped on a document issued by the federal government called a *Carteira de Trabalho* (workbook).

Employees must hold such a *Carteira de Trabalho* in order to obtain a legal work contract in Brazil. It is only granted to those above 16 years of age. It is very similar to the Brazilian passport, and is stamped and signed by employers each time they formally hire or dismiss a worker. Those who do not work under such a formal employment scheme are considered 'informal' and/or 'illegal' workers by the state. Therefore, this legal apparatus establishes different categories of work relations. I would suggest that this legal differentiation of workers has immediate consequences for the way in which certain groups of people recognize people as workers (or non-workers). The 'higher' status granted to those who work with a *Carteira de Trabalho assinada* (a stamped and signed workbook), also creates the expectation that the poorest residents of Rio de Janeiro should strive to achieve the status of formal worker. From this perspective it is a surprise (of the kind expressed by my dentist) when some residents of Rocinha prefer not to engage in formal work.

Nevertheless, for most of the residents of Rocinha whose life I shared, the reasoning was somehow different. These were people who lived in territories of the city that in many ways lay outside the official rule of law. For them, the difference in status between formal and informal work was not the most significant one in their lives. To work under a *Carteira de Trabalho assinada* was sometimes recognized as a good thing, because there were legal protections and social benefits associated with such a legal contract. However, formal employment certainly did not have as much value as my dentist seemed to believe. As we have already discussed, in the favela context the moral status of someone's occupation was not judged primarily on the formal or informal nature of the work, but on the *type* of work that people engaged with. In other words, my friends in the favela saw as wrong (or illegal) activities those performed by bandits (such as drug trafficking, robbery and kidnapping). They did not see other types of informal work as wrong. So in Rocinha people felt perfectly entitled to consider themselves 'workers' and to be proud of their work regardless of whether or not it was done under a *Carteira de Trabalho assinada.*

Nothing to do with criminality

To say that many residents of Rocinha are not enchanted by the prospect of having a full-time formal job is not to say that they prefer to spend their time doing nothing, or that they are necessarily bandits. Adriano, for example, helped a lot in a school that offered a variety of free activities. Moreover, almost every weekday morning he used go to the beach, which was within easy walking distance of Rocinha. There he met friends and exercised for at least an hour. He also used his free time to make contacts and phone calls to facilitate his weekend photographic work. Adriano also studied basic English in a course offered by the same school where he helped as a volunteer.

Ana spent most of her time at home. When she was not doing any house cleaning outside of Rocinha to earn cash, she was working in her home. She cooked for her family, she did all the laundry for them (and also for one of our neighbours) and she also took care of the child of one of her relatives. Occasionally she stopped work to watch television. She loved soap operas. Ana had a sister living in Ipanema, whom she visited often. She liked to talk, and spent a fair amount of time gossiping with and about our neighbours. Ana's husband also liked to stay at home. Ferreira watched a lot of television and loved football. He almost never missed a match on television. The time he spent around the house was also used to fix small problems such as a blocked pipe or a drip from the ceiling. He also liked to play dominoes with friends in a plaza at the entrance to Rocinha.

In contrast to Ana and Ferreira, Gustavo spent almost all his time away from home. He could often be seen hanging out with other teenagers around the favela. Sometimes he disappeared for days. There were quite a few occasions when his family started to get concerned about the lack of news regarding his whereabouts. He was very popular with the girls. There was no need to worry when he disappeared from home, he was having fun – this is what he used to say. Gustavo also loved the beach, and during the summer he would go there almost every day. I used to see him playing beach football with his friends, taking dips in the sea and sunbathing. When Gustavo was short of company, he invited me to go to the beach with him, and he used to tell me that he had a good time, even though money was short for him.

Living more with less

In the years that I lived in Rocinha, I collected enough ethnographic evidence to argue against the taming narrative that the only livelihood alternatives for the urban poor without formal employment are to become rogues, bandits or prostitutes. Such an argument would only hold credibility if all forms of informal work were understood as marginal activities. We have seen that for many people living in Rio de Janeiro this is not the case. But a question remains: how do favela dwellers manage to make a living if they do not have formal jobs on a full-time basis?

Part of the answer can be derived from the vast array of activities in which people engage while they are not formally working. Cleaning the house, looking after children and fixing blocked pipes, could all be seen as non-monetary forms of work that help people make a living. Apart from that, we must not underestimate the benefits of being able to live on few resources. The reduced resource dependence in the life of most favela dwellers may not have been originally by choice. However, when people refuse to work eight hours a day in a formal job, even if doing so would provide them with a lot more resources at the end of the month, they are in effect making a choice: to keep on living with fewer material resources. For example, Ferreira was able to watch as many football matches on television as he wanted, and still survive without resorting to criminal activities. Rather than seeking the highest possible income by selling as much of their labour as possible, many people in Rocinha worked just enough to be able to afford the basic costs of everyday life. Rather than bothering to accumulate money, many people preferred to have free time to enjoy. Therefore, it could be said that time did not necessarily convert into money for many of my friends in Rocinha. Often, they perceived that more money would not make up for the value and priority that they attributed to free time in their lives.

What puzzles most people who do not live in favelas is why a population historically stigmatized as 'poor' would choose 'wealth in time' over 'wealth in goods'. Reisch (2001: 369) argues that 'economics tends to be exclusively focused on material wealth'. The same focus seems to dominate the concerns of much of the middle class in Brazil. In expanding his reflections on the concept of 'time wealth', Reisch (2001: 369) suggests that 'new models of wealth call for a new balance of "wealth in time" and "wealth in goods"'. In many ways, my friends in Rocinha recognize the trade-off between these two forms of wealth.

Tracey Warren (2003) provided a very interesting analysis of the relationship between time poverty and class stratification in the United Kingdom. She argues that couples with a higher overall income (usually because both individuals are working) seem to have less free time available for their family lives. However, if we consider that there are many factors to time wealth, it is not necessarily the case that lower-class couples are better off in terms of time resources than other classes in her study.[1] What seems to be distinctive about the position defended by my friends in Rocinha is the high value that they attribute to their autonomy over personal time, as opposed to people working in upper-middle-class São Conrado across the road, for example.

One possible reason many favela dwellers can afford 'wealth in time' is that many of them do not expect much in terms of 'wealth in goods'. The differences between the cost of living in Rocinha and São Conrado (which is just across the street from the favela) are striking. While in Rocinha it was possible to rent a small one-bedroom apartment for around BRL300 (Brazilian reais) (around US$150) per month in 2010, in São Conrado it would be hard to find anything cheaper than BRL1,500 (around US$750) per month. This was not only because the rent price per square metre was much higher in São Conrado, but also because there were few very small apartments for rent in that area. Another important consideration is all the extra costs of living in the neighbourhood on top of rent. In São Conrado residents paid a lot for tax, electricity, water, sewage, security, insurance and condo fees. In Rocinha, I did not meet anyone who paid any form of tax on their property. Furthermore, there was no charge at all for the public water and sewage (where these services were available). Most of my friends did pay for electricity (although some had illegal connections), but there was a special 'social' rate for favela dwellers, so the cost was low. Indeed many of my neighbours owned their houses in the favela, and did not have to spend anything on rent or mortgage payments. Many of those who did not own their houses shared their living space (and the rent) with friends or family, greatly reducing their fixed costs.

Food prices in Rocinha were similar to those elsewhere in Rio. The large supermarkets, for example, were both located in São Conrado adjacent to the favela. These are examples of spaces where both favela dwellers and the upper middle class shopped side by side, although the consumption patterns of both groups were often very different. Although I did not come across alternative productive food arrangements along the lines of those discussed by Edwards (see Chapter 20 of this volume), most residents of Rocinha bought much cheaper products than those purchased by their neighbours in São Conrado. I noticed this in observing people's shopping baskets while waiting in line to pay for my own purchases. There was also a food market in Rocinha on Sundays, where Ferreira worked. Fruits and vegetables were more affordable there than at the supermarket, especially during what was known as the *xepa* time – the final hours, when prices dropped considerably. Ana, for example, was a master in taking advantage of the *xepa* time. She always had lots of fruit and vegetables in her home.

In addition, a strong network of help operated among residents of Rocinha. Larissa Lomnitz (1975) argues that in Mexican shantytowns social networks based both on residence and kinship serve as means to guarantee the basic livelihood of the poor. I was able to observe similar processes in Rocinha. With fewer expenses, less excitement about accumulating wealth and a denser social network of neighbours and friends to rely on, people in Rocinha had more freedom to choose how much to work and whom to work for. The poorer ones in terms of monetary resources in Rio de Janeiro were also the wealthier in terms of time available for family and other activities. In Rocinha it was possible to make a living, to be a worker (in the favela sense of the word), and still have a lot of time available for friends and to go to the beach, for example. Perhaps, this could be an answer to the questions that deeply bothered my dentist in São Conrado. I was sorry I could not articulate any of this while sitting in her chair.

For an untamed urban future

One point of agreement among scholars concerned with a more sustainable urban life is that we need to explore our creative potential as we face challenges that arise from daily life in cities (Doherty and Mostafavi 2010). The broader goal of this chapter was to show that, although certain alternatives to current urban social arrangements seem to be unavoidable (such as marginality as the alternative to 'legitimate' employment), a closer look at everyday encounters in our cities might reveal otherwise.

Prompted by a broken tooth, the reflection that I proposed on the theme of employment in Rio de Janeiro sparked a fortuitous urban dialogue between topics of concern in Favela da Rocinha and some topics that preoccupy people living and working in the neighbourhood of São Conrado. To sustain my argument, I used ethnographic evidence obtained during my long-term fieldwork engagement in Rocinha. Through many urban conversations and my own everyday life experiences in the favela, I discussed themes such as who counts as a 'worker', what are the alternatives to formal work, and how people's time is allocated when they are less dependent on monetary resources for their livelihoods.

More historical evidence suggests that there is a master narrative that permeates the constitution of metropolitan life. This cuts across different places and centuries, from London in the nineteenth century to Rio de Janeiro in the twenty-first century. This narrative establishes a labour scheme for ideal life in cities: that all people should work (except those with sufficient resources to not need to work). Those who cannot work are often excused under certain conditions, and may even be deserving of philanthropic and/or state assistance. Those who will not work have been accused of all sorts of social evil, and became objects of intense concern and scrutiny from those who do work. (Of course, embedded in this narrative we also find a particular version of what counts as legitimate work.) In both London and Rio de Janeiro, those who will not work are marginalized and treated as a social problem, if not a social disease. At least since the nineteenth century, there seems to have been an implicit understanding that a fundamental objective of urban studies is to enforce taming scripts regarding the identification, regulation and management of the undesirable consequences of life conditions in urban environments.

The pervasive taming narrative that this chapter challenges is one that prescribes that the urban poor do not just have to work, but have to work under conditions that are often determined by others. As such, this narrative aims to regulate the work regime of those considered too poor to not work. If we are to expand our repertoire of alternatives for a more sustainable future, there could be much to be learned from favelas, and how some people manage to live satisfying lives that are at once less resource-intensive and more filled with time for friends and family. This move implies a deep process of resignification. We need to stop seeing the excess of free time in the life of favela dwellers as a social problem, and become open to new interpretations, such as the interpretation put forward by Reisch (2001) – for whom free time becomes a new form of wealth. Certainly, such wealth could be seen as being at odds with material wealth. Perhaps this is a good thing, too, considering that experts have long been suggesting that the increasing patterns of consumption in the world are unsustainable, and we will have to undergo a dramatic downshifting, with a serious impact on current forms of social organization (Nelson *et al.* 2007).

Cities are rarely thought of from the point of view of those living in areas considered informal, marginal and illegal: with notable exceptions such as Chiweshe's analysis of spatial dynamics in Zimbabwean cities from a feminine perspective, and Sotiropoulou's discussion of urban property from the point of view of Greek grassroots movements (both in this volume). The formulation of urban theories and policies tends to take place in circuits that are often disconnected from (or at best asymmetrically connected to) the daily life experiences of certain 'marginalized' urban groups. There is currently a serious lack of adequate knowledge regarding the quotidian details of how those considered 'poor' actually make a living in our cities despite all the challenges they face. For example, the understanding of favelas as urban depositories of cheap labour for the formal city proves to be very limited when confronted with the complex dynamics of life in a large city such as Rio de Janeiro. It is time to consider more seriously how the wealth of knowledge, time and experiences of the so-called 'urban poor' can help inform our push towards untamed forms of urbanism: in this particular case, less resource intensive and, we can hope, with more freedom and time for friends, family and the beach.

Note

1 'Reisch [2000, cited in Warren 2003] has usefully highlighted a number of components to time wealth. These include the chronometric dimension (having the right *amount* of time), the chronologic dimension (having time at the *right* time of the day, week or season), the personal time autonomy/sovereignty dimension (*control* over time) and the synchronization dimension (time that *fits* with the time rhythms of family and friends).'

References

Applebaum, H. 1981. *Royal Blue: The Culture of Construction Workers.* New York: Holt, Rinehart & Winston.
Doherty, G. and Lino e Silva, M. 2011. Formally informal: daily life and the shock of order in a Brazilian favela. *Built Environment*, 37(1): 30–41.
Doherty, G. and Mostafavi, M. 2010. *Ecological Urbanism.* Zurich: Lars Müller.

Fine, G. 1996. *Kitchens: The Culture of Restaurant Work.* Berkeley, CA: University of California Press.

Koonings, K. and Krujit, D. 2007. *Fractured Cities: Social Exclusion, Urban Violence and Contested Spaces in Latin America.* London: Zed Books.

Lomnitz, L. 1975. *Como sobreviven los marginados.* Mexico City: SigloVeintiuno.

Lyons, A. and Lyons, H. 2004. *Irregular Connections: A History of Anthropology and Sexuality.* Lincoln, NE: University of Nebraska Press.

Mayhew, H. 1861–2. *London Labour and the London Poor: A Cyclopaedia of the Condition and Earnings of Those That Will Work, Those That Cannot Work, and Those That Will Not Work*, 4 vols. London: Griffin, Bohn.

Mintz, S. 1960. *Worker in the Cane: A Puerto Rican Life History.* New Haven, CT: Yale University Press.

Nelson, M. R., Paek, H.-J. and Rademacher, M. A. 2007. Downshifting consumer = upshifting citizen? An examination of a local freecycle community. *Annals of the American Academy of Political and Social Science*, 611(1): 141–56.

Ong, A. 1987. S*pirits of Resistance and Capitalist Discipline: Factory Women in Malaysia.* Albany, NY: State University of New York Press.

Reisch, L. A. 2001. Time and wealth: the role of time and temporalities for sustainable patterns of consumption. *Time and Society* 10(213): 367–85.

Warren, T. 2003. Class and gender-based working time? Time poverty and the division of domestic labour. *Sociology*, 37(4): 733–52.

Winefield, A. H., Montgomery, R., Gault, U., Muller, J., O'Gorman, J., Reser, J. and Roland, D. 2002. The psychology of work and unemployment in Australia today: an Australian Psychological Society discussion paper. *Australian Psychologist*, 37(1): 1–9.

Zaluar, A. 2002. *A Máquina e a Revolta.* São Paulo: Editora Brasiliense.

17 Contested taming spatialities

The micro-resistance of everyday life in Buenos Aires

Jorge Sequera and Elvira Mateos

Introduction

Recent neoliberal urban policies and the containment of the excluded in Latin American cities create a paradox. This is apparent at Costanera Sur in the city of Buenos Aires, Argentina, a long walkway between two worlds. On one side is the Buenos Aires Ecological Reserve on the shore of the Rio de la Plata, which adjoins Rodrigo Bueno, a slum in danger of eviction due to political pressure from the city government and real estate developers. On the other side is Puerto Madero, the most expensive neighbourhood in the city, with skyscrapers, state-of-the-art security systems, exclusive shops, luxury hotels, international banking, opulent houses and so on.

The promenade that separates these two adjoining areas that exemplify a fragmented city, is radically transformed every weekend (Centner 2012). On those days, the Costanera is filled with activities (*parrillitas al paso* or street barbecues, informal markets, music and dance) that attract the working classes from throughout the city. In this chapter we contrast these practices with the symbolic construction of the 'right bourgeois use' of the public space by the upper class, and its recounting of the legitimate subject to enact a civilizing process. We argue that the encounter of these ways of being in the city confronts the everyday life practices of the working class but also slows down the production of hegemonic urban subjectivity (Sennet 2006; Wortman 2004, 2010; Lash and Urry 1994; Bourdieu 1979; Wright 1992, 1994).

In this regard, we examine popular informal activities as counter-hegemonic practices in opposition to urban neoliberalisation, constituting new actors that develop and produce alternative geographies of citizenship. Resistance through the intensive use of public space by different rituals from those planned by the creators of Puerto Madero somehow breaks certain government technologies (Foucault 1990) that respond to private interests, instead of being governed by the common use of public space (Stavrides 2010). In this way, such practices are considered as 'anomalies' (or untamed practices) by the upper and middle classes and managed by urban policies that restrict socializing acts and the social relations that they embody.

In order to elaborate our central analytical purpose, we have chosen to examine an urban conflict that is unfolding in this area today and that is likely to continue in the future. A walk through the two antagonistic places, Puerto Madero and the slum of Rodrigo Bueno, allows us to capture a polymorphic imaginary that includes a multiplicity and diversity of subjects as triggers of a spatial transformation in the use of the area.

The Rio de La Plata (or River Plate) bounds the city of Buenos Aires on the east. In the early twentieth century, a number of reforms that modernized the area made it a lively port, but those attempts were made obsolete years later, when the docks became unsuitable for foreign vessels that had typically increased in size. The area remained practically ignored by the public authorities for many years, which led to a gradual degradation of its appearance, complicating its original function as a place of public use. Nevertheless, Costanera Sur was never fully abandoned. Both low-income groups and the middle and upper classes gathered on the shore of the river during weekends to enjoy what was usually known as the Costanera Sur Riverside Resort (though the classes were always separated, in different spaces). Gradually parts of the route to the river became inaccessible, and this resulted in a decrease in the leisure activities performed in the area, although they never totally disappeared. However, at the end of last century, the area became the locus of ambitious interventions.

Everyday life contains resistance practices which are traversed by processes of both personal and collective subjectivities, as argued by Stavrides (2007: 119) 'molecular spatialities of otherness can be found scattered in the city'. Our case study takes us to explore a space understood as a common area which confronts the exception policies that residents and politicians try to implement in Puerto Madero. As Díaz and Ortiz (2003) have contended, the interaction between different social and ethnic groups is limited by the condition of fragmented and fragmentary spatial use, which weakens social cohesion. Public space can increasingly be read as a gap between buildings to be filled in accordance with the objectives of developers and governments: aseptic spaces to enforce the notions of utility, safety and control (Delgado 2011: 9). Following the same line of thought, Delgado (2004) highlights the fact that different prevention policies have institutionalized the new design of urban spaces and social control, as exemplified through the development of new forms of urban surveillance, such as those materialized through the expanded use of video cameras and closed-circuit television (CCTV).

The research informing this chapter was designed precisely by the interest that these images and radically different practices aroused in us, as visitors to the city, and it soon became the subject of scientific inquiry. The methodology adopted included participant observation in these public spaces, in-depth interviews with residents and users of Puerto Madero and the slum of Rodrigo Bueno, and various audiovisual techniques such as photography and video analysis, which were designed to nourish and supplement the analysis of discourse. We also used secondary sources, especially engaging with the analysis of the mass media (newspapers, websites and television).

Puerto Madero: the construction of a class taming discourse

We have already mentioned that the city is a multiple concept that is configured through different subjectivities, which sometimes come into conflict. Naturally this does not mean that the mixture of conception, realities and urban uses occurs in a space of freedom, as the influence of different agents in giving sense to space, and the results, are very unequal. Domínguez (2008: 8) stated that the city is a central node in the global economy, for there are usually very few areas where social spaces escape the logic of capitalist exploitation and domination. This dynamic facilitates the creation of devices to discipline the citizenship (Delgado 2007: 54). In the cases of gentrification and requalification these bring market players into connivance with the public authorities, a process that Harvey (2010) depicts as *urban entrepreneurialism*.

Puerto Madero is the paradigm of a planned urban project of this kind, which has been designed from the beginning to run as the perfect joint venture between business, political power and the needs of the middle and upper classes. We are referring to the relocation in the central areas of the city of these social sectors that could have chosen to live in gated communities. This formalized the transformation of the old harbour into an archipelago of privilege and the privileged, through strategies that were used to create an 'other space' (Foucault 1980), seemingly perfect, meticulous and orderly, which clashes sharply with the existing space; that is, a series of administrative policies managing this new civility, in which the middle and upper classes impose their hegemony on the inner city, as the only acceptable form of social behaviour.

One of the most significant issues in the Puerto Madero project was that it involved a public–private partnership. Large urban projects are widespread throughout Latin America. This dynamic can be encompassed within what was previously defined as 'the new entrepreneurship paradigm' or urban entrepreneurialism. The *Corporación Antiguo Puerto Madero SA* was conceived as a state development company, under the guise of a public limited company, governed by private law (Cuenya and Corral 2011), bringing together the state and the municipality along with private companies and architects through a clear example of public–private partnership.

This phenomenon exemplifies a new form of urban governance, which different local political parties have also adopted elsewhere (Harvey 1989, 2001; Borja and Castells 1997; Rodríguez *et al.* 2001; De Mattos 2009), and whose principal goal is to maximize private profit. As other authors have already highlighted, nowadays these large-scale urban projects create new economic areas with environments protected from violence and urban poverty, which encourage national and international private investment (Lungo and Smolka 2005).

Puerto Madero's design involved an intense dialogue with Catalonian planners, and it has been called the Argentine 'Catalonian project' (Corral 2009; González 2011; Jajamovich 2012). Initially land prices in this area were low, but the project's planners knew there would be an immense appreciation in value due to its strategic location. As a result this was considered an 'opportunity area' (Cuenya 2001). From a speculative viewpoint, Puerto Madero is nearly completed, and nowadays it is exhibited as a planning success. It is considered as a new symbol of the city of Buenos Aires, which pushes the city up to the same level as other leading metropolises around the world, epitomizing power and money (Cuenya and Corral 2011).

Puerto Madero is exceptional mainly because many of its features are totally different from those characteristic of the contiguous neighbourhoods: it is an island of order and security. This has been achieved not only by providing an exclusive security force for this area, the Argentine Naval Prefecture (*Prefectura Naval Argentina* or PNA), a comprehensive security system and a morphology that makes it seems a like a fortress (there are only four entrances by foot), but in a more subtle and effective way. The strong regulation of green areas, and the monopoly of high-class shops and buildings have led to segregation, hampering the use of this area by a large proportion of the population, and restricting alternative uses of the space. In this sense, concepts such as De Giorgi's 'punitive metropolis' (2006) and Smith's famous 'revanchist city' (1996) are fit to describe these surveillance strategies of recovery as a key process in the global city. Roughly, we can identify in Puerto Madero some of the most characteristic features of the privatization model of public space that have been emerging during the last few decades in many other cities in which neoliberal urban policies have been dominant, such as the commodification of public space, video surveillance and architectures of control (Sequera and Janoschka 2012).

Puerto Madero is physically a peninsula of Buenos Aires, separated from the main city by an arm of the river. There are only four bridges providing access, all with checkpoints staffed by the PNA. This public security force does not operate anywhere else in the city, and the proportion of security personnel to population is far higher here than elsewhere in Buenos Aires. According to field data, it is well known that the Prefecture operates more effectively against insecurity that the Federal Police. In addition, Puerto Madero is the only place in Buenos Aires with an integrated CCTV system. There is such a dense network of cameras that every square metre is monitored 24 hours a day, 365 days a year (www.ntsmadero.com.ar/servicios.html).

Public space in Puerto Madero is being increasingly regulated. The aim appears to be to avoid any 'alternative' or traditional (cultural) uses, by creating or designating exclusive spaces, which are in effect public 'private' spaces (Low and Smith 2006: 21) or semi-public spaces. Many references to Europe can be drawn from the discourses and practices in Puerto Madero, including those related to security, as well as the transnational promotion of an upper-class lifestyle. Often, parallels are established between this project and the architecture and aesthetics of the 'European urban model', with Barcelona seen as a paradigm of this. This is seen, too, as a security issue: a local bodyguard told us reassuringly (perhaps noticing that we had the look of residents of the global North): 'this is Europe'.

We are looking here at the concept of a citizen as a consumer of signs, constantly marked by new forms of exclusive consumption. Precisely because of their exclusive characteristics, these make this fragment of the city a commodified product. In this way we witness the materializing inequality in the everyday life of major cities. Admittedly in Puerto Madero – mainly to the east, around Costanera Sur – some goods and services are offered at prices most people can afford, but the general trend is towards exclusive goods and services. Puerto Madero aims to become a new central example of the affluent lifestyle. In complete contrast to the daily practices that have developed in the periphery, in shopping malls, entertainment complexes, parks, major supermarkets and so on, the urban reconfiguration here has been redirected to commercialize public space. We see the proliferation of a similar aesthetic that converts certain urban places into specialized areas for consumption by casual tourists and suburban citizens.

In addition to the leisure model devoted to consumption (and mainly targeted at the middle and upper classes), there is hyper-regulation of the public space in this area of the city. Our analysis of this will focus on three aspects.

First, there is a new project to install parking meters throughout Puerto Madero.[1] Currently many cars are parked there without charge, apparently by people living in peripheral areas who come to work in the capital, as well as by families who come at weekends to enjoy the waterfront. This causes endless jams around the bridges. Parking meters would discourage these individuals, but it also implies the replacement of a public use of space with a paid private use. Many less affluent people would effectively not come, because they cannot afford to pay parking fees. Some residents also resent the 'gorillas' (people who work informally, finding parking spaces in return for a tip), and this would eliminate them. The area also lacks public transport, so whatever the arguments advocating the introduction of parking meters, the result would be further segregation, removing the less well-off from this area.

The second issue is surveillance, part of the securitization trend that we have found in Puerto Madero. According to Janoschka (2005), there are two fundamental criticisms of modern surveillance methods. One is the lack of 'success' of the strategies used, and the other is that they destroy anonymity as one of the bases of coexistence in modern urban life. Increased use of CCTV and similar techniques can be seen as a refinement of the knowledge-power strategies employed by governments. The new technologies used in Puerto Madero are radically different from those practised in the rest of Buenos Aires, and elsewhere in Argentina.

The third regulatory issue concerns crime prevention through environmental design. The current city government has made it clear that this is an objective, and to this end since late 2012 it has fenced off Centenario Park followed by another green area called Lezama Park. Many believe that Puerto Madero will be the next area to be 'gated', as was suggested by the city government at a meeting with local residents. Security here is seen as a multi-faceted concept: as a legal, regulatory, political and social value.

The Rodrigo Bueno slum: a history of resistance

If Puerto Madero exemplifies the 'first world' vision of Buenos Aires, the developing-world vision is not far distant (Cuenya and Corral 2011). In fact, before the new Puerto Madero was built there was a slum called Rodrigo Bueno in the same area, and its residents and stallholders are resisting eviction even today. Two areas of the natural reserve were initially encroached in the mid-1980s, and are now home to 1,795 families according to the last census, many of whom are Peruvian or Paraguayan. After a social and judicial struggle for the settlement to be acknowledged, which lasted ten years, in 2010 a group of legislators proposed the 'redevelopment' of the Rodrigo Bueno neighbourhood. They recognized that this informal neighbourhood existed, that the residents had a right to remain there, and that the local government had an obligation to intervene to ensure decent living conditions (Lekerman *et al.* 2012).

However, the rehabilitation proposal has still not been implemented. In Buenos Aires, the dangers are obvious when lower-income sectors occupy strategic areas where gentrification would make it possible to realize 'surplus value' (García and Sequera 2013; Herzer 2008). As happened in Puerto Madero, modernization and urban regeneration can displace the existing population, leading to social and spatial fragmentation, with very specific characteristics in the case of Latin America (Janoschka *et al.* 2013). This can be seen as a battle over the meanings of legitimacy and illegitimacy in the urban context. Those managing the urban project of Puerto Madero have tried acquiring the land occupied by Rodrigo Bueno's slum through many means (including evictions, subsidies, police surveillance, soil walls built encircling the slum, power cuts). To date these strategies have had no more success in displacing the residents than the residents have had in obtaining a firm legal status.

Jurisdictionally, residents of the slum would come under *Comuna 1* of Puerto Madero for electoral purposes, but they have instead been regrouped with the neighbourhoods of Barracas and La Boca to the south of Buenos Aires city, which are predominantly inhabited by the working classes. However, the links with Puerto Madero are much more evident. Most residents of Rodrigo Bueno not only live near the Costanera Sur, but also make a living in the neighbourhood: in construction, maintenance and care work, at the Retiro fair, in the food stalls along the promenade, collecting cardboard (Rodríguez 2010), or working in restaurants.

The history of Rodrigo Bueno is a history of grassroots resistance and challenge to government policies, which have changed over the last few decades. At first the government's approach seemed to be apathy or disregard, but later it turned into harassment. Several strategies of subordination and intimidation and coercive mechanisms have come into play in recent years (Carman and Yacovino 2008). Among other actions, the settlement has been enclosed by a 30-foot-high wall, built with the earth excavated for the construction of Puerto Madero. We have already mentioned the use of security personnel to guard the entrances to Puerto Madero. Residents of Rodrigo Bueno also had to contend with the suspension of cleaning cesspools, garbage collection and pest control, power outages and so on (Carman and Yacovino 2008).

On top of that, there is now a new urbanization project in the area. The Santa María del Plata proposal from the IRSA[2] development company proposes a hotel resort and residential towers, as well as the opening of internal channels and lakes, creating public and private parks and boulevards. The total estimated cost of this project is US$500 million. Once more we find in this intersection a conflict between two approaches and sectoral interests. On the one hand, the profitability of this new project is threatened by the presence of the nearby slum (Szajnberg, Sorda and Pesce 2006), and on the other hand, the invasion of bulldozers threatens the slum's residents.

The promenade of Costanera Sur: discourses and practices disputing public space

Public space is both a physical concept – the configuration of streets, squares and parks in the city – and a political concept. In the public sphere it is also a site of democratic deliberation (Aramburu 2008). The liberal sense of public space as somewhere for everyone equally avoids a palpable reality: that there are differences in allowed uses and restrictions on certain social groups. Social relations are conditioned by the kinds of access to and use of public squares and streets, as well as social gatherings in private or privatized places. However, this theoretical model does not necessarily fit easily onto a city bustling with life. The aseptic nature of the model becomes a reality of noise, colour and bustle, in a mixture of informal work and partying, at weekends around the Costanera Sur. Through discursive and non-discursive practices, there is a fight for the territory involving a variety of actors, such as the promoters of Puerto Madero, its inhabitants, the municipality, and the inhabitants of Rodrigo Bueno, users and sellers of the Costanera Sur promenade and the mass media.

These practices constitute the heart of a conflict whose dominions extend to the symbolic, and where we can see the materiality of a dispute between meanings. It is in the articulation of the different discourses and practices, which have different points of view of the space, that the conflict of interests acquires full meaning. A study of the recent history of this dispute should help us better understand two discourses. On one side, conceptions and justifications of the present are based on certain versions of the history of Puerto Madero. On the other side, memories are continually shaped by the present conditions.

A first narrative to be considered is that articulated by one of the most influential players in the urban conflict: CAPMSA,[3] the company in a public–private partnership that is responsible for fulfilling the megaproject of Puerto Madero. Since its inception, the company has maintained a discourse concerning social policies that some regard as fake. We can find three basic themes. First, it has always focused on the value of public and green space as one of its main targets. However behind these arguments in defence of the 'public space', urban dynamics of a business nature prevail, in a context where urban requalification processes generate an even greater need to expel certain people from certain areas of the city (Rodríguez 2010).

The second strand concerns the pursuit of zero cost to the state. This discourse was necessary for a fundamental reason: the land on which Puerto Madero was built was public. Some authors have argued that this too is a false discourse from a political standpoint: private investors and high-income consumers were subsidized by public funds (Cuenya and Corral 2011). Some critics of the project have complained that the land was provided without any promised return. The corporation passes the profits from the operation to its partners, the municipality and the national government. The original promise that benefits would accrue to other social areas was never fulfilled (Cuenya and Corral 2011).

Third, we find a narrative that describes the area as one of 'social mix', used as a legitimation in response to those voices that warned Puerto Madero would operate as a gated community (in ways more symbolic than physical) and lead to exclusion. There is no mix of classes in Puerto Madero: it is an island of exclusivity. The working-class activities during the weekends along Costanera Sur are usually cited as refutation of this claim. What we observed is a subtle urban segregation, where different social classes have different uses for the area on different days of the week.

In short, the promoter's discourse tries to suggest that there have been urban improvements for Puerto Madero's neighbours, offering a model that contrasts with what seems to be happening in Costanera Sur. This latter model includes both the social periphery (Zibechi 2007) and the city centre, which is the social complex construction of the working classes, where the following concepts can be found: *dirty*, *dangerous*, *slum dweller* (these are terms taken from recorded interviews and the media) and *invasive* (Carman 2011).

In many cases, the symbolic frontiers are held to impose or maintain social frontiers. In accordance with this, social differences materialize in the unequal and different access to the material and immaterial resources in the urban space (Rodríguez 2010). In Puerto Madero, most of the characteristics of the neighbourhood relate to a quite exclusive use: poor access by public transport, very expensive restaurants and cultural activities, luxury housing supply, absence of public schools and so on (Pico and Yacovino 2010). These are some of the remarkable characteristics of the neighbourhood, which additionally has the PNA and a kind of security system never seen before in the city of Buenos Aires.

Today, Puerto Madero has the tacit support of the city government, plus it is reinforced by the mainstream media, which continue to reproduce its symbolic frontiers. In contrast, the government continues to question the permanence of Rodrigo Bueno, representing its inhabitants as enemies or even usurpers of a public space, while the media in many cases sensationalize the slums, criminalizing and stigmatizing their inhabitants. The segregation policy of the public authorities is expressed mainly in a set of discourses and practices that strengthen the physical and symbolic distance of the urban settlement from its immediate neighbours (Yacovino 2010). Puerto Madero builds its own notion of exclusivity based on this contrast, which is linked to security and differences in lifestyle. Although not all residents of Puerto Madero are rich, the lifestyle promoted is that of the upper classes. Moreover, as stated by Svampa (2001), the *structural weakness* of the Argentinean middle classes is based on the middle place they occupy. They are characterized politically by a conservative and reactionary mentality, and culturally by a mimetic culture and ostentatious consumption. From another perspective, we can appreciate the contrast of tastes and its imposition by the upper classes using Bourdieu's concept of *habitus* (Bourdieu 1988). Among the features of Costanera Sur is the contrast between the habits of different classes (Bourdieu 1979), exemplified for instance by fancy expensive restaurants, and street stalls selling cheap food.

Additionally, the neighbours of Puerto Madero have an important role in the imposition of the rules which aim to 'order' public space (Pico and Yacovino 2010). We were able to verify this in several political meetings with neighbourhood associations. Although the original plan for the neighbourhood proposed to restructure the public space as 'modern', the rules – both explicit and implicit – that regulate the use of these areas, and the expectations of residents enforce a specific kind of public space, structured as a contemplative space, with enjoyment 'regulated' under certain parameters. At the same time the council has reinforced the importance of surveillance and official control in these areas (Pico and Yacovino 2010). Therefore we witness here an unequal dispute that confronts different visions of what public space should be.

As we have seen, the discourse defending the public space by developers and supporters of Puerto Madero in many cases ends up stigmatizing the merchants and users of the Costanera Sur as well as the population of Rodrigo Bueno. They cite public order, care of the environment, cleaning and security as if these were threatened by non-residents of Puerto Madero, who have even been described as 'invaders'. When the use of public space is so tightly regulated, activities that are outside the norm can constitute a counter-hegemonic articulation, a symbolic struggle for the reappropriation of the area. This leads us to argue that in the Costanera Sur, there is a 'spatiality of emancipation' (Stavrides 2007: 119), which is constructed by a series of appropriation practices, new meanings and the responses of daily life to ongoing processes of gentrification.

We refer to a discontinuous space strongly marked by the extreme situational dimension of class. This is very apparent in the contrast between services for the working classes and for the upper classes along Costanera Sur. Hence, 'the space identifies and is identified through its use' (Stavrides 2007: 121). Stavrides developed the concept of a city composed of *thresholds* (2010), or gaps. At weekends the Costanera Sur loses its planned legibility, while *vanishing points* allow the working-class practices to reclaim a different urban sense of the area. These informal practices have correlations in social movements (Zibechi 2012), in contentious fights and in the construction of new citizenship paradigms (Isin 2009). Therefore, these political and social subjects have the ability to raise up urban life models that are non-hegemonic. The main merit of these individual and collective actions is to unmask government technology models imposed on citizens which are rooted in individualism and precariousness. There is a clear intention to depoliticize the measures taken by managing urban appearance from the standpoint of 'technical, non-ideological solutions' (Stavrides 2010; Ong 2006). Hence, everyday life along Costanera Sur, populated by street *chacareras* (Argentinean folk musicians) and street vendors of all kinds, can be read as attempts to counter the effects of neoliberalism, reclaiming new social conditions in contested neighbourhoods.

Conclusions

Through this chapter we have studied the use of public spaces that are constructed in an unequal and conflictive manner, generated by a specific appropriation by some social groups with different types of capital (cultural, economic and symbolic). We have not only reconsidered the way in which a commoditized logic produces and reproduces hegemonic social structures and positions, but also explored a social tension between antagonistic class representations within the neighbourhood, rather than just between the capitalist management of urban space in Puerto Madero and Costanera Sur.

Consequently, the management of contested areas, such as the Costanera Sur which is shared by Puerto Madero and Rodrigo Bueno, in a Foucauldian (1990: 48) sense, reveals the use of true public power 'technologies'. Policies that attack the most vulnerable individuals of the societies are adopted, prioritizing hegemonic social practices and socially cleaning 'undesirable' individuals from defined areas. Through prevention strategies, some practices are legislated as misdemeanours in an attempt to regulate and naturalize this reconstruction of 'the public' as the 'civic'. This explains some of the consequences of neoliberal spatiality for the (re)construction of the city through public space. Through the processes of subjectification of citizenship, urban power discourses are materialized and we see the emergence and consolidation of classic policies of 'Haussmannization' (Low and Smith 2006: 25; Harvey 2008). These are responsible for reorganizing the public space to promote the free movement of capital, goods and population around areas of the city. These policies are not casual, and they turn shops, bars and other enterprises into defining elements of the public and private space as well as ways of controlling it.

This type of ideological urban practice legitimizes tough actions against certain types of behaviour, including punitive (legal), deterrent (CCTV) and preventive (urban planning) measures (Galdón Clavell 2010: 5), while also facilitating the processes of gentrification and urban segregation. In all these policies we find a bias towards an economic view of public space, making each parcel a commoditized object, and finally making the city a class project. It is precisely in these areas where actors express their position in the social system, or in other words, where we see classification and declassification (*classement–déclassement* in Bourdieu's terms – Bordieu 2000), or what is the same, social stratification materialized in a strong urban segregation.

To conclude, we face two models of citizenship and other social stratification in the evolving city. The city is never a finished territory in consensus, but it is always shaped by different representations of the same, different subjectivities that co-produce what ultimately is spatially and socially. These disputes that generate the urban can be observed through the practices, discursive or otherwise, that different groups use to defend their territory. The conflict that occurs here is the result of a symbolic process in search of discursive legitimacy, and beyond that, of social and political legitimacy. Thresholds can become urban porosities that allow the existence of the untamed 'in-between zones', supplying permeable flows of a community defined through its practices in the urban space.

Acknowledgement

The research outlined in this chapter was part of the research project 'Contested Cities: Contested Spatialities of Urban Neoliberalism: Dialogues between Emerging Spaces of Citizenship in Europe and Latin America', financed by the European Commission (Grant Agreement: PIRSES-GA-2012-318944).

Notes

1 Source: www.puertomadero.com/not1.php?id=331
2 Inversiones y Representaciones Sociedad Anónima: http://www.irsa.com.ar/irsa/index_eni.htm
3 Corporación Antiguo Puerto Madero Sociedad Anónima: see www.corporacionpuerto madero.com/

References

Aramburu, M. 2008. Usos y Significados del Espacio Público. *Arquitectura, Ciudad y Entorno*, 3(8): 143–50.
Borja, J. and Castells, M. 1997. *Local y global, La gestión de las ciudades en la era global*. Madrid: Taurus.
Bourdieu, P. 1988. *La distinción. Criterio y bases sociales del gusto*. Madrid: Taurus.
—— 2000. *Esquisse d'une théorié de la pratique*. París: Seuil/Points.
Carman, M. 2011. *Las trampas de la naturaleza: medio ambiente y segregación en Buenos Aires*. Buenos Aires: Fondo de la Cultura Económica.
Carman, M. and Yacovino, M. P. 2008. Los 'usos intolerables' de la tierra en la ciudad de Buenos Aires. El caso del asentamiento Rodrigo Bueno. In *II Congreso de la Asociación Latinoamericana de Antropología*.
Centner, R. 2012. Microcitizenships: fractious forms of urban belonging after Argentine neoliberalism. *International Journal of Urban and Regional Research*, 36(2): 336–62.
Corporación Antiguo Puerto Madero. *Memoria y Estados Contables al 31 de diciembre de 2009 presentados en forma comparativa*. Available at: www.puertomadero.com
Corral, M. 2009. Grandes Proyectos urbanos. Actores públicos y privados en el emprendimiento Puerto Madero (1989–2009). Available at: webiigg.sociales.uba.ar
Cuenya, B. 2001. Las cuestiones centrales de la investigación urbana en cada época. http://www.mundourbano.unq.edu.ar/index.php/ano-2001/61-numero-11/110-1-las-cues-tiones-centrales-de-la-investigacion-urbana-en-cada-epoca
Cuenya, B. and Corral, M. 2011. Empresarialismo, economía del suelo y grandes proyec-tos urbanos: El modelo de Puerto Madero en Buenos Aires. *Revista Eure*, vol. 37, May.
De Giorgi, A. 2006. *El gobierno de la excedencia: postfordismo y control de la multitud*. Madrid: Traficantes de sueños.
De Mattos, C. 2009. *Modernización capitalista, Metamorfosis Urbana y Competitividad en América Latina*. Presentation for Seminario Internacional La Investigación Urbana:

Perspectivas y Desafíos, Lima, Perú. Available at: www.uarm.edu.pe/Docs/investiga cion/. . ./competitividad_mattos.pdf

Delgado, M. 2004. De la ciudad concebida a la ciudad practicada, en Crisis y Reinvención de la Ciudad contemporánea. *Revista Archipiélago*, no. 62. Available at: http://es.scribd. com/doc/57990419/Manuel-Delgado-articulo-de-Internet-sobre-espacio-publico.

—— 2007. *La ciudad mentirosa. Fraude y miseria del 'Modelo Barcelona'*. Madrid: La Catarata.

—— 2011. *El espacio público como ideología*. Madrid: La Catarata.

Delgado, M. Díaz Orueta, F. and Ortiz, A. 2003. Ciudad e inmigración: uso y apropiación del espacio público en Barcelona. In L. López, C. E. Relea and J. Somoza (eds), *La Ciudad: Nuevos Procesos, Nuevas Respuestas*, pp. 399–407. León, Spain: Universidad de León.

Domínguez, M. 2008. Trabajo material e inmaterial. Polémicas y conceptos inestables, marco teórico y estado de la cuestión, Youkali, Revista Crítica de las Artes y el Pensamiento, Madrid. Available at: www.youkali.net/5a1-YOUKALI-Dominguez-Sanchez-Pinilla.pdf

Foucault, M. 1980. *El ojo del poder*. Available at: www.elortiba.org/panop.html

—— 1990. *Tecnologías del yo y otros textos afines*. Barcelona: Paidós.

Galdón Clavell, G. 2010. La pulsió securitària a la ciutat contemporánia. In *Políticas Públicas y Modelos de Ciudadanía*. Barcelona, Spain: CIDOB y Diputació de Barcelona.

García, E., and Sequera, J. 2013. Gentrificación en centros urbanos: Aproximación comparada a las dinámicas de Madrid y Buenos Aires. *Quid 16: Revista de Área de Estudios Urbanos*, (3), 49–66.

González, S. 2011. Bilbao and Barcelona 'in motion': how urban regeneration 'models' travel and mutate in the global flows of policy tourism. *Urban Studies*, 48(7): 1397–418.

Harvey, D. 1989. From managerialism to entrepreneurialism: the transformation in urban governance in late capitalism. *Geografiska Annaler: Series B, Human Geography*, 71(1): 3–17.

—— 2001. *Spaces of Capital: Towards a Critical Geography*. London: Routledge.

—— 2008. The right to the city. *New Left Review*, 53(5): 23–40.

—— 2010. *A Companion to Marx's Capital*. London: Verso.

Herzer, H. 2008. Acerca de la gentrificación. In H. Herzer *et al.* (eds), *Con el corazón mirando al sur. Transformaciones en el sur de la Ciudad de Buenos Aires*. Buenos Aires: Ed. Espacio.

Isin, E. F. 2009. Citizenship in flux: the figure of the activist citizen. *Subjectivity*, 29(1): 367–88.

Jajamovich, G. 2012. Del Parque España a Puerto Madero: circulación del' urbanismo de los arquitectos' y la planificación estratégica entre Argentina y España (1979–93). *Cuaderno urbano*, 12(12): 7–25.

Janoschka, M. 2005. Discursos de inseguridad y la ciudad cerrada: mitos, realidades, barreras y fronteras de un producto inmobiliario 'perfecto'. *Revista de Investigación Social*, (2): 11–35.

Janoschka, M., Sequera, J. and Salinas, L. 2013. Gentrification in Spain and Latin America: a critical dialogue. *International Journal of Urban and Regional Research*. Available at: http://onlinelibrary.wiley.com/doi/10.1111/1468-2427.12030/abstract

Lash, S. and Urry, J. 1994. Economies of signs and space (vol. 26). London: Sage.

Lekerman, V., Yacovino, M. P. and Carman, M. 2012. Una mirada antropológica del caso 'Urbanización de la villa Rodrigo Bueno'. Available at: www.adaciudad.org.ar/docs/

Congreso_derecho_administrativo_Lekerman_y_Yacovino_final1-final.ppt (accessed 20 May 2014).

Low, S. and Smith, N. 2006, *The Politics of Public Space*. London: Routledge.

Lungo, M. and Smolka, M. 2005. Suelo y grandes proyectos urbanos: La experiencia latinoamericana. *Land Lines*, 17(1).

Ong, A. 2006. *Neoliberalism as Exception: Mutations in Citizenship and Sovereignty.* Durham, NC: Duke University Press.

Pico, M. and Yacovino, M. 2010. Orden y caos en el espacio público: planificación, expectativas y usos del espacio en Puerto Madero y Costanera Sur'. Presentation for the 6th Jornadas de Investigación en Antropología Social. FFyL, UBA, 3–6 August 2010.

Rodríguez, A., Moulaert, F. and Swyngedouw, E. 2001. Nuevas políticas urbanas para la revitalización de las ciudades en Europa. *Ciudad y Territorio, Estudios territoriales*, 33(129): 409–24.

Rodríguez, M. F. 2010. ¿Espacio público vs. Asentamiento? La Costanera Sur Rodrigo Bueno. *Intersticios, Revista sociológica de pensamiento crítico*, 4(1).

Sennet, R. 2006. *La cultura en el nuevo capitalismo*. Barcelona, Spain: Anagrama.

Sequera, J and Janoschka, M. 2012. Ciudadanía y espacio público en la era de la globalización neoliberal. *ARBOR Ciencia, Pensamiento y Cultura*, 188(755): 515–27.

Smith, N. 1996. *The New Urban Frontier: Gentrification and the Revanchist City*. London: Routledge.

Stavrides, S. 2007. Espacialidades de emancipación y la 'ciudad de umbrales'. *Bajo el Volcán*, 7(11), 117–24.

——2010. *Towards the City of Thresholds*. Trento, Italy: Professional dreamers.

Svampa, M. 2001. *Los que ganaron: La vida en los countries y barrios privados*. Buenos Aires: Editorial Biblos.

Szajnberg, D., Sorda, G. and Pesce, L. 2006. Privatización desuelo público y especulación inmobiliaria en Buenos Aires: Crónica sobre el pasado, presente y futuro de los pobladores de laVilla Rodrigo Bueno, ciudad de Buenos Aires. Buenos Aires: Universidad de Buenos Aires.

Wortman, A. 2004. *Comp Imágenes publicitarias, nuevos burgueses*. Buenos Aires: Prometeo Editoria.

——2010. Las clases medias argentinas, 1960–2008. In R. Franco, M. Hopenhayn and A. de León (eds), *Las clases medias en América Latina*. México: Siglo XXI.

Wright, E. O. 1992. Reflexionando, una vez más, sobre el concepto de estructura de clases. Revista, *Zona Abierta* (59–60).

—— 1994. *Clases*. Madrid: Siglo XXI.

Yacovino, M. P. 2010. Alcances y limitaciones del derecho a la vivienda: Los asentamientos Rodrigo Bueno y la Aldea Gay y los programas de recuperación de terrenos. *Intersecciones en antropología*, 11(1): 3–13.

Zibechi, R. 2007. *Autonomías y emancipaciones – América Latina en movimiento*. Lima: Universidad Nacional Mayor de San Marcos.

Zibechi, Raúl. 2012. *Territories in Resistance: A Cartography of Latin American Social Movements*. Oakland, CA: AK Press.

18 Public spaces and transformative urban practices in Cape Town

Diana Sanchez Betancourt

The urban space is both a product and a medium, created by social praxis and a structuring element of society (Haydn and Temel 2006: 47). Public spaces are vital geographical and social spaces in the city; platforms for individuals and diverse communities to interact and come together as equal citizens and for civic agency to manifest and be exerted. They are also the main stages for collective political expression (marches) and battle sites over scarce resources such as land. They are the primary scenery where urban diversity either shines or is obscured and where the heterogeneity of urban practices is either tamed or expressed through different ways of '*producing the city and living it*'.

In this chapter I look at some citizen-driven initiatives and practices that have emerged in Cape Town over the last decade. These in my view illustrate disruptions to dominant urban practices and understandings. As a Colombian residing in South Africa, a researcher interested in diverse intellectual approaches and a citizen involved in some of these initiatives, I offer a *translocal* perspective and narrative which is stirred by experiences and knowledge from different places and disciplines. This paper is driven by my curiosity to explore how citizens interact; how could they shape more human-centred and accessible spaces in highly fragmented urban environments, and by my interest in exploring urban public spaces and understandings. I therefore focus my attention on processes of social transformation and the humanity *of* and *within* cities by sharing the journeys of a few urban actors in Cape Town.

I use public space as a lens to explore emerging urban practices at the micro level (street and neighbourhood scales), proposing that these are local expressions of resistance to the current urban form and likely to make urbanization processes more sustainable by integrating notions of equity, as explored by Lawton in Chapter 14. Sustainable urbanization is here understood as a dynamic process that is shaped as local actors respond and try to adapt to the challenges posed by scarce resources and complex economic and social urban conditions. The practices and agency of the urban intermediaries here analysed illustrate the significance of public spaces as sites of social experimentation and transformations. These are in my view aspirational practices that although related to existing notions of urban resilience and innovative urbanization, resist the taming narratives that dominate many urban practices, uses and understandings of public spaces in a city like Cape Town.

Drawing on interviews with some of the individuals involved in these urban initiatives and on personal experience and observations as a participant and/or follower, I argue that these practices, which are staged in, or use public spaces, offer an opportunity for alternative and more integrative social and physical spaces. They do so in tune with ideas of resilience and the innovative urbanization framework which, as explored by Harris in Chapter 9, invites to embrace urban problem-solving through an approach that moves away from technological fixes towards a focus on the daily realities of urban life and *the mechanics of creativity, human agency and transformative change* (see page 00).

I explore these practices as expressions of the human story of an urban land-scape deeply marked by the legacy of racial segregation (Cape Town) and embrac-ing the *everyday urbanism* approach (see Chase *et al.* 2008) to help unpack the implications of these actions, the social relations and networks of the individuals driving them and the new urban opportunities they offer.

Social fragmentation and resilience in Cape Town

> New social relationships call for a new space, and vice versa.
>
> (Lefebvre 1991: 59)

The Apartheid system which dominated South African politics and development from 1948 until the 1994 democratic elections was implemented through institu-tionalized practices of racial segregation and forced removals, which shaped the urban form and fabric of cities. The legacy of violent dispossession is especially visible in the overcrowded settlements that characterize South African cities. These artificially engineered human settlements were developed under Apartheid primarily as labour locations, separated from white suburbs and from each other as coloured, black and Indian families were dumped to live parallel yet separate lives on the periphery of the growing city. While 1994 marked the beginning of a new system of inclusive governance, cities have remained fragmented, with most of the poor and non-white confined to these overcrowded settlements (see SACN 2011). Twenty years after the first democratic elections, uneven density patterns and racial boundaries still dominate local/neighbourhood realities, while socially mixed communities remain a distant dream. The social resilience of urban communities in South Africa has been deeply affected as generations of urban dwellers have grown in an urban system that rejected diversity and social and racial mixing, and slowly undermined the potential for cultural diversity in a rich cosmopolitan city.

In the South African context urban resilience, and the social aspects of it, refer to the capacity of a city to embrace a different pathway in challenging condi-tions, and the human capacity to assimilate and embrace change. While resil-ience involves adapting the urban development trajectory, which may also imply '*transforming local conditions based on experimentation, creativity and innova-tion*', social resilience refers more specifically to '*the ability of urban communi-ties to tolerate and assimilate diversity and the capacity of diverse communities to interact and build trusting relationships*', therefore strengthening the potential of cultural diversity (SACN 2011: 12–13).

Today Cape Town remains a city of stark contrasts. It is made up of sepa-rate enclaves populated by different and often antagonistic racial and income groups, as Figures 18.1 and 18.2 illustrate. It has a population of 3.4 million (Kane-Berman 2012), with about 44 per cent classified as coloured, 35 per cent as black African, over 19 per cent as white and under 2 per cent as Asian (Bekker and Fourchard 2013: XIV). It is also a linguistically diverse and young metro-politan area, where 35.69 per cent of Capetonians have Afrikaans as their first language, 29.8 per cent have isiXhosa and 28.40 per cent have English as their mother tongue. Over 30 per cent are aged between 18 and 34 and another 30 per cent are 17 years and younger (Bekker and Fourchard 2013: XIV). With post-apartheid development still failing to build a more integrated and just city, 35.7 per cent of the households live below the poverty line, 8.8 per cent have no access to sanitation on site and the unemployment rate stood at 24 per cent for 2012–13 (Statistics South Africa 2012).

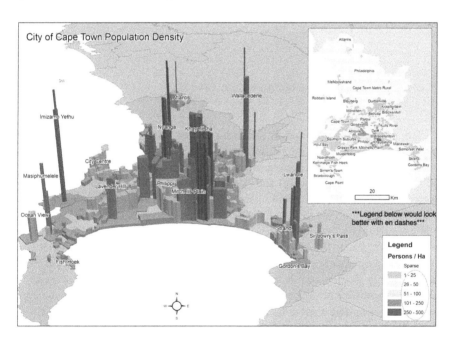

Figure 18.1 City of Cape Town population density: while the average population density is 39 persons per hectare this varies between 4 and 12 in the former white suburbs and 100 and 150 in the shack areas.

Source: SACN (2011: 59).

Figure 18.2 Racial self-identification in Cape Town in 2011.

Urban public spaces, and in particular streets, have often served as sites of protests for discontented urban dwellers. In the South African context these contestations are commonly known as service delivery protests dealing with issues of access (mainly to housing) and poor delivery of basic services, and in some cases they are a call for specific redress. For instance, the Occupy Rondebosch Common action organized by local social movements in 2012, which questioned the unequal urban form and access to land in Cape Town, called citizens to 'liberate public spaces for everyone and not only for the privileged' (Sacks 2012). While the participants aimed to temporarily and peacefully appropriate the common (a large green space at the heart of a wealthy suburb which was a site of forced removals under Apartheid), the gathering resulted in heavy confrontation with the police and local authorities. According to Van Donk, as the levels of frustration keep rising it could be expected that these protests will be increasingly defined by violence (Van Donk 2013: 11).

   While many of these contestations express frustration at the grassroots levels and are usually staged on townships, others are driven by middle-class activists and residents who are challenging urban development decisions around public land use issues. This is the case of the challenge posed to the mayor by the Cape

Town Civic Alliance around the political support of the city for the construction of a shopping centre in the Princess Vlei Wetland (a functional public space with great social and environmental significance for working-class communities). The proposal was challenged on the grounds that this move would further reinforce inequalities by privatizing a functional public space, calling for the protection of public spaces as integral elements of a just and sustainable city. As a local activist explained:

> Critical to the psychological health of a community is access to recreational spaces where people can connect with nature; interact with each other in a relaxed way . . . For those living in over-crowded homes with no gardens, [this] can only be found in natural public spaces . . . these spaces become the pressure valve that enables people to cope with the stresses of social and economic hardship in densely populated environments.
>
> (Pitt; 2013)

These types of contestations unfolding across Cape Town are illustrative of the discomfort and agency of various actors, including wealthy middle-class individuals and organizations. They are evidence of the gap between citizens and policymakers, they show the struggles of communities to exercise the right to participate in the shaping and utilization of public spaces (as explored by Sequera and Mateos in Chapter 17), and they highlight the importance of public spaces as a last resort for less advantaged communities (as discussed by Sotiropoulou in Chapter 19). Overall, these practices and other initiatives not explored in this chapter are expressions of social resilience, urban heterogeneity and examples of forms of civic agency that go beyond assimilating change, to igniting urban change.

Human agency and public spaces

The concept of public space is a complex and multi-layered one. Its importance is situational and it has social, physical and political dimensions (see Staeheli and Mitchell 2007). The physical dimension refers to tangible spaces such as streets, parks and squares which are made and controlled (at least in legal terms) by government bodies. The political dimension refers to spaces (mainly physical but also virtual) where democratic freedom is exercised and where gathering enables political deliberations, mobilizations and contestations. Lastly, the social dimension refers to public spaces as sites where social contact with strangers occurs, where communities are forged and social and behavioural modifications are possible (see Staeheli and Mitchell 2007; Aramburu 2008).

In this section I look at some emerging initiatives that illustrate the potential of utilizing existing public spaces (such as streets, parks and public transport) as instruments to challenge dominant practices and create experiences of inclusion and integration in public spaces.

While all dimensions are relevant and inform each other, the social dimension of public spaces is particularly relevant in socially fragmented cities where public spaces have been sites of segregation (like whites-only parks/beaches during Apartheid rule) and where rapid processes of commercialization and privatization are unfolding without much interrogation. In his research, Aramburu (2008) notes how urban spatial developments in the form of malls, gated communities or public amenities that require citizens to pay are resulting in more homogenous spaces where encounters with socially different people are more unlikely. In Cape Town, while the abundant natural beauty still offers a broad array of open public space options, political and economic forces are pushing to convert natural public spaces (like Pincess Vlei wetland) into privatized commercial hubs.

This trend towards retrieving into 'safe' controlled areas and the privatization and commercialization of public spaces is an issue of concern; it restricts the social life of the city in ways we still need to understand and is slowly diluting the *socialization* function of public spaces. Initiatives that propose alternative uses of public spaces and urban infrastructure as places 'to be' and not only to 'pass by', potentially maximizing their capacity as sites for community socialization (see Aramburu 2008) need to be encouraged.

Since 2005 several urban practices carrying this spirit have emerged or gained force in Cape Town. Some are linked to global processes of urban contestations or urban development trends, while others are rooted in local practices responding to local needs. They express emerging dynamics that might require new concepts rather than recycling old categories to box them somewhere (see Isin 2009). The four initiatives here explored range from politicized actions to *fun* initiatives with no developmental aim, but with urban implications nonetheless. They manifest themselves through specific sites (the streets, social media and networks) and are expressed through particular acts (bicycle rides, car-free streets, urban mobs and open cultural spaces). As they promote small transgressions in the traditional utilization of public space and resources, I argue that they have the capacity to transform realities at the micro level (of streets and neighbourhoods) and potentially beyond, and they offer in my view, disruptions to conventional and hegemonic urban practices and understandings.

In the first place, representative of the power of temporary public spaces but lacking a developmental agenda is the monthly (every full moon) bicycle ride Moonlightmass.[1] It was started in January 2012 by two individuals as 'a social experiment on Twitter', and the small group has grown rapidly to include thousands. They are primarily about enjoying a fun activity in the Atlantic seaboard and central area of the City, and to a lesser extent about raising awareness for cycling and promoting non-motorized commuting (see www.moonlightmass.co.za/moonlightmass/About.html). The action has resulted in the temporary appropriation of central public spaces, prompting the city to provide costly resources such as traffic officers, but it has fallen short of promoting urban agendas such as non-motorized transport.

There is no formal organization or legal entity behind the initiative, and while this has provided great flexibility for the individuals behind it and fluidity to the experiment, it has made it challenging for the city to relate to it. This was illustrated by a fall-out between the City and the organizers/participants around the need for an event permit for the ride. While for the City the individuals advertising the ride on Facebook were event organizers and therefore responsible for road safety, for the moonlight riders and supporters this was not an event and they rejected being boxed into the 'event organizers' category. In their view they never intended the social ride to become an event and it was therefore for the city to manage road safety aspects. Furthermore, in an interview with local media the founders argued that the experiment was now community owned and driven, therefore beyond political or individual control:

> We founded the event but if Daniel and I don't arrive on Sunday or at any other ride, it will continue, the community will come because even the marshals and the paramedics were organised by the community. We have just been the channel between the city and the community.
>
> (Kirshenbaum 2013)

Following the public exchanges, hundreds of individuals expressed their support and commitment to do the ride on social media (regardless of a permit), airing their frustrations with city structures and the city's 'inflexible approach to community-driven initiatives' (Lewis 2013). This episode shows the willingness of urban communities to appropriate spaces for alternative utilizations and the difficulty of streamlining emerging social practices in public spaces into existing institutional structures.

This initiative further shows that a large number of residents are craving for such spaces and are eager to contest traditional uses of urban infrastructure and obsolete city processes, highlighting the difficulty of dealing with new resident-driven initiatives in public spaces. It also shows, by creating a new practice and narrative, how public spaces could be transformed on a temporary (yet sometimes regular) basis as spaces for social gathering. However, it is important to note that although the social ride is an integrative space, it operates in isolation from other areas of the city, standing as a bubble, and therefore limited in addressing physical and social divisions. While the aim of the ride has never been to engage with the geographical and economic divisions of the city, the absence of a progressive urban agenda hampers the transformative potential of this exercise.

The second example takes temporary activations and social encounters to the next level. Open Streets Cape Town is a volunteer-based and citizen-led organization founded in 2012, inspired by the international Open Streets movement and particularly influenced by Bogota's Ciclovia model in Colombia. It has an urban agenda summarized in a manifesto that invites people to embrace the concept of Open Streets as a way to:

> Build shared places that embody respect for all and help bridge the social and spatial divides of the city . . . through streets that; (i) enable safer and more cohesive communities, (ii) provide platforms for creative expression of local

cultures and values, (iii) are places for recreation and social interaction and (iv) contribute to job creation and choice in how to move around the city.
(http://www.openstreets.co.za/about/manifesto-open-streets-cape-town)

This initiative is an example of individual and collective agency to transform the utilization of public spaces. Building upon international experiences of activating the 'recreational' space and economy in major shared public spaces (such as streets), it highlights the potential of temporary public spaces to bring communities together in a platform that encourages organic social, cultural and economic interactions. With no financial resources it has been powered by the agency of five volunteers who rely heavily on personal and professional networks to engage with communities and key stakeholders (such as city officials) in an attempt to get institutional support to roll out public space experiments in the form of Open Streets Days.

The organization implements localized participatory interventions like their Talking Streets[2] community engagement series, where residents engage to do observation and reflective walks around a local street. They have piloted four Open Streets Days where stretches of public roads (around 1 km long) have been transformed into temporary car-free corridors that provide free and safe recreational spaces for everyone (at least in principle). Their aim is to slowly build through experimentation, community participation and partnerships a major network of car-free corridors that will eventually connect distant (socially and physically) areas of the city. They have effectively and intensively use social media tools such as Twitter, Facebook and the crowdsourcing platform Thunda-Fund to reach out to residents (those using social media), inviting them to utilize streets differently, and have successfully and quickly channelled significant public support.[3]

While in most cities around the world Open Streets movements are dominated by cyclists and other forms of non-motorized transport (NMT), in Cape Town these events so far have been dominated by recreational and artistic activities staged and delivered by local residents and newcomers. The temporary urban space that is created on the street is shaped through community meetings with local residents (but open to everyone) preceding the events. In these physical gatherings, and the virtual interactions that inform and complement them, individual agency is encouraged and later on materialized into free activations (games, music and performers), spontaneous acts on the day (e.g. people rolling out their living rooms into the street) and improvised home-street businesses. While the pilots have been small in scale, their impact and significance has been widely recognized in local media and captured the imagination of various urban stakeholders who see the potential and see this as a call for action 'to go beyond the tendency to sit back and wait for delivery' (see Mkalima-Ngewana 2013).

But although the City has acknowledged the potential of this platform (following intense lobbying from the organization), vowing financial support to implement an Open Streets Days Programme in 2014, implementation has been a bumpy road. As one of the co-founders explains, it has been very difficult to work with the City and to overcome the administrative and financial challenges to utilize the streets as places of urban experimentation (Sanchez Betancourt 2014). Tensions between the City and organizers were aired in the media at the early stages of the process, further illustrating the difficulties of citizen–city engagements (see Williams 2013). No Open Street Days Programme was rolled out in 2014, and the first event only happened in January 2015 at a major street in the City's CBD.[4] Overall, the complex regulations and institutional processes illustrate the struggle of the City to do things differently, to utilize urban infrastructure in different ways and to support community-driven initiatives that fall outside traditional institutional boxes.

Similar to the Moonlightmass initiative, Open Streets illustrates the power of temporary uses of public spaces, hinting at the potential of non-motorized corridors to create socially mixed areas and communities, even if temporarily. Streets are the largest publicly owned urban asset, and in the South African fragmented urban setting they could be reshaped (in their use and accessibility) to become places of gathering and spaces to develop new social relations (see Borja, Aramburu 2008). The political agenda reflected in the Open Streets manifesto and their capacity to activate civic agency and volunteering shows the untapped potential of opening new urban spaces even with limited human and financial resources. These two initiatives illustrate both the strength and potential of actions at the micro level, but also the challenges of taking them forward under traditional urban governance structures.

As a third example, following a similar urban agenda, aiming to integrate distant urban socio-economic spaces through grassroots entrepreneurialism, inter-institutional collaborations and the arts, we find initiatives such as the 'coffee mob' (from the Department of Coffee) and the Maboneng Township Arts experience.

The Department of Coffee (DOC) is a small township coffee-shop officially launched on July 2012 by three local residents. It is located in Cape Town's biggest township, Khayelitsha, and operates on the premises of a major urban upgrading project. The infrastructure has provided a *neater* platform for local entrepreneurs to experiment on ways to expand their business beyond the township borders and economic limitations. According to the founders, the aim is 'to help boost economic and social development, shatter class and cultural barriers, establish the township as an integral (and visit-worthy) part of the city . . . and to break down the wall between Khayelitsha and Cape Town'.[5]

With this in mind and with the networking and marketing skills of a city-based partner (a middle-class white young Capetonian), the group is trying to run regular open days where, using Facebook and Twitter, they invite residents from the wealthy city centre area to join an organized 'coffee-mob' to experience the township. The coffee-mob idea emerged through a Twitter conversation between individuals who did not know each other but 'followed' each other on cyberspace and had coinciding agendas; the coffee shop which wanted to get consumers from wealthy suburbs to visit the shop, an urban think tank researcher who wanted to implement a flash-mob experiment in Cape Town, and the marketing manager of the public train company who wanted to broaden its marketing scope and make use of the under-utilized tourist train (Ingram 2013).

Closely aligned to this ethos is the Maboneng Township Arts Experience, which first happened in Cape Town in November 2012 in the Gugulethu township:

> A national public arts exhibition that turns homes in townships into galleries and the outdoor spaces into performance districts, it aims to integrate the township and the city and end the negative notion of townships through the arts. The Maboneng experiment has turned over 70 townships homes in the country into galleries. The exhibition happens annually over two days and includes film screenings, visual art, dance, theatre and music.
>
> (www.maboneng.com/)

Local artist and founder Ngwenya says, 'I'm hoping to foster an artistic culture that connects the township and the city into one creative bubble. I see this as a great opportunity to create social cohesion through a shared experience.'[6]

The experiments of initiatives like Maboneng offer a new terrain for exploring the possibilities of the creative economy, utilizing the space in between the private (homes) and the public (streets) while offering opportunities for social encounters between divided communities (townships and the wealthier city). Similarly, coffee-mob experiments offer a small but practical opportunity to establish new urban practices to address social fragmentation by bringing township and city together in a space of playful interaction. They are evidence also of the potential of creating new social and economic spaces through the arts, shifting the barriers between public and private spaces, and changing perceptions of 'the other' through public space platforms. Lastly they illustrate the power of social media to connect human agency and transformative change. While all of these initiatives operate individually, they have converged on specific occasions as individuals driving them keep contact physically or virtually in their search for synergies.[7]

Overall, although these experiments should not be boxed into static categories, they share certain elements worth noting. They propose to utilize public spaces and cultural infrastructure in new ways, they build on informal social networks and social media, and lastly, while they operate at the micro scale (street and neighbourhood level) they have broader urban implications.

Urban agency and alternative public spaces

Public spaces, when strategically used, offer a platform where new social relations are likely to emerge and be reinforced, where environmentally sound practices could be rooted (like the NMT agenda) and where *untamed* and more sustainable urban narratives could be strengthened through the actions of new urban intermediaries and evolving forms of civic agency. These spaces and the human interactions that unfold within them could help to transform the polarized, hierarchical and fragmentary social urban spaces of cities like Cape Town.

The interventions analysed here illustrate the power of temporary interventions as a way to start opening permanent spaces of change, the possibilities of social media in community action and the potential of small interventions, volunteering and interdisciplinary collaborations to build collective efforts from individual agency. They also illustrate the 'rich reservoir of voluntary activism' available in Cape Town (Pieterse 2012), highlight the need to utilize existing urban infrastructure differently, and show the emergence of a younger generation of urban intermediaries (activists?) who advocate for urban changes by doing things themselves. In other words, they seem to be part of a broader global generation of DIY (do it yourself) citizens who as identified by Iveson are 'not content with lobbying for a better city sometime in the future, and they often refuse to wait for permission to do things differently' (2013: 945).

These citizen-driven initiatives resist being categorized as social movements, social enterprises or activism in the political sense. They are expressions of the horizontal dimensions of urban agency (citizens engaging with and among themselves) as explored in the South African context by Van Donk (Van Donk 2013), but seem to go beyond this concept, illustrating the potential of citizenship as a practice rather than a status (Isin 2009). They are in an *in-between* or *untameable space* where, although lacking a rights discourse, they promote actions that enhance the right to the city and represent the voices of discontent residents and passionate citizens pushing for better spaces for participation and to use urban assets differently. They are part of a broader range of micro-spatial urban practices that are reshaping urban spaces (Iveson 2013: 941) and that require further interrogation. They could be seen as *acts of citizenship*, which Isin (2009) defines as efforts to make a difference: breaking routines, understandings and practices, and using public space as their central stage and tool.

Concluding remarks

The practices examined in the previous section could be defined as expressions of untamed urbanisms insofar as they propose new physical and social spaces and therefore narratives to address historical legacies and current urban practices that reinforce fragmentation. As pointed out in the book introduction, they are significant as they navigate new urban spaces and tensions to bring about transformative change. These initiatives propose different utilizations of public spaces and the creation of new ones; they are an invitation to transgress physical and social borders (township and city); they are opening new spaces for creative and social economy experiments; and are providing alternative forms of citizen engagement, particularly through social media and grassroots level networking.

While their narratives are not purposefully framed under sustainable urbanization or untamed urbanism discourses, their actions call for more sustainable urbanization processes by challenging spaces and practices of segregation and building urbanization from the micro level. They are illustrative of the hetero-geneous practices and contestations that make cities and urban life and that are shaping the city. Thus, they require further investigation and mapping to help us understand emerging processes and opportunities to bridge urban divides and to shape more meaningful forms of civic engagement.

As cities continue to adapt their development trajectory, these initiatives offer opportunities for experimentation, creativity and innovation to transform local conditions. They are valuable expressions of urban resilience as they create shared spaces that welcome diversity to harness its potential, which is likely to increase the social resilience of the urban system over time.

Positive and sustainable urban changes are likely to emerge not from pol-icy impositions but out of organic and day-to-day initiatives and social spaces grounded in urban communities. The alternative utilization of urban spaces and resources as discussed here is opening up new spaces and tensions that will bring about some form of change. This is the promise of public spaces as incubators for urban change in Cape Town and of these initiatives as liberating alternatives and expressions of untamed urbanism.

Notes

1 Inspired by the critical mass rides now common in cities around the world.
2 The Talking Streets series (see the Open Streets Cape Town website) involves research and engagement at the street level through walking seminars, as people are invited to share their experiences, perceptions and knowledge of local streets and propose ideas and take ownership in reshaping them. Intense advocacy work with local government and other stakeholders is also done to advance the streets/public spaces transformation agenda.
3 Together with the Observatory Improvement District (OBSID), Open Streets Cape Town managed to raise R41 500 in 30 days by utilizing the crowd-funding platform Thundafund. The entire event was paid for by Cape Town residents, with contributions from local businesses (http://westcapenews.com/?p=6757).
4 http://www.dailymaverick.co.za/article/2015-01-19-car-less-bree-street-brings-colour-and-life-to-cape-town/#.VMs_SGiUeSo
5 www.capetownmagazine.com/cafes/department-of-coffee-in-khayelitsha/93_22_18910 (accessed 20 June 2014).
6 www.creativecapetown.com/maboneng-township-arts-experience-turning-homes-into-galleries-in-gugs/ (accessed 20 June 2014).
7 For instance, Maboneng and Open Streets joined forces in October 2013 to stage a shared initiative in the Langa township, and there are current conversations with the Department of Coffee to extend the experiments in the Khayelitsha area.

References

Aramburu, M. 2008. Usos y Significados del espacio público. *Arquitectura, Ciudad y Entorno*, 3(8): 143–50.
Bekker, S. and Fourchard, L. (eds). 2013. *Governing Cities in Africa: Politics and Policies*. Cape Town, South Africa: HSRC Press.

Chase, J., Crawford, M. and Kalisky, J. (eds). 2008. *Everyday Urbanism*. New York: Monacelli Press.

Department of Coffee in Khayelitsha. n.d. Spreading the joys of java: Cape Town's first township-based artisan coffee shop. Available at www.capetownmagazine.com/cafes/ department-of-coffee-in-khayelitsha/93_22_18910 (accessed 13 September 2013).

Haydn, F. and Temel, R. (eds). 2006. *Temporary Urban Spaces: Concepts for the Use of City Spaces*. Basel, Switzerland, Boston, MA and Berlin: Birkhauser.

Ingram, M. 2013. Personal interview, 2 September.

Isin, E. F. 2009. Citizenship in flux: the figure of the activist citizen. *Subjectivity*, 29(1): 367–88.

Iveson, K. 2013. Cities within the city: do-it-yourself urbanism and the right to the city. *International Journal of Urban and Regional Research*, 37(3): 941–56.

Kane-Berman, J. 2012. *South Africa Survey: 2012*. Johannesburg, South Africa: South African Institute of Race Relations.

Kirshenbaum, E. 2013. Mass dismay as impasse kills ride. *Cape Times*, 15 November. Available at www.iol.co.za/capetimes/mass-dismay-as-impasse-kills-ride-1.1607554#. UvubAPv3M09 (accessed 5 February 2014).

Lefebvre, H. 1991. *The Production of Space*. Oxford: Blackwell.

Lewis, A. 2013. Cape events 'strangled by red tape'. *IOL*, 26 November. Available at www.iol.co.za/news/politics/cape-events-strangled-by-red-tape-1.1612526#.Uv3___ vxo08 (accessed 5 February 2014).

Maboneng Township Arts Experience. 2012. Turning homes into galleries in Gugs, 7 November. Available at www.creativecapetown.com/maboneng-township-arts-experi-ence-turning-homes-into-galleries-in-gugs/ (accessed 2 September 2013).

Mkalima-Ngewana, B. 2013. Citizen-led projects can forge a unified Cape Town. *Cape Argus*, 4 June.

Pieterse, E. 2012. Urban age award should inspire collaborative efforts in Cape Town. *Cape Argus*, 13 February.

Pitt, B. 2013. The desecration of a temple. *Cape Times*, 25 October. Available at www.iol. co.za/capetimes/the-desecration-of-a-temple-1.1597419#.Uvse5_mSxoE (accessed 30 January 2014).

Sacks, J. 2012. Rondebosch Common: An occupation not a land invasion, 26 January. Available at http://www.politicsweb.co.za/politicsweb/view/politicsweb/en/page7230 8?oid=277182andsn=Marketingweb+detailandpid=90389 (accessed 29 August 2013).

Sanchez Betancourt, D. 2014. Personal interview/reflections, 5 December.

South African Cities Network (SACN). 2011. Towards resilient cities: a reflection on the first decade of democratic and transformed local government in South Africa, 2001–2010. Available at www.sacities.net/

Staeheli, L. A. and Mitchell, D. 2007. Locating the public in research and practice. *Progress in Human Geography*, 31(6): 792–811.

Statistics South Africa. 2012. *Income and Expenditure of Households 2010/2011*. Pretoria: Government of South Africa.

Van Donk, M. 2013. Citizenship as becoming, ch.1 in Active *Citizenship Matters: Perspectives from Civil Society on Local Governance in South Africa*. Good Governance Learning Network (GGLN).

Williams, R. 2013. City's aversion to risk is stifling original thought. *Cape Argus*, 16 October.

19 Everyday practices in Greece in the shadow of property

Urban domination subverted?

Irene Sotiropoulou

> The more difficult and more disappointing the conditions of life are and the more discouraged the Conscious gets, the more the Shadow is empowered until, finally, its darkness has become overwhelming.
>
> C. Jung (1972: 94)

Introduction

This chapter is a first attempt to explore the stance towards property in urban space adopted by grassroots everyday practices in Greek urban centres. The schemes do not use official currency, and neither do they follow the rule of obligatory (re)payment in kind. The discussion also examines mainstream perceptions of property, because on the basis of those perceptions the sharing practices are attacked, suppressed and accused of illegality.

The research question of this chapter is whether grassroots perceptions and practices about property have any potential to defy or subvert the mainstream private property institutions and the mentalities that are linked to them. The complexity of the issue, as well as the attempt to use psychoanalytical tools to explore collective efforts and arrangements, show that untameness in the city may take various forms, mixing the symbolic with basic needs and the institutional with collective unconscious and conscious behaviours.

Consequently, half of the chapter is dedicated to theory. The next section presents the theoretical framework adopted for the analysis. Given that the use of psychoanalysis in studying economic phenomena is still at experimental stage, the following section contains a number of reflections on my theoretical caveats and the methods I used to access the empirical data. Three contrasting case studies are presented so that we can have a concrete picture of how our analytical tools can give us useful insights on the perceptions of property. Those same case studies are further discussed in the final section with the intention to explore whether grassroots initiatives may offer new thinking and practices in contrast to private property establishment.

Theoretical background

Private property as a patriarchal institution in capitalism

Private property can be understood as a patriarchal institution, which has been reconstructed through capitalism to support, sustain and promote a set of behaviours which can be performed only by specific people from the general population, and which reinforce the hierarchical superiority those people enjoy within our society. In other words, capitalist private property is not only an institution related to men. It is also a construction in favour of men who are white, middle-class, possibly engaged in entrepreneurial activities, and of course Western European or Anglo-Saxon. These individuals tend to favour their own privilege and the hierarchical system which privileges them (Richardson 2010; Pateman 1988: 60–4, 148–52, 185).

As a result, perceptions of self, freedom and citizenship are built on and around this private property axis, which is sexualized and politicized in such a way that various hierarchies are reproduced and reinforced through the idea that a free man can treat as his private property everything he mixes his effort or works with. Conversely, no person can acquire rights through their personal work and effort unless they are a free man. To this, the class axis adds the fact that people who do not already have private property titles in their hands are unable to acquire property over what they mix their personal effort with. Commodification and privatization are based on this perception: that the private property owner is able, even by contracting for the work of other people, to mix this bought human work with his property and augment his property instead of having the other people establish claims over what they have produced (Bhandar 2011; Mayes 2005; Pateman,1988: 1–17, 39–153).

No matter how problematic it sounds, the feminization of the working class and of anyone and any social group that is not what capitalist private property describes as an owner proves that the main axis of social inequalities is still that of gender. This means that gender inequality and subordination is reproduced on various levels of economic activity and institutional structures, and it transcends other inequalities, such as class, ethnicity and educational level. In other words, to treat *homo economicus* as the private property owner and producer/ entrepreneur means that all people who are not like him are subjected to the binary constructions of patriarchy. If you are not a *homo economicus*, whether you lack the 'homo' or the 'economicus' part, or both, you enter the economic space as a second-rate citizen.

An additional deeply ingrained assumption within capitalism is that owners of private property do not have any obligations to or (inter)dependencies with society, or social connections to other owners. In economics, this is expressed technically with the term 'externalities'. Therefore, all social costs of private property and its use by its owner are calculated independently of the enactment and performance of private property. This is one aspect of the private–public divide, where the private owner is deemed to be self-constrained and independent in theory, but in practice he treats his private property as non-constrained over the commons, and as dependent on the suppression of the other members of society and on the (ab)use of the public or common resources (Agathangelou and Ling 2006; Baland and Francois 2005; Fitzpatrick 2006).

Private property as the shadow expression of a suppressed archetype

The second theoretical approach about private property stems from this ambivalent or contradictory aspect of private property. The private property owner is institutionally without dependencies and social bonds, but practically he bases again and again his private income or profit on all the other people who produce but cannot acquire property over their effort, given that they are not already property owners. His social bonds establish and reinforce inequalities and exploitation, which are full of deprivation and violence if seen from the point of view of the non-owners (Pateman 1988: 39–115).

On a collective level, the property institution is part of an economic structure which is based on scarcity and greed. Private property is never enough if freedom is constructed through owning things, particularly if each private property has its individual and collective externalities, passed on to other members of society and the public or common spaces and resources. Then, owners and non-owners are forced to seek private property, obviously with much better results for the former than for the latter. And if private property is never enough, then land and urban space are never enough either, no matter what the size of the population is or whether humans have certain needs for social survival and reproduction which cannot exceed certain levels imposed by their mere biology.

However, instead of resolving the contradictions which lead to so much poverty and exploitation, it seems that people are more prone to enhance the contradictions and perform them again and again. To understand this effect over people's behaviour and how the private property institution might influence their perceptions and economic activities, I use B. Lietaer's adaptation of Jungian analysis theory to economic issues (2011). Lietaer explains how the suppression of women and of an archetype directly connected to them (the archetype of mother goddess) in our society leads to behaviours which tend to reinforce economic problems at the expense not only of women, but of all people who are less advantaged in terms of power and/or finances. This Jungian analysis shows that economic institutions, patriarchy and economic injustice are intertwined and form a trap for all of us, programming our behaviour so that we remain in the trap and reinforce those same institutions that trap us.

The symbol of mother goddess (and the women behind it) is the archetype which mostly affects our productive activities or our economic life in its broad sense. A suppressed archetype, just like any other major symbol of human societies, cannot disappear, but turns into its shadows – that is, its negative, aggressive and anti-social alter ego. In other words, it is transformed within the collective psyche (and in individual psyches too) into negative aspects of will which cannot be avoided by people and societies, but affect them deeply and unconsciously. Sometimes there are completely destructive results because those suppressed psychic forces are uncontrollable (Jung 1980: 18–103; 1988: 17–63). Then, a suppressed mother goddess becomes either a condition of scarcity or a condition of greed (Lietaer 2011: 55–121, 133–9, 366–87; Jung 1972: 94–5). It seems that in a crumbling capitalist patriarchy, both scarcity and greed can coexist at the same time, in the same economy.

Theoretical caveats and methods used for this project

In terms of typical private property rules, there is no need for authorities to suppress the two initiatives I present in my first two case studies, as they do not defy private property directly and turn to common spaces for their activities to take place. While it could be argued that such collective activities are practised by a marginal group of people in comparison with the total population of the urban areas examined, I believe their analysis can be illuminating. In other words, my intention here is to use the theoretical approach outlined in the previous section in order to examine why people undertake such initiatives, and why public authorities and individuals appear to be compelled to try to ban or expel them from public space.

Theoretical caveats

To analyse my case studies, I used a feminist critique of property and the Jungian analysis of capitalism, as an analysis of a suppressed feminine archetype. I hope both theoretical approaches complement each other, in the sense that the first describes the situation as it is and the second explains forces which work against or for collective efforts to supersede capitalist problems.

Such an approach comes, however, with a number of risks. My worries lie particularly with the second approach: that is, with the use of psychoanalysis to understand capitalist economic activity and its alternatives. First, the last thing I want is to depoliticize my topic, much less to make it a vague new age discussion about new consciousness and an individualist stance in the face of collective problems. Second, I am aware that Jung's theory, just like all psychological theories, is embedded in patriarchy, just like all the episteme we have in academia. I do not want to replicate stereotypes about which activity or social stance is feminine and what is masculine – something that is not easy to avoid when using archetypes. Third, no matter whether I think that stereotyping genders does not help in any analysis, I cannot close my eyes in the face of a situation where people still live collectively through such stereotypes. Much less can I close my eyes to the fact that the archetypes we have are ones that have been embedded for thousands of years in patriarchy (San Miguel 2011). Therefore, bringing into consciousness archetypes and shadows could be seen as a first step to being able to escape collectively from the trap of the unconscious (Jung 1912: 163–230).

Fourth, social struggles not only include psychological conditions, but also include stereotypes, either as points to fight against, or as ideas to develop and use in movements and political debates. To ignore this aspect of a struggle does not make the analysis more militant; rather it makes it more shallow (Beverley 2004; Icaza and Vazquez 2013). Fifth, to my knowledge, even if we accept the Marxist distinction that our capitalist societies consist of production relations which create the base structure on the one hand and cultural constructions like ideas or artistic expression which are the social superstructure on the other hand, there is no satisfactory explanation on how base structures and superstructures interact. In other words, how are people affected by production relations and how do they then construct their ideas and arts accordingly? And if we are trapped into base and super-structure spaces, can we create new base/infra-structures if the existing ones are inescapable in mental and psychic terms? The Jungian school has worked extensively on the relationships between collective and individual psychology, and even if we could say that the direct use in economics of this school's work might be quite risky, we cannot refine this theory to discuss the economy unless we actually use this theory to discuss the economy.

Finally, just like all academic explorations, I expect this one to be refined, corrected or rejected by further research in the future. For this reason, and taking into consideration the aforementioned caveats, I take a number of analytical risks as I believe it is necessary to challenge the privatization and masculinization discourses here and now (Talpade Mohanty 2002).

Methods used

In constructing this chapter, I decided to use concrete examples and data originating in my own empirical research to understand the implications of the theoretical arguments previously outlined, with the intention of raising more elaborate questions for further research.

In the discussion that follows, I have used two case studies for which I have collected data through field observation and participation between 2011 and 2013. The schemes that are the subject of both case studies have also their own Facebook pages and member listings from which I obtained regular information on their activities. In addition, I regularly have free discussions with people who participate in these schemes, not only concerning problems arising from the function of the schemes, but also with reference to general issues in Greek society and economy which affect the schemes and their members.

I have made extensive use of internet tools and Facebook discussions not only because the scheme members use those tools for their internal issues, but also because negotiation and debate with local authorities and private businesses takes place through mass media and online/social media. The use of the internet permitted me to have a shadow case: in other words, to have data available from extensive public debates concerning a gentrification project where artists participate and defend the gentrification policies. This third case epitomizes a number of key aspects underpinning everyday discursive practices on private property. As such, this case offers an opportunity to explore the contrast with the everyday practices examined through my initial two case studies.

I have always conducted my empirical research in the open, which means that I announce my researcher identity so that collectives and their members are aware of my work. The initiatives described in the first two case studies are groups with which I have had regular collaboration and discussions and which have been very positive to my participating and observing. Public debates are accessible to all, while if a debate takes place on an individual Facebook wall, even if this is public, I also announce that I am researching the topic and I am interested in the discussion for research purposes. However, it is a basic principle that I maintain the confidentiality required to protect individuals and communities. I access the material through my Facebook research account, where people can access my name, contact details and writings.

The case studies

Case study 1: Sharing food in a small city

The first case study concerns a social kitchen which emerged from the 'movement of the squares'[1] in the summer of 2011 in a small city in Greece, a long way from Athens. It is run and supported by individuals, local food producers and inhabitants of the city who contribute work, money and raw food, or run artistic events to raise money to buy food for the kitchen. The kitchen group uses one room for the purpose of food sharing, communal meals and the gatherings of the social kitchen assembly. This is located at the back of the downtown school building complex, but is independent of the rest of the complex.

The meals are not cooked in that room, except in emergencies. Many people have their meal delivered to them, and therefore only some of the people benefiting from this scheme actually eat in the room. Only one meal is served each day, and in total more than 200 households receive a meal every evening. To avoid disturbances to the commercial stores which are located on the same street, the organizers share food after 20.30 in the evening, and the meal is served in the room after 21.00.

However, the shop owners in the area have not been happy with this arrangement. They have complained publicly many times that the social kitchen should not be in this location, as people who wait outside could disturb their business and discourage locals and tourists from shopping. The shop owners found official support from the local chamber of commerce and the city mayor. Both pressed to have the kitchen relocated to a public building well outside the town centre (which would make this scheme less accessible to those who need it most). However, plans to relocate the kitchen did not succeed despite the claim made by the chamber and the mayor that the kitchen disturbed the happy celebratory atmosphere of the street. The shop owners then blamed two thefts that had happened in the area on the social kitchen and the people who receive meals there. In reality it was very unlikely that any illegal act would have taken place during the hours when the kitchen is open (around 20.30–22.30) because there are plenty of people around at that time, and they would have noticed any activity of that kind.

Case study 2: Sharing used goods in Athens

The second case study concerns a regular free-exchange bazaar, a kind of initiative which also emerged from the 'movement of squares' in the summer of 2011. This is a give-and-take gathering which takes place regularly at a designated public place in Athens. People bring and give for free unused and unwanted items, and take what they need out of the things other people have contributed to the bazaar (Sotiropoulou 2012: 44–6). This bazaar is run by a citizens' assembly, and it has been organized many times over about two years in Syntagma Square, which is the central downtown square of Athens.

Problems with the local mayor started as far back as late 2012. The bazaar plan to hold a New Year's Eve event was suspended because the city council organized a charity event with the same purpose in Syntagma Square. Apart from the obvious crowding out of the bazaar organizers by the official charity, the main difference was that those organizing the free-exchange bazaar did not perceive the activity as charity, but as an act of solidarity. In contrast, the official event was an explicitly charitable venture, directly based on the discourse that 'rich people give to the poor'.

In late April 2013, the Athens Municipal Police forced the bazaar organizers to cancel their next planned bazaar and retrieve the goods that had already been accumulated in Syntagma Square. These consisted primarily of second-hand books, which were transferred to an artists' squat near Syntagma Square. After this incident, the bazaar never took place in the square again.

The mayor of Athens justified this action by claiming that the square is the property of all citizens and that the organizers did not have a permit to hold a bazaar there. (Of course, no permit would have been granted for a bazaar had they applied for one.) Syntagma Square is well known as a downtown meeting place and a site of political struggle. It is situated in one of the main commercial areas in Athens, and is also a space where non-governmental organizations (NGOs) and also private companies can set up kiosks to promote their services. Many private companies use the subway entrance in the square as a location to give away leaflets, offers and sample products. None of those activities has been considered as a trespass against citizens' property, and the mayor has not as yet replied to citizens' questions about whether these activities all had the necessary permits.

By contrast, in the case of the free-exchange bazaar, the mayor declared that he would not tolerate anomie, while portraying the exchange of books in a public space as an occupation of the square. This means that, in effect, the ban applied only to non-commercial free-exchange but not to the established commercial activity that takes place in the square. In other words, what became questioned through this conflict was whether people can collectively exchange things with each other for free in a public space.

Case study 3: Nothing belongs to the people?

The third case study emerged quite late, in early September 2013, when I had already written the first draft of this chapter, and is related to an artistic project and real estate development plan in one of the oldest and most disadvantaged neighbourhoods of downtown Athens. This area is undergoing gentrification, with real estate investors and companies showing an increasing interest in investing there. The artistic project was one of the first to be openly and privately funded by a real estate company that had bought properties in the area.

I decided to include this case study for a number of reasons. It is clear that the poverty and the poor people of the area are considered 'the problem' for any revitalization of the neighbourhood by the municipality who sent the police and by the real estate investors of the area who demanded such handling (Chatzistefanou 2013). The gentrification requires police action against the poor people who live and work in the area, usually under very bad conditions. My main reason, though, was that some of the organizers of the artistic project publicly defended the project in online debates using the discourse of private property. In particular, they insisted that the poor people who live around this area were degrading the property and the work embedded in the artistic private spaces.

One of the organizers complained publicly about homeless poor people living on the streets and against sex workers working in the same area where the artistic event is taking place. She clearly did not like their lifestyle, although she focused on issues of hygiene. Another organizer wrote in public that she would be happy to see the poor homeless people persecuted and displaced to other areas. Nevertheless, I stuck with the case once I read the written statement of another organizer that 'nothing belongs to the "people" (and to their beloved "immigrants"), much less in the name of their misery, and nothing belongs to Art in the name of Art'.

I included this case study as a shadow case, in the sense of the Jungian shadow of archetypes (Jung 1972: 94–5, Lietaer 2011: 37–54, 119–21). In other words I treated it as an opposite, or as the mentality against which the organizers in the first two case studies try to fight back. That is, they try to stand against the prevailing power of private property in structuring public space, or at least this is what they differentiate themselves from. The organizers of the artistic event (all the three who publicly expressed such views were women) were furious with poor people because they used the streets and the public space to live in, while the private property owners needed that same public space to make their private business and space accessible to the wider public, sponsors and the mass media.

Beyond property in urban space?

Private property's aggressiveness towards non-property-demanding practices

It seems that, in general, the private/public divide still works for private companies and businesses. Private property is private, while public property serves profit-making private agents (Atkinson 2003). This stance has been adopted by the local authorities in all three case studies: they seem to support the idea that public space is better fitted to be used by private, often profit-making, businesses rather than by all city dwellers. This stance is also very problematic in practice, because the commons and public resources are in every community the last resort of the least advantaged who in many cases face not only poverty, but also gendered poverty (Bayat 2000; Baland and Francois 2005; Platteau 2006; see also chapter 15 by Manase Chiwese).

Therefore, the property discourse works both as public property and as private property, against the public spaces and urban commons (Zick 2006) and, in real terms, against those people and/or groups who have no property of their own or have very limited material resources within the urban space (Atkinson 2003). As a result, the contrast becomes evident between, on the one hand, institutional and legal rights which frame social relations through the paradigm of property, and on the other hand, the grassroots perceptions of using urban space, which implicitly or explicitly reject such paradigms.

The three case studies also make evident that the policy summarized as 'there is no space' for grassroots initiatives and everyday survival enforces the constructed scarcity of urban space, which in turn is linked to the shadow archetype of the suppressed producer (mother goddess). I have already mentioned in the theoretical section how the archetype of mother goddess is the archetype of producers, and what its suppression means for our societies. The social kitchen and the free bazaar shake up our programmed behaviour to seek property and entitlement for everything: anyone, irrespective of their economic or political status, can participate in one way or another in the sharing. Contrary to this, the people who run the gentrification artistic project perceive that there is not enough urban space for all, much less enough for the most disadvantaged.

As a result, even if practices like the ones described in the first two case studies might not have emerged as a direct resistance to capitalism, they might form a type of deep resistance to capitalism and patriarchy, and to all those connotations working together in favour of an old and complex system of injustice. Such practices are negotiated and persist, even when displaced, without arguments over property entitlement. They are at the same time a practical attempt to de-stereotype poor people and all activity that takes place without the rule of obligatory payment or reciprocity. They decolonize alternative practices of resource use and sharing from being signs of poverty, ignorance and marginal lifestyles (Thelen 2011), (re)constructing them as signs of abundance, inventive thinking and solidarity among different people and social groups. In other words, the two first case studies reveal that abundance exists where poverty does not, making possible such a thing as a free meal and a free book (Lietaer 2011: 55–126).

At the same time, we can see from all the case studies that the shadowy property archetype continues to exert aggression and to expand to colonize every aspect of associational urban life. Capitalism displaces people in the city and suppresses collective coping strategies attempting to recolonize it, both as living proofs of lower status or even as activity which devalues and destabilizes the prosperity of privatized urban space. The persecution of such practices takes place through property discourse and violence institutions (typically the state or municipal police), and it in the process reproduces and increases poverty and scarcity (Atkinson 2003).

First, we need to take into account the systemic violence by property owners using a public discourse of 'being attacked' by the poor people who just use the urban space for dwelling or survival. Second, we need to notice the support this discourse receives from official associations and authorities (Blomley 2003; Garnett 2009). Both aspects combined make us see that private property becomes weirdly, incommensurately aggressive to people and activities which apparently do not demand or attack property. This is increasingly the case in cities, where the commodification and privatization of space and life often reaches its most overt and intolerant expression.

The revival of a suppressed archetype as possible collective subversion of private property

What could be underneath this aggressiveness? As already mentioned, *homo economicus* and privatization are institutionally normalized shadows which attack humans, urban space and communities under the TINA (there is no alternative) assumption of neoliberal policies. Every practice that conscientiously revives the suppressed archetype of compassion, creativity, sharing, abundance, sociality and justice without entitlement and ownership shakes the shadow (suppression of the archetype) and disturbs the psychological programming that capitalism and private property institutions have imposed over the urban space and its inhabitants.

However, just as material claims over the communal resources are not enough to achieve communal life, it also takes loads of collective conscientious effort to refurbish, develop and free the archetypes that are not shadowy and aggressive (Jung 1972: 36–97). The extremity of official retribution and persecution towards those practices mirrors some very interesting features of the grassroots sharing schemes:

– *Scarcity and greed as institutional results of private property.* A first conclusion is that grassroots sharing schemes reveal that there is some potential to reverse the situation of believing that scarcity and greed are normal behaviours or human instincts against which it is impossible to fight (Lietaer 2011: 345–92). Both the social kitchen and free-exchange bazaar case studies expose how scarcity and greed are institutionally created and sustained. The third (shadow) case study shows that the perception of public space as something that should serve private property and its owners is not based on any instinct but on the deeply ingrained archetype of private property itself. The tautology which is implied in the third case study discourse is that 'as a private property owner I have the right to decide about public property too, and this right does not exist for the people who have no private property in the area where I have private property'. This tautology or circular argument reveals the class aggressiveness that can be publicly and unapologetically exerted in the public domain, and also how and why property owners feel entitled to ask for more rights over the rest of urban dwellers.

– *The practicality of small, grassroots, marginal experiments.* A second observation emanating from the previous analysis is that grassroots initiatives which are organized beyond institutional structures and beyond property agreements seem to have the potential for new conditions to be created for social and economic collective action (Fafchamps 1992; see also chapter 20 by Ferne Edwards). Food is secured for people in the first case study. This does not only ensure their survival within a framework of harsh capitalist conditions, no matter whether they are examples of *homo economicus* or not; it also reinforces their potential to think of resources and human effort in a way far from the individualist approach of the 'survival of the fittest' and 'the winner takes all'. The first two case studies show that reproduction of humane living conditions stems from collective arrangements that function beyond strict reciprocity which is actually linked to the ideas that what we need to reproduce ourselves as social beings (food, books, etc.) is scarce and that all humans are greedy if they are not restrained by a pay-back rule. Securing this biological and social reproduction requires complex arrangements that small experiments can try to improve and educate communities about (Weiner 1980). As argued by Jung (1972: 94), securing a main reproduction resource every day creates a collective condition where the collective shadow of scarcity is gradually disempowered.

– *Private property cannot really work if it is not absolute.* Privatization of everything is ideally what capitalism (and the suppressed shadowy producer archetype) wants (Demsetz 1964; Webster 2007). The case studies analysed indicate that total privatization is not only about destroying the lives of humans and natural resources, but also about eliminating any human creativity which might be able to resist this absolutism. Public spaces are then renamed and reconstructed as addenda to private property, and they get privatized in the name of the people who cannot access them. The negative stance adopted by the authorities and private business, and their discourse in all three cases, show that even small-scale demonstrations that people can survive in many ways other than by negotiating with private owners can be detrimental to the capitalist privatization project.

– While privatization of urban space expands, *the free archetype of the mother goddess who is not a private property owner is remembered and practised.* According to the Jungian analysis, the archetype re-emerges not only to reverse destruction but to create from scratch new resources, spaces and communities (Lietaer 2011: 55–139). Women prevail in this type of grassroots practices, in the first two case studies as both members and coordinators, and so do they in most similar schemes across Greek cities (Sotiropoulou 2014). The interesting thing is that in the third case study, the ideology of aggressive property ownership was also promoted by women [artists running the artistic event]. However, just as capitalist patriarchy is not only about suppressing women and people from outside Europe, the mother goddess archetype of prosperity and abundance refers to all people, regardless of their gender. While private property attempts to eliminate the inventiveness and the resources of people trying to survive, the ideas that stand for collective arrangements based on common resources and spaces proliferate and become more resilient than expected.

Conclusion

Returning to the title of this chapter, it could be argued that subversion is too narrow a notion to describe social forces and everyday practices working outside the paradigm of private property in contemporary cities. Moreover, it might be premature to put this label on the grassroots everyday sharing schemes analysed in this chapter. Nevertheless, the emergence of abundance, non-property-sharing and feminine archetype practices such as the ones explored here show that those same practices are not for mere survival only. The people of the schemes negotiate and resist publicly the property discourse, showing that what they do exceeds the limits of property thinking and the institutional frameworks which regulate public space and other commons within cities.

Whether such practices will eventually become subversive in the future against the shadows and capitalism itself is not known. That is of course the very nature of the 'untamed', which means that control by the powerful is not entirely succeeding in the first place, without, at the same time, anyone being able to foresee what the resisting groups will decide to do after that. Further research could explore and reveal their potential, or at least it could refuse to turn a blind eye to the attacks those practices face and to the reasons for those attacks.

Acknowledgements

I am grateful to the people who run and participate in the social kitchen and the free-exchange bazaar, Mr Panagiotis Koustas who brought into my attention the public online discussion concerning the banning of the free bazaar, and Mr Panagiotis Chatzistefanou and his Facebook page guests for their extensive debates on gentrification. I would like to thank all teachers and fellows from the Quito WSS workshop, particularly the Quito WSS Freeing Alternatives group, the group leader Ferne Edwards, the group editor Adriana Allen, our editing coordinator Sharon Verwoerd and our language editor Susan Curran for giving generously the inspiration for this topic, their comments, support and ideas. The data concerning the social kitchen was gathered for a team research project titled 'Covering immediate needs with solidarity economy and redefining the role of trade unions', conducted for and funded by the Labour Institute of Athens.

282   *Irene Sotiropoulou*

Note

1 In late May and the entire summer of 2011, people were gathering in the main square of big cities in Greece demanding the cancellation of austerity policies, discussing alternatives, organizing demonstrations and other events, and opening the political space to people who were until then quite far from collective efforts. The entire movement has been called the 'movement of the squares', and concerning Athens it has been brutally suppressed. By the end of summer 2011 the entire effort started to mutate into other collective initiatives.

References

Agathangelou, A. M. and Ling, L. H. M. 2006. Fear and property: why a liberal social ontology fails postcolonial states. International Affairs Working Paper 2006–07. Paper for a panel on 'Contesting modern state: stateness in the postcolonial world', International Studies Association, 22–26 March 2006, San Diego, CA.

Atkinson, R. 2003. Domestication by cappuccino or a revenge on urban space? Control and empowerment in the management of public spaces. *Urban Studies*, 40(9): 1829–43.

Baland, J.-M. and François, P. 2005. Commons as insurance and the welfare impact of privatization. *Journal of Public Economics*, 89: 211–31.

Bayat, A. 2000. From 'dangerous classes' to 'quiet rebels' – politics of the urban subaltern in the urban South. *International Sociology*, 15(3): 533–57.

Beverley, J. 2004. El subalterno y los limites del saber academico. *Revista Aktual Marx*, 2 (August), trans. M. Beiza and S. Villalobos-Ruminott.

Bhandar, B. 2011. Plasticity and post-colonial recognition: 'owning, knowing and being'. *Law Critique*, 22: 227–49.

Blomley, N. 2003. Law, property and the geography of violence: the frontier, the survey and the grid. *Annals of the Association of American Geographers*, 93(1): 121–41.

Chatzistefanou, P. 2013. Το όνειδος που αυτοαποκαλείται σκηνή σύγχρονης τέχνης στην Ελλάδα [The shame that is self-named contemporary art stage in Greece], IEfimerida online magazine, 15.10.2013, http://www.iefimerida.gr

Demsetz, H. 1964. The exchange and enforcement of property rights. *Journal of Law and Economics*, 7 (October): 11–26.

Fafchamps, M. 1992. Solidarity networks in preindustrial societies: rational peasants with a moral economy. *Economic Development and Cultural Change*, 41(1): 147–74.

Fitzpatrick, D. 2006. Evolution and chaos in property rights systems: the Third World tragedy of contested access. *Yale Law Journal*, 155: 996–1048.

Garnett, N. S. 2009. Private norms and public spaces. *William and Mary Bill of Rights Journal*, 18(1), Article 7: 183–98.

Icaza, R. and Vazquez, R. 2013. Social struggles as epistemic struggles. *Development and Change*, 44(3): 683–704.

Jung, C. 1912. Αναλυτική Ψυχολογία: Ι – Ψυχολογία του ασυνειδήτου, ΙΙ–Σχέσεις μεταξύ του «εγώ» και του ασυνειδήτου. *[Analytical Psychology: I – Psychology of the Unconscious, II – Relations Between Ego and Unconscious]* Μτφρ. Πην. Ιερομνήμονος Π. Athens: Εκδόσεις Γκοβόστη [Govosti Publishing].

—— 1972. Η ολοκλήρωση της προσωπικότητας *[The Integration of the Personality]*. Μτφρ. Σοφία Αντζάκα. Athens.

—— 1980. Ο άνθρωπος και τα σύμβολά του. *[Man and His Symbols]* Σύλληψη and εκτέλεση συλλογικού τόμου: Κ.Γιουνγκ, επιμέλεια: Τ.Φρήμαν. Μτφρ. Χατζηθεοδώρου. Athens: Εκδόσεις Αρσενίδη [Arsenidi Publishing].

— 1988. *Τέσσερα αρχέτυπα – Μητέρα, αναγέννηση, πνεύμα, κατεργάρης [Four Archetypes – Mother, Rebirth, Spirit, Trickster]*. Μτφρ. Γιώργος Μπαρουξής. Athens: Εκδόσεις Ιάμβλιχος [Iamvlihos Publishing].

Lietaer, B. 2011. *Au Coeur de la monnaie – Systemes monetaires, inconscient collectif, archetypes et taboos*, trans. M. Ickx. Gap, France: Editions Yves Michel.

Mayes, E. 2005. Private property, the private subject and women – can women truly be owners of capital? In: M. Albertson Fineman and T. Dougherty (eds), *Feminism Confronts Homo Economicus – Gender, Law and Society*. Ithaca, NY, and London: Cornell University Press, pp. 117–128.

Pateman, C. 1988. *The Sexual Contract*. Stanford, CA: Stanford University Press.

Platteau, J.-P. 2006. Solidarity norms and institutions in village societies: static and dynamic considerations. In: S. Kolm and J. Mercier-Ythier (eds), *Handbook on Gift Giving, Reciprocity and Altruism*. North Holland: Elsevier.

Richardson, J. 2010. Feminism, property in the person and concepts of self. *British Journal of Politics and International Relations*, 12: 56–71.

San Miguel, P. 2011. Sobre el subalterno, su conocimiento (local y global), su 'traductor' y el exotismo. *A Contra Corriente – Una revista de historia social literatura de America Latina*, 8(2): 298–310.

Sotiropoulou, I. 2012. *Exchange Networks and Parallel Currencies in Greece: Theoretical Approaches and the Case of Greece*. PhD dissertation, Department of Economics, University of Crete.

— 2014. Women in alternative economy – or, what do women do without official currency? *Women's Studies International Forum*, 47: 339–348.

Talpade Mohanty, C. 2002. 'Under Western Eyes' revisited: feminist solidarity through anticapitalist struggles. *Signs*, 28(2): 499–538.

Thelen, T. 2011. Shortage, fuzzy property and other dead ends in the anthropological analysis of (post)socialism. *Critique of Anthropology*, 31(1): 43–61.

Webster, C. 2007. Property right, public space and urban design. *Town Planning Review*, 78(1): 81–101.

Weiner, A. 1980. Reproduction: a replacement for reciprocity. *American Ethnologist*, 7(1): 71–85.

Zick, T. 2006. Property, place and public discourse. *Washington University Journal of Law and Policy*, 21: 173–223.

20 Free-ing foods?

Social food economies towards secure and sustainable food systems

Ferne Edwards

The current global industrial food system is being challenged by incidents of insecurity, as food supply is at risk from weather extremes in times of climate change, as fluctuating prices dictated by the global market result in food riots around the world, and as food scares from hidden production processes cause consumer concern and food loss. Rather than recognize the industrial food system as the *only* food procurement option, in this chapter I draw attention to the persistence of non-capitalist food economies and the emergence of new, innovative models. These untamed – in the sense of unfunded, unregulated and diverse – *social* food economies are found in cities both where issues of food insecurity and sustainability are paramount, and where the people and resources required to resolve these issues can be found. I tell the stories of people who are gleaning, growing and gifting foods in Sydney, Australia, to ask how social food economies contribute to secure and sustainable food systems.

The rise of the urban food movement

Since the 1990s, there has been a resurgence of interest in urban agriculture in the West. This was previously predominant in the developing world, accompanied by discourses of survival, cultural diversity, food poverty and insecurity (see Abrahams 2006; Crush *et al.* 2011; Egziabher *et al.* 1994), while food was abundant in the cities of the Global North (see Gaynor 2007). But now citizens across the developed world have started to acknowledge issues of the global food system and look for possible alternatives.

Cockrall-King (2012) identifies three phases of the new urban food movement. The first is epitomized by Tim Lang's coining of the term 'food miles' in 1993, with its message supported by the research papers 'The food miles report' (Paxton 1994), 'Eating oil' (Jones 2001) and 'In praise of slow' (Honoré 2004). In addition to urban agriculture, alternative food networks (AFNs) also emerged during this period as a reaction against the globalization, standardization and unethical nature of the global industrial food system. AFNs represent a wide range of alternative food pathways that build on ethics of sustainability, social justice, animal welfare and the aesthetic values of local food cultures. AFNs seek to transform and diversify modern food provisioning by connecting ethical producers and consumers in more localized and direct ways (see Goodman *et al.* 2011).

In the second wave of the urban food movement in the 2000s, consumers became more aware of the political implications of their diets, with farmers' markets and community-supported agriculture projects growing in popularity, as the Slow Food movement pushed for 'consumers' to become 'co-producers'. We saw the introduction of the term 'locavore', to describe people who eat foods grown close to where they live, in 2009. In the third wave, cities became central to food politics when for the first time in history more people lived in cities than in the countryside. In late 2007 and 2008 global food insecurity reached new heights when food riots erupted in over 30 countries, with the United Nations announcing that in the world 862 million people were hungry (FAO 2009).

While there is now greater focus on the role of the city to address food insecurity challenges, the transformative capacity of many so-called 'alternatives' to the industrial food system has been questioned by scholars and activists. Among the issues raised are that 'alternatives' remain within the *capitalist* market, remain dependent on the capitalist state for funding to exist, or are created to fill a gap of need left by capitalism as part of the welfare state (see Goodman *et al.* 2011; Guthman 2004; Tregear 2011). Rather than contest issues embedded within the industrial food system, green capitalist and social welfare models may instead reinforce existing, unequal capitalist power relationships and dynamics. By ignoring political relations and issues of equity, they continue to overlook issues of class, race and privilege.

Indeed, from my perspective as both an academic researcher in sustainable cities and a participant in many not-for-profit sustainability organizations, when attending conferences and workshops I have been constantly struck by how many organizations devote much time and energy to seeking funding rather than questioning the narrow forms of dealing with these issues and how they could get beyond them. At other events I have witnessed comprehensive discussions that have omitted the topic of who holds the power to determine access to funding. Indeed, in these ways such organizations are being 'tamed' – herded to act in specific ways to conform to funding requirements. This taming process reduces complexity in order to homogenize and push ahead 'progress', quietening alternatives that could be perceived to threaten dominant interests, rather than allowing for diversity and difference. I argue that such complexities offer possible solutions and innovations that are essential in a dynamic world. As an anthropologist, I recognize that political-economic systems change, and that it is crucial for people to constructively criticize current practices and to consider aspects from emerging radical examples in order to adapt well to changing circumstances.

To bypass issues of capitalist dominance and constraints, I focus instead on social food economies: food economies that are non-capitalist in that they are unregulated and non-monetary, and social in that they directly connect people with procurement processes and prioritize social and environmental justice over economic values. Social food economies are often overlooked or trivialized in the media and by government bodies because of their small quantities and scattered distribution, with other economic priorities such as increasing house size, falling wages, food as an export commodity and urban development coming first. Instead, this paper employs a 'weak theory' perspective from economic geography (see Gibson-Graham 2006: 71) to look beyond assumed, 'known' facts to recognize the space 'in-between', where relationships and actors not dominant in the capitalist market can be found.

Case studies: gleaning, growing and gifting food

I have chosen three case studies from Australia to represent a food systems approach, providing examples from production through to distribution, exchange and waste that occur across a range of ecosystems, urban forms, social demographics and modes of participation. 'Gleaners' are people who collect edible or medicinal weeds, surplus fruits and nuts overhanging people's fences or found on public land. Those I studied operate primarily in the central south-west of Sydney (NSW), and obtain edible mushrooms from state forests on Sydney's fringes. 'Growers' are people who grow a substantial part of their own food: in this case, in Sydney's peri-urban region of the Blue Mountains, Mount Tomah and the Hawkesbury. 'Gifters' are people who redistribute processed foods discarded as waste from the capitalist food system. They include 'dumpster divers', people who choose to retrieve edible food discarded by retail outlets as a protest against overconsumption and waste, and those involved in two organizations: Food Within, a not-for-profit micro-enterprise that helps disadvantaged people by bartering access to fresh, healthy food; and OzHarvest, a charity that rescues food from function centres, caterers, offices, restaurants and cafes to donate to charities for people who are disadvantaged or at risk.

From January to August 2011, I interviewed 8 'gleaners', 21 'growers' and 4 'gifters' in addition to conducting participant observation of activities. The gleaners were identified from 'weed tours' and 'food mapping' websites, online maps that reveal the availability of uneaten foods. The growers were selected from food-sustainability groups, and the gifters from food rescue and barter organizations.

How 'free' are they? Exploring alternative economic theory and concepts of autonomy

Alternative economic theory contributes to an understanding of social food economies by acknowledging social and environmental values, space and concepts of autonomy. Calling to first 'step away' from the capitalist economy, degrowth economics, proposed by Georgescu-Roegen in 1971, challenges capitalism's prioritization of economic values over others to recast 'economic activities in *political* terms' (Fournier 2008: 534). Gibson-Graham (2006) then challenges capitalism as the *only* political-economic system to acknowledge the diversity of economies that exist both within and outside of capitalism. By acknowledging the validity of diverse economies, they argue that people can exist in a 'zone of cohabitation and contestation among multiple economic forms' (Gibson-Graham 2006: xxi). Such economic alternatives posit 'a renewed interest in the possibilities of alternatives to capitalism that go beyond the failed models of state socialism' (Leyshon *et al.* 2003: 12).

The concept of 'autonomous zones' then broadens alternative economic *geographical* spaces to encompass social, political and ecological dimensions. Cattaneo (2011) identifies three stages towards autonomy away from the capitalist system: that of social autonomy of thought, where people learn to question the authority of the media and assumed capitalist values; autonomy from money, where people trade time for money, reducing their need to spend and hence work; and autonomy from the 'system', where rural squatters with access to material resources 'drop out' of the capitalist market. The topic of social food economies emerges from a critique of AFN literature, drawing on Gibson-Graham (2006) to recognize the existence of diverse food economies. These social food economies are then discussed through the lens of autonomy.

Autonomy from money: do social food economies meet food security needs?

Food security is defined as when 'all people at all times have physical and economic access to sufficient, safe and nutritious food to meet their dietary needs and food preferences for an active and healthy life' (FAO 1996). This concept is often broken down into the aspects of quantity, quality, access and health. Social food economies are not food secure in terms of supply, with foods procured complementing rather than replacing supermarket-bought foods. However, in terms of quality, they add diverse new flavours, textures and nutritional elements which often better suit alternative procurement due to freshness, time and knowledge required for harvesting, and supply and demand. Although they provide a diversity of crops, there is much potential to grow even more, with motivations including inquisitiveness, environmental and social justice, community and pleasure preceding food security concerns.

Foraged foods include edible weeds such as sorrel, saltbush, wild fennel, warrigal greens and mushrooms, while growers produce many unusual fruit and vegetables, and animals for consumption such as fish and squab. Alternatively, gifters rescue and redistribute food from the commercial sector, including fruit and vegetable markets, supermarkets, wholesalers, corporate events, catering companies, distributors, warehouses, shops, delis, film and television shoots, and restaurants. The amount of food that would normally go to waste is staggering: OzHarvest delivered 5.34 million meals nationally in 2012, diverting 1.6 million kilos from landfill (OzHarvest 2012).

Foods from social food economies offer a fresh source of nutrients, adding fruit, vegetables and salad to conventional diets, while foraging in Sydney provides greens in spring, mulberry, fruits and fennels in summer, and mushrooms, fennel seeds and dandelion roots in autumn. Furthermore, many wild plants are highly nutritious. For example, 100 grams of dandelion greens contain 11,000 mg of potassium, 18 mg of vitamin C and 42 mg of calcium (see Wild Edible and Medicinal Plants n.d.). They also offer substantial indirect health benefits which include herbal remedies, mental health benefits and opportunities for social engagement and physical exercise.

However, food safety can be an issue, with consumption of unregulated foods requiring sufficient knowledge for harvesting and preparation. Likewise, foragers may also encounter collection sites that are polluted or poisoned. To counter food safety concerns, foragers are encouraged to first eat what is found in backyards before foraging in public areas. Likewise, companies that donate foods to organizations such as OzHarvest are protected under the Civil Liability Act 2002. Dumpster divers are largely protected from food poisoning because of the wide variety of stock, their vegan or vegetarian diets, food preparation knowledge and excessive packaging, and by applying the senses of touch, taste and smell (Edwards and Mercer 2007).

Although social food economies are economically 'free', access to these may be hindered by time, interest and energy, in addition to required technologies, such as computers for food mapping. Furthermore, members are predominantly middle class, well educated, and have strong political beliefs which can exclude others from participating. Food Within is an exception to this trend, offering disadvantaged people a 'Hand up, not a hand out' (Food Within 2012) through a ten-week education and food bartering programme.

Autonomy of thought: reinterpretations of diet free from corporate control

Key motivations behind these diets include gleaners' strong desire to reconnect to the landscape, to explore new flavours, and to prevent feral food from going to waste; growers' environmental, social and economic concerns, with some striving to grow extensive self- and community-sustaining gardens; and gifters' desire to rebalance issues of greed and need, voicing urban food security concerns. Foraging appeals to people who want to learn more about their environment, and to immigrants who wanted to continue their cultural traditions in Australia. The inclusion of edible or medicinal 'weeds' or mushrooms to their diet adds both cultural and biological knowledge to it. Stefanie explained how foraging continues to link her to childhood:

> We use to go mushroom picking with my grandparents in Poland too . . . I think everybody in Poland goes mushroom picking. It's a cultural thing . . . When they brought the pines, they brought the mushrooms rhizomes, whatever they are, and the two species that came with it. And we have beautiful mushrooms here.

Bonetto, an environmental artist with an Italian background who runs weed tours in Sydney, had the aim 'to rediscover traditional knowledge, to celebrate the multiplicity of cultures in botanical terms' (Radio National 2012). Furthermore,

Bonetto desires to delve into the socio-cultural framing of 'weeds' – to ask why non-indigenous plants are considered illegal. Bonetto comments:

> Weeds are defined by a nation's law, and what is declared weed in one place may be a precious resource in another. There is a significant metaphorical connection between this definition of 'weed' and the arbitrary restriction imposed on human migration by national governments.
>
> (Wild Stories n.d.)

For other gleaners, rather than represent an alternative to the capitalist food system, harvesting wild resources allows them to participate and profit within it, with top-end restaurants placing unusual ingredients on their menus at exorbitant prices. Such wild produce offers new tastes and textures that often cannot be matched by commercial sources, as was explained by Jaimie, a young restaurant forager:

> What was growing there was the flavours. Really wild flavour. Anything foraged obviously, its wild nutrients. No fertilizer obviously. It's always tasting like very different compared to anything commercially grown because it's just wild. Obviously a lot of it's a lot stronger, bitter.

While some believe that wild harvesting contributes to an environmental awareness (see Ellena 2012), it is unclear to what extent the environmental value of foraged food reaches customers. When asked about customers' reactions to the food, Jaimie stated, 'I'd hate to say this but 90 per cent don't actually know. They're there for the "wow" factor. There is also the wow factor of having found something that no one knows. You say, "wow, what's that?!"' Instead, it is the foragers themselves who explore Sydney's hidden corners that benefit most from knowing where the produce comes from.

Food mappers' motivations are clearly labelled on their websites: for Scrumpers Delight it is 'a community mapping project to share the joys of scrumping', for Urban Food Maps it is 'to encourage selfless collaboration and foster kindness of strangers', for the Blue Mountains Fruit and Nut Network it represents an 'informal (non-monetary) economy network [that] connects growers and consumers', and for LandShare Australia it is an initiative that 'brings together people who have a passion for home-grown food, connecting those who have land to share with those who need land for cultivating food'.[1] Additional motivations include reducing food waste and the demand for lengthy food chains, and encouraging the sharing of public and private space to free up urban land for food. They also strive to encourage healthy lifestyles through greater exercise, consumption of fresh food, social interaction and community. These latter food maps thus reflect a different way to read the city as a proactive, engaged space where resources both do and can exist.

Nearly all growers garden with environmental or animal welfare motivations in mind. Aspects include maintaining biodiversity, caring for the soil, and caring humanely for chickens and other livestock. Many participants also practise per-maculture, a design philosophy that espouses the ethics of earth care, people care and fair share (Holmgren 2003). The involvement of some surfaced from a perception of crisis or uncertainty, with some citing 'peak oil' as a motivation, the belief that maximum petroleum extraction has been reached with expected catastrophic implications for agriculture and transport. Hence, many respond-ents desired to learn how to be self-sufficient in their food production. Growers explicitly voiced their desire to be less dependent on the capitalist food system, and are often identified as 'downshifters', 'people who make a voluntary, long-term, lifestyle change that involves accepting significantly less income and con-suming less' (Hamilton and Mail 2003: 8). Downshifters had experienced a shift in values from making money to pursuing a better quality of life for themselves and others. As expressed by Lance, a grower in peri-urban Sydney, it's about revaluing people and the land:

> I just felt that from an environmental point of view, I didn't think the way we were living was a particularly good way of living, society in general, so I wanted to change the way I lived that reflected what I though was important and not what society was telling me was important . . . I see value in working, and that is why I call this work, but it is a different type of work, and I see value in community work and doing work that is not paid.

Gifters' motivations were strongly focused on urban food security concerns, redistributing food to disadvantaged communities in a range of ways. For exam-ple, OzHarvest donates food to agencies that prepare meals for those in need, and Food Within offers local residents places to work in its not-for-profit organiza-tion so they can barter for food, effectively training and empowering people to get beyond their food insecurity state. Dumpster divers, the most radical of the 'gifting' examples, also redistribute food among their social, often activist, net-works, often foremost for political and fun reasons. Commenting on her political motivations for dumpster diving, Kelly, a young 'diver' also living in the Blue Mountains, exclaimed:

> I just can't just believe the stuff that's thrown away. It's all so edible and so fit for consumption. And it makes me angry that they're doing that and it makes me proud to be involved in getting it back out again. Bringing it back into circulation.

Hence, the three social food economies analysed offer a disparate autonomy of thought, ranging from those that incorporate social food economies *into* the capi-talist market, selling foraged foods to restaurants, to those (such as OzHarvest) that revalue once 'conventional' foods with new social and environmental moral values through the process of rescuing and redistributing food to those in need, to those who consume a largely different diet to set them apart from capitalist constraints, such as growers, food mappers and dumpster divers. Regardless of their variable motivations, representatives of all social food economies valued their produce beyond dominant economic values, and included cultural, social, economic and environmental justice values.

Autonomy from the system: how alternative are alternative food economies?

The social food economies in my sample with the least autonomy from the system are OzHarvest, which works closely with corporations to redistribute waste, and foragers who sell wild harvest to restaurants. OzHarvest recognizes its role in assuaging corporations' 'green guilt'. However, although it represents a social food economy *within* and dependent on capitalism, its involvement provides a means to revalue waste as a resource, with this message being accepted by a mainstream audience, while providing extensive support to many in need. The food rescue model has now been replicated throughout Australia, with OzHarvest branches in Adelaide, Brisbane, Melbourne and Newcastle, adding recognition to a new wave of independent food rescue agencies such as SecondBite and Fare Share.

However, for foragers who sell wild harvest to restaurants, this practice appears to represent simply yet another green consumerist trend with some dubious consequences. For example, once wild harvest ingredients become popular, rather than benefit the environment, they may instead harm it. Jaimie explains:

> If it's on the menu on one of the Three Hats restaurants in Sydney . . . The little guys will go, 'Well, these guys have got Three Hats. They must be serving something that we need.' So they'll go, 'OK, they're serving saltbush.' And everyone knows everyone, so they'll find out where this restaurant gets it and it will be on their menu. And it will keep going through and then it will be on twenty people's menu. And after that the resources will go because everyone would have got it from the same spot.

The people with the most autonomy from the system are growers in the Blue Mountains who, through their everyday gardening and sharing of skills through like-minded social networks within a geographically bounded territory, are effectively creating an autonomous food zone towards a more productive city. These spaces of change extend to working with local councils, which have agreed to not spray poisonous chemicals on public land to encourage foraging, and to grant permission for people to grow food on street verges. Growers also have the most developed vision of what an alternative food future could look like. This desire for change often extends beyond the individual to care for the local community and to consider the establishment of new political-economic systems and territories. Visions of a sustainable food future from a number of growers included these comments:

> What we need to do, from our point of view, is we need to live with as much local sufficiency as possible. Our vision would be, you have to get rid of

money, right? Organize what we need and how much can we produce right here. We need to swap [with] a neighbour, [with our] neighbouring region[s to meet] their basic needs . . . The internet can be employed very usefully. It can mean that every household can work out what it might consume over a six to twelve month period. And if you take twelve months – that's the natural season – so that's a natural thing to look at and if people are really clear about what they need and what the substitutes are, then you can get together a bigger list of all the people in a bioregion and you could start planning in such a way so people are as self-sufficient as possible and then collectively sufficient.

These social food economies thus illustrate a range of autonomy from the system: from those who make profit from the city's free natural resources, such as foraging for restaurants, to those that remain *within* the capitalist model to address major socio-ecological needs with the potential for transitional change, such as OzHarvest and Food Within.

Discussion: how are social food economies productively disruptive?

From the research, it is evident that the case studies represent diverse food initiatives with examples both coexisting with the conventional system and remaining outside it. These diverse economies on the whole use very few resources, re-reading what can be considered useful or edible from the local environment, such as foraging, to reuse resources that would often go to waste. In the case of growing, this includes employing techniques of permaculture, composting and wastewater reuse, while for gifting this entails collecting and redistributing discounted or free food from the commercial sector. Hence, in some ways, social food economies are parasitic in resource use by taking away from, rather than contributing to, further production.

However, although participation in social food economies does little to increase monetary incomes (with the exception of foraging for restaurants), it reduces – and hence raises questions about – the need for a constantly accelerated economy. In this way, social food activities actively 'de-grow' the economy by using what resources are already available. This downshifting requires access rather than ownership, as some foods are grown on public lands and others on private lands that share rights for collection and harvesting, with non-monetary costs incurred including time, energy, knowledge and an ability to access that land.

These social food economies are thus economically disruptive, in challenging the logic behind economic growth while revaluing food in different ways ahead of economic values. For example, 'gleaned' revalues food as cultural heritage, as a way to understand the environment, to appreciate new flavours, and to question land management and dietary practices; 'grown' values food's diversity, its link to community and to the environment, as a channel to voice a personal politics, and to step away from outside control; and 'gifted' revalues food in the case of dumpster divers as an independence, as a political and social outrage, and for dumpster divers and all other gifters here recasts food as a resource and not a waste. For those who obtain food through OzHarvest and Food Within, the cost of food becomes one less pressure that needs to be navigated every day.

Social food economies are also socially disruptive in their integrative features of bringing people, product and place together to foster social change. Growers represent the best example of potential transformational change, as they incorporate aspects of autonomy of thought, money and the system into their everyday practices. Their clustered location in peri-urban Sydney further represents the creation of autonomous zones, which could possibly – with the development of future social networks – be scaled up and out to other regions. This integrative potential for change is encapsulated in Gabrys' concept of 'sinks' (2009). This proposes that sinks possess transformative power not simply to close the resource loop, but through their uniting of various features to give rise to 'new systems, and new natural–cultural relations' (Gabrys 2009: 668). Such sinks can then be used to 'mobilize and transform our environmental practices and imaginings' (Gabrys 2009: 668). Urban food could be considered to be such a catalyst or sink: reusing wasted resources, reuniting people and reappropriating space to reconsider, redesign and react to issues embedded within the conventional food system.

Returning to Gibson-Graham's concept of diverse economies, the social food economies discussed here might then lead to all of the above outcomes. They could complement, overtake, and be overtaken by the conventional system, offering many avenues for change (and integrative feedback loops) to the conventional food system from both inside and outside. Hence, this story of social food economies that represent a wide diversity of people, places and products highlights the importance of nurturing diverse, untamed urbanisms and their associated energies, entrepreneurialism, innovations, and assemblages that emerge from the frictions and contestations in the untamed city (as expressed in the Introduction).

Furthermore, social food economies are disruptive methodologically. They highlight the dangers of dualisms between the city and the country, and the formal and the informal. Dualisms are both value-laden and blind the dynamism of form, preventing acceptance of new assemblages and the changes they bring. Our diets also are not confined to one place, nor should they be, recognizing that urban, peri-urban, rural and global environments all contribute in specific ways. In a similar way, social food economies also contest the boundaries of mainstream definitions of food security, which evaluate social food economies against the extent to which they do or do not fulfil a need. Rather, 'food security' in my view needs to consider how food can be valued *and revalued*, while acknowledging food's role for social change.

Importantly, this analysis goes beyond the romanticization of 'local, quality, direct, and organic food' to consider their specific historical, socio-cultural and environmental contexts and to ask questions of social exclusion, audience and politics. Finally, for me personally, 'untamed urbanisms' represents a way to explore pertinent issues of food security and sustainability beyond capitalist constraints, to recognize dynamism, networks and a diversity of approaches that challenge and rethink how our cities are run. Through the rupturing of inflexible concepts and theories, new attitudes and approaches can be acknowledged and applied to emerging situations to address the real issues at hand.

Conclusion

Thus, non-capitalist food economies contribute to socio-ecological change by providing alternative understandings and values embedded within the procurement of food, in addition to providing greater urban food security through dietary diversity and access seldom offered by capitalist enterprises. The study of social food economies also reveals new social networks, new ways of reading and extending the city as a site of resource, and new ways of reaching a wider breadth of society to address both urban food security and sustainability concerns. Admittedly, the social food economies examined here still only provide a limited food supply, but they demonstrate the possibility to do more. By embracing more untamed spaces throughout the cityscape, social food economies could reach a greater range of people and places, to break down barriers of mind, culture, the legal system and bureaucracy, towards a more socially and environmentally just food-productive city.

Note

1 The website addresses in order are: http://scrumpers.heroku.com/about, http://thevery hungryrevolution.com/2011/08/09/urban-food-maps/, http://bmfruitandnuttreenetwork. blogspot.com/, and www.landshareaustralia.com.au/about/

References

Abrahams, C. 2006. Globally useful conceptions of Alternative Food Networks in the developing south: the case of Johannesburg's urban food supply system. In D. Maye and M. Kneafsey (eds), *Alternative Food Geographies: Representation and Practice.* Bingley, UK: Elsevier Science.

Bonetto, D. 2012. Urban foraging. *Off Track*, ABC Radio National. Available at www.abc. net.au/radionational/programs/offtrack/urban-foraging/4268428 (accessed 10 March 2014).

Cattaneo, C. 2011. The money-free autonomy of Spanish squatters. In A. Nelson, A. and F. Timmerman (eds), *Life Without Money. Building Fair and Sustainable Economies.* London: Pluto Press.

Cockrall-King, J. 2012. *Food and the City: Urban Agriculture and the New Food Revolution.* New York: Prometheus.

Crush, J., Hovorka, A. and Tevera, D. 2011. Food security in southern African cities: the place of urban agriculture. *Progress in Development Studies*, 11(4): 285–305.

Edwards, F. and Mercer, D. 2007. Gleaning from gluttony: an Australian youth culture confronts the ethics of waste. *Australian Geographer*, 38(3): 279–96.

Egziabher, A., Lee-Smith, D., Maxwell, D., Memon, P., Mougeot, L. and Sawio, C. 1994. *Cities Feeding People: An Examination of Urban Agriculture in East Africa.* Ottawa: IDRC.

Ellena, R. 2012. Wild edible plants: an overview. Nordic Food Lab. Available at http://nordicfoodlab.org/blog/2012/9/wild-edible-plants-an-overview (accessed 25 September 2013).

Food and Agriculture Organization of the United Nations (FAO). 1996. Rome Declaration on World Food Security and World Food Summit Plan of Action. World Food Summit, 13–17 November, Rome.

——2009. Number of world's hungry to top 1 billion this year – UN Food Agency. UN News Centre, 19 June 2009. Available at www.un.org/apps/news/story.asp?NewsID=31197 (accessed 14 August 2013).

Food Within. 2012. A hand UP not a hand out. Available at www.foodwithin.withinfood.org/articles/a-hand-up-not-a-hand-out.html (accessed 19 September 2013).

Fournier, V. 2008. Escaping from the economy: the politics of degrowth, *International Journal of Sociology and Social Policy*, 28(11/12): 528–45.

Gabrys, J. 2009. Sink: the dirt of systems. *Environment and Planning D: Society and Space*, 27: 666–81.

Gaynor, A. 2007. Animal agendas: conflict over productive animals in twentieth-century Australian cities. *Society and Animals*, 15(1): 29–42.

Gibson-Graham, J. K. 2006. *A Postcapitalist Politics*. Minneapolis and London: University of Minnesota.

Goodman, D., DuPuis, M. and Goodman, M. 2011. *Alternative Food Networks: Knowledge, Practice and Politics*. Abingdon, Oxon and New York: Routledge.

Guthman, J. 2004. *Agrarian Dreams: The Paradox of Organic Farming in California.* Berkeley, CA and London: University of California Press.

Hamilton, C. and Mail, E. 2003. Downshifting in Australia: a sea-change in the pursuit of happiness, Discussion Paper 50. Canberra: Australia Institute.

Holmgren, D. 2003 *Permaculture: Principles and Pathways Beyond Sustainability*. Burlington, VT: Chelsea Green.

Honoré, C. 2004. *In Praise of Slow: How a Worldwide Movement Is Challenging the Cult of Speed*. Toronto, ON: Vintage Canada.

Jones, A. 2001. Eating oil: food in a changing environment. A Sustain/ Elm Farm Research Centre report. London: Sustain.

Leyshon, A., Lee, R. and Williams, C. (eds). 2003. *Alternative Economic Spaces*. London: Sage.

OzHarvest. 2012. OzHarvest Annual Report. Available at www.ozharvest.org/ourimpact.asp?pageID=615 (accessed 5 September 2013).

Paxton, A. 1994. The food miles report: the dangers of long-distance food transport. London: SAFE Alliance. Available at www.sustainweb.org/publications/?id=191 (accessed 20 May 2014).

Radio National. 2012. Urban foraging, with Diego Bonetto. Off track, Radio National. Available at: www.abc.net.au/radionational/programs/offtrack/urban-foraging2c-with-diego-bonetto/4268498 (accessed 28 May 2014).

Tregear, A. 2011. Progressing knowledge in alternative and local food networks: critical reflections and a research agenda. *Journal of Rural Studies*, 4(27): 419–30.

Wild Edible and Medicinal Plants (n.d.) Wild edible and medicinal plants. Available at: http://wildedibleandmedicinalplants.blogspot.com.au (accessed 10 January 2014).

Wild Stories (n.d.) Wild stories. Available at: www.wildedibles.info/database/ (accessed 1 March 2014).

Untamed Urbanisms

Enacting productive disruptions

Adriana Allen, Andrea Lampis and Mark Swilling

There is currently little disagreement within contemporary debates on sustainable development on the fact that we now live in an urban world. This is epitomized by the now highly popular claim that 'the sustainability battle will be lost or won in cities', an argument that in turn has inspired over the last two decades multiple planning pathways to tame 'unsustainable cities'. However, whether this just signifies a world demographic shift, the expansion of capitalist urbanization, a fundamental socio-political change or the dominance of cities in shaping nature at planetary scale raises different interpretations of emerging realities and the practices and regimes that make the urban world.

The notion of untamed urbanisms was posed throughout this book as a provocation to tease out how we make sense of the ongoing urban transition and such socio-political urban practices and regimes. What is untameable – capitalism, nature or urbanites' agency? Is untameability to be regarded as a negative or positive condition? If the former, what is to be tamed, by whom and why? If the latter, where do untaming practices live? In the lived and unregulated urbanisms of ordinary women and men? In the realm of more progressive planning? In insurgent urbanisms and the conscious and unconscious search for alternative ways of producing the city?

If we accept that there are many urbanisms that produce cities, then each of them might reveal different answers to the above questions. In searching for such answers, this book could be read through different streams of consciousness, such as *Hopscotch*, the famous novel by Argentine writer Julio Cortázar. But unlike Cortázar's novel, *Untamed Urbanisms* does not include a 'Table of Instructions' but leaves the reader the option of choosing her/his unique thinking-path through the different chapters. Some chapters might appear 'expendable' to different readers, but upon closer examination they might reveal crucial clues to what untamed urbanisms mean to them within their particular context. In this final chapter, we offer some of the paths that we found more productive and exciting in travelling through the book.

Swilling and Annecke (2012: 121) contend that at least four differentiated but interdependent urbanisms or 'ways of life' can be identified in the contemporary production of cities. *Inclusive urbanism* inspired the materialization (at least in part of the world) of the 'modern networked city' and the Keynesian vision of universal 'rights to cheap, good quality and accessible infrastructure services and its associated obligations of prompt payment and respect of technical boundaries' (Graham and Marvin, 2001: 29, cited in Swilling and Annecke, 2012: 122–3). *Splintering urbanism* emerged in the late 1970s out of the neoliberal assault and dismissal of the social democratic contract and the aspiration to reconfigure cities as globally networked hubs and markets shaped by profit-seeking corporations and the capacity and willingness to pay. *Slum urbanism* captures the 'quiet encroachment' (Bayat, 2000) of the one-third of the world urban population often defined as 'the urban poor' who live mainly in self-built largely unregulated settlements. And *green urbanism* that more recently has become firmly positioned as a viable project to control and minimize the impact of cities and urban life styles on the environment to fit the contemporary urban transition into the constraints of one planet.

The next section takes these four 'plots' as a navigation map to reflect on the ways in which untamed and untaming urbanisms are explored by the different contributions in this book in conversation with other voices 'outside' the book. This is followed by a discussion of the potential of writing as a political methodology and an act of untaming in its own right. The chapter concludes by examining the emerging threads to reclaim the materiality of urban transitions in planning theory and praxis

Hopscotching through the book

Without forcibly shoehorning the cities and processes analyzed throughout the book into single categories derived from deductive theories of urban change, here we seek to identify and explore common threads that reveal crucial tensions between the malleability and obduracy of the city.

Inclusive urbanism: taming injustice?

A key message emerging throughout the book is that urbanization is not a process that automatically delivers justice through agglomeration; instead justice is a moral compass that should guide the way we thinking about alternatives. Thus, untamed urbanisms are not about rejecting all framings – a sterile and probably impossible task – but rather about exposing the many faces that unjust urbanization has and the processes and actions that counteract them. Quite often justice in the city is equated with inclusion, the most significant achievement (in some parts of the world) of the Keynesian project of inclusive urbanism. Inclusion, however, is not the same as justice. Not only was the justice of inclusive urbanism associated with inclusion, in assuming 'growth' and 'material affluence' as the closest epigones of modernity; it also denied the significance of unjust exploitation of natural resources. If, as suggested by several contributions in this book, justice is accepted as a key value to guide both the assessment of our understanding and action, what are the governance implications? How is a commitment to justice guaranteed or ensured in a world that may have become too complex to envisage the re-assembly of strong unitary states of the kind that were built by post-WWII social democrats? How can social and environmental justice be successfully claimed if space, flows and processes within the city are strongly influenced by global actors and institutions, whereas the defense of rights largely remains within the jurisdiction of weakened national and local governments?

All the chapters in this book grapple with the consequences of accelerated urban expansion, decay and renewal in the wake of an era characterized by sustained assaults on the notion that the state has a positive to role to play in guiding the evolution of society. Like many other books on cities, the lament in this one is the same – the second urbanization wave is a process of social transformation that is unprecedented in scale, and yet the state will more than likely remain incapable of responding appropriately if it continues to reproduce the economistic tropes of neoliberalism. Similarly, in the so-called global North, the disillusionment with government stems from a pervasive belief that states did not prevent the economic crisis and seem incapable of resolving it. In short, there is an implicit and explicit call for the state to be rebuilt as an instrument for interventions based on justice and sustainability, especially across the cities of the world. But is it possible to imagine a relational approach that results in the incremental assembly of new institutional arrangements to deal with the challenges at hand?

Some of preceding chapters relate directly or indirectly to this challenge. For instance, Lawton's chapter explicitly tackles the challenge of conceptualizing modes of political power that are appropriate for promoting just forms of sustainable urbanization. Proceeding from the 'right to the city' principle, he ends up calling for an 'enabling state' that is derived from relational dynamics that favor the urban poor rather than derived from technocratic assumptions. Obeng-Odoom's contribution extends this call for a reconceptualization of the state with reference to Georgist perspectives on collective investments and benefits. Swilling calls for a reconceptualization of urban infrastructure governance on the grounds that urban infrastructures cannot be governed by institutions that were invented in the nineteenth century. Haysom suggests that food supplies might well be the Achilles heel of traditional modes of governance that left them mainly to market dynamics and argues that in a world of rampant market failures in the food sector, the state will be forced to intervene. Mukherjee's case study of Kolkata clearly reveals the role the state has historically played in abetting the destruction of eco-systems that sustain livelihoods and treat urban sewage on scale and ends up calling for a state that acts in the public rather than the private interest. Rosales questions whether urban planning has caught up with the need for a new set of tools that can cater for urban sustainability. In short, these are all calls to tame the city using progressive means and frameworks.

And yet many chapters also give emphasis to the enormous complexity – indeed, untamability – of the city. Many of the contributions in Parts II and IV refer to processes that will not easily be tamed to fit into a consolidated governance framework, no matter how legitimate or progressive. Maybe it is time to recognize that there is no return to the golden era of the social democratic Weberian state that tended to establish integrated publicly funded and controlled service delivery institutions. Although it remains a powerful imaginative attractor, it is more than likely a distraction. It might be time to accept that institutional bri-colage is here to stay, that institutional heterogeneity is not just a passing phase, but potentially the best way to build a governance arrangement that is appropri-ate to the complex realities of contemporary cities. This theme emerges in many papers: from the chapter by Lampis where social security is decoupled from a state-centric discourse, to Sotiropoulou's discussion of alternative and non-cur-rency schemes, to Lawanson's call to transcend the formal-informal dualism that suffocates incrementalism, and finally to Hajer's reflections on developed coun-try cities where states will not be the most effective actors to transform the socio-cultural templates of highly industrialized cities.

This discussion raises a very tricky challenge: if an inclusive urbanism cannot be built by a return to strong states with integrated service delivery systems, can it be built by working with rather than against institutional heterogeneity? The answer to this question will depend on whether it will be possible to jettison a deep-seated belief that heterogeneity is a symptom of state failure when in fact it might reflect the realities of highly complex untamable urbanisms that will need to be gathered together not into a new institutional uniformity, but into institu-tional assemblages that are profoundly relational, negotiated and therefore always provisional. If this results in a sense of vertigo because all the desired securities of hierarchy have fallen away, then so be it – that may be the governance implication of an era of untamed urbanism. It would be a mistake, however, to assume that this is a weaker option, with less potential than 'strong states' to effect change. If supported by new relational leadership capabilities well trained in facilitation, vision building, coalition making and conflict resolution, this might be the most effective way to tackle the challenges.

Splintering urbanism: untamed apartheids?

Oren Yiftachel (2009) argues that across the South-East, contemporary urbani-zation takes place through the 'grey spaces' for the unregulated and stubborn urbanisms of those who 'are neither integrated nor eliminated, forming pseudo-permanent margins of today's urban regions' (89). These gray spaces, he claims, are facilitated by a process of 'creeping apartheid' in which large segments of the poor and marginalized 'are only partially incorporated into the urban community, economy and space, and are excluded from membership in the city polity' (ibid.).

This permanent temporariness is produced as much by state action as non-action and vividly describes not just those marginalized in the Beer Sheva metro-politan region (Israel/Palestine) – that is, the scene where Yiftachel unravels his notion of emerging urban apartheids – but equally the experience of peri-urban farmers in La – towards the east of Accra – who for decades have supplied the city with most of the perishable vegetables it consumes and yet are awaiting to be evicted from the customary land to which they belong; or the 5,000 women and men who call Cantagallo – a small spit of land alongside the River Rimac in central Lima – home, despite many living informally for over 50 years and under the periodic threat of being evicted.

Across the global South or 'South-East', as Yiftachel puts it, splintering urbanism is indeed producing grey spaces and urban apartheids along multiple lines of ethnic, class, religious and gender exclusion. These apartheids are of course not just shaped by outside forces but also permeated by practices of 'slum real estate' (Gulyani and Talukdar 2008) and countered by practices of 'occupancy urbanism' and 'actually existing urbanisms', rooted in alternative social dynamics that 'resist worlding practice' (Watson 2012).

Many chapters in this book capture case studies of struggles against the consequences of splintering urbanism that are representative of a growing tide of local struggles across the globe and, perhaps more significantly, that have the potential to coalesce into regional and global movements for change with varying degrees of efficacy. Without going into the intense current debates about how to achieve this, some of the book chapters provide insights into the diverse ecology of actors that populate movements for change towards less splintered post-neoliberal cities. The case by Sequera and Mateos provides the most dramatic insight into how micro-resistance builds up against neo-liberal property markets that local states allow to roll out across urban space to the detriment of historically embedded communities. In a very different context, Edwards describes the emergence of socialized food economies in Australian cities that challenge the commodification of food. It is activist practices like this that shock one into realizing how far the commodification of food has really gone and what the consequences of market failure at scale might be.

However, it would be mistake to impose a 'resistance' lens on the wide range of actors that engage the implications of splintered urbanism. Lino e Silva's case reveals how urban cultural practices emerge within quite mature urban niches like Rio's favelas that resist the logics of capitalist work discipline, wage-based time and the notion that freedom is defined by market positionality. By contrast, the case by Harris reveals how it is possible to 'work with the market' to realize social objectives in a context of endemic state failure. Sanchez Betancourt's discussion of active interventions to claim public space in Cape Town is possibly another typical way of contesting the commodification of space – it is not resistance of the type discussed by Sequera and Mateos, but rather similar to socialization of food movement discussed by Edwards. It is a multi-class movement that wants to make a statement about the value of non-commodified spaces that symbolically value a sense of the public, a sense of community – a sense of freedom from both regulation and the market. In short, a sense that splintering can be transcended.

Whether these various responses coalesce into local-global movements that reinforce Lawton's call for an enabling state that guarantees the 'right to the city' remains to be seen.

Slum urbanism: the quiet encroachment of the untamed?

All across developing world cities in Latin America, Africa and Asia there are millions of transactions underway that result in a distinct social formation referred to here as slum urbanism. Because slum urbanism is distinct rather than merely a stepping stone towards urban modernity, it deserves close scrutiny and understanding. In particular, it is necessary to comprehend the agential drivers of quiet encroachment across spaces that are at one level remarkably similar (unregulated, self-built, poorly serviced, home to groups that tend to be poor although not always) while at another level each settlement is embedded within a unique political, cultural, economic and spatial context best understood by those who live there. Attempts to impose templates on these fluid and complex environments to implement development projects invariably come to grief. Although slum urbanism is often depicted as the spatial manifestation of splintered urbanism in developing countries, the chapters in this book suggest that the story is more complex than this. Even without neoliberal commodification of urban services, large parts of the urban population in developing countries would most likely have ended up in slums. Furthermore, the assumption that slum urbanism will disappear under the forward march of a state-managed or market-driven urban modernity creates unrealizable expectations about what is possible. Even in China, a state-driven urbanization programme that delivers millions of formal housing units has not been able to prevent the build-up of de facto slums of temporary workers in the hidden nooks and crannies of a highly regulated urban regime.

Several chapters in this book have attempted in various ways to engage the challenge of slum urbanism. Drawing down the global discourse on climate change vulnerability into the Tanzanian context, Mubaya *et al.* discuss the dynamics of agency in the slums of Dar es Salaam. While there is plenty of evidence of self-organized quiet encroachments, the potential for this to translate into longer-term processes of incremental upgrading are limited by the historical legacy of institutions and policies that subvert the best efforts of slum dwellers. Aguilar and Castro develop similar arguments with respect to Merida City, Mexico. Slum dwellers find a way to survive, but the potential to go beyond survival will depend on the emergence of new modes of engagement with state agencies. Lawanson's study of Nigerian slums confirms this when she argues: 'It is important that the rhetoric go beyond formal–informal labels and the idea of informality as unacceptable within the urban fabric, towards a view of informality as a dynamic pointer to shifting urban relationships between the authorized and unauthorized.' All three case studies are underpinned by optimistic assumptions about the potential of incrementalism – that is, that progress from the current condition to an improved mode of urban living is not just desirable but also possible. Swilling and Harris build on this optimistic logic by demonstrating that there are examples of 'co-production' where slum communities have successfully engaged state agencies to configure improvements in service delivery systems. This includes the Water Justice movement in Latin America analysed by Swilling, and the community-cum-market-based sanitation projects in Accra examined by Harris. Both provide examples of the kinds of institutional reconfigurations through state–community engagements that are anticipated in the case studies drawn from the Tanzania, Nigeria and Mexican contexts. Drawing on the work of Allen (2012) and Allen *et al.* (forthcoming), Swilling argues that co-production should be considered as a key element of the post-nineteenth-century modes of infrastructure governance that will be required to handle the complexities of urbanization dynamics in the twenty-first century.

The chapters by Lino e Silva, Chiweshe and Sotiropoulou, however, raise critical questions about the modernist logic that underpin the notion of incrementalism. Based on ethnographic work in Rio's favelas, Lino e Silva identifies sub-cultures that subvert the Victorian notion that all slum dwellers would like a job, a proper house and a place in the formal urban system. In short, it is not possible to assume that there is a shared interest in incrementalism and, ultimately, in urban modernity. Chiweshe, on the other hand, argues that urban spaces are masculinized in ways that differentiate between the potentials available to men and women as they negotiate their everyday lives in the city. Like Lino e Silva's message, Chiweshe's argument is a significant cautionary that highlights the importance of incorporating a gender analysis into an understanding of slum urbanism. Sotiropoulou invites the reader to explore not only how and why the patriarchal institution of private property reinforces the hierarchical superiority of some urbanites at the expense of others, but also re-enacts highly sexualized and politicized perceptions of self, freedom and citizenship that are paradoxically rendered as neutral and enjoy almost naturalized legitimacy to attack and suppress those everyday practices that live outside the rule of obligatory (re)payment. These three contributions remind us of the pervasive scope of multiple forms of 'othering' that are equally reproduced by morally, functionally or aesthetically superior practices taming the quiet encroachment of women and the urban poor within and beyond slums.

Green urbanism: taming the cyborg?

Green urbanism has become mainstream over the past two decades. To a large extend this closely follows the belief that the city is by definition a 'cyborg' entity – a hybrid composed of organism and machine – which opens simultaneously the possibility to enhance urban performance beyond physical limitations and to expand the boundaries of human creativity and innovation (Gandy 2005). Green urbanism is, however, miles away from the intellectual project triggered by Donna Haraway when she coined the cyborg metaphor back in the 1980s (Haraway 1992), opening the scope to articulate feminist epistemological strategies into science, technology and urban studies and to develop new sensitivities in the understanding of the material interfaces between bodies, cities, nature and culture.

Driven largely by the property development industry and the architectural profession, green urbanism is about minimizing the environmental damage of built spaces, infrastructures and landscapes, a project underpinned by the promise of the possible ecological modernization of our urban future. This tradition has now been absorbed into aggressive smart city discourses that have been packaged and marketed by the IT industry with amplified vigor since the start of the global economic crisis in 2007/8. Echoing the profound impact on urban imaginaries of the Crystal Palace project in the early twentieth century, Siemens has built The Crystal in London as a museum of the future to make an equally significant impact on the twenty-first-century urban imaginaries. Significantly, these IT companies tap into research on the potential efficiencies of urban systems of the kind discussed by Reusser *et al.* to mount their arguments. Hajer's chapter critically engages with the smart city discourse by equating it to the sanitation syndrome of the late nineteenth century and the highway boom of the mid-twentieth century. His is a cautionary argument that questions the power role of the IT companies in the building of urban imaginaries, but accepts that more inclusive and sustainable options will in future depend heavily on IT systems that might drastically reduce transaction costs and distribute the data flows that future economic activities will depend on. But as the chapter about Mexican urban planning by Rosales points out, none of this will be possible if sustainability is not incorporated into urban planning processes in more meaningful ways. For Mukherjee this involves not just the re-engineering of planning to become more efficient and effective but, above all, the need to reflect 'more on the ecology "of" cities rather than ecology "in" cities'. Mainstream interpretations of green urbanism appear by contrast to focus on mastering the morphological and functional malleability of the machine, and the commodification of nature, body and space, overlooking the sensitivities developed in recent years from the field of urban political ecology.

Writing as untaming

In assembling this book, we have taken a number of risks. Conceptually and ideologically, the authors depart from different and often contrasting framings of what constitutes desirable and undesirable urban trajectories. Analytically and methodologically, they choose very different means to respond to the provocation of untamed urbanisms, ranging from the examination of grand narratives through discourse analysis, the interrogation of big data and the analysis of long-term trajectories of socio-ecological change all the way to the ethnographic interrogation of spatial, mediatic and embodied urban micro-practices.

As argued in the Introduction, this book was not produced through a pre-selection of akin thinkers but rather as an open encounter that does not seek agreements or shy away from dissonance. In doing so, we have refrained from harmonizing views but insisted on the importance of pausing to explain where we write from. Brazilian scholar Marcelo de Souza (2012: 315) reminds us that '[n]o contribution in the field of social sciences, urban studies included, is free of 'accent', since every piece of knowledge directly related to social life is both culturally embedded and historically-geographically situated'. Most authors in this book have taken the risk to be explicit about their accents, not just in terms of the multiple 'wheres' from which they write but above all their political–philosophical choices and affiliations.

Situated writing has in our view untaming power, and this transcends the global north–south divide, inviting a reflexive engagement with the multiple geographies of difference from which we write, upon which we write and to whom we write – even if unfortunately, this is often an approach more systematically adopted by those who write from outside Europe and North America. In other words, our writing can be highly performative in reclaiming a plurality of urbanisms, thus, writing can indeed be a site of untaming. However, not all accounts of untamed urbanisms have untaming power, in the same way that not all untaming writing focuses on the untamed. Let us clarify this apparent tongue-twister.

On the one hand, a now robust body of urban literature focuses on the urbanisms of the poor, or, as suggested in Section 2, their 'untamed everyday' practices. While revealing the agency of the urban poor and, more widely, the typically marginalized from prevailing urban regimes is valuable, we are often confronted with the risk of romanticizing their struggles or, even worse, of feeding into the economization of their lives, as reflected by a plethora of urban policies underpinned by the assumption that substandard living conditions can be overcome by tapping more effectively into the human and social capital, adaptive capacity and resilience of the urban poor. In short, if slum urbanism is the urbanism of the untamed, then the pragmatic response to it is to tap into the untameability of the urban poor – their inexhaustible ingenuity, elasticity and capacity to innovate under stress – to foster the further internalization of the production of the infrastructures and services required to secure their place in the city, and thus enhancing the viability of splintering urbanism. But there is more in this book connecting the 'untamed everyday' with the 'liberating alternatives', insofar one cannot exist without the other. As chapters in Parts I and III are connected by the uneasiness with mainstreamed narratives and policy-making practices, those in Parts II and IV are linked by the attempt to shake off social labelling and common academic insights that at the end tend to pity the poor and the excluded, trying to rescue the dignity embedded in their agency and in every person and community who attempts to live a freedom not necessarily defined by others, by frameworks, by master-plans or strategic developments often proposed by people who do not even know the places they are planning for.

Thus, on the other hand, untaming through writing might be effected when we seek to generate new understandings by recognizing 'the importance of different kinds and levels of epistemic (and political) "otherness"' (Souza, 2012: 316). This is not an easy enterprise and requires constant and critical reflection on the world of ideas in which we seek to understand how cities work. Marxist urban studies have been perhaps the most significant and long-lived source of inspiration for radical urban theory and updated readings of the urban condition. However, it could also be argued that reading urban change as a series of endless expressions of capitalist urbanization seems to strike almost always the same cord and to marginalize what Souza defines above as 'epistemic (and political) "otherness"', often also alienating the possibility of engaging with action beyond the boundaries of what might be regarded as radical or insurgent. Most chapters in Part IV take a careful approach not to fall into this trap, interrogating the very notions of freedom, rights and autonomy through quotidian practices and in the process repoliticizing how ordinary men and women carve different ways of being in the city by quietly rejecting formal work, monetized interactions or the masculinization of urban space.

Thus, what makes writing an act of untaming is not necessarily its subject but the epistemological risks we take. In other words, untaming urban narratives might often be found not necessarily in writings about the marginalized but written from the margins of mainstream urban theory. But is it then possible to simultaneously enact critical analysis and reclaim actionable urban theory?

Reclaiming the materiality of urban transitions in planning theory and praxis

Much has been written in recent years about the need to move our understanding of a world of cities beyond the realm of Western urban theory (Edensor and Jayne 2012), and this is particularly urgent in the field of planning. Vanessa Watson (2012) argues that the gap in non-Western theorizations of urban planning is rapidly being addressed by a body of incipient but fast-growing work. She groups this work in two strands: 'those which aim to understand and explain (South-East) urban contexts from a planning perspective, and those which move to normative or action-oriented positions' (86). The notion of untamed urbanisms might be fruitful in this respect as a means to bring both strands of work into more explicit dialogue. Untamed urbanisms call for a simultaneous epistemological, axiological and methodological interrogation of the ways in which we seek to understand different forms of urbanism and to transform them. Or, in other words, for deploying a conscious and systematic effort to engage explicitly with the tension between analysis and action. Such enterprise talks directly to planning theory and praxis and invites explorations that acknowledge that transformative change resides not in conceptions of the state, markets and communities as coherent and monolithic agents but on fluid and spatially and socially embedded webs that might equally challenge the fruitfulness of grand theorizations and the pragmatism of best practice approaches. Furthermore, bringing nature – and the material flows of energy, water and food that make any urbanism possible – into the repertoire of the untamed is essential, as this continues to be a dimension of urban life either forgotten or brought to the fore as an overriding taming and operational narrative.

To sum up, the notion of untamed urbanisms creates a conceptual space for searching for a synthesis between actionable theory and aspirational practice. Such an enterprise can only be activated if we – urban practitioners and academics – take the risk to actively question hegemonic practices, their scope and limits, abandoning the comfort equally granted by domesticating projects and grand narratives, while simultaneously developing our sensitivity to capture and nurture more relational and materially grounded pathways to transformative change. Such pathways are likely to look patchy, imperfect and incomplete to the eyes of many, but the reassurance provided by contemporary taming urbanisms may prove to be false promises that lure cities in, resulting in contrived reproductions of unsustainable and unjust urban development pathways.

Rupturing historical and contemporary representations of the urban world involves – as argued by Ananya Roy (2014: 18) – 'an analysis of the worlding of the world but equally an effort to imagine other worlds'. Such analysis and imaginations do not just live in the realm of urban theory and planning; they exceed the epistemic boundaries of urban professionals and encompass the ways in which ordinary citizens make sense of the everyday, of the past and of the future to come. Untamed urbanisms is therefore above all a call to engage with a more reflexive approach towards the relative unknowability of the city, of nature and of human agency and to tender the possibility of transformative change beyond the undifferentiated 'we' that often permeates the actions proposed by green and inclusive urbanisms and the differentiating 'them' denounced by splintering and slum urbanisms.

References

Allen, A. 2012. Water provision for and by the peri-urban poor: public-community partnerships or citizens co-production? In Vojnovic, I. (ed.), *Sustainability: A Global Urban Context*. East Lansing, MI: Michigan State University Press, pp. 309–40.

Allen, A., von Bertrab, E. and Walnycki, A. forthcoming 2015. The Co-Production of Water Justice in Latin American Cities. In Allen, A., Griffin, L. and Johnson, C. (eds), *Environmental Justice, Urbanization and Resilience*. London: Palgrave.

Edensor, T. and Jayne, M. 2012. *Beyond the West: A World of Cities*. London and New York: Routledge.

Gandy, M. 2005. Cyborg urbanization: complexity and monstrosity in the contemporary city. *International Journal of Urban and Regional Research*, 291: 26–49.

Graham, S. and Marvin, S. 2001. *Splintering Urbanism: Networked Infrastructures, Technological Mobilities and the Urban Condition*. London: Routledge.

Haraway, D. 1992. 1992. Promises of monsters: a regenerative politics for inappropriate/d others. In L. Grossberg, C. Nelson and P. Treichler (eds), *Cultural Studies*. London: Routledge

Roy, A. 2014. Worlding the South: toward a post-colonial urban theory. In Parnell, S. and Oldfield, S. (eds), *The Routledge Handbook on Cities of the Global South*. London: Routledge.

Souza, M. L. de. 2012. Marxists, Libertarians and the City. *City*, 16(3): 315–31.

Swilling, M. and Annecke, E. 2012. *Just Transitions. Explorations of Sustainability in an Unfair World*. Cape Town and Tokyo: UCT Press and United Nations University Press.

Watson, V. 2012. Planning and the 'stubborn realities' of global south-east cities: some emerging ideas. *Planning Theory*, 12(1): 81–100.

Index

'n' refers to end of chapter notes.

For Product Safety Concerns and Information please contact our EU
representative GPSR@taylorandfrancis.com
Taylor & Francis Verlag GmbH, Kaufingerstraße 24, 80331 München, Germany

www.ingramcontent.com/pod-product-compliance
Ingram Content Group UK Ltd.
Pitfield, Milton Keynes, MK11 3LW, UK
UKHW021018180425
457613UK00020B/979